TEACHING BASIC ENGLISH COURSES

Readings and Comments

TEACHING
BASIC ENGLISH
COURSES

Readings and Comments

Edited by RICHARD M. BOSSONE
Baruch College of The City University of New York

Foreword by ROBERT F. HOGAN
Executive Secretary, National Council of
Teachers of English

VAN NOSTRAND REINHOLD COMPANY
New York   Cincinnati   Toronto   London   Melbourne

Van Nostrand Reinhold Company
Regional Offices:
Cincinnati New York Chicago
Millbrae Dallas

Van Nostrand Reinhold Company
International Offices:
London Toronto Melbourne

PE
1065
B6

Published by Van Nostrand Reinhold Company
450 West 33rd Street, New York, N. Y. 10001

Published simultaneously in Canada by
Van Nostrand Reinhold Ltd.

10 9 8 7 6 5 4 3 2 1

To Walter Loban and Francis Christensen
— master teachers, who educate
their students to realize that a conflict
of ideas is not a disaster but an opportunity

Foreword

In times of crises our vision and our rhetoric lose almost any semblance of fit. We focus our sights narrowly on one crisis or another, and with our rhetoric we are prodigal. Part of the problem is that we look to the language of space technology for the metaphors we use, and the metaphors govern the programs we envision. We draw up "task force" models that "zero in" on "target" populations; and we "launch educational moonshots" powered by all the "thrust" we can "mount." In mounting that thrust (which in the long run means mostly people and funds), we squander our superlatives. We argue that the need is at least "desperate," that the priority is nothing less than "imperative," that the situation was "critical" yesterday and "worsens" by the hour.

The response of the educational world when Sputnik went into orbit in 1957 was a vivid example. Educators reacted as to a forest fire. Federal, state, and local programs sprang up overnight, focused on academic reform and scholastic renaissance to insure that, even though Russian technology had produced the first earth orbiting satellite, the United States would accomplish the first successful moon landing. Arguments for subject matter reform in teacher preparation and in the school curriculum, first in science and mathematics but before long in most school subjects, were tied directly and urgently to the national interest. They were inextricably coupled with the "National Defense," the banner which flew over the first new major legislation in recent memory aimed at nation-wide educational change.

Yet before that first moon landing was accomplished, before that first educational forest fire was under control, other fires flared up—literal rather than metaphorical fires, in Newark, in Watts, in Chicago, in Washington, D.C., in Milwaukee. As the "fires" grew more literal, the "moonshots" became more visionary: equality of educational opportunity, universal literacy, at least two years of post high school education not only available to anyone who might want to take advantage of it but designed for all those who might. While the targets of the task forces changed, however, the stridency of the rhetoric did not. It was as if the fires were increasing while the water supply was shrinking and the trick was to make any one fire seem more threatening than any other.

It was only natural that we should grow weary of the visions and the rhetoric. The danger in attempting to cope with problems of great magnitude is that we come eventually to see how real they are and, for the moment, how insoluble. Consequently, we are likely in the last analysis to shrug off our guilt or sense of failure and continue with business as usual.

One of the commendable features of the essays collected here is that they do not shrug. Nor do they attempt to douse every educational forest fire. To back away from the concentration on separate crises is not to deny the existence or the urgency of any one of them. Rather, it is to wonder if acting upon one crisis now and another later is a sane or productive pattern of response. It is wondering whether we ought to continue spending so much money and so many man hours (and man lives) in extinguishing forest fires, while our chief effort at prevention consists of committing much of our faith and considerable advertising money to an animated bear.

No one in education today would deny the failure of our instructional programs for children born into the black community, a failure which rightly commands much of our effort and resources at this time. But these children are not the only victims. In cities and suburbs and small towns across the country are tens of thousands of young people, many still in school, whom we have failed to teach read and write adequately. And we continue to teach them our subject in a way that taxes most severely the two clusters of skills we have failed to teach—reading and writing. It is to this issue that the present book addresses itself. It does not ignore the problem of minority group youth, but it keeps in focus all the young people upon whom our unsuccessful efforts to teach the skills and joys of literacy have been visited.

To be sure, the problem involves issues other than those treated in this volume. Financial support, for example. One city school system, supported by federal funds, has contracted with a private agency at the cost of $250,000 per year to remediate problems of reading and arithmetic for approximately 140 children in the junior high years. That averages out to about $1,800 per child. In the meantime, other children in the system, including those in the elementary schools that feed the junior high schools, enjoy the fruits of a program that costs about $520 per child per year. At that latter level of expenditure, the supply of remedial cases in the junior high school will never be exhausted.

There is also the question of the crippling of a child's aspiration when he is the third generation on relief and sees no prospect of escaping that milieu. There is the need to explore more fully the psychological implications of trying to teach behavior patterns (e.g., voluntary reading for pleasure) and linguistic patterns (some form of standard English) to those whose value systems and linguistic loyalties, whose very self-image, cannot accommodate these patterns. We might ask, as well, what adjustments we must make in a basically competitive educational system to elicit anything except seeming lethargy from children who consciously and perhaps commendably turn away from an opportunity to make a friend "lose" by doing better than the friend can do—particularly when the victory is determined by an adult over 40 who shares neither the social nor the ethnic heritage of the victor or the loser in the competition.

The authors represented in this collection, clearly, have pondered these sobering issues. At the same time, they have retained, in the articles gathered here, a sharp focus on the equally sobering task of classroom instruction in the fundamental skills of English. And the suggestions and recommendations that they offer call neither for $1,800 per child per year nor for a school or college building fashioned after the geodesic dome.

The writer of this foreword is for one third of his time and with all his heart an English teacher. He approached this collection of essays in the fashion of any caring English teacher. It was not *his* collection. He thinks he might have added other pieces, though he is not sure which. He suspects he might have omitted one piece or another with which he does not fully agree. But in the end he triumphed over ambivalence and censorship. Being forced to entertain seriously a contrary position is, in Frost's best sense, educational. It "rumples the mind." Although the invitation to write the foreword included the invitation to suggest adding or subtracting from the body of the volume, neither option was taken.

Most teachers, however much some may seem to fail, teach as well as they know how to. They would teach better if they knew how. The essays that follow were written by teachers who have something of value and substance to share with prospective teachers and with other teachers who want to reach and teach students. There is nothing here for anyone who thinks teaching would be a noble calling if it were not for the students. Or for anyone who thinks it is the responsibility of the admissions and counseling departments to steer to him students who will watch in joy and wonder while he does his thing—whether that thing be Victorian novels or multi-media happenings. But for the rest, for those present and future English teachers who will not shrug off as someone

else's failure the immediate need of students to learn more about reading
and writing, there is much.

Robert F. Hogan
Executive Secretary,
National Council
of Teachers of English

Preface

This book deals with a problem of growing concern in the teaching of English. It addresses the question of how to conduct English courses for the increasing numbers of students who, for many reasons, come to the English program in high schools, two-year colleges, four-year colleges, and various nonschool-affiliated retraining programs with major deficiencies in basic English skills. The book is intended primarily for the pre-service methods course, as well as a guide and reference for in-service use. It may also prove an appropriate addition to graduate courses, institutes, workshops, and in-service training programs for teachers who wish to be informed about practices in teaching basic English courses: that is, reading, remedial English, terminal English, and composition in high schools and two-year or four-year colleges. Further, it may be of interest to anyone concerned with the relationship between high-school and two-year or four-year college English programs and how greater articulation between them can be achieved.

Few four-year colleges or teacher-training institutions today prepare prospective English teachers to teach basic English courses. As a result, teachers are often in a quandary when confronted with their first teaching assignment, which often consists precisely of the teaching of such courses. These teachers need ideas and concrete suggestions about how to conduct these courses. They need to be exposed to a broad range of alternative rationales and a variety of specific methods which will help them develop their own approaches to teaching such courses. Although a number of excellent texts dealing with the teaching of English in secondary schools do furnish a general basis for teaching English, none concentrates heavily enough, in this editor's judgment, on teaching, or reteaching, the fundamental skills of English; nor do textbooks, as a rule, present diverse viewpoints about teaching upon which today's teachers can draw as they strive to evolve programs tailored to the students they encounter in their classrooms. In both these respects current professional education skirts an important issue, especially as it affects newly appointed teachers of English everywhere.

Having worked with both prospective English teachers and practicing teachers of English in senior high schools and junior colleges, the editor is aware that the proliferation of periodicals, books, and inexpensive reprints dealing with the teaching of English now renders it almost impossible for teachers to devote the requisite time and energy to identifying the best from the current flood of material. Inevitably, many outstanding articles or works relevant to the teaching of English courses go unread or unstudied. To help resolve this problem and to bring some order to the isolated pieces which constitute an expanding literature on the subject, the editor asked prospective English teachers and practicing teachers of basic English courses to identify all particularly instructive materials they had read. The prospective teachers were then asked to react critically to the selections submitted, and any gaps were filled in with the original essays prepared especially for this collection. The present volume is the result.

Part I presents an overview of English programs in high schools and junior colleges, as well as a general profile of the students attending these institutions; Parts II, III, IV, and V present ideas about how to teach, respectively, reading, remedial English, terminal English, and composition. A general commentary precedes each section.

All selections were chosen primarily for the assistance and insight they would give to unprepared teachers of basic English courses. Accordingly, articles on the teaching of literature were omitted—not because literature is unimportant, but because English teachers are generally well prepared in this area, and then, too, they are rarely given a literature class to teach, initially. The majority of articles presented here appeared originally in *The English Journal, College Composition and Communication,* and the *Journal of Reading* during the past ten years. As authoritative representations of viewpoints in the English teaching world, they should give the reader an opportunity to participate in the accumulated experience and knowledge of outstanding teachers and scholars. Thus it is hoped that the present collection will provide fresh insights into the vital responsibilities of teaching basic English courses.

R. M. B.

Contents

**PART TWO   READING: IN HIGH SCHOOL
AND COLLEGE**

**PART THREE   REMEDIAL ENGLISH:
READING AND WRITING FOR
DISADVANTAGED HIGH SCHOOL AND
COLLEGE STUDENTS**   185

PART ONE

AN OVERVIEW

This introductory section is concerned with the current state of basic English courses in high school and junior college. It provides an overall picture of English programs in these institutions and the students who, in general, attend them.

Many articles have been written about high school English programs; but, until Squire and Applebee's large-scale national study of high school English programs, no comprehensive analysis existed. The article by Squire, in the opinion of the editor, not only presents a lucid summary of that study but also provides a penetrating analysis of the characteristics of outstanding programs which "deserve emulation elsewhere."

The Merson article gives a thoughtful picture of the two-year college movement, including types of instructional programs and implications for instruction in English. When read in conjunction with the *Summary, Conclusions, and Recommendations* of the Weingarten-Kroeger report, this article should give the reader not only an overview of English instruction in the junior college but also a considerably broad-based evaluation of such instruction.

Because successful teaching depends on a thorough understanding of the student population, any book attempting to present an overview of English instruction in high schools and two-year colleges should certainly include material which strives to delineate the students who attend these institutions. Two such selections have been included here.

In a searching essay analyzing the various high school student subcultures in relation to external pressures exerted upon them by contemporary society, Ashe explains how a student's resources are often enervated by forces in and out of school. This article can give teachers who truly wish to contribute to the heuristic development of their students a better understanding of forces that may be operating against the teaching and learning process.

Bossone's article on *Understanding Junior College Students* advances the view that a sympathetic attitude toward junior college students may well be the most important personal characteristic necessary for success in teaching this student group but that one cannot develop such an attitude unless one has an understanding of the traits and milieu of the average junior college student.

In sum, the five pieces in this opening section explore implications for teaching, counseling, and the academic program in general as it confronts the teacher of basic English.

The English Program
in High Schools

National Study of
High School
English Programs

A SCHOOL FOR ALL SEASONS

JAMES R. SQUIRE

IF, AS THE report[1] by Roger Applebee makes abundantly clear, we cannot commend to the attention of the profession any single cluster of perfect English programs, we can at least point to those characteristics which seem so widespread or so desirable in the schools we have visited that they deserve emulation elsewhere. Clearly the benchmarks of a great English program are found in the administration and supervision of a program; in the English faculty itself; in the nature of the program of studies in English. Here I shall discuss all three.

I

The greatest single strength—the most all-pervading characteristic—which any school can develop is its administration. By administration, I mean not jealous, autocratic centralization of all power and authority in the hands of a single principal or single department head with the

From *English Journal* (March, 1966), pp. 282–290. Reprinted with the permission of the National Council of Teachers of English and James R. Squire.

[1]Dr. Squire, [former] Executive Secretary of the National Council of Teachers of English, served as Director of the Project reported in this . . . article; Roger Applebee was Associate Director. [Their] articles, based on presentations made at the Boston [1965] Convention of NCTE, are [complementary]. See Roger K. Applebee, "National Study of High School English Programs: A Record of English Teaching Today," *English Journal*, 55, March, 1966, pp. 273–281.

inevitable result of class demarcation of supervisors and subordinates. Nor do I mean an administration devoted solely to the service function, to the elimination of barriers, hurdles, and red tape so that teachers can be completely individualistic. Rather I mean to indicate the effectiveness which strong leadership of a department chairman and a building principal can bring to English teaching.

A strong, responsible department chairman, given adequate time and resources, can do much to free teachers to teach and students to learn. The special qualifications of a chairman and the ways in which he may operate have been carefully delineated in the Project's report on *High School Departments of English: Their Organization, Administration, and Supervision,* just published by NCTE. Here I say only that the chairman's essential responsibility is one of providing vigorous, intellectual leadership—stimulating ideas, organizing for curriculum development, conferring with teachers, visiting classes, opening classrooms to intervisitation among teachers, assisting in placement and evaluation, of *not,* as is often found, *merely* servicing the department in a most passive sense—distributing books, passing out papers, filling out forms. Such might better be done by the department's clerk or secretary, a necessary staff member, and one required at least full-time in every department with as many as 14 or 15 teachers.

To do all of these things, the chairman must have time. In even the smallest school he will require at least one class period for departmental duties, in addition to his regular preparation period. In larger schools, he should have an additional period for every five or six teachers, but always, we think, the chairman should teach one class. Thus, in a school of, say, 2,500 students, the chairman teaches only one class and then is free for departmental responsibilities during the rest of the day.

We are convinced, too, that his class assignment should rotate—at one time the teaching of slow students in Grade 9, at another, bright students in Grade 12. So, too, should the assignments of all teachers of English. The assumption of specialization—"I am a tenth grade teacher," "I teach senior honors"—leads only to interrupted sequence and fragmented curricula. Not infrequently we found eleventh-grade teachers possessing little conception of where students had been in English or where they might be going. To avoid specilization so complete that it undercuts departmental unity, we recommend that part of the assignment of every teacher, including the chairman, be regularly rotated according to level and class so he may better understand the problems and purposes at all levels of instruction. In the school we envision, the chairman—in consultation with the principal and his fellow teachers—will be responsible for all assignments in English.

But the chairman can operate as an instructional leader only if he has the complete support and confidence of the building principal. Our visits demonstrate again and again the significance of the principal in determining the intellectual tone of the school. If the principal supports a strong English program—one that emphasizes the disciplined understanding and expression of human thought—if he views the cultural contributions of mankind with at least the same interest and involvement that he devotes to athletic prowess or school architectual problems—then his faculty will respond accordingly.

Have you ever eavesdropped on a faculty lunchroom conversation? To what extent does the staff move beyond small talk in its exchange? How often do you hear discussed an important new book? Significant affairs? A new scientific theory? A new idea of any kind? (One of the reasons we strongly recommend a separate lounge in an English Center is to bring together those interested in language and literature. We have seen in many schools how an informal grouping of teachers will spark a continuous intellectual dialogue.)

Too often we found that the "static" atmosphere on a school faculty resulted directly from a principal uninterested in ideas and/or learning. Conversely, a special concern—the "spiral curriculum" in one school, computerized scheduling in another, perhaps even "'Great Books" or the humanities, to mention several we found widespread—these can provoke faculty interest. No college dean nor department head exerts nearly the influence on his faculty according to our college observers, alternately appalled and then enthusiastic over the role of the principal in America's secondary schools.

But to provide the rich atmosphere of intellectual ferment needed in the secondary school, a principal and a chairman must have reasonable freedom of operation. This freedom is not always present. The evidence in our study points to the enveloping, strangling pressures of administrative practices in large city and multiple-school districts. In one high school, for example, a chairman was asked to prepare 28 copies of an evaluation report on a simple one-hour visit to a single teacher. In another, a 25-year effort to get *The Grapes of Wrath* on the approved district list for school library purchase, a substantial portion of this time resulting from administrative red tape rather than censorship.

Again and again our observers reported principals and teachers meeting at the opening of a term new faculty members whom they had never seen before—and about whom they knew next to nothing. We found English teachers selected and assigned by a central district personnel officer who rarely even visited schools. We found district

English supervisors losing their way in driving to particular schools, assistant superintendents who showed up at a school for the first time in two or three years (for the purpose of seeing us, not visiting the students or the teachers), audio-visual depots and textbook supply centers so cumbersome in operation that they seemed designed less to get good new learning aids into the hands of students and teachers than to prevent much use of such materials.

Not all practices in multiple-school districts are as bad as those I have mentioned, and not all district-level personnel are unaware of the problems, but the majority certainly are. And seldom indeed did we find the quality of instruction or the intellectual tone of a school in the multiple-schools districts approaching the quality of the program of the single high school, no matter how large it may have become. As a second and third high school are created, district administration moves away from the school, the administrative decisions become detached from the classroom, and the elaborate special paraphernalia and personnel of the Education Establishment come into being—separate offices, separate architectural and building specialists, separate community relations specialists, even separate district librarians and separate audio-visual coordinators—all removed from the schools, yet vested with vast decision-making powers which directly and seriously affect classroom teaching. With the Commission on English of the College Entrance Examination Board, we have firmly concluded that the real decisions *must* be made in each school, by each English faculty, involving every English teacher.

What does this seem to mean for the administration of a program? Surely, insofar as possible, school administrators should cling to the single school site, resisting the temptation to build a second plant as long as they are able. The decision at Evanston Township High School seems to me an important one, expanding the present plant rather than creating a new one.

But multiple-school districts will remain in medium and larger cities. What can be done there? Attempts, I think, must be made to return authority and decision-making to the teachers, to department chairmen, to administrators in the individual schools—in ways perhaps not yet even understood. English supervisors can perform a vital *service and consultant* function, and in some districts they serve this function magnificently. But the central staffs of large districts most clearly need to recognize that it is the function of the administrators and supervisors to make schools easier for teaching—not to make them cumbersome and difficult—that the quality of an instructional program is more directly related to the smoothness and ease with which each classroom teacher operates, than to the efficiency of district supervision and administration. In many ways I suspect there is a close correlation between the difficulties incurred in administering a program and the excellence and quality of the program itself.

II

The English faculty of a department need not be uniformly excellent. This would be too much to expect. Rather it must be composed of well-prepared English teachers of good quality and reasonable vision, encouraged to "stand on tip toes" through the interaction of sound departmental leadership and the catalytic effect of a small cadre of outstanding, creative teachers within the department. That is to say, if it is too much to expect all 90,000 high school teachers of English to be pacesetters in the profession, it is not too much to try to recruit and retain five or six such leaders within every department and then to promote their interaction with the other teachers. The excitement which such a group creates, the ideas which they spark, the standards of teaching they set, the projects they incite, the programs they develop —these will create an atmosphere for learning that is vigorous and bracing. Far more frequently than departments of uniform excellence, we found groups of "middlin' average" teachers sparked by inner-leadership. Far more often than completely inadequate teachers, we found the "static" atmosphere, the disappointing lethargy, the diffidence created in departments which lacked such "inner fire."

But recruiting teachers is one thing; retaining them is another. More important than many goals of education which enlist far more attention from our professional leaders is the crisis in leadership apparent everywhere in education. If we can agree that fundamental to our aims and purposes is the retention of outstanding teachers in teaching positions in our schools, then we must provide adequate status and salary to offset the blandishments of school administration, supervision, and college teaching, to say nothing of the attractions of publishing and industry. Again and again promising young people, potentially gifted teachers, told us in confidence that they wished desperately to remain in classroom teaching but could not impose the permanent financial burden on their families. Talented, educated, obvious leaders, they are seduced from their natural calling by the lure of money and prestige.

To provide inducement for truly gifted teachers to remain in the classroom, no alternative seems open but to pay them what they are worth, no matter how sensitive the profession to the issue of differentiated compensation or merit pay itself. Whether by creating special "chairs" for outstanding teachers or by increasing the compensation offered selected individuals above and beyond published salary scales, appropriate ways must be found, ways fair to all teachers, which separate the wheat from the chaff. I conceive of schools in which a few outstanding teachers with considerable experience may be paid even more than their supervisors and administrators. It is not unusual in a college or university, for example, for two or three truly distinguished scholars to earn several thousand dollars more than their deans or department chairmen. It should not be unusual for the distinguished high school teacher to earn more than his department head, more even than his principal, if we wish to retain him in teaching. It is the qualities of the person—rather than the status of the position he holds—which should characterize the individual to be retained in teaching from his colleagues slated for administrative and supervisory positions.

Some schools are making progress. In New England, we found one principal stepping down after three years to assume the chairmanship of a department—and, I believe, at no loss in salary, and certainly not in status. In one California school, three "Teacher Executive" positions have been created. Each individual so designated receives a special stipend of $1,500, travel expenses of up to $3,000 to attend professional and scholarly meetings and to visit experimental schools, and a full-time paid intern with whom he spends much of his time working and who is present to take over classes whenever the teacher needs to visit out of the school. The appointments are for three years—a time limitation that may be necessary for any special position to permit periodic reassessment and reconsideration.

Who will select these superior teachers? Aye, there's the rub! Under our present system of supervision and evaluation, competent selection may seem influenced more by political considerations than by merit. But in the school envisioned here, adequate protection for all teachers will be built in. With a strong chairman and school administrative support, the pacesetters would be clearly visible. Joint committees of teachers, supervisors, administrators, perhaps a parent or two, could make reasonable, popular selections. With classrooms open, with much interaction among the faculty, and given the conditions we outline as necessary prerequisites for excellence, such processes would not be difficult to achieve. They seem difficult only because the present system imposes so many barriers to obtaining a real knowledge about one's fellow teachers.

I would set no firm ceiling on the salary or the conditions of employment for these truly gifted teachers. If it is necessary in retaining teachers, as it was in a State of Washington school, to schedule a teacher for two honors classes within the school and for one sixth-grade humanities class in a nearby elementary school, then I should certainly make the attempt. But I would set a floor. Salary schedules, basic conditions—these are standards from which schools must be ready to depart, but they exist to help us all. I would want most English teachers to have at least five years of education, largely in the liberal arts, and I would expect continual renewal through additional study, formal and informal. Like the schools that we have studied, we would find more than half of the teachers possessing Master's degrees. Whether M.A.'s, M.A.T.E.'s, or M.Ed.'s seems less important than what the degree symbolizes in terms of academic achievement. More important than a degree is continued enthusiasm for learning.

I would want few individuals without the equivalent of sound undergraduate majors teaching English in any department, but from experiences during these years, I should try to be less doctrinaire in determining the "equivalency" than are many schools today. Naturally, adequacy of background in literature, language, and composition is important, but it should be balanced against other things. Some of the most exciting English teaching that I have seen has been conducted by majors in history, philosophy, majors even in education, individuals concerned with ideas and insights wherever they are found, people who have gone on reading and studying well beyond their academic training. Indeed, for some courses I would demand preparation in other fields. No English major would teach English literature in my ideal school without adequate understanding of the history of the English-speaking people, not because it would limit him to an historical approach but because personal knowledge could free him from too rigorous a dependence on such history. No team in the humanities would be without a specialist schooled in the history of Western thought. No American literature class would be planned and conducted by a teacher uninformed about American cultural, social, and intellectual history. Similarly, special background would be required for the programs emphasizing lexicography, the history of the language, or regional and social dialects.

This is not to say that specialization can go so far that every teacher of English will not need to possess basic understandings about language, literature, and composition and about developing frontiers of our discipline. But schools need a balanced faculty, some members with interests and specialties in aspects of literature and general cultural history, some with the dimensions of language, some in rhetoric or reading or whatever else may be offered in the program. Only with such balance can an English faculty achieve the perspective needed in our time.

Inevitably then, the selection of faculty members for any school must ultimately rest with individuals informed about the nature of English. Regardless of their administrative convenience, everything I have seen in American high schools during the past three years convinces me that general personnel departments, especially those in large districts, have done a permanent disservice to the teaching of English in this country. Necessary as general personnel officers may be for the initial screening of applicants, someone informed about the internal needs of the department, about the problems of staffing, about the essentials of the subject, must play an important role in recruiting, interviewing, and selecting. In most school districts—regardless of the problems involved —this individual should be the department chairman. Working with the principal, the district supervisor, and—if necessary—the central personnel officer, he can look beyond the immediate credits and units on the transcript to the intellectual and academic qualifications of the applicant.

Unrealistic? I think not. Expensive? I suggest it as an economy to schools truly interested in recruiting outstanding teachers. In large districts where expansion or turnover may be so great that a number of teachers are hired each year, the chairman may well make recruitment trips with a member of the administrative staff. To which district is the potentially strong English teacher most likely to go? To the one represented by a general personnel officer? Or to the one in which the representative is a qualified specialist in English? For the possibility of acquiring truly able teachers, the cost of time and trip seem very slight indeed.

III

Our ideal English curriculum would offer a balanced program— balanced in its attention to all students and to all aspects of our program. For want of better or more basic classification of components, we see language, literature, and composition as the three dimensions— but quickly state that teachers do injustice to themselves and their subjects if within language they include not *oral* language; if within literature, not *oral* interpretation; if within composition, not *oral* composition. Speech in the general English program seems basic, albeit at present it receives little thoughtful attention. Reading, too, must be an essential part of English. The reading of literature involves crucial skills, attitudes, and insights; the perceptual, cognitive, and linguistic aspects of reading are important dimensions of the language component of English and must be considered in program planning.

But balance among language, literature, and composition need not demand separate but equal time. However the percentage of time which we have discovered may strike you, I, for one, am willing to suggest that the overwhelming emphasis in literature may be exactly what we need, provided the moments of genuine learning are moments of sufficient intensity and depth.

Our literature programs tend to place far too little attention on the *close* reading of literary texts, far too much on superficial coverage and talking *about* texts. This is not, as we initially hypothesized, because English teachers are uninformed about modern textual criticism. Rather a detailed analysis of the academic background of teachers suggests that most have studied modern criticism. Rather they seem not always to understand how to translate their knowledge of critical approaches to their classroom work. They distinguish not the teaching of *Silas Marner* as a work in itself from the teaching of *Silas Marner* as an example of the novel form; and they tend, too often, to see lessons in literature as ends in themselves, rather than as means by which we can fire students to read widely and well. Thus we find too much lecturing *about* literature—in large groups and small groups both—too little studied analysis. The data we have assembled leads us to recommend more carefully planned attention to teaching the methods and the approaches of close reading of individual texts, far less coverage (of history, works, authors); far more guided individual reading programs built upon the intelligent use of classroom book collections. Indeed, our recommendation is that we strive for 500 appropriate titles for student reading in every classroom—a standard which our observation suggests may well lead to an average expectation that young people read 20 or 25 books a semester rather than the more usual, paltry four or five. Our experience suggests such an approach will lead to greater library use. And we would also provide much school classroom time for reading—at least one hour, if not two, each week—time when the teacher works with individuals and with groups.

For composition we recommend a varied program in writing, not one limited to particular kinds. One of the possible explanations for the success of many of the schools has been variety in assignment. Stampeded neither by the sometime exaggerated emphasis on exposition and analysis, nor by the demand to relate all composition to literature and not to life (as if the two could be separated!), many teachers steer a middle course.

We do think that more should be done to *teach* writing, or better to teach composing, rather than to provide writing activities alone and assume that students will necessarily learn from practice. Students need some understanding of basic rhetorical principles underlying composition; they need, too, the help that can come from rigorous, incisive attention to the processes of thinking and expression which result from careful consideration of their themes. Despite important professional efforts to help teachers annotate student composition more adequately, we find thoughtful analysis of student papers a sometime thing even in the better departments, so we commend this practice again to the attention of the profession.

A word here about creative or imaginative writing. During recent years we have weaned ourselves away from sentimental and undisciplined aspects of creativity; indeed, it has become fashionable to scorn creative expression of many kinds. Several of us on the project team have expressly warned against the danger. But it becomes clear, I think, as we interview the better English students throughout the country, that imaginative writing, especially the writing of poetry and fiction, can serve an important role. Again and again students recall such classroom experiences years before, times when the products of writing may have been far less memorable than the process they underwent. Not until they wrote a poem did they really understand what poetry was. So, at least, they say. The oft-heard argument that much student writing be related to literature is clearly intended to strengthen the students' understanding of and response to literature. By the same logic, cannot well designed experiences in imaginative writing produce students with a unique understanding of literary forms and styles? Perhaps less for its contribution to composition than for the way it can strengthen our offerings in literature, creative writing must be provided for many of our young people.

About programs in language, we have little good to say. In no other area do we find such confusion and concern. Too much of what presently passes for language is little more than a haphazard offering of sporadic usage drills determined solely by errors in students' speech or writing, an important aspect of English to be sure, but an approach to language instruction which in itself is so limited in its conception of what needs to be done that it is clearly out of touch with the prevailing attitudes of our scholars.

Many of the better high school English programs seem to have abandoned any formal and systematic study of English grammar. Unwilling to perpetuate the schoolroom grammar of the past, unable to introduce transformational grammar because of the limited background of the staff, most talk furtively about "structural linguistics" and do little or nothing. In no other basic aspect of English are we so lacking in direction, so subject to the vagaries of a single textbook or a single specialist, so wanting in continuing education. And in only a handful of schools can we report the language program to be more than a euphemism for prescriptive grammar and usage. Here and there we did find units introduced on lexicography, and a few on semantics and symbolic logic, American dialects, or the history of our language. These may be harbingers of change.

One discovery troubles us severely in this area—the tendency of many schools to impose strictures on the language program through large-scale, system-wide adoption of single textbooks and the tendency where this is done, of teachers seldom or never to use these language books with their classes. The overwhelming number of schools in the study purchase these texts by the hundreds; the overwhelming majority of teachers in the study don't want them, don't use them, and don't protest the waste in public funds. In view of the overwhelming shortage of usable books in classroom libraries, in school libraries, in needed audio-visual equipment for the department and classroom, should we not rethink our present practice?

Indeed the entire use and distribution of funds for books and teaching materials requires the most careful study. Last summer it was announced that the average Job Corps Training Center, educating our "dropouts" or "push-outs," would spend some $70.00 per trainee just to obtain needed instructional materials. Compare this with the paltry five dollars or ten spent annually in many high school programs! Even allowing for the cumulative backlog of materials in school which reuse books for several years, the discrepancy is great. We are concerned, too, with the lack of use of such materials by students and teachers even when they are available. Why do students much prefer the public library to the collections in their schools? Why will teachers not use machines, electronic equipment, and films when these are made available through a central instructional materials center? Because we see evidence that the use of instructional materials varies inversely with the distance of these materials from the teacher and the classroom, we thus recommend book collections, overhead projectors, and audio-visual materials in every room and the needed projectors, tape recorders and other essentials in nearby departmental English Centers.

One final curriculum problem may be the most pressing of all—the curriculum in English for the non-college bound, the average learner, the lower middle student. Although everything that I have said thus far applies to this sequence no less than to the others, special problems of motivation remain. Teacher motivation, that is. For no one can travel to 168 high schools in this country without sensing an appalling fact: despite the overwhelming acceptance of the tracking program in America's high schools today, teachers and administrators are giving little attention to the lower tracks. David Holbrook calls the tune in writing of British schools in *English for the Rejected*. Students in our lower tracks are the rejected indeed. Rejected by teachers, by principals, and by supervisors, walled off from any contact with the greatness of our culture. Too often our findings paralleled those of Holbrook in Britain—little attempt to introduce any intellectually stimulating learning, an absence of imaginative literature and excessive reliance on the technological, the scientific, the mechanical; a much greater use of routine drill books, work-books, and "canned" dittoed lessons. Indeed, again and again, we found the same teacher performing brilliantly with her honors students, performing dully and dismally (and I might add without adequately preparing lessons) with the dullards an hour later.

If I speak bitterly, it is because I know we can do better. If I felt we were really trying and failing, I should take a different position. But for teachers of literature not to present literature, teachers of composition to ignore composing, teachers of language to neglect all we know about the social dialects of their pupils—seems to me shocking and shameful. There are exceptions of course—a humanities program for the lower tracks in one school (needed, I think, more than any humanities program, because these students will never get such in college); in another, an extensive paperback collection of good books for slow readers (*The Pearl, Hiroshima,* and *The Bridges of To-Ko-Ri*); a specially equipped English laboratory study hall, well-stocked with books, recordings, listening centers, and inviting reading rooms in the third. But these are clearly exceptions. The overwhelming majority of programs either devote no time to curricular planning for the slow and average or are content merely to "modify" or "adapt" their programs for the college-bound, euphemisms I have come to suspect which merely indicate the failure to devote careful attention to special planning for such students. American teachers seem to believe in the importance of a tracking or grouping system. If so, should not we expect important learnings on each of the tracks? I cannot believe that American society will long support such indifference and lack of concern about the English programs for almost half of our students so evident in this country today.

IV

Here, then, is the story of the National Study of High School English Programs, a study of 168 high schools in 45 states. It is a study of spectacular successes in teaching and of dismal disappointments. It is no less the story about how some 15 staff members and consultants at the University of Illinois learned about what can be done in English instruction as well as what is not being done, from the only individuals in a real position to know: the classroom teacher in the schools. The dazzling moments of brilliant teaching that we have seen will remain with us always; so will the memory of the students themselves. In the vitality and the dedication of teachers that we have met is the true strength of American education; in their imagination and insight resides our hope for the future. If the study in some way points certain directions through which vitality, insight, and imagination can better be released for the benefit of all students, then we shall not fear the future of our discipline and its teaching in tomorrow's schools.

The English Program
in Two-Year Colleges

English in the Total
Context of American
Junior College Instruction

THOMAS B. MERSON

INTRODUCTION

WE CAN ALL find encouragement in the growing attention which is being
given nationally to improvement of instruction in English and the communication skills. We can hope that from this conference and others
like it will come ideas which will hasten the implementation of major
changes in language instruction—changes which are long overdue. The
National Council of Teachers of English is to be commended for its
leadership.

This paper is addressed to a rather broad assignment: to describe
American junior colleges and to infer from the characteristics and
purposes of these institutions particular responsibilities for instruction
in English. The assignment further specified that the paper identify
issues, problems, and potential action and set the tone and basis for
conference discussion.

The scope of this assignment, obviously, requires a selection of emphasis. Arbitrarily, it was decided to concentrate attention on major
issues and on plans for future improvement, anticipating that other
papers presented at the conference would be addressed to more specific
problems. Brief discussion of these major topics follows:

From *Research and the Development of English Programs in the Junior College:
Proceedings of the Tempe Conference,* the National Council of Teachers of English,
1965, pp. 7–20. Reprinted with the permission of the National Council of Teachers
of English and Thomas B. Merson.

1. Community junior college development: present and future.
2. Requisite adaptations of instruction and implications for instruction in English.
3. Recommendations for a nationwide effort to improve instruction of communication skills in community-junior colleges.

COMMUNITY-JUNIOR COLLEGE DEVELOPMENT

Forces of many kinds are directly and obliquely changing the configuration of our society at an unprecedented rate. Change is ubiquitous. Adaptation by individuals and by agencies of society is imperative if we are to profit from new opportunities 'rather than to be overwhelmed by the adjustments new developments demand. Almost no segment of our population, no facet of the life of an individual remains unaffected by these changes. Of all the changes, the most impressive and most portentous is the rate of change itself. Any aspect of our society which seeks to perpetuate the status quo and to entrench tradition faces inevitable failure more surely in the future than in the past.

The day has passed when one can live in isolation. Advancements in transportation and communication make us increasingly individually interdependent. The rapid proliferation of knowledge and the unprecedented rate of application of technology have intensified the need for specialization. Opportunities for those who do not or cannot specialize are diminishing rapidly. Few can escape the impact of these events.

The day has passed when society can be indifferent and unresponsive to these forces and developments. To prosper, a society must initiate, organize, and operate agencies which promote its general welfare. Experience has shown that of all the agencies man has invented none is more basic or more effective in contributing to his advancement, and hence to his welfare, than education.

The day has passed when an elementary education or a high school education will provide sufficient formal preparation for the responsibilities of citizenship, economic independence, or personal well-being. The need for the universal upward extension of educational opportunity for all was never greater. And no impartial analysis of trends in our development can reach any conclusion other than that we are only on the brink of demands for education which will dwarf by comparison all past records of accomplishment, however laudable they may have been.

The day has passed when merely an extension of previous education practices will suffice. Tomorrow's education—at least post-high school education—must relate itself directly to the welfare of individuals and of society. The very definition of "college education" must be modified to embrace new responsibilities which colleges must assume. No longer will a "classical education" or a traditional "liberal arts" education suffice. We must accept the necessity for giving increasing attention to things ordinary and practical in collegiate institutions if these institutions are to serve well the needs of a larger segment of our society. It is interesting to speculate on what might be the form of higher education today had not the land grant colleges been established a century ago. In the opinion of many, the phenomenal advances in agriculture and technology—advances which clearly have made our leadership among nations possible—is attributable almost entirely to the break from traditional education by the land grant colleges and the state universities. The criticism heaped upon these institutions during their efforts of pioneering in educational innovation is well known and should be remembered during similarly trying days of development of community colleges.

The day has passed when a single kind of post-secondary institution can adequately provide all the kinds of education society needs. More than ever before, universities must concentrate their efforts on research and on preparation of persons who can become competent researchers. To do this well, universities must relinquish to other institutions responsibility for other kinds of higher education. Society must provide these other kinds of institutions and define their responsibilities—responsibilities which are clearly different from those assigned to universities toward this end. Several states have made significant headway in developing master plans for higher education. But in spite of the significant progress which has been made in enlightened states, there still persists in the minds of many the impression that all higher education should be university education; the higher higher-education is, the better it is; and any higher education which does not replicate university education is inferior.

In effect, we are groping for means to provide appropriate post-high school education for major segments of our society—to segments which previously have not enjoyed the benefits of higher education. To do this we are creating new institutions with new purposes, and we are redefining the responsibilities of existing institutions. Hopefully, these changes in educational structure and function will not lag too far behind changes in society itself.

It is in this setting that the community-junior college finds itself the youngest member of the family of institutions of higher education. Throughout its early life older members of the family have told it what it could and couldn't do, and just how to do whatever it did. Junior has now grown to the point where his competence in some fields exceeds those of others in the family. By virtue of his youth he is less hampered by habit, more sensitive to current developments, and more eager to demonstrate capabilities which his youth makes possible. His ambition to seek a career in fields previously unknown, but with promising futures, is normal. Society can well afford to give this youngster a chance to test himself, especially while he is still versatile and adaptable.

Visionary leaders have advised Junior to seek his fame and fortune by developing the human intellect of the millions who have been by-passed by his forefathers who happily found the pot of gold at the end of the rainbow. His advisors have encouraged him to set up his mills and shops within easy reach of all, to remove barriers of distance and cost, to display his welcome sign, to leave his latch unlocked, to keep a light in the window—in short, to be a house at the side of the road, and a friend to man.

In educational terminology, junior-community college leaders have sought six major responsibilities for this institution:

1. Transfer programs which provide university-parallel lower-division courses comparable to those provided in the senior colleges and universities to which junior college graduates can transfer with junior year standing in any field.
2. Occupational-technical programs which prepare community college students for gainful employment in any field for which two years or less of post-high school education qualify them to enter competently.
3. Continuing education programs, largely extended day or evening programs, which are as rich and varied as man's need for further education. These programs give special attention to occupational upgrading and retraining, to social, civic, and personal improvement, and through them the college becomes a center of community service and improvement.
4. Repair programs which provide opportunity for students to overcome deficiencies in their preparation, irrespective of the causes, and to qualify themselves for programs which lead to a level of service which their present level of education makes unattainable.
5. General education constituting an appreciable portion of the programs of all students and having as its goals development of knowledge, skills, and attitudes designed to provide students with a scale of values upon which choices would lead to richer and more meaningful lives, and greater service to society.
6. Counseling and guidance services which would assist students in assessing choices open to them, and which would enable students to

obtain maximum value from opportunities provided through college and noncollege experiences.

The success of the community college depends on its willingness to accept all these responsibilities. To slight one will undoubtedly weaken the others. Viewed in broad perspective, society is asking the community college to enroll all high school graduates and to make adequate provision for adults of all ages who can profit from post-high school programs. If community colleges enroll such a wide range of talent, intellect, interest, ambition, and motivation, it must provide an equally wide variety of programs. It must specifically provide for:

1. Several starting points, all providing success expectancy.
2. A wide range of rates of progress.
3. A broad spread of directions of development.
4. Several points of enrollment termination—hopefully, most of them temporary.

Stated another way, the community college cannot enroll and successfully educate a wide variety of students if it offers only one kind of opportunity. To enroll students of such diversity in a single common core program is only to invite failure by the students and the institution. Ideally, program adaptations for each individual are desired. Frequent evaluation, flexible placement, planned exploration, and often redirection are essential requisites to individualizing students' opportunities.

There are critics who say this is too much to expect of any institution. But evidence is plentiful that when programs are properly planned, organized, staffed, and executed, success exceeds all expectations. Junior college graduates are eager to testify to the excellence of all the programs described above.

That the testimony of junior college graduates has been widely heard and heeded is attested to by the phenomenal growth of community-junior colleges in recent years. More than a million students are now enrolled in over 700 junior-community colleges. More than one student in four starts college in a community-junior college; in a few states more than half of the freshmen enroll in junior colleges. The increase in first-time enrollment of students in 1964 over comparable enrollment in 1963 reported by the Office of Education was 19 percent for two-year colleges and 9 percent for four-year colleges and universities. More than twenty new community colleges are being established each year. Furthermore, when new community colleges start in metropolitan areas, their enrollments often rise to several thousand students in only a few years. Fourteen community colleges have enrollments exceeding 10,000.

Junior-community colleges have developed much further in some states than in others. Some states even lack adequate enabling legislation; many states have not adopted a master plan, and most states lack adequate provision for financing these colleges. A number of states have not favored establishing independent junior college districts; rather, they are establishing a system of university branches. Other states are establishing separate area vocational schools instead of comprehensive community colleges. On the positive side, California enrolls 443,000 students in its seventy-nine two-year colleges. Florida in the last eight years has established twenty-five new colleges and is rapidly achieving its goal to have a community college within commuting distance of 99 percent of its population. Texas, New York, and Michigan have substantial numbers of students enrolled in community colleges. Washington, Oregon, Arizona, Colorado, Massachusetts, Mississippi, Missouri, and North Carolina have well-formulated plans for future development. Illinois, Pennsylvania, Kansas, Ohio, and New Jersey have taken substantial strides forward in the past few years.

It is hazardous to try to predict the future development of these institutions. However, if long-range planning is to be effective, estimations of future needs must be made. The preponderance of evidence points toward the expectation of a system of independent, low-tuition, tax supported, open door, comprehensive community colleges in every state. When these colleges reach full development, it will be normal procedure for almost all high school graduates to enroll in them, and, in addition, they will serve as educational centers in an intermittent way for a very large proportion of the adult population in their respective communities.

If these predictions are sound, junior college enrollment will eventually include perhaps 80 percent of each year's high school graduates, and almost as large a percentage of the adult population over every four or five year period. We can expect less than half of the junior college graduates to transfer to senior colleges; we can expect substantial increases in enrollment in occupational-technical programs, and we can expect a phenomenal increase in enrollment in evening programs. Guidance will become an essential service for both day and evening students, and general education will become much more important and effective than it is at present. The future of repair instruction is not clear. It is probably safe to predict that repair instruction will increasingly become a responsibility of the community college because that institution can provide this service better than any other agency. It is certain that advancements in knowledge and technology will make high school preparation increasingly inadequate, and these advancements will require more frequent attention to occupational retraining and upgrading. If these services are categorized as repair in the future as they are now, it seems likely that responsibility for repair instruction in the community college will not diminish.

When these predictions are applied nationally they seem staggering. Actually, they are conservative and unimaginative; they merely describe current practice in states with well-developed community colleges. The only point of uncertainty is how soon well-developed community colleges will become widespread in every state.

REQUISITE ADAPTATIONS OF INSTRUCTION

If society is to be served in so many ways, if the community college is to fulfill its multifold missions and provide universal, realistic post-high school educational opportunity, none of the responsibilities of the community college enumerated above can be abrogated.

To fulfill these varied responsibilities, community colleges must adopt educational processes which are appropriate for these tasks. For these processes to be appropriate they may have to be bold and imaginative deviations from those employed in other institutions with different students and for different purposes. Among the major adaptations which instructors in community colleges must make are these:

1. *Universal Opportunity*—Instructors must openly endorse the validity and desirability of extending educational opportunity universally to both youth and adults. Incessant search must be made for means to assist students to succeed. Expressed reservations about the social worth of the "open door," or inclination on the part of instructors to be interested in and concerned about the welfare of only selected students, will influence adversely any organized effort toward instructional improvement.

2. *Multiple Programs*—Instructors must fully accept the principle that students comprising a heterogeneous student body will require several substantially different programs. Each program must be specifically designed for a group of students whose characteristics differ significantly from those in other programs, and consequently each group will require some variation in instruction.

3. *Individual Differences*—Instructors, institution-wide, must believe that individual differences exist, that they can be identified and measured, that some of them require administrative and instructional variations, and that the expedient of "grouping" students does not

relieve instructors of responsibility for, and concern about, individuals and their progress.

4. *Variable Standards*—Instructors must recognize that differences in student ability, achievement, background, personality, interest, motivation, and objectives are so fundamental as to make it imperative for the college to identify and define a range of reasonable levels and kinds of expectation for students. Instruction must be varied in accordance with different student needs; programs of individual students must be constructed with regard to expected and demonstrated achievement; achievement must be described in terms of both program and level: There cannot be only one standard of achievement, or only one expectancy level, any more than there can be only one program, if equality of educational opportunity is to be a reality in an institution which enrolls a heterogeneous student group.

5. *Professional Competence*—Instructors must strive for competence to fulfill the responsibilities which this complex institution imposes upon them. These responsibilities require, in addition to mastery of the subject they teach, unusual skill in adapting instruction to student differences. Community college instructors currently must learn much of what they teach and most of their technical skills from experience during their first years of teaching. Instructors must take the initiative in instituting innovations which reduce the time they spend inefficiently.

6. *Analytical Evaluation*—The college as a whole, and instructors in particular, must systematically plan ways to improve their instructional effectiveness. This implies far greater application of objective evaluation of the instructional process than teachers are usually willing to initiate or accept. It is the teacher's responsibility to seek opportunity to introduce instructional innovations and to adopt those which prove more effective than procedures which are currently used.

IMPLICATIONS FOR INSTRUCTION IN ENGLISH AND COMMUNICATION SKILLS

Research dealing with instruction in English, particularly in the communication skills, in the comprehensive community college is so limited that one has little basis from that source upon which to make recommendations. There is, however, a substantial understanding of the basic instructional problems by a large corps of experienced community college teachers. Unfortunately, no serious effort has been made to systematically record these experiences so others may profit from them.

The survey of English instruction in two-year colleges recently completed by Weingarten and Kroeger[1] provides us with the only nationwide view of significant elements of general practice. Throughout this report one is impressed by the great range of practices which are in effect. Some of the variations can be attributed to differences in the nature of the colleges themselves, but other differences suggest that many practices in English instruction have been adopted and are being followed because critical evaluation of these practices has not been attempted.

The community-junior college claims excellence of instruction to be one of its major strengths. Compared to higher education institutions generally, this is probably a valid claim. There is, however, a paucity of evidence that imaginative instructional innovations have advanced in their development as rapidly as new demands for innovation have increased. Junior college teachers readily admit that they find themselves ill prepared for the many problems which the diversity of students presents to them. It is precisely this point which makes this conference so timely.

If one compares recent changes in instruction in several fields, he is impressed by the substantial changes in mathematics, engineering, technology, physical science, biological science, and foreign language which have resulted from increased national attention to those fields. Phenomenal daily civic and political developments have served to force instructional adaptations in social sciences even without the incentive of increased financial support. Isn't it fair to say that on a scale of innovation, one would have to place English instruction well down toward the conservative-traditional end of the scale? To the extent this is true, this conservatism is a liability in a versatile, dynamic community college. It can be hoped that the USOE English Programs, NCTE efforts, and other incentives will develop promising innovations which will move English instructors from their entrenchment.

In one respect, English holds an enviable position. Development of student competence is regarded to be of such importance that uninterrupted, sustained attention is given to it for all students for thirteen school years. Surely within that time span, reasonable competence can be developed. Therefore, junior-community college English instructors need not assume all the responsibility for students' competence or lack of it in communication skills. Nor can English instructors expect to correct in one year all the deficiencies which have accumulated over the previous twelve. Furthermore, English instructors cannot expect marked

[1]Samuel Weingarten and Frederick P. Kroeger, *English in the Two-Year College* (Champaign, Ill.: NCTE, 1965).

improvement in one year's time by repeating the experiences students have had in previous years. There is good reason to believe that community colleges are in a strategic position to influence improvement of English instruction in elementary and secondary schools in their communities. Effort along these lines may be one of the most profitable investments which college English instructors could make.

Many community college English instructors declare that their most serious problems stem from the heterogeneity of the students they teach. They claim if they had only selected students in their classes, they would have no problems. This is largely a delusion because "goodness" is relative at any point on a value scale. For example, university professors complain of incompetence in language skills of graduate students, as do professors of engineering and science, yet all teach highly selected students. It seems important to note that, as a rule, successful mastery of a different task provides the master with greater satisfaction than doing something which almost anyone could accomplish. Perhaps our colleges do not provide sufficient approbation and recognition for outstanding *instructional* achievements. Have we neglected the publicity value of the fact that community-junior college instructors succeed with students who would be failures in other institutions?

Many community-junior college instructors hold the view that inordinate loads prevent them from teaching more effectively. If this is valid, it can be proved—and should be proved. The near unanimity of this view marks this point as one to which early research attention should be given. At the time such research is going on, however, other research should be undertaken to determine what activities now performed by instructors might be done as well, or better, in other ways. Any evidence which will lead to improved instructional effectiveness should be sought.

It is obvious that research findings must point the way to solutions of the critical problems facing community-junior college English instructors. Even at the risk of encroaching on other papers being prepared for this conference, brief mention of some of the critical research needs should be made here:

1. Development of screening instruments with high prognostic reliability which would provide a dependable basis for grouping students.
2. Development of diagnostic instruments which would quantitatively identify specific student strengths and weaknesses in communication skills in such a way that repair instruction can be individualized.
3. Systematic search for effective ways to organize and schedule instruction in English in order that the "system" itself does not preclude improvement.

4. Systematic valuation of alternative components of course content in order that needed variations may be provided without unnnecessarily dispersing desirable concentrations of instructional effort.
5. Critical evaluation of all instructional procedures, both traditional and innovative, in order to obtain maximum value from instructional efforts.
6. Critical analysis of student characteristics including motivation and interest which seem to have direct relationship to instructional effectiveness.
7. Deep, penetrating follow-up studies by which the long-range impact of instruction might be assessed.

RECOMMENDED ACTION

The task of substantially improving instruction in English and the communication skills in community-junior colleges nationally is a major one. Only through organized cooperative effort can significant progress be expected. The most promising efforts should be identified at this conference, and the following suggestions are submitted for consideration:

1. *Prepare a statement of goals and objectives of instruction in English and communication skills in junior-community colleges.*

   A small team of experts could compile such a statement relatively quickly and easily. The statement would: (1) identify several different goals and describe each in terms of student competencies sought; (2) view these goals in perspective with references to student characteristics and student objectives; (3) rank major responsibilities of English instruction such as the humanistic responsibility, the communications skills responsibility, the repair responsibility, the specialization (vocational-technical) responsibility and others in terms of (a) numbers of students and (b) importance.

   The statement of goals should consider and be addressed to the implications for English instruction of each of the accepted social missions of the community-junior college.

   The statement of goals should provide a philosophical base and a structural framework on which efforts to improve present practice could be built systematically.

2. *Describe an ideal program with appropriate standards in English and communications skills for community-junior colleges.*

   Content for this publication would be derived from current best practices. A single author with an advisory committee or several authors, all experienced teachers, should be selected for this assignment. The bulletin would make recommendations regarding all facets of English and communication skills instruction including screening and placing students, course content, instructional techniques, and methods of evaluating student achievement. The bulletin would be designed primarily to assist colleges which had made little progress in developing differentiated programs. Without further research the statements on standards would admittedly be difficult.

3. *Compile known facts on teaching English and communication skills in community-junior colleges.*

Such a list will probably be startingly short. Its purpose would be to dramatize the need for research and to stimulate interest in seeking facts to support or refute divergent points of view. These facts would include such items as information about (1) relevant student characteristics, (2) student screening and placement, (3) course content and organization, (4) instructional effectiveness, and (5) impact of instruction.

4. *Develop hypotheses regarding critical aspects of teaching English and communications skills in community-junior colleges in an attempt to direct action toward research, especially experimentation, which is needed to improve programs and instruction.*

Instruction generally, and instruction in English specifically, has reached a point where further progress requires additional research-based information. Precisely worded hypotheses provide one of the best means to channel effort toward finding answers to questions now answered only by opinion. Examples of hypotheses to be tested are:

a. First semester junior-community college students show greater improvement in communication skills when they are enrolled in unclassified classes having uniform content and instruction.

b. Course placement of first semester students in community-junior colleges is most effective when it is based exclusively on a writing exercise administered by college English instructors one month before classes start.

c. Student improvement in communication skills is significantly greater in classes which enroll fifteen students or fewer.

d. Independent study of taped exercises improves spelling performance of students more than spelling taught in the standard teacher-centered classroom.

e. A given amount of money used for theme readers results in greater improvement of student writing proficiency than the same amount of money spent on reduced class size.

f. Students who are assigned themes of less than two pages improve their skills of organization as much as students who write longer papers.

g. Engineering technology students who are enrolled in regular liberal arts transfer courses in English develop greater proficiency in writing technical reports than students enrolled in technical report courses.

5. *Organize research centers and pilot programs to systematically evaluate current practices, selected hypotheses, and long-range impact of programs and instruction in English and communications skills in community-junior colleges.*

These centers should be cooperatively arranged between universities and junior colleges so the university could assist with research design, so the junior college could provide the laboratory for experimentation, and so the professional competence of junior college instructors could be increased by their participation. A cooperative arrangement between graduate students and junior college faculties could provide means for completing longitudinal studies which are usually impossible for individuals to undertake alone.

6. *Analyze the responsibilities of instructors in English and communications skills in community-junior colleges in order to design and initiate programs of teacher preparation which will insure competence for fulfilling these responsibilities.*

No single action will do more to improve instruction in English communication skills than one which will lead to providing an adequate supply of competent teachers. Problems of program reorganization within universities are formidable but not insurmountable. A strong recommendation from this conference on this point, followed by more detailed explication of the preparation sought, together with continued organized pressure at both state and national levels should be influential.

ORGANIZATIONAL PLAN

This conference will be recorded as the fountainhead of major change if the study groups and the summary panel address their attention to *action* which is requisite to change. *Desired action should be clearly stated by this conference.* To insure that this action is taken, plans of organization should also be formulated and recommended. Components of such organization might include the following:

1. Teams of experts, or task forces, to be assigned specific responsibilities such as those suggested in this paper.
2. Research centers and pilot programs to be organized cooperatively by universities and satellite community-junior colleges.
3. National coordination to be provided by the National Council of

Teachers of English, the U. S. Office of Education English Programs, the American Association of Junior Colleges, or other appropriate body, or combinations of agencies.

4. Financial support to be derived from federal funds, foundation grants, or state or local sources.

5. Publicity to be directed to English teachers, to various segments of the higher education community, to other levels of education, to students and parents, to counselors, and to the public generally.

In conclusion, it is my hope that this conference will not adjourn without taking action which will launch a continuing, well-directed effort toward improving programs and instruction in English and communications skills in community-junior colleges. We may have to wait for another Sputnik with "Reverse English" to dramatize our plight. Perhaps we must wait until we meet "little green men" before the need for increased proficiency in communication skills receives adequate attention. Must we wait for such spectacular events to focus our attention on, and direct our efforts toward, solution of basic problems which we recognize so clearly? *Action* taken at this conference can supply that answer.

English in the Two-Year College

SUMMARY, CONCLUSIONS, AND RECOMMENDATIONS

SAMUEL WEINGARTEN
AND FREDERICK P. KROEGER

THIS REPORT has presented a picture of English instruction in the two-year college drawn from the information furnished by 187 department chairmen and 292 teachers in 239 two-year colleges of various types, located in every region of the country. In the eight main sections, the authors of the report have analyzed the data and arrived at conclusions concerning the teaching of English in this unit of the American educational structure in which the largest number of college-age youth will be enrolled in the future.

One of the conclusions arising from data related to the general situation in the two-year colleges is that there is very little democratic procedure in matters relating to personnel practices, such as engaging and dismissing teachers, making recommendations for tenure, and selecting chairmen of departments. Even chairmen who have a voice in the selection of personnel are in the minority. The situation seems to this committee of the National Council of Teachers of English and the Conference on College Composition and Communication an alarming one. Certainly with the two-year college now recognized as a part of higher education, there should be a more democratic spirit within these insti-

From *English in the Two-Year College*, National Council of Teachers of English, 1965, pp. 79–86. Reprinted with the permission of the National Council of Teachers of English, Samuel Weingarten, and Frederick P. Kroeger.

tutions, where administrators should draw on the professional judgment of teachers in making decisions about the selection of staff members and in determining which teachers are to occupy positions of authority within the staff. Edmund J. Gleazer, Jr., executive director of the American Association of Junior Colleges, has called the two-year college "democracy's college of this century." The institutions of a democracy must foster the spirit of democracy in professional procedures if the basic philosophy of our way of life is to flourish. The data revealed by this study concerning present practices point toward a need for reform within the institutions in which faculty participation in policy making will have a larger role, not only in relation to curriculum but also in relation to personnel practices.

Another of the conclusions reached is that providing students with writing practice is a major problem in many two-year colleges. The data demonstrate that many of these schools are substandard in the number of papers which students are required to write or in the small number of words required. It is concluded that this situation is the result of the overloading of teachers with too many and overly large classes. The data on class size and teaching loads reveal that this is indeed the case. This situation is explicitly stated by the teacher respondents to be one of the unique problems of teaching English in this type of institution. Its undesirable effects are felt not only on the students' writing but also on the professional welfare of the teachers. Every effort should be made through the cooperation of teachers and administrators to reduce class size and teaching load. Only by such a reduction can English instruction in the two-year college be on the quality level of such instruction in other types of institutions of higher education. *This NCTE-CCCC committee recommends that an English teacher in a two-year college should have no more than seventy-five students in composition and that he should have only three sections of composition, plus other teaching in literature, speech, drama, or whatever the nature of the program of the school dictates. It also recommends that no English teacher should have more than two different preparations unless he prefers a wider variety of courses.*

The report presents, in all of its complexity, the situation created by the open-door policy: a mass of students varying greatly in preparation, ability, and goals. The situation has baffled many teachers in the two-year colleges where students of such contrasting quality must, because of local conditions, be taught in the same classes. However, in the majority of the schools surveyed, 65.8 percent, the problem is handled by the placement of students in honors (advanced), regular, or remedial classes. The most usual pattern, 32 percent, consists of regular and remedial English. Because of the unselected and heterogeneous student population, proper placement becomes, then, the crucial step in English instruction in the two-year college. The survey of techniques and instruments for placement contained in this report leads us to conclude that the problem of identification of students for placement in English sections has not been solved. As one of the authors of this report says, "Obviously with many students needing much help, proper placement, both in remedial and regular English classes, is the first thing a staff must do for effective teaching." Teachers in the two-year colleges should make the topic of identification for placement a subject for research and discussion at their meetings and in the publications of NCTE and CCCC. They should also apply for funds to support projects in which more reliable instruments for placement can be developed.

Evidence presented in this report reveals the bewildering variety of what is called "Freshman English" in the two-year colleges. The great variation in cut off scores for placement in regular English, the wide range of writing requirements, the variety of patterns in texts and required reading make it impossible to construct an image of the course. It must not be thought that the authors of this report would consider as desirable a uniform course to be taught in all two-year colleges, even though the most frequently heard cry of the teachers in the responses to our questionnaires is for some kind of standard curriculum guide that would serve as an aid for the perplexed. Certainly local conditions warrant variation. Perhaps the publication now offered by CCCC as a presentation of patterns in basic first year English courses would contribute toward some uniformity. To facilitate better communication we recommend that greater opportunities for conference among teachers of English in two-year colleges be made available through local workshops, national study groups, the pages of the official publications of NCTE and CCCC, or even through a new publication devoted entirely to English in the two-year college. Teachers of English in the two-year colleges should take the initiative in organizing and sponsoring such groups and in supplying articles to the publications. Only by such strengthening of the channels of communication can the present bewilderingly varied scene be made one of rational pattern and order.

The incontrovertible fact that emerges from this study is that the remedial function is an integral and indispensable part of the English curriculum of the two-year college which has an open-door policy. The remedial course cannot be regarded as an illegitimate member of the curriculum which we hope some day to exile into the wilderness. It must be regarded as a *sine qua non* of the basic English program; as such we must give it our best resources to strengthen it and make it operative in the improvement of the language skills of the young people who are placed in remedial courses. Adequate funds for supporting such a program must be made available. Every effort must be made to awaken a realization of this need in college administrators, controlling boards, and taxpaying communities.

Fifty-eight percent of the chairmen who contributed data for this study described remedial English courses in their programs and 10 percent said they plan to innovate such courses. Certainly a course that exists to this extent should be examined to determine its effectiveness in achieving its objectives. Eighteen percent of the teachers contributing to this report were of the opinion that remedial courses are likely to be ineffective. The causes of such an opinion warrant investigation.

Many teachers undoubtedly identify remedial English courses with grammar. In spite of evidence that a knowledge of traditional grammar does not guarantee a carry over which leads to improvement in writing, this emphasis persists. Ninety-nine percent of the chairmen thought grammar important to one degree or another in the remedial course. In spite of the prominence today of the study of structural linguistics and transformational grammar, only 3 percent reported any departure from traditional grammar. Our study of the grammar included in regular English courses shows this same prevalence of traditional grammar. The facts of our study point to the simple truth that, on the whole, two-year college teachers of English do not know the newer developments in linguistics. This is confirmed by the fact that most of these teachers say they wish they had more training in linguistics (45.6%) and the history of the English language (30.8%). The ironic fact is that an examination of the years of teaching experience of the participating teachers shows that many of them are young persons whose formal training took place in recent years. We are led by these considerations to recommend:

1. That English teachers in two-year colleges make every effort to bring themselves up to date in the study of language through attendance at workshops and through publications useful in independent study. The facilities that now exist to enable high school teachers to pursue such self-improvement will have to be extended to include two-year college teachers.
2. That efforts be made to establish experimental centers for the development of methods and materials for use in remedial courses. Funds for such centers are becoming increasingly available.

3. That courses which may give teachers expertness in handling problems in remedial teaching be made available to them by university graduate schools.

Questioning of departmental chairmen as to what courses are subsumed under "English" in their schools revealed that such courses as these have, in a limited number of instances for each, been developed to meet the needs of students in various vocational programs: Business Letter Writing, Technical Report Writing, Advertising Copy, Radio and TV Writing. There remains a great opportunity for teachers to devise special English courses to fit the vocational programs that are being introduced in increasing numbers in the two-year colleges. The committee recommends this as an area for research. Undoubtedly teachers of English in the two-year colleges have been of the opinion that the needs of students in specialized vocational programs are best served in the more general terminal English course. The complaint of teachers about having terminal and transfer students in the same English course leads one to infer that the drift is toward differentiating terminal students from transfer students in placing them in English courses. Research is recommended in the development of terminal English courses of a distinctive nature that will serve especially the needs of students whose formal college work terminates at the end of the two year program and whose placement test results indicate that they cannot successfully complete a college transfer English course. The responses to the questionnaires did not yield significant information about any existing courses of this kind which show originality and insight into the nature and needs of students placed in such courses. Undoubtedly further inquiry about such courses needs to be made, and a study of them in depth also seems highly desirable. We recommend that workshops be set up especially devoted to the development of courses of study for terminal English, as distinguished from transfer English and from remedial English. However, the committee recognizes that in some situations grouping with ability alone as a criterion is undoubtedly a preferable procedure. The assumption of a universally applicable dichotomy of terminal and transfer courses would be unfortunate. Much research remains to be done concerning principles for determining the placement of students in English courses in the two-year college.

It is surprising that teachers who feel so strongly the need for help in solving the realistic problems encountered in the community, open-door two-year colleges have an attitude of contempt for schools of Education and their offerings. Yet it is in the field of Education and nowhere else that they can find the answers to their problems. We therefore recommend that a great effort be made to bridge the gap between subject matter respectability and professional training in the minds of English teachers in two-year colleges. They cannot afford to fumble as amateurs in areas of teaching where scientific information about the learning process and knowledge of materials and methods can turn them into proficient teachers of the poorly prepared and the disadvantaged.

They cannot afford to remain disappointed teachers yearning for selected students of high ability. Most of the two-year colleges are quite unlike Oxford ". . . whispering from her towers the last enchantments of the Middle Age." There are far too many teachers of English in two-year colleges who are disoriented persons, failing to face realistically the fact that they must adjust their subject matter specialty to the particular situation that exists in most of the colleges of this kind and that will exist to a greater extent in the future. We must point out to chairmen of English departments in four-year colleges and universities, through their now existing organization, that college teaching opportunities for students majoring in English will in the future increase in the two-year colleges and that these young people must not go into such positions, even if they are accepted, without the skills needed in teaching English in such schools. As Warner Rice pointed out some years ago ("Our Ph.D's—Where Do They Go from Here?" *PMLA*, February, 1952), if the graduate English departments do not give them such preparation, someone else will have to undertake it. We therefore recommend that a course in "The Teaching of English in the Two-Year College" become as standard a part of professional training as the already existing courses of this type for elementary and secondary school English, and that this course, if handled within the English department, be taught by someone as thoroughly acquainted with the two-year college situation as with the subject matter of the field.

We also recommend to chairmen of English departments in four-year colleges and universities that they try to make their students majoring in English aware that Education is not an alien country, but rather, a place where they can attain proficiencies and awareness that are prerequisite for successful teaching in the two-year colleges, especially in the remedial program. The mere fact that such majors in English can read with expert understanding the literary classics does not mean that they can offer helpful instruction to two-year college freshmen, some of whom have reading abilities on the ninth grade level or lower. The challenge remains for Education departments to offer more meaningful courses that will have genuine importance in the professional development of the people who enroll in them.

We recommend further that in the training of teachers of English for the two-year college such cooperation should come to exist among the various disciplines that there will no longer be applicants for teaching positions who only dimly understand what one means in speaking of general semantics, structural linguistics, transformation grammar, remedial and developmental reading, and programed learning. We recommend that courses in semantics, logic, and linguistics be required parts of the training of teachers of English for two-year colleges. We wish also to point out that frequently departments of speech, which place emphasis on the art of rhetoric, its practice as well as its history, offer potential English teachers much light on the art of composition. Unless such auxiliary fields become a part of the training of English teachers, the realistic needs of the open-door, community two-year college will quickly reveal the hoax of English teachers who are trained exclusively in belles lettres and other fine arts, valuable as these may be in other aspects of instruction in English and humanities. We recommend therefore that the four-year colleges and universities train teachers of English through such courses as these that we have mentioned and by an increased amount of training in the composing art itself.

We note with comparison one teacher's sense of regret that he did not have "supervision under a master teacher as a part of training" and "experience in grading compositions under critical supervision." He regrests that his training did not lead him to learn ". . . that I should not teach to impress my colleagues, but teach the students." We recommend an increased amount of practice teaching in two-year colleges as an indispensable part of preparation for such teaching and possibly the establishment of an internship in such teaching. Perhaps such training, as well as some of the courses mentioned above, can be incorporated into the required work for a higher degree in English.

Our study reveals that 54.8 percent of the teachers responding are members of the National Council of Teachers of English, that 32.2 percent belong to the Conference on College Composition and Communication, and 14.7 percent to the College English Association. The study also reveals that 41.8 percent of these teachers have not attended a single national professional meeting in the last five years and that over one third have not attended one local meeting in this same period of time. We must conclude that, at least to some extent, this slightness of attendance can be explained by the failure of the meetings to have relevance to the professional problems of teachers of English in two-year colleges. Certainly in recent times the professional organizations have begun to give time, space, and effort to two-year college English, at national meetings and in the pages of the journals. We recommend that these be increased so that thousands of teachers of English in the hundreds of two-year colleges will find help through their professional organizations in solving their bafflling problems. As such help increases, membership in the organizations will undoubtedly increase.

We recommend that the present two-year college members of NCTE and CCCC take steps to establish affiliate organizations of two-year college teachers which will serve regional needs. There are at present regional organizations of two-year college teachers of English, as in the state of California. Would it not be possible to organize other regional groups of such teachers and to relate them to NCTE as affiliates? We recommend further that chairmen of English departments in two-year colleges seek to organize themselves as a national group comparable with that for chairmen in four-year colleges or as regional groups.

It is not a coincidence that the conclusions which we have reached by the examination of the data and the recommendations which we make are to some extent identical with those explicitly stated by the chairmen and teachers who contributed to this study and with the published conclusions of many workshops at CCCC conventions. These workers in the two-year colleges know what the situation is in the teaching of English to the students who come to this type of school. In most instances they also have the intelligence to know some of the means by which they can be helped, and they will undoubtedly find solutions to most of the problems with which they are now confronted. But it is for the people who are in authority in the professional organizations and in the upper divisions of higher education, as well as for those who control the use of funds by national foundations, to act now to help the teachers of English in the two-year colleges.

Understanding High School Students

ARE THEIR RESOURCES BEING WASTED?

AMELIA ASHE

WHO IS THE much discussed "American high school student"? He may be still in high school, or a drop-out, or someone new to the college campus (in which case he will tend for a while to resemble the high school population more than the collegiate); or perhaps he may be an adult whose last educational experiences were those of high school. In any case, he will not yet have taken his place—either because of a simple age or experience factor, or because of some external interruption of his educational development—among the ranks of the literate college adult population. It is this student whom we meet most often in basic English courses. Because of the low level of his skills in reading and writing, he requires basic instruction in the use of English. And there is much that can be done through written and oral work and through reading to help him gain mastery of the language.

To generalize about the high school population is to attempt a description of more than ninety percent of the adolescent age group, those between the ages of 14 and 18, who are enrolled in high schools. Any generalization will apply only to some members of that population; few or none will apply to all. High school students defy easy categorization. They are a puzzlement! Perhaps because life seems to offer them such a variety of conflicting possibilities and choices, we find considerable diversity in adolescent personalities, life styles, attitudes, values, and behaviors.

Written especially for this volume.

There is, in fact, something in flux about the whole generation. Today's young people have lived with change all their lives, and they seem attuned to it to a staggering degree—whether it be educational, technological, social or political. The majority have grown up in cities; all have grown up in the shadow of nuclear weapons. They have witnessed and vicariously experienced man's first, weird landing on the moon. They perceive the age of the computer, the conquest of space, and the reality of instant communication as part of the natural order of things. (In fact, their sense of wonder is reserved for marvelling at the poor use adults make of their knowledge, rather than for admiring the ingenuity that fashions these marvels.)

Within the maelstrom of the high school population, however, certain commonalities can be identified. On the one hand, we find young persons who demonstrate incredible precocity, intelligence, and self-confidence. Some of these appear sensitive, idealistic, ethical, interesting, tender, and they speak with quiet force about their quest for personal purpose and worth. We also find the bland and the stolid—those who seem to accept the goal of a college degree unquestioningly and who pursue it with a grim determination. In sharp contrast are the rebellious young, seemingly without a cause or a rationale, affecting impudent, fantastic fashions, bizarre manners, and championing ideas outside the mainstream.

ADOLESCENCE AS A LIFESTAGE

To some extent, of course, adolescence in our society has always been that period in an individual's life which provdes an opportunty for exploring alternatives in personal style, interests, and identity. Traditionally, it has also been a time to enjoy a series of dramatic try-on roles. According to anthropologists, the case is somewhat different in other societies. In some cultures situated in distant parts of the world today, one is either a child or an adult. Shortly after puberty, the young person is initiated directly into the company of his elders through a series of rites of passage, sometimes harsh, sometimes poetic, always symbolic. Tests of courage and skill are required at this point, after the early years of imitation and preparation, but there is never much question as to the type of adult the young person will—and wants to— become.

In cultures where the individual's function is somewhat more complicated, an adult social role is not learned so easily. Here the adolescent will need not only the universal experience of sensing his own ability to perform meaningful work, but he will also need to carve out a sense of his new identity and a belief in his own worth. And both are more difficult in a complex society. If the young person lacks some image of himself as an emergent adult he comes to believe that he has no *raison d'être* except to be alive and to grow; this, psychology tells us, is not enough to nurture and sustain a healthy personality. If society asks nothing of the young person, gives him nothing to do which will help him test and prove himself, if it offers no appealing place or places in the adult world, and if it provides no constructive ways for him to achieve an adult identity, the adolescent must fail at his task of individuation and role definition.

Erikson has characterized youth as a period of "psycho-social moratorium" on the way to adulthood and the consolidation of an adult social role. Teachers of English need to be especially sensitive to the fact that this is the time during which the young person engages in a struggle for personal integrity. He strives to know what he is and what he is not, what he wants to be, what he looks like to others, to whom and to what he belongs. He begins to see himself as others see him, yet he wishes to be—and his task is to be—himself, openly and undefensively. This is the time when he needs the security and intimacy afforded by warm interpersonal relationships, but when he must begin to be aware that one's life is one's own responsibility. He will also learn, ideally, that one's personal style may be forged from any beginning, since the crucial determinant tends to be the way in which one copes with the ills inherent in the human condition, rather than becoming submerged in these ills which inhere in one's immediate environment.

THE CONDITIONS OF ADOLESCENCE TODAY

The condition of society itself will have far-reaching effects on the condition of its youth. Above and beyond the more or less universal conditions of adolescence, then, high school students today reflect and respond to situations inherent in this time and this place. Thus many of them manifest certain orientations different from those manifested by young people in other cultures.

Keniston has described one of these as the "here and now" view of the world, in which a hedonism of the moment is selected in lieu of the long-range goals, postponed satisfactions, and deferred rewards offered by society. When adulthood seems hazy or undesirable for any reason, it follows that one may decide simply to enjoy the highest possible number of immediate sensory experiences: drugs, sex, speed, "kicks."

A second generalized reaction to the modern world among young people has been cited by Riesman. Feelings of powerlessness, perhaps self-fulfilling, he believes, have fostered a climate of "privatism" in which young people increasingly value those areas of their lives from which the larger society can be excluded. When predictability and control are hard to come by in a complicated and shifting society, one may opt for a retreat into one's own small sphere where it seems more possible to be in charge, to control events, and to manage what might otherwise be inimical to control. Here again, we see that feelings of helplessness increase when one cannot shape one's future and when, in the great sorting process, one may be assigned no clear rung on the ladder of opportunity.

As a result of their idiosyncratic world views, new kinds of students are emerging on today's high school scene. In the minority are the band of rebellious intellectuals. In pursuit of identity, primarily within the sphere of ideas, these students have been summoned to action by the apocalyptic events in Mississippi, Berkeley, Kent State, Chicago, and elsewhere. The revolutionary aspects of our time, particularly the war on poverty, the civil rights movement, and the crusade against the Vietnam War, attract them and make them more active politically and socially than many preceding generations.

They are insistent about being heard. Much of their criticism is leveled against the institution they know best—the school—and against society's failure to provide satisfactory alternatives for adolescent development outside the college experience. Even as high school students, they are already aware that college is less than Camelot, yet they recognize that failure to pass through college can adversely affect their chances for many kinds of success. Since formal education has long been recognized in this country as the primary means for achieving higher occupational and social status, the college decision is often forced by circumstances rather than by love of learning.

Quite distinct from the group of rebellious intellectuals in motive and in response to the conditions of their lives, are the culturally impoverished youth who are coming increasingly to dominate many of our high schools. Indeed, it is this group which is largely responsible for the upsurge of the need for basic English courses in our schools, colleges, and extra-academic programs. Often a depressing, sometimes a fearful, challenge to their teachers, these disaffected youth see little or no connection between education and either their present or future roles. Basically passive, they note the meaningless work or the lack of work which fills the lives of their own family group members, and they come eventually to view themselves in their pockets of poverty as outsiders with no legitimate or possible way of attaining status or money. But the "outsider" role rankles as they see from their window on the world the affluent society which television, films, and the news media hold up to all. Restless, eventually rebellious, such adolescents flout not only school but also social rules in their challenge to authority. Society itself, as well as the educational enterprise, becomes the enemy, and their generalized hostility erupts into acts of violence. Violence permeates the neighborhoods in which these students live; it filters into home and school. Acts of aggression against persons and property feed the "blackboard jungle" climate in some of our schools.

The highly visible students in this adolescent subculture apparently believe that the social structure is designed to defeat (some say "murder") them. One student, quoted in a Public Education Association report on student grievances, comments:

> I already feel like I'm nobody, and then what they do to you in school says, 'That's right, man. You're nobody!

Another explains the disruptive behavior of his fellow students thus:

> I know why those guys throw rocks and set fires. They found out there's *no* way they can make it. They know that's not right, but it's true, and they don't know what to do about it. If you try to change things, you get put up against the wall for that too. So finally you get mad. That's just human.

THE ROLE OF THE SCHOOLS

There is much support for the harsh indictments of the schools. Friedenberg has charged the schools with the assumption of excessive responsibility for students' intellectual and moral development. According to Friedenberg, the school is not really the agent, but the arena for individual development. He argues that, as arena, the school should be primarily responsible—not for the end results of education—but for setting in motion those processes that are the stuff of which continuing education is made.

Friedenberg's study of American high school youth led him to conclude that the schools appear to stultify the growth of healthy individualism among students when they "Americanize" them, teach them their "place" in the scheme of things, and even equip them with behavioral models for responding to success or to failure. Ultimately, he contends, the schools certify each student not only for his vocational or professional role, through the assessment and nurturance of his intelligence, but also for his future socioeconomic, cultural, and emotional life, through evaluative judgments about his emotional tone, his personality, and his medical condition. As Riesman remarks in his introducton to Friedenberg's *The Vanishing Adolescent:*

> School has become not only a sorting station for academic aptitude, but a monitor for character and personality as well.

Many other studies (see the bibliography following this article) have noted that the increasing complexity of the schools serves, in many instances, to effect greater standardization, bureaucratization, and stratification of students.

BASIC ENGLISH AS A LIBERATING MECHANISM

Certainly any failure of the schools to work with the creative energies and concerns of students at this dynamic lifestage is lamentable wherever it has occurred. But for the teacher of basic English, the challenge of *righting* this situation is particularly imperative. No small task when the very idea of education has become antithetical to self-development in the minds of many young people! Nevertheless the teacher of English, above all, must encourage expressiveness, initiative, spontaneity, imagination, ebullience, creativity. He must contrive somehow to get himself on the side of the students' search for autonomy; at the same time, he must encourage their progress toward the self-discipline that accompanies self-esteem.

But how stimulate them to accept the hard work that we all know good writing requires? In these days of the great "put-on" few of us were especially shocked by a recent story about a new luminary among authors who "wrote" his book by taking a pill, talking at random into a tape recorder, and shipping this effluvia to the luckless editor of his favorite publisher. *Le voilà*, a best seller! A writer like Thomas Mann counted himself productive if he readied five hundred words for his editor on a single day. Good writing is the end product of a painstaking process—a gestative-like activity requiring time for sustained thought, as well as experience and aptitude in organizing and expressing what one has to say.

When we ask a student to write 1,000 words in ninety minutes, or even when we ask him to write only 300 words in forty-five minutes, exactly what are we saying to him about the act of writing? We are encouraging him in the absurd notion that ideas flow from the pen in polished prose, ready for publication, or that anyone experiencing a lack of success in such a task is simply one of those unfortunates who "can't write."

In effect, we make this statement when we imply that good writing springs full-blown, Athena-like, from the brain. Concurrently, we also deny the student the opportunity for disciplined pre-writing or post-writing activities. Small wonder that he is unsure what ideas he wishes to transmit, that he does not organize his material coherently, and that he has no interest in editing it for precision and clarity. The benchmarks of the accomplished writer—order, coherence, power, and style—will continue to evade the scribbler who "writes" to satisfy an inherently impossible assignment rather than from his own need to communicate.

Effective writing grows out of reading. It also grows out of experience. The experience may be personal or vicarious, but it is essential. One must—even today—have something to say. And one must shape his statement to a known audience. All the rest, save the spark of brilliance over which we have no control, is practice. For writing, like human development, is process. The student must be actively engaged in writing, not just talking about writing or filling a prescriptive drill exercise. He must shape all his communication, oral or written, so that its power will make real to others what is real and significant to him. The beginning of this process will coincide with the beginning of thoughtful and honest study of himself; only then can he transmute his imaginative conceptions into something substantial which will be apprehended by whoever cares to hear. He must ask: How do I really feel about that? How has it touched me, perhaps even changed me?

"I am fearfully and wonderfully made," said the young King David marveling at the depth and mystery of his uniqueness. His voyage into self-discovery presaged the modern psychologist's and sociologist's characterizations of youth in search of their own uniqueness. If, as Friedenberg has said, "Personalization is the metièr of adolescence," and the essential task is self-definition, then adolescence is certainly much more than a physical process largely involved with sexual maturation. It is also a social process the primary end of which is a clear and stable self-definition.

The great aim for those who strive to put the student in touch with his language is that he should use it effectively in speaking about the vital issues of the human being in search of self, and also that he should come to use literary works as material for further explorations into the human condition. High school students, one could even say those in the grip of poverty and disaffection in particular, should be able to anticipate that their turn will come soon in our society's new climate of rising expectations.

REFERENCES

Cicourel, Aaron V. and John L. Kitsuse, *The Educational Decision Makers,* New York: Bobbs-Merrill Company, Inc., 1963.

Clark, Burton R., *Educating the Expert Society,* San Francisco: Chandler Publishing Company, 1962.

Clark, Kenneth B., *Dark Ghetto,* New York: Harper and Row, 1965.

Coleman, James S., *The Adolescent Society,* New York: The Free Press of Glencoe, 1961.

Erikson, Erik H. *Childhood and Society,* New York: Norton, 1951.

————, "Identity and the Life Cycle," *Psychological Issue,* New York: International University Press, 1959.

————, (ed.) *Youth: Change and Challenge,* New York: Basic Books, Inc., 1963.

Friedenberg, E. Z., *The Vanishing Adolescent,* Boston: Beacon, 1959.

Goodman, Paul, *Growing Up Absurd,* New York: Random House, 1960.

Hollingshead, A. B., *Elmtown's Youth,* New York: Wiley, 1949.

Keniston, Kenneth, *The Uncommitted:* Alienated Youth in American Society, New York: Harcourt, Brace, & World, Inc., 1965.

Moynihan, Daniel Patrick, "The Impact on Manpower Development and Employment of Youth," in *Universal Higher Education,* ed., Earl J. McGrath. New York: McGraw Hill Book Company, 1966.

Public Education Association, Information Series No. 2, May, 1969, *Student Grievances* in the New York City High Schools, New York: Public Education Association, 20 West 40th Street, New York, N.Y. 10018.

Riesman, David. Introduction to *The Vanishing Adolescent* by E. Z. Friedenberg. Boston: Beacon, 1959.

Understanding
Junior College Students

PROPOSALS FOR MEETING
THEIR SPECIAL NEEDS

RICHARD M. BOSSONE

IN DISCUSSING the qualifications for successful teaching in a junior college, Tyrus Hillway says that "a sympathetic attitude toward students
of the junior college age group may very well be the most important
personal characteristic necessary for success."[1] No doubt the majority
of junior college administrators would agree with this statement. But
do teachers who should have this attitude understand what is meant
by it? Instead of assuming that all teachers do, administrators who expect to avoid disillusionment, frustration, and despair when dealing
with them would do well to explain it clearly.

Having a sympathetic attitude toward junior college students implies,
first, that the teacher has an understanding of their typical traits. Judging
from the statements of administrators and from my own experience
in supervising junior college teachers, I would say that the majority
of them have a very limited understanding of their students. This, of
course, is often not so much the fault of the teachers as of leaders
in the field who have failed to shed light on the subject. Aside from
the usual statistics set forth in textbooks and articles about the student's
age, sex, marital status, socio-economic background, and academic aptitude (most of which reveal that the average public junior college stu-

From the *Journal of Higher Education*, 36, May, 1965, pp. 279–283. Copyright ©
1965 by the Ohio State University Press and reprinted with its permission.

[1]*The American Two-Year College* (New York: Harper and Brothers, 1958), p.
189.

dent is eighteen years old, male, single, a member of the lower socio-economic groups, and somewhat inferior in academic aptitude to those who enter four-year colleges), very little seems to be known about him. Given such lifeless statistics, teachers have noted them casually as findings and have not fully understood the significance of them. What is needed, then, is more information and discussion on the implications of these statistics, in particular those dealing with socio-economic background. In order to get a better understanding of the psychological and academic problems of the majority of junior college students, who come from what Burton R. Clark calls lower white-collar homes (of sales, clerical, and kindred workers) and blue-collar homes (of craftsmen, foremen, operatives, service workers, and laborers),[2] one must examine their milieu.

Such students are likely to come from the wrong side of the tracks, where they live in a physical setting that is unaesthetic and offers little personal privacy. Their parents may be immigrants who tend to be less conservative politically than members of the upper and upper-middle classes, to be somewhat suspicious or fearful of authority, and to be more sympathetic to industrial than to professional groups. They are likely to be dissatisfied with their individual work, pay, and chances of getting ahead; yet generally, they believe that equal opportunities exist for all. Usually they live more in the present than in the future, and it is typical of them to manifest a greater desire for security than for the self-expression which the upper-middle class values.

In this milieu, which is not congenial to academic matters and educational ambitions, the student's limited command of the language skills basic to educational success is a serious handicap. In his insightful and provocative essay "Social Class and Linguistic Development," Basil Bernstein points out that the lower class employs a "public" language which is distinguished by short, ungrammatical sentences (or idiomatic phrases) that do not "facilitate the communication of ideas and relationships requiring a precise formulation."[3] Needless to say, experience in reading and writing is minimal, and the opportunity to acquire basic information and understanding of fundamental concepts is extremely limited.

Now what do all of these findings imply for the staff and administration of the junior college? Let me designate a few of the more important implications they have in connection with the counseling serv-

---

[2]See *The Open Door College: A Case Study* (New York: McGraw-Hill Book Company, Inc., 1960), pp. 51–61.

[3]*Education, Economy, and Society,* edited by A. H. Halsey, Jean Floud, and C. Arnold Anderson (New York: Free Press of Glencoe, 1961), p. 298.

ices and the academic program. The problems they reveal may be
interdependent, but basically they fall into two categories: the psychological and the academic.[4]

Those student problems we might designate as psychological generally stem from early environment and are reflected in insecurity,
occupational and status anxiety, greater concern about the present than
the future, and lack of certain social skills. These psychological problems point up the importance of counseling and guidance in the junior
college and the need for close analysis and intelligent development of
student activities.

Educators ought to make clear what kinds of counseling and guidance
services are available. While it is true that the junior college has committed itself to the importance of counseling, in many instances it does
not live up to the meaning of the word.[5] Administrators should clarify
the counseling policy, objectives, and services to students, staff, and
community. The counselors they employ should be professionally
trained and should understand the problems of students who come
from low socio-economic groups. Too often, counselors are merely
program advisers who want a reduced teaching load. More in-service
training and more frequent staff meetings should be planned to inform
the faculty concerning their counseling responsibilities and to provide
them with assistance when needed. Topics for discussion might center
around the reasons for the tensions and anxieties of students and the
means of alleviating them, as well as the problems involved in reconciling the institution's objectives with those of the student. It may
be necessary to enlist medical and psychiatric help from community
sources for seriously disturbed students, and to invite leaders in a number of occupations to discuss their work, so that students will have
a better understanding of the knowledge and skills called for in the
various pursuits in which they plan to engage. Since many students
face financial problems and find it necessary to work while attending
college, thorough pre-admission counseling needs to be instituted in
order to help them reconcile financial needs with academic responsibilities.

---

[4]The relation between class status and personality adjustment is definite. See
Emil Heintz, "Adjustive Problems of Class Status," *Phi Delta Kappan*, XXX
(April, 1949), pp. 290–93. The relation between class status and academic or
linguistic ability is also definite. See Bernstein, *op. cit.*
[5]C. Gilbert Wrenn defines counseling as "a personal and dynamic relationship
between two people who approach a mutually defined problem with mutual
consideration . . . to the end that the younger, or less mature, or more
troubled of the two is aided to a self-determined resolution of his problem."
See *Student Personnel Work in College* (New York: Ronald Press, 1951), p. 59.

More intensive and extensive research is called for regarding students' interests, attitudes, personality problems, patterns of class attendance, and academic progress. In accumulating information on these subjects, the junior college might do well to work closely with the local high schools. In addition, there should be a thorough analysis of student activities to determine in what ways they contribute to the student's attitudes and values. This might begin, for example, with a thorough study of campus publications. Moreover, activities should be developed which would give students a greater opportunity to learn social skills and become interested in cultural pursuits. Since students whose parents are in the lower socio-economic classes proverbially come from culturally deprived backgrounds, they have far less knowledge of the amenities of life than their opposite numbers in the four-year colleges. Finally, educational and extra-curricular programs should be regularly evaluated so that they may keep pace with the student's changing needs.

One of the major academic problems junior college students face when they have the opportunity of attending what may seem to them a "Cinderella College" arises from their inability to cope with a situation in which language skills are demanded. Some of these students come from homes where broken English is spoken. For many of them, books have been replaced by television. They have probably not had to meet critical academic tests prior to this time but now are confronted with entrance examinations which require reading and writing skills they lack. As a result, they are placed on the remedial treadmill, and they begin what Burton Clark calls the hidden process of cooling-out: "In summary, the cooling-out process in higher education is one whereby systematic discrepancy between aspiration and avenue is covered over and stress for the individual and the system is minimized."[6] In short, the student's hopes are let down gradually, gently, and peacefully, allowing the junior college to keep its cooling-out function hidden and its other functions highlighted.

But need this be the case? Would it not be better to face this problem honestly, understandingly, and openly, so that failure would not frequently follow persistent effort to succeed academically, so that students would not feel inferior, bewildered, and defenseless in a new and demanding linguistic enviromnent? Educators in the junior college should determine the student's command of written and oral English and adjust the program accordingly.

In many cases, a full year of remedial English should be required.

---

[6]"The 'Cooling-out' Function in Higher Education," Halsey *et al.*, *op. cit.*, p. 521

(I doubt seriously that a one-semester course would be adequate to give students all the help they need.) In-service training programs for teachers of remedial English should be conducted in which emphasis is placed on ridding the student of hostility toward language study, developing reading skills, and teaching transformational or generative grammar and expository writing. A specialist in the training of teachers of English should be called in to serve as a consultant in establishing in-service programs. Furthermore, reading and writing clinics should be organized. In the reading clinic, particular attention should be given to improving comprehension of various types of expository prose. No student can write clear expository prose unless he can read well. In the writing clinic, students should have an adequate opportunity for practice in composition and should receive expert advice about their writing problems.

In addition to linguistic tutoring and guidance, students need broader academic assistance in the form of counseling on the development of proper study habits and skills, especially note-taking and outlining. Moreover, they need encouragement to generalize from the knowledge gained in classwork and to relate this knowledge to other subjects and themselves. All teachers, regardless of subject-field, should emphasize these aspects of learning.

Finally, educators ought to engage in more experimentation with methods and materials. They might begin by varying the presentation of subject-matter in order to avoid boring their students: abandoning the exclusive use of long formal lectures, and, instead, alternating them with discussion and question-and-answer periods; using visual aids; and supplementing teaching and reading materials by a wide variety of illustrations. Also they might experiment with programmed instruction if good programs are available in the subject-field. Many of the students under discussion are more likely to grasp the meaning of material when it is presented to them in the small step-by-step procedure of certain linear programs than when traditional teaching methods are used.

These observations regarding public junior college students are more important than they may seem at first glance. Teachers who have no understanding of students from the underprivileged social classes—their psychological and academic problems—are bound to be ineffective. When they are not prepared to cope with these problems the inadequacies of the student are bound to bring out the inadequacies of the teacher. That this is often the case is confirmed by the administrator's perennial search for teachers with "a sympathetic attitude toward students." But empathy is a quality that is not inherent in the teacher. Rather it is developed by leaders in the field of teacher-training who believe that for the student, emotional readiness is a prerequisite of learning; and that for the teacher, emotional acceptance of the student is a prerequisite of good teaching. In short, it is more likely to be developed by educational leaders who believe it is dangerous to assume that the observations about public junior college students set forth in this paper are what every junior college teacher knows.

PART TWO

READING:
IN HIGH SCHOOL
AND COLLEGE

Most high schools need developmental reading programs but very few have them; and in public two-year colleges where the caliber of the student's reading ability is often lower than that of the student in the four-year college, reading programs are even more desperately needed. Too often, students at these institutions are simply not prepared to read much of the material they are assigned. Large numbers of these students need guidance in learning to read the increasingly difficult material that confronts them as they progress from one grade level to another. In order for teachers to offer such assistance, a broad understanding is needed of what is involved in teaching reading in high school and college, as well as specific ideas of what to do in the classroom. The selections that follow are intended to help meet those needs.

More specifically, the articles by Early and Karlin set a basis for understanding the role reading instruction should play in the high school and illustrate the need for providing suitable instruction in reading for all students: Early clearly sets forth the purposes of reading instruction in the secondary school and some possible means by which they may be accomplished, and Karlin underscores the need for promoting reading as "a common denominator of the high school curriculum." Karlin also discusses conditions that influence growth in reading for all kinds of youth.

Shaw's sweeping analysis of *Reading in College* serves as a counterpart to the articles by Early and Karlin by supplying a knowledgeable view of reading programs at the college level. Shaw also stresses the need for sequential

development of a college student's reading ability, an area frequently ignored by college educators.

Moving from this broad understanding of reading instruction to a more
specific understanding, the reader will find that McCullough's article gives
him a thorough insight into the dynamics of the reading process. William
S. Gray has observed that the reading process involves essential understandings, attitudes, and skills most of which are an integral part of one or more
of four interrelated components of reading: (1) word perception (sight
recognition and analysis); (2) comprehension (recognition and construing
of meanings); (3) thoughtful reaction (involving both critical evaluation and
appreciative responses); and (4) assimilation (integration with previous
experience of the ideas acquired through reading). McCullough points out
in her exhaustive report that new research promises to have a most dramatic
impact upon the understanding and teaching of the reading process, and
she offers, in concrete form, ways in which one might apply these new
research findings in the classroom.

The article by Russell on knowing how to read critically serves not only
to give the reader a more thorough understanding of this vital aspect of the
reading process, which was analyzed in the McCullough article, but also
to provide a base for better understanding of the three articles which follow.
Essentially, Russell explains that critical reading can best be thought of as
closely related to critical thinking, which is explained as a three-factor ability:
"an *attitude* factor of questioning and suspended judgment, a *conative* or
functional factor which involves use of methods of logical inquiry and problem solving, and a *judgment* factor of evaluating terms of some norm" [italics
added]; in addition, he adduces reasons why critical thinking ought to be
stressed from kindergarten through college.

Russell's thoughts about critical thinking are taken a step further by
Melnik, who views reading as inquiry, that is, the influential factor of questioning in guiding the reader's understanding of what he reads.

Larson's article on *Teaching the Analysis of Expository Prose* illustrates
Melnik's concept in detail by pointing out that, through the asking of certain
questions, teachers can help students become better readers of expository
prose. Larson strongly underscores Early's statement that the absence of
expository prose in the high school curriculum "proves that reading-study
skills are being ignored," whereas the presence of such skills "indicates at
least the possibility of appropriate instruction."

Hogan's article, *Book Selection and Censorship*, echoes the previous three
writers' views, in particular Russell's, that educators must help young people
decide for themselves what to read. He points out that "censorship usually
involves a decision by a person or a group about what others should read,"
whereas the notion of critical reading suggests that the individual ought
to make this choice. Among his intelligent suggestions for educators on framing a policy concerning book selection, Hogan makes the point that "if
one purpose of the literature program is to build lifetime reading habits, it
will probably rely less on 'restrictive' or 'required' reading lists as a guide to

independent reading and more on 'suggested' reading lists. Beyond this—and here at once is the riskiest, yet the most fundamental principle of all—it will insure that the student can talk with a sensitive teacher or librarian about any book he has read on his own."

Hogan's thoughts about building lifetime reading habits are implemented in Robinson's article, which sets forth specific techniques to foster such habits and cautions teachers against techniques that discourage such habits.

Strang's chapter from the NSSE Yearbook, *Development in and through Reading*, is an appropriate conclusion for Part Two not only because of the appropriateness of its topic, evaluation, but also because of its inclusive discussion of the entire subject of reading in which many of the ideas discussed by previous writers are reviewed.

Reading

IN AND OUT OF THE
ENGLISH CURRICULUM

MARGARET J. EARLY

BECAUSE READING and study skills are basic to every subject in the secondary school curriculum, English teachers do not have exclusive rights
to the teaching of reading. Nor do they want such prerogatives. But
they do have responsibilities for understanding the nature of reading
instruction in secondary schools, for defining the differences between
"reading" and "English," and for giving leadership to schoolwide efforts
to improve reading services. As articulate spokesmen for all-school
developmental programs, English teachers can dispel the notion that
remedial or corrective programs are the answer to all the reading ills in
a secondary school. By clearly defining the role of English with respect
to reading, they can help other members of the faculty understand
their roles and assume *their* responsibilities.

Until this decade, the extension of reading instruction beyond the
elementary school has been slow, haphazard, and piecemeal. Now, with
the aid of state and federal funds, the momentum has increased but
secondary programs are still haphazard and piecemeal. Special reading
classes are being planned overnight and hastily staffed with inexperienced and untrained teachers, recruited usually from the English
department. In such circumstances, confusion and disappointment are
inevitable, but there remains at least the hope of learning from mistakes.
School systems that began by scheduling special reading classes have
become aware of their limitations and are moving now, with the help

From *The Bulletin of the National Association of Secondary School Principals*, 51,
April, 1967, pp. 47–59. Reprinted with the permission of the National Association
of Secondary School Principals.

of ESEA funds, to more broadly based programs involving subject-matter teachers beyond the English department.

IMPORTANCE OF CLARITY OF PURPOSE

False starts can be avoided by long-range planning. From the beginning, administrators and teachers should know the dimensions of reading instruction in the secondary school. Its aim is the extension and refinement of skills, habits, and attitudes which have begun to take shape in the elementary grades. How can this extension and refinement be accomplished? In two ways: (1) through direct skills instruction concentrated in reading and English courses, and (2) through the fusion of reading and study skills with subject matter in all other courses. Of the two approaches, logic lies with the second; it makes more sense to "extend and define" reading and study skills as they are required for subject matter learning. Nevertheless, we can defend direct instruction through reading courses or units of study as an expedient in schools where few teachers are prepared to teach reading-study skills.

Which of these two approaches should receive first emphasis is a point of needless controversy. Obviously, this question of priority has to be settled by the resources available in a given situation. Where a competent reading consultant is available, the approach through subject matter should probably be emphasized. Where there are large numbers of immature readers, and where experienced reading teachers may be recruited or inexperienced ones trained, it would be sensible to begin with direct instruction. Either approach is a safe one so long as the ultimate goal of an all-school developmental program is firmly established with administrators, teachers, and boards of education.

Either approach involves the English department from the beginning, because English teachers are responsible for both skills learning and subject matter. If the decision is to emphasize direct instruction, English teachers will have to staff the program, wholly or partially. If the approach is through subject matter, they will have as much to learn as their colleagues about how to teach reading-study skills instead of merely requiring their use.

DIRECT INSTRUCTION

Direct instruction classes are usually labeled "corrective" or "developmental." These labels are relatively unimportant except as they suggest that the major concern in secondary school reading is *not* with the

remedial. When we define *remedial* precisely, we limit its application
to students of average to superior mental ability who have not learned
to read beyond first-grade or second-grade level, even though they have
had opportunities to learn. In the average American high school, relatively few students fall into this category. Those who do are likely to
be suffering from psychoneurological disturbances requiring specialized
treatment. After years of failure they should not in secondary schools
be assigned to still another reading class. English teachers and minimally trained reading teachers are not remedial clinicians. The school's
responsibility to such severely handicapped students is to help them
to learn through channels other than reading, referring them when
possible for expert psychological and medical advice.

In center-city schools (and in many rural and suburban schools as
well), illiterate or almost illiterate adolescents are found in high school
classrooms. These young people do not fit the restricted definition of
"remedial" we have just applied. Therefore, they may be appropriately
assigned to corrective or developmental classes of limited size, so that
teachers can learn to work with them individually much of the time.
It is arguable that these youth do not need the skills concentration that
is the *raison d'etre* for special reading classes. If, however, the goals
and consequently the methods and materials of instruction are reori-
ented for these pupils, the "extra reading class" is as justifiable for them
as for others.

The most optimistic goal for the average adolescent illiterate is
that he will become a reader, not a student. This means that the total
effort should be to get him to read—anything. Perhaps the worst approach is through textbooks, workbooks, and skill-building exercises.
(One junior high teacher tells me that mimeographed sheets are more
palatable to these pupils than are more legible, better designed workbook pages, probably because the former seem more personalized, even
when they are not.) If textbooks are ever to be used successfully with
these pupils, it will only be after they have learned personally satisfying reasons for reading. Only then will it be possible to develop
orderly sequences for word analysis skills and basic comprehension skills.

So far, success stories involving adolescent illiterates are rare. Those
that have appeared emphasize the importance of motivation and endorse all kinds of unorthodox materials, from menus and racing forms
to hot rod magazines and best selling paperbacks. The program described by Daniel Fader in *Hooked on Books* as achieving varieties
of success in a boys' training school in Michigan and the Garnett-
Patterson Junior High School in Washington, D.C., breaks with tradi-

tions of both reading and English.[1] Apparently, what happens when seeming "illiterates" suddenly begin to read adult magazines and paperbacks is that walls of resistance are shattered and dormant skills are put back into service. The true illiterate has no dormant skills, and for him miracles come more slowly.

HELPING READERS BECOME "STUDIERS"

Dramatic though they may be, the problems of the adolescent illiterate are not the chief concern of secondary reading instruction. Rather, the main thrust is toward students who have acquired the basic skills which need to be extended and refined. They are competent "general" readers by the criteria of standardized grade-level tests. Our aim is to help these readers become students, that is, "studiers"—persons who learn through reading. When we set up special reading courses for these readers, our reason is that they require more direct teaching, followed up by intensive practice, in how to read and study than is being supplied by the teachers of subject matter courses.

The content of the reading course should be dictated by the needs of the students. We analyze the reading tasks required in studying textbooks; we test students' abilities with respect to these tasks and identify where they need help. On the basis of this skills analysis, we select from instructional materials of varying difficulty those lessons needed by particular students. We provide for practice but only after demonstrations and explanations have made clear how to apply the skill. Frequently this teaching is directed at individuals and small groups, but occasionally all students in a class may need teaching preceding differentiated practice.

The focus on skills development dictates a laboratory classroom, equipped minimally with many short sets of textbooks and workbooks on varying levels, dictionaries and other references, and several hundred paperbacks. Ideally, the room should also be equipped with study carrels, tape recorders and headsets, projectors and viewers, and under some circumstances with a few pacers for improving rate of reading. Extensive equipment will not ensure excellent instruction, but neither can we expect dramatic achievement when the teacher is a "floater," with access to a duplicating machine and a box of skills exercises and little else.

As part of the English curriculum, the goals, methods, and materials

[1]Daniel Fader. *Hooked on Books*. New York: Berkley Publishing Corporation, 1966.

of the reading course are similar to those of other English offerings. Periods of instruction are usually shorter, ranging perhaps from two to six weeks of intensive work on reading-study skills, per se. This brief time allotment is compensated for by the fact that English teachers who employ unit methods and laboratory techniques can extend skills instruction to groups and individuals from time to time throughout the year.

MOTIVATION ESSENTIAL

Skills practice in any endeavor—sports, music, typewriting, reading— must be highly motivated and sharply focused on individual needs. Even so, it can be dull or demanding. Students would rather engage in discussion (often lively but irrelevant), or they would rather escape thinking by listening or pretending to listen, or by a type of reading for pleasure which is more closely akin to daydreaming than to think- ing. For teachers, too, skills instruction is more demanding and less interesting than leading a discussion, lecturing, demonstrating, or merely talking. In reading classes, the great temptation is to distribute the mimeographed exercises, get out the skills box, plug in the film or tape recorder, and then escape to the teacher's room for a cup of coffee. No wonder students learn to hate reading classes, even if they like to read.

How can we motivate? This question is often asked in despair by teachers who don't want a usable answer. It is difficult to motivate skills practice unrelated to substantive learning. This is the hurdle we set for ourselves when we organize special reading classes. Since we would not schedule these classes in the first place unless convinced of their usefulness, we must be willing to surmount the hurdle. One way to infuse the skills course with purpose may be to treat it as a course in the psychology of learning, one in which students study themselves as learners. Another way is to teach individuals instead of large groups. Another is to let students see success as they chart their own progress. Nourishing a spark of motivation takes constant attention. The flame can go out while the teacher distributes mimeographed exercises or the student chalks up another failure.

TEACHER MAY LACK MOTIVATION

Perhaps the teacher's own lack of motivation contributes most to failure in skills courses. Just as he needs to offer constant and genuine encouragement to his students, so, too, the teacher needs to have his enthusiasm bolstered. He needs tangible help—materials, ideas, equipment—from consultant and principal. He needs their support in scheduling classes of reasonable size, and in providing time for diagnosis and consultation. Most of all he needs to see progress in the spread of the program throughout the subject classes.

Because skills instruction is a hard job, especially for the novice, many reading classes become something else. In the hands of English teachers they often become extensions of literature courses, weak courses at that.

"Send me an English teacher who knows the difference between teaching reading and teaching literature," pleaded a secondary school principal recently. In too many junior high school reading classes, the bulk of the time is spent in reading novels—in common. When a teacher orders thirty copies of *The Yearling* for a junior high reading class, this is a sure sign that he is unaware of the objectives of reading instruction. (If he orders whole class sets of any textbook, he is doing a poor job of teaching skills, and many believe he is doing a poor job of teaching literature, too.)

Of course, we can justify the inclusion of fiction in a reading course as part of "free reading." One of the aims is to get weak students to read whatever appeals to them, and fiction appeals to many as a relatively undemanding exercise of basic reading skills. Wide reading serves an appropriate skills objective: it is a vehicle for developing fluency, adding to vocabulary, and exercising simple comprehension skills such as the ability to follow sequence. But reading fiction does nothing for the development of essential study skills such as relating major and minor ideas, understanding closely reasoned argument, judging facts, following explanations, and other skills necessary for the assimilation of informative prose.

The study of *how* to read literature can be justified as content for the reading and study skills class only when equal time is allotted to how to read science, history, mathematics, and other subjects. Obviously, equal allotment of time to each subject in the curriculum means that scant attention can be paid to any of them, and thus points up again the need for teaching reading not only in the special class but in every subject area. The teaching of subject-oriented skills in the special reading class sets up an artificial learning situation, takes additional time, lessens the chance that something of substantive value can be learned at the same time that skills are being refined, and puts the burden for the transfer of learning wholly upon students.

English teachers, while claiming to be unprepared to teach reading,[2] assert that they do it all the time. They mean, of course, that they *use* reading in the literature program but are ill equipped to deal with word analysis, basic comprehension skills, and rate of reading—the components they define as "reading." It is the exceptional English teacher who teaches his students how to read imaginative literature. In his disregard of the skills required for reading in his specialty, the average English teacher is no different from his colleagues in other subject fields.

The truly professional English teacher who recognizes his dual role as a teacher of skills and of subject matter distinguishes between reading and literature and gives balanced attention to both. (English teachers of junior high school students or of weaker students in the senior high school give more time to developing reading skills and interests, less time to the study of literature. Teachers of mature students reverse the emphases.)

READING VERSUS LITERATURE

How do we distinguish between "reading" and "literature" in the secondary school curriculum? Differences are evident in the objectives and in the materials of instruction. The development of reading-study skills requires informative or expository prose as its vehicle of instruction, rather than discursive or imaginative writing. If the fare of the English course is exclusively novels, poetry, and drama, the English teacher can fulfill only one part of his dual role. Fortunately, nonfiction articles and essays are found in most anthologies. If these have been abandoned, the teacher must seek other sources of nonfiction, principally periodicals. Materials do not make the program, of course. But the absence of expository prose proves that reading-study skills are being ignored; its presence indicates at least the possibility of appropriate instruction.

Many reading teachers and supervisors are unaware of any confusion between reading and literature. They assume that the narrative-type materials which predominate in elementary school—where individualized reading as well as basal approaches have favored narrative materials—should be continued in junior high school, even though by this time students' needs have shifted from general comprehension to study skills. Fortunately, the current trend in elementary reading in-

---

[2]According to *The National Interest and the Continuing Education of Teachers of English* (Champaign, Ill.: National Council of Teachers of English, 1963), 90 percent of English teachers do not feel well qualified to teach reading.

struction is to correct the imbalance in materials and in methods of teaching. As more exposition is included in elementary materials and as elementary literature programs become more sharply distinguished from basal reading instruction, the tradition of basing developmental reading on narrative prose will die out.

Confronted with the obligation to teach reading-study skills *and* skills for reading literature, English teachers plead the restrictions of time. In junior high school, time limitations are eased by extra reading classes, double English periods, and core or block-time arrangements. In senior high English classes, the time required for direct instruction will become less as more of the reading-study skills are shifted to the content areas. Elective courses in reading-study skills, especially for college-bound students in grades 11 and 12, are another kind of solution. Nevertheless, many English teachers must still decide what to leave out in order to include reading-study skills.

We suggest a hard look at the efficiency of the language instruction and the inordinate amount of time given to the discussion of literature. Fortunately, new developments in language and literature suggest economies in teaching. (See Harold B. Allen's article in this symposium.) Moreover, new methods of organization, such as team teaching and laboratory techniques, provide more time for skills instruction and free reading than do methods which treat a class of 25 or 30 as an inflexible unit.

SCHOOLWIDE READING IMPROVEMENT

Leaving reading instruction entirely in the hands of the English department, even one with a supplementary staff of reading teachers, has proved extremely limiting. The resulting program may be effective but limited, or it may be merely an extension of English and not very effective at all. In either case, the program falls far short of what we mean by teaching reading in the secondary school.[3]

In schools where reading instruction is truly pervasive, it would be inappropriate to talk about reading "programs." Instruction would be clearly visible and measurable, but it would be so thoroughly integrated with subject learning that it would not show on master schedules. There would be no extra classes and no reading teachers and, except in large urban schools, no special clinics or laboratories. But this pervasive instruction, reaching into every classroom where reading

[3]Olive S. Niles. "Systemwide In-Service Programs in Reading." *The Reading Teacher*, No. 19 (March, 1966).

is a medium of learning, would be visible to the administrator who knows what to look for.

For example, the administrator surveying reading instruction in his school would look in every classroom for answers to questions like these:

- Do teachers frequently develop concepts and introduce vocabulary *before* students read an assignment?
- Do teachers help students to identify the reading tasks required by a particular assignment?
- Do they then demonstrate how to apply the necessary skills?
- Is attention paid not only to what a textbook says but to how it is said, that is, to the author's choice of words, his sentence structure, and his organization of ideas?
- Is the author's purpose examined?
- Are comparisons made among treatments of the same subject?
- Are students not only encouraged to make judgments but shown how?
- Are teachers aware of the different kinds of reading abilities their students possess?
- Do they help them to make the best use of their various abilities by providing books and other reading materials on varying levels of difficulty?

SUPERVISORY LEADERSHIP ESSENTIAL

The foregoing questions, by no means comprehensive, suggest what we mean by teaching reading in secondary schools. To initiate and maintain this pervasive instruction in reading requires strong administrative backing and the day-to-day services of a competent coordinator, who may or may not be attached to the English department. Just as scheduling reading classes produces no easy solutions, neither does hiring a coordinator, provided one can be found. But it is well for administrators to recognize the need for schoolwide reading improvement. In large schools, the English chairman's hands are too full to undertake this task even though, if he is competent, he will understand and give support to the movement. The near-impossibility of finding a reading coordinator leads most schools to select one of their own staff, perhaps a reading-English teacher, and to subsidize his further study. We recommend a year if possible of full-time study at a university near enough to his school that its students, teachers, and resources can be subjects of his study.

Educating teachers to teach reading is the main job ahead. State and federal funds have presented us with opportunities for greatly expanding in-service education; what we need now are ideas for spending this money effectively. Among the least effective methods is transplating the university course intact to the school cafeteria for 15 weekly meetings from 4 p.m. to 6 p.m. Nor is the currently popular plan of bringing in a series of guest lecturers from hither and yon likely to prove any more effective—if by effective we mean producing changes in the classroom. Even lecture courses that are well planned and intelligently presented probably do little more than supply background information, spark interest, and soften the attitudes of recalcitrant teachers, getting them ready to have someone else do the job that needs doing!

Along with or instead of the credit course or lecture series, some schools get the most from their government grants by concentrating attention on a few teachers at a time and freeing them, by hiring substitutes, to work intensively with the reading consultant. For example, three small school systems in central New York have selected key teachers from their secondary school faculties to attend a series of three week-long workshops conducted at intervals during the first semester at a nearby university reading center. Three days of each week are spent in the center in intensive study of reading methodology applied to the teachers' own textbooks; two days are spent in local schools observing preplanned reading lessons in the content areas, in examining other phases of the reading program, and in teaching demonstration lessons to "borrowed" classes. Between the weeks on campus, these teachers spend regularly scheduled days in their own schools demonstrating for each other and for the university personnel who are consultants to the project. In each school, these teachers are becoming the nucleus for subject-centered reading instruction.

The Reading Center staff at Syracuse University has produced a series of 10 films on teaching reading in secondary schools. These films, accompanied by 15 manuals, constitute the core of an in-service workshop to be directed by a school's reading consultant, supplemented perhaps by university personnel. The films are meant as an introductory step in developing an all-school program. Like the customary course, they will prove minimally effective unless followed up by work in the teachers' own classrooms. However, the film package can be used with considerably more flexibility and economy than can the university course. For example, the films may be viewed by a single department, with discussion restricted to the special concerns of this particular group. Teachers study the film content through viewing and reviewing, discuss with each other the implications for their classrooms, turn to the manuals and suggested references for more information, and try out recommended procedures. The films appear to offer another approach to in-service education without straining further the overextended resources of the universities.

Administrators about to embark upon schoolwide efforts to improve reading instruction would do well to study the recommendations made by Olive S. Niles in her article previously cited.

SUMMARY

In an all-school reading program, English teachers have responsibilities comparable to those of other subject specialists. Additionally, they are responsible for the direct instruction of reading-study skills as part of regularly scheduled English courses or in extra classes. In spite of the fact that reading is one of the skills of language which, with literature, constitutes the discipline of English, the majority of teachers of English seem neither better prepared nor more willing to teach reading-study skills than their colleagues on secondary faculties. Because of lack of preparation, English teachers assigned to reading classes tend to teach literature or promote wide reading and to ignore reading-study skills.

There is no standard pattern for reading instruction in secondary schools nor should there be, but readily observable features distinguish excellent from mediocre direct-skills instruction. Chief among these are the attention given to individuals, the diversity of materials for skills instruction, the preponderance of expository prose in skills exercises, and collections of paperbacks and periodicals for wide reading.

Similarly, reading instruction in subject matter classes does not follow fixed patterns, but is easily identified by the ways in which those teachers direct students towards the process of learning through reading.

Schemes for improving reading instruction in the secondary school should probably concentrate first on the preparation of teachers in inservice action programs, since preservice courses are rare and in any case theoretical and introductory. English departments should play leading roles when a whole school faculty undertakes reading improvement. Along with helping others to understand the rationale of a whole school program, English teachers should decide upon the relative emphases to be given direct instruction in reading-study skills and in how to read literature.

What Does Research in Reading Reveal—About Reading and the High School Student?

ROBERT KARLIN

IN SPITE of the fact that there is an increasing awareness of the wisdom in establishing reading programs in high school, a comparatively small number of our youth receive systematic instruction in reading. Educators who studied this phenomenon have speculated about instructional explanations for the apparent omission: the belief that responsibility for teaching reading belongs solely to elementary schools; the lack of well-prepared personnel to direct and staff programs; an unawareness that large numbers of high school students might profit from direct help.

Our purpose in this section is to underscore the need for promoting reading as a common denominator of the high school curriculum, to provide a base for appreciating some conditions that influence growth in reading, and to encourage efforts in behalf of all our students.

READING ABILITY OF HIGH SCHOOL YOUTH

How well do our high school students read? What evidence do we have of the relationship between reading achievement and academic success? Just what are the reading needs of most youth? Research offers us some answers to these questions.

Reprinted with permission from *What We Know About High School Reading*, A Research Bulletin Prepared by Committee of the National Council of Conference on Research in English. Champaign, Illinois: National Council of Teachers of English, 1969, pp. 19–28.

READING ACHIEVEMENT

A number of investigations, as well as observations, provide information about the reading ability of students we teach. One large metropolitan school system studied the reading status of its freshmen and sophomores and reported that over 40 per cent were reading below their potential ability. More than 23 per cent were found to be reading two to five or more years below grade level (12). The reading scores of over three thousand high school students in a midwestern state showed why its schools should establish developmental and remedial programs without delay (43). Cooper (8) reported that 30,000 test scores drawn from a southern state showed a greater variance between reading ability and grade placement at secondary level than at elementary level. Ramsey (45) found in his state that eighth-grade students achieved reading levels significantly below grade norms.

These and other studies demonstrate quite conclusively that a considerable portion of the high school population does not read as well as it should or could. Another way of stating this well-established fact: perhaps as many as one-fourth (and in some areas an even higher proportion) of students lack the reading skills they need to read the books with the comprehension expected of them. Is it any wonder so many boys and girls fail to grasp bare essentials, not to mention deeper meanings?

SCHOOL SUCCESS

It is no small wonder that large numbers of high school students do poorly in English and other subjects. Many fail to complete their textbook and supplementary reading satisfactorily. That success in school is tied directly to reading achievement has been documented by the findings of research and experiences of teachers and administrators. The influence of reading ability even on such a subject as mathematics is recognized. Call and Wiggin (5) compared the results of instruction in understanding word meanings and tying them to mathematical symbols with no comparable help in solving word problems. They found that the students who received the instruction (from an English teacher!) achieved better results than did the students who did not receive such instruction from their mathematics teacher. Fay (14) studied the relationship of reading ability to different achievement areas. He reported that students of superior reading ability achieved significantly better in social studies than students who did not read as well. Carter (6) found that better readers have higher averages, study better, and are happier in school than poorer readers.

Perhaps one of the most telling studies that sought to appraise the effects of reading ability on school performance was conducted by Penty (42). She found that of the students whose reading was in the lowest quarter, close to 50 per cent left school before the twelfth grade, while just over 14 per cent in the highest quarter of reading left before graduating. She interviewed the dropouts six years later and discovered that in most cases they gave poor reading as the cause of their problems. Frustration, embarrassment, and boredom were products of their condition. Penty noted also that a very large percentage of the poor readers who dropped out of school as well as those who remained had the ability to read better. She deplored the fact that proper help in reading was not available to them. Penty's findings are corroborated by Bledsoe (2), Nachman (36), and Whitmore (64).

Who will deny a close association between reading ability and school achievement? What hope is there for our poorer readers to derive some satisfactions from their efforts? What is the school's responsibility to all students? The answer to each question seems clear; if we can send a man to the moon, it ought to be possible with persistence to make a real impact upon the lives of our youth through better reading. Surely we ought not settle for less.

READING NEEDS

Naturally, teachers of English spend a considerable amount of time in the reading and study of literature. It is hardly necessary to explain the reasons for the emphasis they give to this effort. But how much time do they spend in teaching their students *how to read* literature? A recent survey of English teaching practices reported by Squire (56) covered 168 high schools. In the tenth grade less than 5 per cent of the instructional time was devoted to the teaching of reading and in the twelfth grade less than 3 per cent. Obviously, the teachers in these high schools saw little reason to devote more time to reading instruction. As Squire suggested, it is possible they expected their students to become discerning readers of literature merely from reading. But the evidence shows the contrary; comparatively few students achieve without guidance. And in view of the fact that so many of them are deficient in reading, it becomes even more necessary to help them overcome their weaknesses and achieve to the extent of which each is capable.

What are the skills needed by students to read literature and other content? Spache (54) lists the following: understanding and interpreting the content and grasping its organization, developing special vocabularies, concepts and symbols, evaluating what is read, selecting materials, recalling and applying what is read, and broadening interests, tastes, and experiences. Some of these are often included among the study skills. It is apparent that students with general reading ability possess some of these skills. However, we know now that all of them cannot be taken for granted, and that it is necessary to offer direct instruction in most. Even students themselves are keenly aware of their reading and study weaknesses. Michaels (34) reported how eleventh-grade students perceived their reading difficulties in literature, history, chemistry, and plane geometry.

A number of investigations provide support for direct instruction in specific reading skills and for reading in the content areas. Maney (33) and Sochor (53) found that interpretative reading ability appears to be independent of literal reading ability in science and social studies, respectively. The results of a previously cited study (5) underscore the importance of dealing with the vocabulary of mathematics in solving word problems. McDonald (31) in summarizing the research on reading flexibility concluded that there is need for systematic instruction in developing ability to read for different purposes. Strang and Rogers (58) studied the responses of high school juniors to a short story and concluded that there are marked differences between good and poor readers in their ability to respond to literal and implied meanings. Husbands and Shores (24) reviewed the literature and concluded that reading consists of different abilities that are needed for specific purposes in various content areas.

DeBoer and Whipple summarized the implications of these and related studies. "Thus, reading is not a generalized skill that, once developed in an English class, can be applied in a special field. Rather, reading involves the ability to interpret this or that particular area of experience. Basic instruction, no matter how excellent, is not enough. Reading abilities must be developed in the areas where they are to be used (10)."

PERSONAL FACTORS AND READING

Is it realistic to expect equal performances in reading of all our students? Perhaps the answer to this question will be found in another: Are all our students of equal height and do they possess the same athletic prowess? We know they are quite different in many respects, not the least of which is reading ability. The studies cited earlier (8, 12,

43, 45) as well as others yielded results which underscore the existence of significant differences in reading performances, not only between grades but also within grades. A number of personal factors among which are intelligence, sex, interests and attitudes, and language development account for some of these differences.

INTELLIGENCE

There appears to be a significant relationship between reasoning ability and reading achievement. Paterra (41) suggested on the basis of her findings that reading should be improved through programs that stress verbal reasoning. Jan-Tausch (25) reported that his advanced readers were better able to do abstract thinking than his poorer readers. Braun (4) reported a significant difference in concept formation between her superior and poor readers. Harootunian and Tate (19) obtained correlations between reading test scores and seven intellectual abilities described by Guilford. Both Harris (20) and Fransella and Gerver (15) concluded that the relationship between IQ and reading as measured by such tests as the Stanford-Binet and WISC, respectively, increases with chronological age.

At this point it is necessary to affirm that some intelligence tests fail to distinguish between slow learners and poor readers. Experimenters have noted the truth of this observation, especially when group verbal tests are used to assess mental ability. Such tests usually require reading ability to insure high performance; obviously, poor readers are penalized under these circumstances. Too often students of average and superior ability are classified as inferior learners on the basis of the results from inadequate tests.

Another caution: We ought not to assume that slow learners are unable to profit from reading instruction. What they require is a more moderately paced program with carefully-selected materials and proper guidance. The fact that this group of students seems to learn well through programmed instruction which combines the aforementioned conditions suggests reasonable returns from real efforts to teach them.

SEX

Girls seem to have a slight edge over boys in reading development. Whether or not the difference exists because of constitutional and/or environmental factors remains to be determined. The differences, however, seem to be more marked in the formative years rather than during the later ones. Singer (50) reported superior achievement in reading speed for girls in the sixth grade. Seventh-grade girls in the below and above normal ranges of intelligence surpassed boys of comparable ability in reading vocabulary (51). Another investigator (30) obtained similar results in the above-average IQ range but the differences between boys and girls decreased with age.

Boys with serious reading problems outnumber their female counterparts by about four to one. Whether or not this phenomenon is the product of physical, cultural, and other societal conditions is a question whose answer is unknown. Speculation persists in the absence of hard facts.

INTERESTS AND ATTITUDES

The interests and attitudes which adolescents possess seem to have a profound influence upon their reading behaviors. Such personal factors have their origins in home and other environmental settings. Past and ongoing experiences account for variations in motivation to learn and in actual performance.

There is an accumulating body of evidence about the influence of home conditions on students' reading development. Hughes and Willis (22) found that parents of students who read widely, read more, and had more interests than parents of another group of students matched for sex and intelligence. Watson (62) found that poor reading dropouts came from less stable and lower socio-economic homes than did successful high school graduates. Keshian (26) concluded that successful readers had parents who had shown great interest in reading and books and in school work and who built solid family units. MacDonald (32) reported that parents of unsuccessful male readers who attended public schools possessed significantly more negative attitudes than found in parents of successful students.

The development of wholesome attitudes toward reading has been the subject of much discussion and research. Many writers have suggested that if reading is to have a place among favored activities in which adolescents engage, basic human needs must be met through it. Perhaps the one need which is met most directly by reading is the *need to know*. Research on the reading preferences of high school students tends to support this judgment. Shores (49) sought to determine what they seek in books. He concluded that information about national and international problems rather than about personal and social matters dominated their interest. Whitman (63) polled large numbers of superior high school students and found that they selected books which helped shape attitudes and provided information.

Perhaps one of the most significant outcomes of research on the interests of high school students is the recognition that reading preferences of boys and girls vary and that these preferences do not seem to be greatly influenced by reading ability or intelligence. As a group, boys prefer books which contain elements of excitement, suspense, adventure, action, and humor. Girls look for books which deal with love, sadness, home, and mystery (38, 57, 60). These differences in reading preferences could have some bearing upon the outcomes of our efforts to teach reading and instill in youth a love for reading. Materials which fail to satisfy are not likely to promote either goal.

LANGUAGE DEVELOPMENT

Differences in language abilities seem to account for some of the variability in reading achievement. A longitudinal study of oral language by Loban (29) in which he contrasted high and low achievers in language development showed definite relationship between competence in the latter and reading. Strickland (59) recorded the spoken language of children and after analyzing structural patterns concluded among other things that those who made more use of them ranked higher in reading, both oral and silent.

Vocabulary development and reading achievement have been the subjects of a number of investigations. The conclusions that vocabulary and reading comprehension are closely related and that word knowledge is one of the significant contributors to meaning have been confirmed (39, 47). Holmes and Singer (21) reported that vocabulary played a very important role in accounting for high school students' power in reading. Knowledge of vocabulary both in and out of context helped to differentiate between good and poor readers.

Research on listening and reading, both receptive skills, has been summarized by Duker (13) and Devine (11). They reported positive and high correlations between them and concluded that it would be useful to study further the nature of this relationship. Both point out the distinct possibility that similar mental processes account for reading and listening skills and that additional research on these questions might provide guidelines for teaching strategies.

READING FOR ALL YOUTH

Inasmuch as our free society requires youth to attend school until the age of sixteen or seventeen is reached, it seems fairly obvious that aside from the commitment we have to education generally, we must be equally committed to the proposition that every boy and girl has a right to instruction from which they can profit. Acceptance of this tenet precludes any justification for not providing educational programs that serve youth. Thus it is not difficult to explain measures designed to aid the disadvantaged and the slow learner as well as the gifted. The fact that these populations are difficult to reach is no excuse for ignoring them.

THE DISADVANTAGED

Efforts to describe disadvantaged or culturally different adolescents had led to the conclusion that they exhibit similar characteristics but that there is sufficient variation among them to warrant consideration of appropriate educational environments. Studies show that they generally are weak in the use of spoken and written English (28, 52), that they are generally educationally retarded (16, 40), and that they possess a low level of self-esteem and aspiration (1, 18). Hunt and Dopyera (23) found that their degree of self-determination was lower than that of middle-class adolescents but that they showed great variation in conceptual level. Others (17, 35) also point out variabilities among culturally disadvantaged youth.

The fact that many disadvantaged adolescents are weak in English and reading has produced specific recommendations regarding this aspect of their educational programs. Bloom (3) reviewed the research and recommended greater emphasis upon language development and reading. Wachner (61) described the Detroit Great Cities Project and its adoption of the core program in English and social studies and the establishment of reading improvement classes and reading rooms. A task force of the National Council of Teachers of English (37) observed more than fifty programs for the disadvantaged and noted the traditional use of anthologies with students who were neither capable of nor interested in reading the selections. It recommended literature appropriate to the abilities of students and de-emphasis of traditional grammar. Spiegler (55) described different programs for the disadvantaged which included reading of books and magazines to build a better self-image and reading skills, using "experience stories" for corrective reading, and introducing "traditional" literature through oral readings, films, tapes, TV, and recordings.

It should be obvious that there are no magical formulas for overcoming deficits in culturally disadvantaged students. Much more has to be known about the interrelationships of factors that distinguish this school population from others and how teachers can best deal with them. However, this state of affairs should not be used as an excuse for indifference and inaction. Some inroads into language and reading deficiencies have been made; our continuing efforts through practice, demonstration and research are likely to have a salutary effect upon the achievements of all our students.

THE SLOW LEARNER

Slow learners are not to be confused with the mentally retarded or educable mentally retarded. "The slow learners are the highest intellectual group of retarded children and are largest in number. They form the 15 to 17 per cent of the school population that cannot quite 'keep up' and are usually doing the poorest work in the regular classroom. Slow learners are essentially normal in their emotional, social, physical, and motor development. Even in intellectual development, the slow learners are at the lower fringe or range of the normal group. Thus, while they are retarded and consequently have difficulty in 'keeping up' with the rest of the class, their deviation is not so great that they cannot be adequately educated in a regular classroom situation" (9).

From this description it appears obvious that slow learners are capable of mastering many reading skills and sharing the joys of reading for pleasure. Their reading needs at the high school level will be as varied as those of other students, but a larger proportion of slow learners will be found at the lower ranges. A number of disadvantaged students are known to be slow learners, and programs for them require adjustments on more than a single level.

For a number of reasons, a slow learner is bound to be behind the "normal" reader by the time he enters high school. And he is likely to fall behind further unless he receives help—but at a slower pace—that most of his age-peers also require. Not unlike other youth, he probably has some weaknesses in word identification, study skills, and/or comprehension. Although he is not likely to engage in higher academic study, he needs the same opportunities to develop and take his place in an increasingly complex society. Teaching him how to read better through programs suited to his abilities and requirements will enable him to experience some successes in school as well as prepare him for the responsibilities he must assume later.

THE GIFTED

Do all our gifted students achieve in reading to the extent of which they are capable? Can they profit from reading instruction? That there are underachievers among the gifted has been documented by Combs

(7), Shaw (48), and Rippert and Archer (44), among others. Krippner and Herald (27) conducted an investigation to determine if the causes of poor reading among gifted students differed from those of average students. They found similar explanations for reading difficulties for both groups. Woolcock (65) studied the reading habits of gifted high school girls. He reported that their evaluation of reading weaknesses included deficiencies in vocabulary and skimming. A metropolitan school system organized an intensive reading program for gifted students. Immediate and delayed results confirmed the values that such programs offered (46).

From data secured from these and other studies, it seems reasonable to conclude that the reading abilities of gifted students vary, and that instruction to help overcome any deficits these students might have will be as beneficial to them as to other school populations. To exclude gifted students from developmental and remedial reading programs is unrealistic and possibly damaging. Our responsibility is to provide for all youth; to do less fails to serve them and society.

REFERENCES

1 Ausubel, David and Pearl Ausubel. "Ego Development Among Segregated Negro Children," in Harry Passow, ed., *Education in Depressed Areas* (New York: Bureau of Publications, Teachers College, Columbia University, 1963), pp. 109–141.

2 Bledsoe, Joseph. "An Investigation of Six Correlates of Student Withdrawal from High School," *Journal of Educational Research*, 53 (Sept. 1959) 3–6.

3 Bloom, B., A. Davis, and R. Hess. *Compensatory Education for Cultural Deprivation* (New York: Holt, Rinehart and Winston, 1965).

4 Braun, Jean. "Relation Between Concept Formation Ability and Reading Achievement at Three Developmental Levels," *Child Development*, 34 (Sept. 1963) 675–682.

5 Call, R. and N. Wiggin. "Reading and Mathematics," *Mathematics Teacher*, 59 (Feb. 1966) 149–157.

6 Carter, Harold. "Over and Underachievement in Reading," *California Journal of Educational Research*, 15 (Sept. 1964) 175–183.

7 Combs, Charles. "Perception of Self and Scholastic Achievement in the Academically Capable," *Personnel and Guidance Journal*, 43 (Sept. 1964) 47–51.

8 Cooper, Bernice. "An Analysis of the Reading Achievement of White and Negro Pupils in Certain Public Schools of Georgia," *School Review*, 72 (Winter 1964) 462–471.

9 Cruickshank, W. and O. Johnson, eds. *Exceptional Children and Youth* (Englewood Cliffs: Prentice-Hall, Inc., 1958).

[10] DeBoer, John and Gertrude Whipple. "Reading Development in Other Curriculum Areas," *Development In and Through Reading*, Sixtieth Yearbook, Part I, of the National Society for the Study of Education (Chicago: University of Chicago Press, 1961), p. 57.

[11] Devine, Thomas. "Listening," in *Language Arts and Fine Arts, Review of Educational Research*, 37 (April 1967) 152–158.

[12] Donovan, Bernard. *Survey of Reading Abilities of Pupils Entering the Academic High Schools* (New York: Board of Education, 1955).

[13] Duker, Sam. "Listening," in *Language Arts and Fine Arts, Review of Educational Research*, 34 (April 1964) 156–163.

[14] Fay, Leo. "The Relationship Between Reading Skills and Selected Areas of Sixth Grade Achievement," *Journal of Educational Research*, 43 (March 1950) 541–547.

[15] Fransella, F. and D. Gerver. "Multiple Regression Equations for Predicting Reading Age from Chronological Age and WISC Verbal IQ," *British Journal of Educational Psychology*, 35 (Feb. 1965) 86–89.

[16] Goldberg, Miriam. "Factors Affecting Educational Attainment in Depressed Urban Areas," in Harry Passow, ed., *Education in Depressed Areas* (New York: Bureau of Publications, Teachers College, Columbia University, 1963), pp. 68–99.

[17] Goodman, Paul. "The Universal Trap," in D. Schreiber, ed., *The School Dropout* (Washington: National Education Association, 1964), pp. 40–53.

[18] Gottlieb, David. "Goal Aspirations and Goal Fulfillments: Differences Between Deprived and Affluent American Adolescents," *American Journal of Orthopsychiatry*, 34 (Oct. 1964) 934–941.

[19] Harootunian, B. and M. Tate. "The Relationship of Certain Selected Variables to Problem Solving Ability," *Journal of Educational Psychology*, 51 (Dec. 1960) 326–333.

[20] Harris, Albert. "Reading and Human Development," in *Development In and Through Reading*, Sixtieth Yearbook of the National Society for the Study of Education, Part I (Chicago: University of Chicago Press, 1961), pp. 17–34.

[21] Holmes, Jack. "Speed, Comprehension and Power in Reading," *Challenge and Experiment in Reading*, Conference Proceedings of the International Reading Association, (Newark, Delaware: The Association, 1962), pp. 143–149.

[22] Hughes, M. and P. Willis. "Personal Reading: A Study of a Seventh Grade," in *On Becoming a Reader*, Proceedings of the Claremont Reading Conference, 29 (1965) 90–101.

[23] Hunt, D. and J. Dopyera. "Personality Variation in Lower-Class Children," *Journal of Psychology*, 62 (Jan. 1966) 47–54.

[24] Husbands, K. and J. Shores. "Measurement of Reading for Problem Solving: A Critical Review of the Literature," *Journal of Educational Research*, 43 (Feb. 1950) 453–465.

[25] Jan-Tausch, James. "Concrete Thinking as a Factor in Reading Comprehension," *Challenge and Experiment in Reading*, Conference Proceedings

of the International Reading Association (Newark, Delaware: The Association, 1962), pp. 161–164.

26 Keshian, J. "The Characteristics and Experiences of Children Who Learn To Read Successfully," *Elementary English,* 40 (Oct. 1963) 615–616, 652.

27 Krippner, S. and C. Herald. "Reading Disabilities Among the Academically Talented," *The Gifted Child Quarterly,* 8 (Spring 1964) 12–20.

28 Loban, William. "Stages in the Acquisition of Standard English," *Social Dialects and Language Learning,* U. S. Dept. of Health, Education and Welfare, Office of Education, Cooperative Research Project No. F-059 (Champaign: National Council of Teachers of English, 1964), pp. 75–103.

29 Loban, Walter. *The Language of Elementary School Children* (Champaign: National Council of Teachers of English, 1963).

30 Loughlin, L., H. O'Connor, M. Powell, and K. Parsley. "An Investigation of Sex Differences by Intelligence, Subject-Matter Area, Grade and Achievement Level on Three Anxiety Scales," *Journal of Genetic Psychology,* 106 (June 1965) 207–215.

31 McDonald, Arthur. "Flexibility in Reading Approaches: Measurement and Development," *Combining Research Results and Good Practice,* Conference Proceedings of the Annual Convention, Vol. II, Part II (Newark, Delaware: The Association, 1966), pp. 67–71.

32 MacDonald, D. "An Investigation of the Attitudes of Parents of Unsuccessful and Successful Readers," *Journal of Educational Research,* 56 (April 1963) 437–438.

33 Maney, Ethel. "Literal and Critical Reading in Science," *Journal of Experimental Education,* 27 (Sept. 1958) 57–64.

34 Michaels, Melvin, "Subject Reading Improvement: A Neglected Teaching Responsibility," *Journal of Reading,* 9 (Oct. 1965) 16–20.

35 Miller, S. M. "Dropouts—a Political Problem," in D. Schreiber, ed., *The School Dropout* (Washington: National Education Association, 1964), pp. 11–24.

36 Nachman, Leonard, Russell Getson, and John Odgers. *Pilot Study of Ohio High School Dropouts, 1961–1962* (Columbus, Ohio: State Department of Education, 1963).

37 National Council of Teachers of English. *Language Programs for the Disadvantaged* (Champaign: National Council of Teachers of English, 1965).

38 Norvell, George. *The Reading Interests of Young People* (Boston: D. C. Heath, 1950).

39 O'Donnell, Roy. "Awareness of Grammatical Structure and Reading Comprehension," *High School Journal,* 45 (Feb. 1962) 184–188.

40 Osborne, R. "Racial Differences in Mental Growth and School Achievement," *Psychological Reports,* 7 (Oct. 1960) 233–239.

41 Paterra, Mary. "A Study of Thirty-three WISC Scattergrams of Retarded Readers," *Elementary English,* 40 (April 1963) 394–405.

42 Penty, Ruth. *Reading Ability and High School Dropouts* (New York: Bureau of Publications, Teachers College, Columbia University, 1956).

43 Peyton, J. and R. Below. "The Need for Reading Instruction in Kentucky High Schools," *School Service Report*, 6 (Oct. 1965) 2–7.

44 Pippert, R. and N. Archer. "A Comparison of Two Methods of Classifying Underachievers with Respect to Selected Criteria," *Personnel and Guidance Journal*, 41 (May 1963) 788–791.

45 Ramsey, Wallace. "The Kentucky Reading Study," *The Reading Teacher*, 16 (Dec. 1962) 178–181.

46 Rochester City School District. *The Tutorial Reading Program: A Second Year Progress Report for an Exploration in Small Group/Individualized Reading for Above-Average Pupils* (Rochester, New York: Rochester Public Schools, 1963).

47 Russell, David. "Six Studies of Children's Understanding of Concepts," *Elementary School Journal*, 63 (Feb. 1963) 255–260.

48 Shaw, M. and G. Alves. "The Self-Concept of Bright Academic Underachievers," *Personnel and Guidance Journal*, 42 (Dec. 1963) 401–403.

49 Shores, J. Harlan. "Reading Interests and Informational Needs of High School Students," *The Reading Teacher*, 17 (April 1964) 536–544.

50 Singer, Harry. "Substrata-Factor Theory of Reading: Grade and Sex Differences at the Elementary School Level," *Improvement of Reading Through Classroom Practice*, Conference Proceedings of the International Reading Association (Newark, Delaware: The Association, 1964), pp. 313–320.

51 Sinks, N. and M. Powell. "Sex and Intelligence as Factors in Achievement in Grades Four Through Eight," *Journal of Genetic Psychology*, 106 (March 1965) 67–79.

52 Smiley, Marjorie. "Research and Its Implications," *Improving English Skills of Culturally Different Youth*, U. S. Dept. of Health, Education and Welfare, Office of Education Bulletin 1964, No. 5 (Washington: Government Printing Office), pp. 35–61.

53 Sochor, Elona. "Literal and Critical Reading in Science," *Journal of Experimental Education*, 27 (Sept. 1958) 49–56.

54 Spache, George. "Reading in Various Curriculum Fields," *The Reading Teacher*, 11 (Feb. 1958) 158–164.

55 Spiegler, Charles. "Provisions and Programs for Educationally Disadvantaged Youth in Secondary School," *The Educationally Retarded and Disadvantaged*, Sixty-sixth Yearbook of the National Society for the Study of Education, Part I (Chicago: University of Chicago Press, 1967), pp. 184–210.

56 Squire, James. "Reading in the American High Schools Today," *Reading and Inquiry*, Proceedings of the Annual Convention, International Reading Association (Newark, Delaware: The Association, 1965), pp. 468–472.

57 Stanchfield, J. "Boys' Reading Interests as Revealed Through Personal Conferences," *The Reading Teacher*, 16 (Sept. 1962) 41–44.

58 Strang, Ruth and Charlotte Rogers. "How Do Students Read a Short Story?" *English Journal*, 54 (Dec. 1965) 819–23, 829.

59 Strickland, Ruth. *Language of Elementary School Children: Its Relationship to the Language of Reading Textbooks and to the Quality of Reading of Selected Children,* Bulletin of the School of Education, Indiana University, 7, No. 4, (July 1962).

60 Vaughn, Beryl. "Reading Interests of Eighth-Grade Students," *Journal of Developmental Reading,* 6 (Spring 1963) 149–155.

61 Wachner, Clarence. "The Detroit Great Cities School Improvement Program in English," *Improving English Skills of Culturally Different Youth,* U. S. Dept. of Health, Education and Welfare, Office of Education Bulletin 1964, No. 5 (Washington: Government Printing Office), pp. 123–133.

62 Watson, R. L. "Early Identification of High School Dropouts," *Reading and Inquiry,* Proceedings of the Annual Convention, International Reading Association (Newark, Delaware: The Association, 1965), pp. 265–267.

63 Whitman, Robert. "Significant Reading Experiences of Superior English Students," *Illinois English Bulletin,* 51 (Feb. 1964) 1–24.

64 Whitmore, P. and R. Chapman. *Dropout Incidence and Significance at Modesto High Schools, 1961–64* (Modesto, California: Modesto Public Schools, 1965).

65 Woolcock, Cyril. "Guiding the Reading of Superior Students in a Special High School," *The Reading Teacher,* 16 (May 1963) 448–451.

Reading in College

PHILLIP SHAW

NEW INTELLECTUAL CLIMATE OF COLLEGE

AN ENTERING college Freshman at once is aware of greater freedom than he enjoyed in high school. He is given assignments without being told what to look for. His homework is not checked regularly. Course syllabi are without limiting specifications; some teachers mention titles of books that he may or may not read or consult. In the classroom, he takes notes when and how he wants to, and outside of class he reads and studies as he chooses. Never before has his personal development depended upon skills and attitudes operating in so continuously permissive a setting. With his new freedom, the college Freshman is confronted with new responsibilities for self-direction and self-discipline in working toward his academic goals. For many students, this new responsibility stimulates personal development and inspires greater intellectual effort than he formerly exerted.

The permissive yet demanding intellectual climate of college poses the question: "Are students getting maximum personal development out of their college experience?" Some educators have lamented that American students tend to pursue mediocrity rather than excellence at college. According to many observers and critics, academic mediocrity is widespread, and they acount for it by the failure of too many students to realize their potential.

PREVALENCE OF READING DEFICIENCIES AMONG COLLEGE FRESHMEN

Estimates of the prevalence of reading and study deficiencies among college Freshmen are quite alarming. Observations and criticisms of the

From *Development in and through Reading*, the Sixtieth Yearbook of the National Society for the Study of Education, 1961, pp. 336–354. Reprinted with the permission of the National Society for the Study of Education.

situation by educators and laymen are confirmed by Carter's study of 1,029 students completing the Freshman year of college. Of these students, "68 per cent reported that they had never been taught how to read a chapter effectively, 70 per cent indicated that they had not been taught to concentrate upon a reading activity, 64 per cent had not been shown how to develop an awareness of problems, and 70 per cent had not been taught how to critically evaluate a writer's bias and use of preconceived ideas."[1]

Halfter and Douglass concluded, after eight years of carefully controlled testing, that two-thirds of their entering college Freshmen lack the reading skills required for academic success.[2] Hadley estimated that "95 per cent of college entrants lack adequate study skills." He noted that "a relatively small percentage have reading speeds and comprehension skills adequate for handling all college assignments" and that a great proportion are weak in note-taking.[3]

A MISCONCEPTION ABOUT READING DEFICIENCY

Many college educators believe that the mediocre reading ability of American college Frenshmen is the result of poor preparation in the high school. They deny that colleges have responsibility for teaching students the reading and study skills and attitudes needed by them for college work. These college educators do not recognize the need for a sequential development of a student's reading ability. As a student ascends the educational ladder from elementary school through the university, he encounters increasing demands and opportunities for development. As expressed by Townsend, "many of the reading skills, habits, and attiudes which are effective in producing good high-school achievement are inadequate tools for college reading, even though they are still necessary and still constantly in use."[4]

COLLEGE READING PROGRAMS DURING THE 1950's

Despite some misconceptions concerning the responsibility for developing the reading ability of college Freshmen, it is evident from six

[1]Homer L. J. Carter, "Effective Use of Textbooks in the Reading Program," in *Eighth Yearbook of the National Reading Conference for Colleges and Adults,* p. 156. Fort Worth: Texas Christian University Press, 1959.

[2]Irma T. Halfter and Frances M. Douglass, " 'Inadequate' College Readers," *Journal of Developmental Reading,* I (Summer, 1958), 42.

[3]L. S. Hadley, "New College Students Lack Study Techniques," *School and Society,* LXXXV (November 9, 1957), 353.

[4] Agatha Townsend, "How Can We Help College Students Develop Critical Reading of Textbooks and Resource Materials," in *Better Readers for Our Times,* p. 112. International Reading Association Proceedings, 1956. Edited by William S. Gray and Nancy Larrick. New York: Scholastic Magazines, 1956.

surveys of college reading programs reported in the yearbooks (1954–59) of the National Reading Conference for Colleges and Adults[5] that, during the 1950's, hundreds of American colleges provided reading-improvement programs and enrolled thousands of students in them. By 1956, almost three-fourths of the 418 institutions replying to Causey's questionnaire reported reading programs in progress. This study also reported a total enrollment of 57,052 students, as compared with 33,341 students noted in a survey made the previous year. In 1959, Miller summarized a total of 233 responses to questionnaires representing the returns from 372 colleges that had reported reading programs in 1955:

> In terms of growth of program in the last five years, 49 schools indicated that their programs had more than doubled, 67 indicated that they had had moderate increases, 34 indicated no increase at all, 20 indicated that they were limited by college policy and would not grow, and 2 indicated that they were unable to tell about growth.[6]

The surveys made portray a considerable development of reading programs at the college level during the 1950's. But, it is evident that, during that decade, numerous colleges failed to provide any reading programs even though it had been quite well established that pratically all college students can increase their reading efficiency through instruction.

The "cut-off" points established by colleges for the selection of students for reading-improvement programs obviously affect the reading enrollments. Blake noted that "most programs offer services to a limited segment of the school population.[7] According to Jones,[8] in many institutions about two-thirds of the entering class fail to take the course because of limitations placed upon enrollment. Usually selected Freshmen are admitted first.

It appears that the majority of American college administrations do not have a systematic policy of, or extensive program for, the improvement of the reading ability of their students. The concept of the "Freshman year" as a period when college youth are helped to establish a springboard for their subsequent education has become increasingly current. However, the policy of guiding Freshmen to gain maximum

[5]Yearbooks of the National Reading Conference for Colleges and Adults (Prior to 1956, Southwest Reading Conference for Colleges and Universities). Fort Worth: Texas Christian University Press, 1954–59.
[6]Lyle L. Miller, "Current Use of Workbooks and Mechanical Aids," *Eighth Yearbook of the National Reading Conference for Colleges and Adults, op. cit.* p. 67.
[7]Walter S. Blake, "College Level Study Skills Program—Some Observations," *Junior College Journal,* XXV (November, 1954), 148.
[8]Ernest Jones, "Selection and Motivation of Students," *Eighth Yearbook of the National Reading Conference for Colleges and Adults, op. cit.,* pp. 27–30.

personal development in and through reading has not been widely adopted. In view of the predicted increase in college enrollments during the next decade, the need for the adoption of such a policy is more urgent than ever.

It is to be hoped that the 1960's will witness not only an increase in the numbers of American students who receive a higher education but also a change in the attitude of college administrators toward *all* academic "failure," particularly failure of students to realize their potentialities. To achieve the aim of development in and through reading during college years, college reading programs that represent a broad rather that a narrow mechanized view of reading are necessary.

ORGANIZING A COLLEGE READING PROGRAM

After scrutinizing questionnaires returned by the colleges reporting that their reading programs had been discontinued, Miller surmised that, in some of these schools, the staff members concerned with reading had not been persuasive enough, while in other schools they had apparently failed to establish the value of the program in a way "readily recognizable to those in positions of administrative responsibilty."[9] In another article, Kingston expressed the opinion that "it probably was easier to 'sell' a reading program to college administrators and faculty in the late 1940's and early 1950's than it is today [1958]."[10] These observations suggest the dynamic role that a reading staff must act on a college campus.

ORGANIZATION AS A SEPARATE COURSE

No conclusive study has yet been published concerning the number and advantages of each of the three basic kinds of organization of college reading-improvement programs: (*a*) a separate, special service; (*b*) a part of a language-arts course; (*c*) an intrinsic part of each subject. At present, organization of reading courses as a special service seems to be the most common. In Barbe's study of forty-eight colleges, thirty offered reading instruction in a separate reading course.[11]

When a college reading program is organized as a separate course,

[9]Miller, *op. cit.*, pp. 68–69.
[10]Albert J. Kingston, Jr., "Problems of Initiating a New College Reading Program," in *Eighth Yearbook of the National Reading Conference for Colleges and Adults, op. cit.*, p. 16.
[11]Walter B. Barbe, "Reading Improvement Services in Colleges and Universities," *School and Society*, LXXIV (July 7, 1951), 7.

the over-all objectives and practices of the program can be determined primarily by the reading staff. Otherwise, the traditional departments, such as English and speech, are likely to control the total language-arts offering.

Further study is needed concerning the advantages and disadvantages of college developmental reading programs that are organized as a separate service for all Freshmen. In view of the mediocre performance of so many American students, an all-Freshman reading-improvement service would seem to be as important as Freshman composition. Unless the all-Freshman reading course has the status of a course, such as composition or speech, conditions like those in the situation described by Sandberg can threaten its effectiveness:

> Budgetary limitations make it impossible at present to engage a reading specialist on a full-time basis. Secondly, it is impossible to find a free hour each day when the Freshman class as a whole can be given reading instruction. Thirdly, there is not at present even one free period a week at which the entire class can meet since the only hour now available is used for Freshman orientation. Consequently, the Freshman staff had to consider all these problems and, in the light of them, establish a program which could be operated within the limitations.[12]

The greatest threat to a policy of admitting to a separate reading program all of the students who are likely to benefit from it is budget considerations. Too often class size, course duration, and available facilities of classroom space and materials are determined by the budget rather than by the needs of students.

A separate reading program, unlike the program that is integrated with regular instruction, does not always involve required enrolment and attendance nor is credit commonly given for it. As to whether required enrolment and credit constitute advantages or disadvantages, there is a difference in opinion. Jones definitely opposes forced enrolment in a special course:

> The selection of students for college and university reading programs should be *entirely* on a voluntary basis. At this level, students will be successful only if they want to be and not because they are forced.[13]

On the other hand, a study by Blake supports the opposite view that college students, at least Freshmen on probation, will benefit from a

---

[12]Edwin T. Sandberg, "Reading Program at Wartburg College," *Journal of Developmental Reading*, II (Winter, 1959), 60–62.
[13]Jones, *op. cit.*, p. 25.

compulsory reading-improvement course.[14] According to the judgment of the present writer, who has supervised and taught reading classes that were completely voluntary and classes for which both enrolment and attendance were required, it is a mistake to assume adequate insight on the part of each lower Freshman as to whether he should enrol and, once enrolled, as to whether he should attend regularly. Of course, if a student resists the course, he should be allowed to drop it as he would any other course.

As to the wisdom of establishing a special reading service as a credit course, opinions differ. Scott[15] wrote of an especially unhappy experience with a noncredit but required course. According to Miller's recent study of 233 colleges reporting reading programs, somewhat less than half granted credit for the course. This is a goodly number, in view of the newness of the field of reading improvement on the college level. The writer hopes that increasingly on American college campuses a reading program carrying credit will take its place alongside other "personal development" courses, such as English composition and speech.

Staffing presents a particular problem in setting up a separate reading program. The following statement by Miller suggests the seriousness of this problem:

> Staff changes seem to be a significant factor in the discontinuation of several programs. In these cases, one individual has taken the interest and the time, often in addition to his regular staff assignments, to develop a reading program. When this staff member left, no one else seemed ready to take over these responsibilities. They had never been established as a part of the on-going university program, but only as a special-interest area of an individual or a small group of staff members. In a few cases there was some indication that the university would like to employ another person with similar interests, but that they had not had much success in locating such qualified personnel.[16]

Behind the staff changes just described is the lack of adequately trained personnel in the field of reading improvement. The proportion of college reading personnel who are "specialists," according to the usual educational requirements of specialized study of a field, and of those who are "specialists" only on the basis of teaching experience in the field can perhaps be guessed from statistics concerning the spon-

---

[14]Walter S. Blake, "Do Probationary College Freshmen Benefit from Compulsory Study Skills and Reading Training?" *Journal of Experimental Education,* XXV (September, 1956), 91–93.

[15]Frances Deane Scott, "Evolution of a College Reading Program, 1952–56," *Journal of Developmental Reading,* II (Autumn, 1958), 39.

[16]Miller, *op. cit.,* p. 68.

sorship of college reading programs. Woods' recent Wisconsin study[17] reveals considerable variety in the sponsoring departments. In Causey's first report, twenty-seven different campus agencies are listed as sponsoring college reading programs. In his second report he notes: "Departments responsible for instruction in the courses were reported as follows: English 126, Education 122, Psychology 48, Reading Clinic 21, Communications 10, Humanities 5, not named 86."[18] This breakdown suggests a dilettantism in the field. These studies indicate the lack of university centers for the preparation of college reading teachers.

COMBINED WITH A LANGUAGE-ARTS COURSE

Some colleges offer reading-improvement instruction as a unit integrated with a course in language arts. Organization of such a reading program has been supported on several grounds. First, not being subject to the limitations of a separate course, the reading program can reach all students.

The second reason usually advanced to support the organization of a reading program within the framework of a language-arts course takes into account the optimum personal development of the students. The relation between general semantics and adjustment and the evidence of inadequate reading and study skills as a cause of failure in college point to the importance of systematic instruction for personal development. Research also indicates a positive relationship between reading-study ability and other skills ordinarily taught in language-arts courses. A striking evidence of this relationship pointed out by Durkin is that films for reading improvement can be used to teach college students clear and forceful writing.[19] Thus the student is more broadly served than in a separate course on reading skills. Moreover, language-arts teachers are more specifically trained to contribute to personal development through the interpretation of literature, the building of mature reading tastes and interests, and the development of a critical and intelligent attitude through reading. However, as Cosper observed, "few teachers of high school or college English have had formal training in the teaching of reading."[20]

[17]Kieth Woods, "A Survey of Reading Programs in Wisconsin," in *Sixth Yearbook of the National Reading Conference for Colleges and Adults*, pp. 134–28. Fort Worth: Texas Christian University Press, 1957.

[18]Oscar S. Causey, "College Reading Programs in the Nation," in *Fifth Yearbook of the National Reading Conference for Colleges and Adults*, pp. 135–37. Fort Worth: Texas Christian University Press, 1956.

[19]Brian Durkin, "New Values in College Reading Films," *Journal of Developmental Reading*, II (Summer, 1959), 17–25.

[20]Russell Cosper, "Improvement of Reading in Colleges and Secondary Schools," *North Central Association Quarterly*, XXXI (October, 1956), 199.

INTEGRATED WITH REGULAR INSTRUCTION

A third kind of college reading-improvement program is carried out by subject-matter teachers in their own classrooms. Besides avoiding the limitations of a separate course, such an integration is supported by the fact that reading abilities vary in different content fields. It has long been recognized that all secondary and college teachers should be teachers of reading in their subjects. This position is reinforced by research studies which, according to Spache, show that reading specialists "are not discovering methods or materials for teaching students to read or study more effectively in mathematics, in physics, in economics, in history, and any of the half-dozen other fields."[21] However, we have more knowledge than we use. Some college teachers need to become aware of their students' needs. Many students fail to read effectively because their teachers are so occupied with outside-the-classroom activities and with large classes that they do not take time to consider which instructional techniques and materials would best meet the students' needs.

Elsewhere, the present writer has asserted that the proper teachers to train college students to develop their reading ability are instructors of lower Freshmen. He developed the following thesis:

Each instructor of lower Freshmen should (1) help his students to increase their ability to read textbooks and reference materials in his particular field, (2) lead his students to develop their vocabulary in his field, (3) aid his students in developing other skills leading to proficiency and scholarship in his field, (4) anticipate the special needs of his deficient students, (5) induce his students to utilize their precourse experiences in his field, (6) create in the minds of his students a strong impression of design in his courses, and (7) cultivate his students' interest in voluntary reading.[22]

A series of intradepartmental, perhaps even interdepartmental seminar meetings of classroom teachers and a college-reading specialist (already on campus or brought in for the purpose) could result in the formulation of a body of basic information that the teachers would carry back to their classrooms.

[21]George Spache, "Improving Reading Skills in the Subject Matter Areas," in *Seventh Yearbook of the National Reading Conference for Colleges and Adults*, pp. 32–33. Fort Worth: Texas Christian University Press, 1958.
[22]Phillip Shaw, "Teachers of Lower Freshmen Are Specialists," *Bulletin of the Association of American University Professors*, XLIII (Summer, 1953). 345–52.

The seminar method is an informal way of repairing a deficiency in the training of subject-matter teachers. Preferably, these teachers should receive this instruction as part of their regular educational background. Instruction in the teaching of reading skills in a particular subject and exploration of the opportunities for personal development and self-improvement through reading in every content field could very well be a unit in a general course on the principles and methods of teaching at the college level.

COLLEGE-LEVEL OBJECTIVES

STATING OBJECTIVES

A general objective of most college reading programs, stated in terms of proficiency, is "to help the students to read to capacity"; in terms of academic performance, "to help the students gain personal development in and through reading." In a protest against exclusively general expressions of aims, McDonald and Byrne urged that objectives of college reading programs be stated in "operational terms," "in terms of the observable behavior of pupils." Centi proposed that the college reading teacher should actually "talk to the teachers within his own institution to determine the type of reading which is required of the students." To sum up, Srs. Fridian and Rosanna declared:

> Reading programs should begin with objectives which are of immediate practical concern to those who participate. Only when developed on such a basis can they be expected to become effective in all departments and to receive the enthusiastic support of the administration, the faculty, and the student body.[23]

The functional approach to setting up a reading program leads inevitably to differing objectives among various institutions. These stem from differences in the curriculum, administration, interests and qualifications of teachers, textbooks used, library facilities, and the student body itself. These variables may partly account for the diversity of practices found in college reading programs. Marked differences of opinion as to the scope of the objectives of a college reading program abound in the

[23]Sister M. Fridian and Sister M. Rosanna, "A Developmental Reading Experiment in a European History Class," *Journal of Developmental Reading*, I (Winter, 1958), 7. [See also Arthur S. McDonald and James A. Byrne, "Four Questions on Objectives," *Journal of Developmental Reading*, I (Spring, 1958), 46–47, and Paul Centi, "What is College-Level Reading?" *Catholic Educational Review*, LXII (November, 1959), 549–52.]

professional literature. On the one hand, visual skills are emphasized; on the other hand, interpretative or "thinking" skills. Surveys of American programs reveal differences in practice with respect to inclusion of vocabulary lessons, paragraph-structure exercises, and concentration-improvement exercises and as to the use of reading films, the tape recorder, and the classroom approach. To sum up with Bliesmer's statement, based on an examination of research in 1958: "As in the past, the reported programs continue to represent considerable variations in types of programs, procedures employed, evaluation instruments used, length, and the like."[24] One common objective that emerges, however, is that of inculcating the study-type of comprehension skills. These skills have already been described in the professional literature, but one of these is, in the opinion of the present writer, so much the core of a college reading-improvement program that it deserves special emphasis.

THE CORE STUDY-TYPE SKILL

Ability to identify main ideas.—Many college students are not convinced of the importance of grasping main ideas and are not sufficiently alert in noting them. This deficiency is to be noted in the manner in which they think in connection with many activities, of which reading is but one. Yet, ineptness in reading easily reveals to students this weakness in their mental habits.

Poor readers usually fail to demand full meaning from books. They plunge into a particular chapter assigned in an unfamiliar textbook. They neglect to examine the preface for a statement of the author's point of view, scope of subject matter, place of this book in a certain genre of academic writing, and so on. They fail to examine the table of contents to observe the design of the textbook. They do not examine such items as the appendix, glossary, bibliography, and index until they are actually referred to them. They do not thumb through a new textbook to satisfy a curiosity about the author's editorial characteristics. But they might want to know if the text contains exercises, charts, pictures, or subject matter in outline form. If so, how are these edited items related to one another?

Simple exercises can alert students to identifying main ideas of textbooks. They can be asked to skim through a given preface to select the best one-sentence statement of the author's purpose. They can be given

[24]Emery Bliesmer, "Review of Recent Research on College and Adult Reading," in *Eighth Yearbook of the National Reading Conference for Colleges and Adults," op. cit.,* pp. 171–92.

a table of contents with the items in scrambled order and asked to restore the original table. From a few given pages of a textbook, they can be required to pick out words in bold face, in italics, and in capital letters. Students can unscramble headings and subheadings prepared in haphazard order; an obviously irrelevant heading can be introduced for the students to identify and discard.

While reading literature, students with poor habits neglect to look for clues to main ideas needed for a full appreciation of the work. As for alerting students to main ideas that contribute to their appreciation of literature, the following devices may be helpful. Have students suggest new titles and endings for written works. Ask students to put checks in margins next to statements of the theme. Consider how a work would be affected if one of the characters were removed, if the setting (place and period) were different, if the work began later or ended earlier. For narratives, ask students to sketch a "scenario." For a play already read, have students read *only* the words spoken by a leading character throughout the play. For a poem, have students rewrite several lines. For an essay, single out fair and objective statements of controversial issues and have students deliberately rephrase the statements so as to "slant" them.

Ability to grasp main ideas.—When poor readers attack an assignment, they may begin by studying the details at once. These students underline as they go along instead of first reading ahead and then returning to underline ideas that fit into the over-all pattern of thought.

Emotional and visual difficulties do, indeed, result in poor reading, but among untrained average readers, failure to use techniques of grasping the "whole" meaning is a more common cause of ineffective reading. The chief weakness of a "slow" reader may simply be that he *must* plod over the page, word by word, because he has not grasped the main ideas that make the words meaningful. Similarly, anyone attempting to understand a library or a botanical garden would have to proceed ponderously, item by item, if he has not already glimpsed the general organization of the contents. The ability to use one's eyes either for rapid understanding or for slow study, either for general comprehension or for specific comprehension, is the attribute of the so-called "flexible" reader. He adjusts his speed of reading to his purpose for reading.

The basic principle of reading a textbook is "whole learning." The capable reader avoids study of details before he has grasped the main idea that integrates them. The term, "main idea" has a double meaning: It is a *whole* idea (main idea of a section), and *part* of a whole idea (one item of the author's outline). Thus, a paragraph heading

expresses the key point of a paragraph both *out of* context—a meaning
it would have in any book—and *in* context—the particular meaning it
has because of the other ideas in the chapter.

Almost every reading specialist recommends that a careful reading
should be preceded by an overview. Students' neglect of this Gestalt
approach may reflect the lack of agreement among specialists as to
the nature of the overview. Some, like advocates of alphabetical systems
of reading textbooks, advise a survey or a preview as the only step to
precede careful reading. Others recommend two different readings, a
quick one for main ideas only and then a careful reading for fuller
comprehension.

Much can be said in favor of the attack by two different readings
when the student encounters subject matter that is not easy for him.
The average student must read his textbooks quite carefully just to
understand them. If first he concentrates on grasping only the main
ideas, he will not be in danger of acquiring scraps of information without gaining knowledge. A bizarre spectacle of the school world is the
student who "learns" thoroughly without understanding thoroughly.

Advocates of two different readings can be found for all types of materials, including literature. For example, the poetry editor of *The
Nation* suggests that William Faulkner and T. S. Eliot will be more
"available" to the general reader if approached as indicated in the statement: "For most works, a first, largely uncritical but alert reading is
helpful simply to get an overall sense of the set, the feel, of the
whole."[25]

College reading manuals are available for special practice in grasping main ideas. Simple, informal devices that should be useful are as
follows: Have students select the most general sentence of a paragraph
and then the least general. Provide a paragraph from which the topic
sentence has been removed and have students locate the missing sentence from a list of sentences. Ask students to locate added sentences in
a paragraph that do not keep to the topic. Provide sentences of a paragraph in haphazard order, and have students put them in the proper
order. Call for a statement of the topic of a group of consecutive
paragraphs. Have students reorder scrambled paragraphs.

A teaching approach to inculcate this core skill is to conduct lessons *deductively*, as opposed to *inductively*. Call first for expressions of
the main ideas of the whole passage read before asking students to discuss in detail any part of the passage.

[25]M. L. Rosenthal, "On Teaching Difficult Literary Texts," *College English,* XX
(January, 1959), 155.

THE PERSONAL DEVELOPMENT OBJECTIVE

In college, students have access to a wide variety of reading materials that should contribute to their growth in self-understanding and social relations. It is not enough for them to obtain merely an intellectual grasp of the author's meaning. They should read with the expectation of experiencing a feeling of kinship with notable characters of literature and history and should carry away from their reading modified values and standards.

To develop judgment, the reading of presentations by authorities who differ sharply is an excellent exercise. This type of critical reading requires not only grasping the main ideas set forth by each authority but also determining the validity of the pronouncements of representative authorities and weighing the relative importance of each with reference to the problem. Books that present ideas in conflict with the student's habitual way of thinking likewise require the exercise of logic and judgment.

Deeper levels of interpretation of literature should be acquired during college years. Through the study of great books and stories, students may develop ideals and courage to face the complexities and difficulties of life.

ADOPTING PROCEDURES AND MATERIALS

A college reading-improvement program usually can be classified according to one of three basic orientations around which its procedures and materials are structured: (*a*) "mechanical-aid oriented," (*b*) "textbook oriented," and (*c*) "counseling oriented."

The "mechanical-aid-oriented" programs are described in detail in chapter xii.

"TEXTBOOK-ORIENTED" PROGRAMS

The second type of reading program, one that is "textbook-oriented," employs expository "how-to" books, reading manuals, or the students' textbooks in the content fields—usually combinations of these kinds of material. The number of textbooks published for students in college reading programs, according to Fulker,[26] more than tripled during

[26]Edmund L. Fulker, "A Decade of Progress in College and Adult Reading Improvement," in *Seventh Yearbook of the National Reading Conference for Colleges and Adults, op. cit.,* p. 15.

1946–55. In 1956 alone, Miller[27] noted, at least ten such textbooks appeared. And reading-improvement textbooks are being widely used on the college level; Miller's study revealed that 88 per cent of four hundred institutions employed them. A later study by Miller disclosed the following facts:

> By far the most popular basic plan of instruction, as indicated by 96 [of a total of 233] responding institutions, was the basic group practice of using workbooks for the whole group, supplemented by individual practice with mechanical aids. The next most popular pattern, as followed by 51 institutions, was one of basic group practice with mechanical aids supplemented by individual practice in workbooks.[28]

A special kind of "textbook-oriented" reading program uses the students' regular textbooks. These textbook materials are characteristically used in certain specialized reading programs and also in reading programs which are integrated with content courses.

One kind of "textbook-oriented" reading program has been criticized by several writers. It has been labeled the "skills-drill" course by Spache and has also been stigmatized by Carter as seeking an *accumulation* rather than an *integration* of skills. McDonald and Byrne declared that these programs "seem to be predicated on the implicit attitude of 'there they are—give them the skills *you* know they need.' "[29] In this kind of program, excessive reliance is usually put upon a single textbook. Thus, there is failure to take into account the fact that the many manuals and expository textbooks in the field differ, in some cases considerably, as to purpose, design, emphasis, and uses. Berg[30] rightly insisted that the variety of instructional material used in a reading program should match the range and complexity of the reading process.

"COUNSELING-ORIENTED" PROGRAMS

"Counseling-oriented" programs take cognizance of the increasing attention given in the 1950's to the relationship of emotional problems

[27]Lyle L. Miller, "Evaluation of Workbooks for College Reading Programs," in *Sixth Yearbook of the National Reading Conference for Colleges and Adults, op. cit.,* pp. 75–85.
[28]Miller, "Current Use of Workbooks and Mechanical Aids," *op. cit.,* p. 71.
[29]George Spache, "Trends in College Reading Programs," *Fourth Yearbook of the National Reading Conference for Colleges and Adults, op. cit.,* pp. 46–47; Homer L. J. Carter, "The Role of Evaluation in Understanding the Usefulness of Reading," *Journal of Developmental Reading,* II (Spring, 1959), 45–51; McDonald and Byrne, *op. cit.,* p. 48.
[30]Paul C. Berg, "Motivation and Specific Instructional Materials in the Reading Program," in *Eighth Yearbook of the National Reading Conference for Colleges and Adults, op. cit.,* pp. 113–21.

to reading difficulties. McDonald wrote that "group psychotherapy contributes significantly to a college reading improvement program. Serious consideration should accordingly be given to the utilization of group psychotherapy as part of the various services offered in connection with reading improvement programs."[31]

Whether the directive or nondirective method is most appropriate for college students having anxieties has also been investigated.[32] Spache has summarized the procedures of the "counseling-oriented" type of college reading program:

> Some students will be assigned to directive textbook-oriented courses, others to supportive machine training courses, others will be offered a laboratory course with a minimum of direction and still others will be given an individualized but closely supervised program. In these various groupings, emphasis upon particular reading skills will also vary according to the personality needs of the students.[33]

EVALUATING A COLLEGE READING PROGRAM

DIFFICULTIES

Reading is such a complex process that measurements of reading potentiality, achievement, and attitudes are extremely difficult to make. Throughout the 1950's, strong doubt was cast on the reliabilitiy of both evaluations and the instruments for evaluation of college reading programs. In 1950, an article by H. Allan Robinson[34] pointed out a marked absence of adequate validation in the whole field of reading, in particular at the college level. Robinson noted three successive stages in program evaluation during 1930–50 characterized in turn by (a) the tendency to rely upon simple, subjective evaluations; (b) an overworking of standardized testing; and (c) matching of supposed equivalent groups of students without regard to motivational factors. This article stimulated several subsequent critical descriptions by other writers.

[31]Arthur S. McDonald, Edwin S. Zolik, and James A. Byrne, "Reading Deficiencies and Personality Factors," in *Eighth Yearbook of the National Reading Conference for Colleges and Adults, op. cit.,* p. 48.

[32]Donald E. P. Smith *et al.,* "Reading Improvement as a Function of Student Personality and Teaching Method," *Journal of Educational Psychology,* XLVII (January, 1956), 47–59.

[33]George Spache, "Reading Improvement as a Counseling Procedure," in *Eighth Yearbook of the National Reading Conference for Colleges and Adults, op. cit.,* p. 129.

[34]H. Allan Robinson, "A Note on the Evaluation of College Remedial Reading Courses," *Journal of Educational Psychology,* XLI (February, 1950), 83–96.

Eight years later McDonald and Byrne pointed out that current reports were still being made on the basis of evaluation procedures that Robinson and other researchers had condemned.[35] A similar lack of progress was reported by Bliesmer in 1955 and in 1959. In the 1959 investigation, the use of standardized reading tests and/or statistical analyses of gains were indicated in about half the reports. Control groups were utilized in only two evaluations of the reported programs.[36] Finally, some critcis have been skeptical about the prevailing optimism of reports on individual reading programs. Barbe, for example, did not find a single report in the literature on a plan which failed.[37]

During the 1950's the professional literature was as critical of the instruments of evaluation of college reading programs as of the evaluations themselves. In 1950, Robinson[38] questioned whether reading tests measured the objectives that investigators were trying to attain. In 1951, Traxler cautioned that no test had yet been constructed to make the weight of each skill in the total score proportionate to the weight of that particular skill in the total reading process.[39] During the next year Triggs explained that investigations in this area are seriously hampered by the scarcity of reliable and valid instruments on which to base judgments.[40]

The above criticisms of instruments and findings suggest that an individual responsible for justifying a reading program to his college administration is between a professional Scylla and Charybdis. On the one hand, he is vulnerable to criticism if he fails to conduct scientific evaluations of the program, and, on the other hand, he lacks the precision instruments needed for valid evaluations. Consequently, seeking to meet the dilemma by testing achievements that are more easily measurable, such as reading speed and academic achievement, he exposes himself to the criticism that his evaluations, if not unreliable, are narrow.

[35]McDonald and Byrne, *op. cit.*, p. 49.

[36]Emery Bliesmer, "The Status of Research in College Reading," in *Fourth Yearbook of the National Reading Conference for Colleges and Adults*, pp. 28–35. Fort Worth: Texas Christian University Press, 1955. See also, Bliesmer, "Review of Recent Research on College and Adult Reading," *op. cit.*

[37]Walter B. Barbe, "A Reading Program That Did Not Work," *Journal of Developmental Reading*, I (Autumn, 1957), 17.

[38]Robinson, *op. cit.*, pp. 86–88.

[39]Arthur E. Traxler, "Critical Survey of Tests for Identifying What Is Read," *Promoting Growth toward Maturity in Interpreting What Is Read*, pp. 195–200. Supplementary Educational Monograph No. 74. Chicago: University of Chicago Press, 1951.

[40]Frances O. Triggs *et al.*, *Diagnostic Reading Tests: A History of Their Construction and Validation*, New York: Committee on Diagnostic Tests, 1952.

SOLUTIONS

For this perplexing dilemma, a solution can be found. First, if a program purports to influence the personal development of its students in and through reading, it is obvious that objective tests are not the only means available. Evaluations, in part subjective and using informal inventories, observations, and academic history, are valuable. Three formal subjective evaluations of the college reading program of which the present writer was in charge were conducted by educators from outside the reading program. In one of these evaluations, a committee of senior instructors of different departments interviewed a sample of students to assess their personal development as a result of taking this improvement course. In another evaluation, a committee of graduate students in the field of testing and research studied the influence of the course on the skills and attitudes of participating students, by means of a questionnaire which was prepared under the supervision of an instructor trained in evaluation. The third subjective evaluation consisted of class observations of and interviews with reading instructors by an experienced evaluator. Besides these formal subjective investigations, the writer, while directing the program, sought informal appraisal by continuing to teach at least one of its sections. In this connection, it is fitting to quote Smith's advice to reading teachers:

> Don't expect to find the answers to your questions in books. . . . Don't expect the specialist to know the answers to your problems either. He doesn't. The answers lie in the behavior of your clients, waiting there for you to discover them.[41]

The other cause of the dilemma, the lack of a scientific approach to evaluating reading programs, appears to be a serious professional weakness. As noted by Sommerfeld, controlling research conditions presents difficulties: "They are not insuperable, however, and they must be handled more skillfully if reading research is to show improvement in quality—if our evaluation is to achieve scientific stature."[42]

Herein lies the undermining cause of the whole problem of evaluating reading programs. A noticeable deficiency occurs in both the quantity and quality of published research on college reading improve-

[41]Donald E. P. Smith, "Clay Idols in the Reading Business," in *Eighth Yearbook of the National Reading Conference for Colleges and Adults, op. cit.,* p. 170.
[42]Roy E. Sommerfeld, "Problems in Evaluating College Reading Programs," in *Fourth Yearbook of the National Reading Conference for Colleges and Adults, op. cit.,* p. 26.

ment. A great volume of "action research" (reports on classroom teaching experiments) is inadequately balanced by "scientific" research. In "Some Unanswered Questions in the Psychology of Reading," Dechant pointed out numerous questions concerning reading comprehension, rate, teaching, and testing that remain unanswered in the research literature. To sum up in Blake's words: "Research is needed particularly in these areas: program evaluation, program improvement, and validation of diagnostic instruments."[43]

[43]Emerald Dechant, "Some Unanswered Questions in the Psychology of Reading," in *Eighth Yearbook of the National Reading Conference, op. cit.*, pp. 99–112; Blake, "College Level Study Skills Programs," *op. cit.*, p. 149.

What Does Research in Reading Reveal—About Practices in Teaching Reading?

CONSTANCE McCULLOUGH

THE PRESENT article is a supplement to that which appeared in the *English Journal* of November 1957. Because of linguistic and cognitive developments which have affected research and theory in the field of reading in the past few years, it seems unwise to attempt a repetition of the earlier report. The present article will be confined to those events which, in the writer's opinion, promise to make the most dramatic difference in practice.

The status of practice in the field was reviewed by James Squire and Roger Applebee (56) in a report in 1966 on 158 selected high schools which consistently educate outstanding students of English. They found that teaching methods showed little variation, that there was little innovation or experimentation, and that there was less use of audiovisual aids then availability seemed to warrent. Reading programs appeared to lack soundness, purpose, organization, and impact. Slow learners and non-college-bound students seldom received enough attention.

In the past ten years, on the other hand, there has been an explosion of new research relevant to reading. The well-publicized study by Holmes (32) has suggested the tremendous importance of experience as a preface to reading. Bloom and others (9) have produced their taxonomy of educational objectives. Guilford (28) has reported his theo-

Reprinted with permission from *What We Know About High School Reading*. A Research Bulletin Prepared by Committee of the National Council of Conference on Research in English. Champaign, Illinois: National Council of Teachers of English, 1969, pp. 54–72.

retical construct of the intellect. And a number of linguists have come forth with theories, materials, and practical ideas for the teaching of reading.

The organization of the 1957 report had been in terms of vocabulary, comprehension, and speed. These dimensions were now both too gross and too unrelated in treatment to represent the newer insights into the dynamics of the reading process.

The present report is divided into parts representing activities in the reading process, many of which are simultaneous in occurrence, as well as interdependent. They are:

Word Recognition (including sight recognition and analysis)
Analysis of Sentence Structure
Determination of Word Meanings
Determination of Sentence Meanings
Determination of Sentence Functions
Determination of Meanings of Larger Units of Composition
Determination of Function of Larger Units of Composition
Evaluation and Interpretation of Ideas
Use of Ideas

While each of these will be treated in turn, each has a bearing on the others. In fact, the major message of the newer knowledge is the relativity that pervades all language and language-related activities. It should be reflected also in our teaching.

WORD RECOGNITION: SIGHT WORDS

Recognition of words as wholes is not the immediate result of a first encounter (23). Apparently it is the result of a number of encounters in contexts which require the refining of observation while they permit more and more rapid recognition, until it would be impossible to say that one had studied every letter in sequence in the time taken for reading the word. Obviously, we could not read so rapidly as some of us do if we were not pattern-conscious (as well as meaning-conscious) in relation to words, phrases, and sentences.

Word meanings affect the ease or difficulty of learning word forms. Walker (67) in a study of nouns and verbs found that, while usage frequency had some effect on retention by seventy-two high school freshmen boys, concrete nouns seemed to be much easier to recall than either abstract nouns or verbs. It follows that more attention needs to be given to the learning of abstract nouns and to verbs than to forms which represent concrete ideas.

Marianne Frostig (27) has identified several kinds of visual perception required in the observation of forms, one or more of which may be deficient in the case of a retarded reader, and capable of improvement by exercise. However, the student who can already recognize a variety of words, no matter how simple they may be, has shown that he can achieve the recognition of forms. His problem may be more a need for application of techniques of learning words—techniques that work for him—and motivation to apply himself, rather than specific deficiencies in perception.

C. C. Fries (25) has promoted the idea of having students learn whole words by means of noting their contrastive feature. With an established pattern contrast such as *pet: pat; met: mat; set:—*, the student can derive *sat*. The application of this technique is limited to regularly spelled words.

Some programmed materials use the presentation of a word in association with a picture, and the gradual establishment of consciousness of the parts in relation to the whole by the omission of parts, to be filled in by the student: *cat; ca, c t, at, —*. The cloze procedure (29), which is the omission of a word or word-part to be supplied by the student, has shown itself to be a useful testing and teaching device. As a follow-up of the *cat* word-parts omission, the student can insert *cat* and other words in appropriate places in the context. In this way the student is required to associate meaning and form.

WORD RECOGNITION: FORM ANALYSIS

May Hill Arbuthnot (2) has written that "Printer's ink is the embalming fluid of poetry," expressing figuratively what linguists are saying to reading teachers: that the written form of English words is an approximation of the sounds of those words, at best; that the spoken word is the living form (25). Thus, although *lamb* is spelled with a *b*, it is correctly pronounced as /lam/. Only when the *b* initiates the second syllable in *lambent* does the *b* produce a sound in this sequence of letters. *Lambkin* and *lambda* are examples of the silent *b* condition, with the *-mb* completing the first syllable.

The student must recall the spoken form in order to be sure of the sound and stress represented by the printed form. If he has never heard the word, he has to make informed guesses based upon similar word patterns.

Basic to the ability to evoke the sound of an English word is the ability to discriminate and produce the sounds of English. Wepman's test of auditory discrimination (71) yields data on the student's ability to notice such differences. But to know which sounds the student does not discriminate is not always enough, for the question is, "Why does he not discriminate?" Treatment will be different according to the answer.

Lado (36) and Fries (25) have shown the efficacy of teaching to the need in the case of dialect or foreign speech. Foreign language speakers tend to substitute for an English sound in a word the sound most like it in their own language or the sound in their own language which usually holds that position in relation to other sounds in the word. So some speakers say *so* for *show*, *lather* for *ladder*. In Spanish, *-rd* is nonexistent as an ending; hence *card* becomes *car*. In the same language, *st-* never initiates a word without a vowel before it; thus, *star* becomes *estar*.

Labov (35) in his study of a Harlem Negro dialect has shown how dialect can increase the number of homonyms in the spoken language, with consequent confusion in the observation of the written language, and a great dependence upon context. The omission of *r*'s makes homonyms of *guard* and *god*. *Yeah* rhymes with *fair*, *idea*, and *fear*. The omission of *l*'s creates the homonyms *toll* and *toe*, *help* and *hep*, *fault* and *fought*. Final clusters tend to lose the final *-t,-d,-s*, and *-z* sounds. *Pass, passed*, and *past* are all pronounced /pas/. Final consonants *-t,-d,-g*, and *-k* are weak or missing, while *-m* and *-n* are nasalized. Voiced final *-th* becomes *-v*, and unvoiced final *-th* becomes *-f*. *E* and *i* are not distinguished before nasals (*pin, pen=pi (n)*.

Initial consonants tend to be pronounced as in standard English except for the *d* substitution for *th-* and the substitution in certain clusters, as in *steam* (pronounced *scream*). The plural form of a word ending in *-st* deviates from the standard English addition of /s/: the word *test*, pronounced /tes/, follows the rule which applies to *bus* (*buses*) and becomes *testes*. Labov suggests that the teacher will have to treat omissions of letter sounds much as he does the silent letter in standard English, stressing the different spellings for the different meanings intended.

He makes the very important point that the student may not hear the difference between his pronunciation of the word and the teacher's pronunciation of it. Mere correction does not do the trick. Pointed speech and hearing exercises may.

Dialect is spoken in a setting which supports identification of the specific meaning intended, whereas printed material demands the fabrication of setting from the print. Essentially, we either make the learning of reading harder by trying to teach it from the dialect, or give the dialect speaker an equal chance with the standard English speaker by first helping him master the spoken standard English substitutes for the dialect deviations. Doubtless the poor academic performance of some Negro dialect speakers can be traced at least in part to this initial handicap. The solution on the secondary level is to give special attention to word endings and letter-sound omissions, with much emphasis upon speech. This is not to suggest that all reading be oral.

The Labov study simply illustrates a much larger problem: that of meeting the needs of dialect speakers of all sections of the country, and the needs of foreign language speakers learning English (53).

One of the aids students unconsciously use in the solution of polysyllabic words is the knowledge of the patterns of letters usual in the English language. In solving the word *fitful,* the student accustomed to the visual patterns of English knows that *t* is not followed by *f* in the same syllable. Therefore, he divides the word after *t* and before *f.* He can do this whether or not he knows *-ful* as a suffix. Obviously, students of foreign language background or students vastly inexperienced in reading English have not developed this skill.

Looking at the word as a pattern instead of as a sequence of single letters, the student can avoid the blending pitfall. He can determine the sound of *a* in the closed syllable *cat,* and associate it with both consonants: *ca-at,* instead of inserting unrelated noises: *kuh-at* or *ka-tuh.*

Sound relationships within monosyllabic words have been explored by Cassidy (17), who shows the mathematical possibility of the occurrence of certain sound patterns within English words. While his suggestions are made in relation to the development of a lexicon organized by sound patterns rather than by alphabetical order, they may be valuable to the teacher and students who wish to learn by discovery.

The patterns of vowels and consonants (VC) which he lists represent sounds, not letters, so that *fast* and *taste* are both of the pattern CVCC; and since *ch* represents the sounds *t* and *sh,* the word *crunch* has the pattern CCVCCC. By possible frequencies (not actual count), there are more than eight thousand opportunities in the language, according to Cassidy, for the occurrence of the pattern CVCC (*fast*), 6,000 for CCVC (*step*), 4,000 for CVC (*pit*), 3,000 for CCCVCC (squirt), and more than 1,000 for CCVCCC (*crunch*), CCCVC (*splash*), CVCCC (*wasps*), and CVVC (*boil*). Other patterns are of less frequency.

He also lists the vowels and consonants which can be final or initial and consonant clusters which can be final or initial. He further suggests a grid somewhat comparable to the syllabaries used extensively in some countries, except that this one contains complete words. For example, his grid for the CV sound combination includes *dee day do doe daw da,* and *he hay who hoe haw ha.* This is a way to see how many English words there are for a particular consonant sound in combination with the possible (in this case single) vowel sounds. Imposed upon the students, it can become a meaningless ritual. Developed by students, it can become an impressive discovery (13).

In somewhat similar vein, Fries (25) has proposed exploration of CVC patterns. Given the pattern P-1, and adding diphthongs to the vowel possibilities, the student can produce *pail* and *pale, peel* and *peal, pile, pole* and *poll, pule, pal, pell, pill, poll* (parrot), *pul* (pit), *paul, pull,* and *pool.* There is no *powl* or *poil.* This activity yields awareness of variant English spellings for the same sounds, while it designates openings for new words in the language. The next rocket might be named *powl*—a pow with a howl.

The pronunciation of letters is a matter of relativity. In the sentence *The bear lunged at the tourist,* the *th* in *the* could be voiced or unvoiced. Only the student's experience with the spoken word assures him of the voiced sound. The *e* in *the* could be long or schwa, depending upon the beginning sound of the next word, or upon the stress (It is *the* best.).

The word *bear* could be pronounced *beer, bare, bur,* or *bar.* A student who did not know it as a sight word would have to read farther before deciding on the pronunciation:

> The _____ branch = bare.
> The _____ barrel polka = beer.
> The _____ stuck to his clothing = bur.
> The _____ was closed = bar.
> The _____ can lunge = bear.

Lunged could have a hard g, except that bears do not lung anything. The *e* sound in *lunged* is omitted, and the *d* is pronounced as it is spelled because of the preceding *g* sound.

Pronunciation is also a matter of history, as in the case of *tourist.* The pronunciation of *ou* could not be predicted by a student unfamiliar with *tour,* which retains its French spelling.

Far from being a crutch to be shunned, the use of context is, in some instances, as important to the revitalization of the spoken word as it is to word meaning.

For many years teachers have had some faith in the utility of phonic generalizations. Burmeister (15) reported the findings of seven studies showing the relative dependability and the extent of utility of phonic generalizations. Clymer (19) had found eighteen of high utility, but with many exceptions. Emans (24) and Bailey (5) largely supported his evidence.

The findings by Hanna, Hanna, Hodges, and Rudorf (30) on 17,310 words in a computerized study showed that the spelling of words is subject to several factors: phonological, morphological, and syntactical. The use of phonic generalizations would be less discouraging if they were applied in sequence rather than alone. For example, when *ea* is followed by other consonants than *r*, it probably represents either the long or the short *e* sound; when followed by *r*, it may in addition be sounded as in *hearth* or *heard*. Burmeister (15) proposed that in words like *have* and *rave*, the student be told that the *e* usually is silent and the preceding vowel long or short, and that the long sound should be tried first.

When followed by *r* plus consonant plus silent *e*, as in *terse, purse, sparse, horse*, the preceding vowel ordinarily has the sound it would have if the word ended with the *r*. Weir (70) investigated the effect of environmental factors on the sound of *e* in *er*. In *term*, where it is followed by a consonant; in *experiment*, where it is followed by *i*, and a consonant, or *heresy*, where it is followed by *e* and a consonant; in *experience*, where it is followed by *ie*, or *period*, where it is followed by *io*; and in *her*, where it ends the word. As some of the newer findings on spelling and pronunciation are released, English teachers will be able to be much more helpful to their students, and the task of decoding the printed word will be more rewarding. We still, however, must think in terms of how much the rules are worth.

Syllabication has been torn by strife between lexicographers who divide words by structure, and linguists who divide them by pronunciation. *Expect* is a case in point. While it is necessary to divide as in the dictionary between the *x* and *p* in order to see that the first *e* is in a closed syllable and therefore short, the pronunciation of the word divides between the *k* and *s* sounds: *ek spect*. For some time it has been the practice to teach, for purposes of determining vowel sounds in pronunication units, the following divisions: *la bor, lad der, lit tle, mas ter, mail man, look ing, ex pect, an chor*. *Labor* and *mailman* tend to be pronounced as they are divided above. For the others, however, the students must learn to shift for pronunciation: *la (d)der, li (t)tle, ma ster, loo king, ek spect, ang ker*. The teacher must literally "play it by ear" in regions in which the standard pronunciation is *lit (t) l*.

Venezky (66) in a computerized study of 20,000 most common English words pointed out that *a* tends to be short when followed by a final consonant or series of consonants, as in *rat* and *annals*. The long *a* occurs in *rate, anal,* and *sane*. "What must be acquired," he stated (66: p. 103), "for the proper pronunciation of *a* is the ability to differentiate the environments and suffixes; final consonant vs. consonant plus final *e* (*rat*: *rate*), double medial consonant vs. single medial consonant (*annals:anal*), and the base form vs. particular suffixed forms (*sane: sanity*)." He went on to say that he believes a differentiation approach will yield more understanding of the conditions controlling the sound of *a* than will separate treatments of *rat: bat: sat* and *rate: bate: sate*. He proposes *rat: rate, mat: mate*. In this view he parts company with the authors of a good deal of currently used linguistic material.

The discovery method such as described above, in which the student may derive certain principles from an observed pattern, continues to have support in the research in teaching methods, while it does have the drawback of being based upon limited data. Burmeister found both inductive and deductive approaches effective with eighth- and ninth-graders (14).

SENTENCE STRUCTURE

It is surely true that sentence structure has something to do with the reading comprehension of sentences. The questions are whether specific training in the recognition of sentence structure is useful, what form it should take, and for whom it should be. One handicap is that we still have no instrument which measures kinds of comprehension and which also takes the critical points of structure important to the answers and asks the meaning of those.

Beaver (8) collected mistakes in oral reading, some of which involved changes of meaning: The sentence, "I gave my sister to you to protect," was read, "I gave my sister to protect you." Word order is an important clue to meaning in English sentences. Misreading of order might well be followed by a discussion of the change in meaning which it precipitates.

Many children enter school with awareness of the basic sentence types in English (61, 41). They do not need ear training for this purpose. But even in the secondary school there are many youngsters whose backgrounds have not supported the signals to English structure.

Labov (35) found that when Harlem Negro boys, ages ten to seventeen were asked to read the sentence, "When I passed by, I read the posters," most of them read *passed* as *pass,* and pronounced *read* as *reed,* showing that they not only failed to read the ending of *passed* but failed to get its signal to tense. Others misread *passed* but clearly caught the signal of *-ed,* reading *read* as *red.* Labov pointed out that the teacher who merely rereads the sentence according to standard English is wasting his time if the student cannot hear the difference.

The student of Chinese background, who is accustomed to sentences like "Boy go barn," may be completely unaware of the importance of the article and preposition:

A boy went into a barn.
The boy went into the barn.
from the barn.
by the barn.
behind the barn, etc.

The Hindi speaker will find both order and structure a problem, when in his language he would think, "I Curzon Road on live," and he reads in English, "I live on Curzon Road."

It is quite possible that the English speaker does not realize that his interpretation of the preposition is influenced by its object:

I shall come by noon (up to, not later than: time)
by bus (on a: means)
by the house (past: place)
etc.

This lack of realization is relatively unimportant until the student reads unfamiliar topics. Then he needs to be ready with all the possible meanings which a word like *by* can have in relation to the unknown word. Dictionary definitions of some of these so-called "little" words should remind the student of their varied meanings and roles in sentence structure.

Fries (26) for at least thirty-five years in this writer's memory has shown how signals to structure can be put into relief by the use of Lewis Carroll inventions in the place of nouns, verbs, adjectives, and adverbs: *The iggled oggles aggled an eggle ugglely.* Structural signals are: *The -ed -s -ed an -ly. The* predicts a noun. The verb form following *the* must be an adjective. The *-s* ending of the next word suggests the heralded noun. The *-ed* of the next suggests the past form of a verb. *An* predicts another noun, which could be *eggle,* and must be *eggle* as the next word ends like an adverb. To show their mastery of these signals, the students can insert likely meaningful substitutes for the artificial words:

The armed robbers raided an arsenal boldly.

LeFevre (37) has assembled pertinent linguistic facts in his book, *Linguistics and the Teaching of Reading*. Fries (25) offers insights into reading problems with his book on a similar topic, *Linguistics: The Study of Language*.

It is too soon to say that research has shown the value of transformational grammar and generative grammar to reading comprehension. There is, however, a strong possibility that a student faced with a complicated sentence which he cannot comprehend could be benefitted by a way to break it into digestible pieces, which, understood separately, could then be seen in relationship to the other parts. Whether there is need to reconstruct these fragments into whole sentences remains a question. Perhaps there is a shorter way. And there is also the question of whether the student who cannot understand the long sentence can understand transformational grammar.

It is conceivable, too, that the generative experience would provide a creative approach which might give the student readier insight into complicated structures, and, further, might help him realize the many ways in which an author may express the same thought. Whether it can do this remains to be seen. If transformational and generative grammars do prove beneficial to reading comprehension, both will gain in motivation from being associated with the student's immediate need to comprehend what he is reading.

Buswell (16) in a study of the relationship between perceptual and intellectual processes in reading found that when training on word discrimination was followed by recognition of phrase patterns and functional reading units, the correlation of training with reading achievement increased a great deal. This finding is an encouragement to the idea that there is value in dealing with patterned language beyond isolated word drill.

O'Donnell (46) constructed a test of recognition of structural relationships of words and administered it to high school seniors along with the Cooperative Reading Comprehension Test. He concluded that there was not a strong enough relationship between scores on the two tests to warrant teaching linguistic structures as a major means of developing reading comprehension. Another reasonable interpretation might be that the points of structure emphasized in the structure test were not those required for getting the right answers in the comprehension test; or perhaps structure plays a minor role which is nonetheless important.

The two-year study by Bateman and Zidonis (7) of the effect of the study of transformational grammar on the writing of ninth- and tenth-graders showed that the study of transformational grammar was accompanied by improvement in sentence complexity and reduction of errors.

They expressed the thought that grammar is perhaps never fully mastered—another way of saying that the possibilities in English will always race ahead of the experience of any one individual.

Darnell (20) experimenting with twenty college students, used different word-order constructions in varying degrees of disorganization, and reported, not surprisingly, that the amount of loss of clarity becomes greater as the degree of disorganization becomes greater. The reader apparently does lean on word order, on meaningful groupings of words, and upon words or word parts which signal relationship.

A further consideration is whether students find comprehension more difficult when certain signals are missing. In one sense that has already been proved by the Labov study. Beaver (8) found that students reading aloud sometimes inserted words showing relationship, when the author had omitted them:

> Author: *He was as wiry and skinny as a spider.*
> Student: *He was as wiry and as skinny as a spider.*

> Author: *He put down the bag he was carrying.*
> Student: *He put down the bag which he was carrying.*

WORD MEANING

In a language of the versatility of English, in which the same words can play different roles (*The bare branch could bear the bear no longer*), students must know the role of the word in order to assign the proper meaning. In some cases, as Deighton (21) has shown, the student may have to read to the end of the sentence before he realizes which meaning to apply. In "The bear clung to the tree as though he were real," the last word makes a toy out of the bear. Change the last word to *afraid*, and the bear is genuine again.

Bormuth (12) in an extensive review of newer techniques of appraising the readability of material stated (p. 130), "Without question the most important advances should come through the development of better linguistic variables developed through the study of psycholinguistics, linguistics, and literary style." In earlier studies he showed the value of the cloze procedure (10) and a measure which he calls "mean word depth" (11) as ways of determining comprehension difficulty.

In discussing mean word depth (11: p. 87), a method of computing sentence difficulty introduced by Yngve, he used the illustration: "*The dark brown bear sniffed hungrily.*" Word depth is a matter of how many more elements (adjective, noun, verb) the student can anticipate in the sentence structure from the point at which a particular word is. *The* has the value of two because a subject and predicate must still come to complete the sentence. *Dark* has the value of three because it requires an adjective before the noun and predicate. *Brown* again has the value of two, *bear* of one, and *hungrily* of zero. You add all numbers total depth (9), and divide by the number of words in the sentence to find mean depth (1.5). The technique is described here not as a suggestion for classroom work but as an indication of the way the wording of the sentence holds the reader in varied degrees of suspense as he progresses and as the thought unfolds.

Thayer and Pronko (63) had 112 college students react to five fiction excerpts, and concluded that responses of students concurred to the extent that they had common backgrounds.

Russell and Saadeh (52) studied the qualitative levels of children's vocabularies in third, sixth, and ninth grades with a multiple-choice test. The concrete choices preferred by the third-graders gave way to abstract and functional preferences in Grades 6 and 9.

That the general development is toward less concrete wording should not blind us to the fact that students vary in their tolerance of abstraction among themselves and among different areas. Ausubel (3) states that the culturally deprived child "suffers from the paucity of abstractions in the everyday vocabulary of his elders." Because each individual has had different degrees of exposure to the levels of thinking in different aspects of the environment, he may operate comfortably with abstract terms in one subject and cast about desperately for concreteness in another. This suggests the value of group discussions in which insights can be shared, as well as the great need for vocabulary development and concept development.

McCullough (45) has summarized data on desirable teaching practices in the development of concepts. Karlin (34), reviewing research and classroom practices, recommended direct vocabulary instruction, incidental attention in building word meanings, and wide reading, although, as he said, there is little evidence to support the conclusion that wide reading alone leads to increased vocabulary. He proposed a combination of approaches: meaningful dictionary work, word study in context rather than in isolation, uses of context clues for specific word meanings, attention to multiple meanings and figurative language, study of history and etymology relevant to current reading, and application of new words in oral and written language.

Ames (1), after a study of 334 contextual situations and readers' responses to them, offered a new extensive classification of context clues: clues derived from language experience or familiar expressions, clues using modifying phrases or clauses, clues using definition or description, clues provided through words connected or in a series, comparison or contrast clues, synonym clues, clues provided by the tone, setting, and mood of a selection, referral clues, association clues, clues derived from the main idea and supporting details pattern of paragraph organization, clues provided through the question and answer pattern of paragraph organization, preposition clues, clues using nonrestrictive clauses or appositive phrases, and clues derived from cause and effect pattern of paragraph and sentence organization (pp. 66–67).

Lieberman (38) developed concepts through direct experience with an experimental group of fifth-graders, with the result that the gain in reading achievement was as great as for students whose instruction had been in diction, structural analysis, antonyms and synonyms, and context clues. The concept achievement of the former group was greater. Livingston (39), using tenth-grade students, found that instruction in general semantics was accompanied by an increase in critical reading ability. Thus, it can be seen that vocabulary study does not need to be considered time taken away from comprehension, though in the extreme it could be.

New developments in theory of the structure of the intellect (28) suggest the addition of a dimension to word study (59: pp. 247–248). There is a linguistic dimension in synonyms, antonyms, homonyms, derivation, derivatives, multiple meanings including figurative meanings, uses in the structure of the sentence, and pronunciation. There is a conceptual dimension dealing with behaviors, qualities, and uses of the thing itself (such as an apple). And there is a cognitive dimension dealing with relationships within the thing itself or to other aspects of the environment (whole-part, cause-effect, sequence, comparison-contrast, coordination-subordination), and with products of intelligent consideration of it (theories, laws or principles, generalizations, summarizations, definitions, classifications, procedures). All of these, of course, are modified by an affective factor.

Comprehensive study of a word, including these linguistic, conceptual, and cognitive-affective elements, conceivably would equip the student for any aspects of meaning an author would feature in its use. Carried to the -nth degree, it would equip the student with too few words. Yet, he deals with many words in the study of one, by this pattern. Certainly the conception of this three-dimensional study of words should give us pause when we dismiss a word with a synonym, or when we find ourselves employing consistently only one or two of the aspects of word meaning.

SENTENCE MEANING

Weaver (68) claims that words are not self-evident or functionally valid units of meaning. Like LeFevre (37), he recognizes the influence of the environment on the word.

The meaning of a word is determined by attention to the form, the way it is used, the setting in which the use exists, and the information the reader brings to it as it is used. In the sentence, "Consumption has been one of the great problems of the modern world," the word *consumption* has to be analyzed physically to be identified as a pattern of sound. Sentence analysis shows it to be a noun equated with modern problems. Whether it is consumption of goods and services or the consumption of pathology depends upon a larger setting: the surrounding sentences, the magazine or book in which the statement appears, the heading if the book is an encyclopedia. The reader may or may not have had the varied experience with the label, *consumption*, to think that more than one meaning might be applied to it.

Multiple meanings of words dictate a process of selection as relationships are observed in written material (48). In "The bear lunged at the tourist," *The* can designate a particular bear or the classification "bear," as in, "The bear is a mammal." *Bear* as a noun can mean a person of a particular type of behavior on the stock market, a shaggy mammal, a person with a growly disposition, or a portable punch press. *Lunge* can mean to move in a leap or to move in a circle. *At* can mean *in, on, by, near, for,* or *because of. The* can designate a specific tourist or a classification. *Tourist* can mean a traveler, literally or figuratively.

It is in relation to each other as well as the larger environment that these words develop firm meanings, and yield the meaning of the sentence. *The* in relation to *lunged,* past tense, suggests a specific bear rather than a classification. *Lunged* implies the action of a living thing. *Bear* thus becomes alive, and, in combination with lunging and a tourist, suggests action unbecoming a dealer in stocks. Since one does not lunge something but lunges *at* something, *at* is a part of the verb expression, and carries the idea of pursuit, threat, or attack.

A particular bear, which must have been mentioned earlier (or it would be *a* bear), attacked a previously mentioned individual in the process of travelling or with the reputation of having travelled. *Tourist* could be a humorous reference to an animal which has strayed into this particular bear's territory—a poacher on the berry, honey, or fish supply.

Intonation possibilities are narrowed as the reader decides upon a particular meaning for the sentence. Edfelt (22) has reported that silent speech occurs in the reading of all persons. Far from being something to be eradicated, it is a part of the revitalization of the print. Intonation depends upon the setting of the sentence as well as upon the content. If a previous sentence had established that two animals threatened the tourist, then the intonation might be:

Bea

ear   lunged at the

The   tourist.

If only one animal confronted the tourist, then the stress and pitch might feature the action instead:

LUNGED

The bear

at the tourist.

While all good oral readers do not give the same rendition to the same meaning, the patterns above might be rough approximations of the range within which renditions would vary.

Lloyd (40) believes that study of intonation may ultimately prove to be more useful than the word-sound relationships now stressed. Lubershane (43) has evidence from matched groups of fifth-graders that auditory exercise is associated with reading growth. Cleland and Toussaint (18) concluded in their study of interrelationships among reading, listening, arithmetic computation, and intelligence, that the relationship between listening and reading justifies more stress on listening activities in the reading program. Listening to sentences to discuss their meanings, and offering sentences of like meaning, can lift the words out of the printed page and permit concentration on meaning itself, and the intonation support for it.

Taylor (62) found the cloze procedure to be a valid measure of students' understanding of material they had not previously seen. It could well be prefaced by exercise in listening to insert the desired word. Since sentence meaning is often based upon clues beyond the sentence, exercise should not be confined to single sentences entirely.

The relation of spoken language to understanding of what is read was the concern of a British study of Baranyai (6). She reported that Hungarian children were discriminated against in 40 to 52 per cent of the questions asked on tests of verbal comprehension in English. This does not support a revision of comprehension tests to suit any one language group, but it does point to the need for sensitivity to usage which bafflles the foreign language speaker.

SENTENCE FUNCTION

Consciously or subconsciously the good reader is aware of the kinds of ideas the author is presenting and the directions in which he is proceeding. The author does not say, "Now you should look for this," as many exercise books do, depriving the student of the natural task of identification. Nor does he say, "What question does this sentence answer?"—which is one way of arriving at the kind of idea it presents.

In "The bear lunged at the tourist," the reader has a statement of accomplished fact and a particular event. If the verb were *lunges*, it might instead express a general principle of bear behavior in relation to a general class of creatures called "tourists." Nothing specific would have occurred. *Is lunging* could express present action—a play-by-play account by a radio or television commentator.

Sentence function is influenced by setting. If the preceding sentence had been, "A tourist shot at a bear," and then, "The bear lunged at the tourist and killed him," these two sentences would have been statements of fact or event. The first sentence states a cause and the second, an effect, in a sequence of two steps. Also, the second sentence just may be a capsulated cause-and-effect relationship itself: the killing being the consequence of whatever was done in the lunging. But the killing may have required a number of steps, also.

Notice that there are no structure words, such as *because* or *first*, to suggest causality or sequence, as is handily the case in so many contrived exercises. The reader must gather these relationships from his experience with the language, with cause-and-effect and sequence, and with at least the reputation of bear-tourist encounters. Notice also that *shot at* and *lunged at* are specifics, whereas *killed him* is a generalization which leaves details to the reader's imagination.

Many students fail to realize the function of the sentence, reading as though they were stringing unrelated beads. Some of them do this because of the backgrounds from which they come. Impoverished homes are frequently language-impoverished, much being expressed in action rather than words (53). Students from such homes themselves resort to action rather than words, and may even reach the secondary school without having had sufficient speaking or listening experience with thought patterns in standard English.

Students who do not recognize the function of a sentence in a setting of other sentences or in a physical or affective situation, can benefit by listening exercises in which they identify kinds of idea, pose the question which the sentence answers, or add the possible next sentence. One thing they will surely learn is that there is almost no telling what the next sentence will be, or what its effect on the function and meaning of the preceding sentence will be. They will begin to realize that just as words may express cognitive relationships, so sentences can be statements of cognitive relationships; and only as statements are considered together can the relativity of those statements to each other be determined. Amazingly, they will find that one situation's generalization is another situation's fact: that there are hierarchies of idea. They will learn that the difference between "Once a bear tastes blood . . ." and "Once a bear tasted blood . . ." (a difference which Labov's Harlem youngsters did not notice) may well be the difference between a generalization and a particular event, with a changed meaning for "Once" and a crucial signal in the tense endings of the verbs. These discoveries can be highly interesting if the teacher will resist the temptation to tell all he knows.

Russell (51) reviewed research on the processes of thinking, with some applications to reading. Strang (59: pp. 247–257, 300–320) offered a classification of sentences and types of content in larger units of composition. Reedy (47) found high correlations between the ability to organize expository writing and critical thinking, reading, and recognition of well-organized writing. He concluded that for promoting ability to organize expository writing, direct teaching of organization is more effective than indirect teaching.

In an experiment with a prose passage from Poe and a fairy tale, MacGinities (44) used six hundred college students. His purpose was to study the effect of omitting every third, fourth, fifth, or sixth word, on the students' ability to supply the word. He found that the omission of every third word created difficulty, and that a context more than five words distant has relatively little effect upon restoration.

This study might warrant replication with different material, for in some prose passages a pronoun in the tenth line may refer to a noun in the first. Also, we need more studies which show the effect of certain types of omission on comprehension, not in terms of parts of speech or regularity of omission but in terms of strategic elements.

The deer were very _____.

_____ went down to the stream to
look for _____.

_____ the stream bed was
_____.

Finally, _____ wandered _____
somebody's garden and _____ the
_____ out of the bird _____.

This passage reminds us, among other things, of the importance of associated meanings of words in the student's mastery of context. The linguist would classify this as part of the redundance of English. For simpler souls it can be referred to as the "echo effect," an assurance that the author is still on the same subject. Weaver and Kingston (69) found that redundancy in writing can improve the readability of a selection. Jenkinson (33) used the cloze procedure in a diagnostic test at the secondary level, questioning the student on the reasons for his choices to fill the blanks.

MEANINGS OF LARGER UNITS OF COMPOSITION

Reading instruction seems on the one hand to be influenced by a consideration of word form, word meaning, and sentence meaning, and on the other hand to be caught in a historic concern for the précis or general outline of extended prose. From the reading of a sentence to the determination of the main idea of a paragraph is quite a leap.

Only in recent years have we begun to have teaching material which makes some effort to help the student derive the main idea instead of just demanding it of him. Much of our instructional material is still on a "Did you get it? Didn't you get it?" basis—a good thing, perhaps, once the student understands the process. As it is, the student knows he was right or wrong, but not why. To support the kind of testing which much of such teaching material really is, we need to take teaching time to develop the understandings which lead to recognition of main ideas.

In a study of the effect of the presence of synonyms upon comprehension, Ruddell (49) found that the paragraph with the greater structural redundancy was the easier to comprehend. The following example illustrates some of the factors of a redundancy which help a reader determine a main idea:

The gatekeeper explained why tourists were not to harm the animals in the park. Only last week a tourist had shot at a bear. It had lunged at the tourist and killed him.

A study of this passage for redundancy may result in this:

The gatekeeper explained
   why tourists were not to harm the animals in the park.

     ↓   ↓   ↓   Only last week
   a tourist   had shot at a bear.

                               ↓
                             It

              had lunged at
    ↓   ↓
   the tourist   and killed
    ↓
   him.

Such a diagram can be developed by students to clarify for themselves the relationships among ideas. *Tourists* in general are reduced to *a tourist, the tourist,* and *him* in subsequent sentences. *Animals in the park* dwindle to *a bear* and *It.* The general term, *harm,* is reflected in specifics: *Had shot at, had lunged at,* and *killed.* Notice the past of *explained,* the future of *were not to harm,* and the remote past of *had shot,* etc.

The gatekeeper explained is not repeated. *In the park* is assumed the setting of *Only last week,* which cues an example. *Only* in this context means "as recently as."

The second sentence of provocation and the third of retribution explain *why.* The main idea is not in the first sentence but in a combination: "The gatekeeper explained that tourists were not to harm animals in the park, lest the tourists, themselves, be killed." It would take more than one example to derive a broader term than "killed," such as "harmed" or "victimized."

FUNCTION OF LARGER UNITS OF COMPOSITION

In 1957 Lorge (42:18) stated that one of the most promising techniques for evaluating the structure of written material seemed to be to ask children to rearrange randomized sentences into the best order. "One of the best helps toward better thinking is to give children some kind of plan to help them organize material so that they can learn to see relationships." If the teacher suggests questions which the child's material might answer, "The very questions direct the child's attention to a thinking and reasoning process which may give the basis for an adequate mastery of supplementary reading."

The questions answered by the example in the preceding section of this article are: "What did the gatekeeper do? What did a tourist do? What did a bear do?" The following are some details of the thinking which might take place in a careful analysis of these sentence relationships:

The gatekeeper explained (not explains)=single past event
why=reason (cause for effect).
tourists . . . harm . . . animals=general terms; a law or rule
Only last week=a specific time
a tourist . . . a bear=specific characters
had shot (not simply *shot*)=reinforcement of *Only last week.*
as prior to *explained*
a tourist had shot at a bear=example of harm to animals; hence generalization or law is followed by example (specific cause and first step in a sequence of events)
It=bear; *the tourist*=a tourist; therefore, subject not changed
change of action from tourist to bear=signal of effect, second step in a sequence of events

So the gatekeeper explained the reason for a park rule by citing a cause and effect.

One might ask what kind of paragraph this is. It contains specific facts, a generalization, a law, an illustration, a sequence, and cause and effect. It does not fit nicely into our typically hopeful patterning for paragraphs which can be trusted to be one thing or another, but not a medley. The author of the paragraph above is stating a cause to support an effect (law). The cause is expressed in a cause-and-effect illustration.

The upshot is that the student must be taught to detect the kinds of thought the author is expressing, for no two authors can be depended upon to maintain the same pattern. Even the same author may be versatile in the directions he takes to make his point.

We cannot even be sure that an author will tell a sequence of events in chronological order. Did the bear attack first or did the tourist? The cue other than sentence order is experience: You don't shoot after you have been killed, and park gatekeepers do not warn against shooting if someone has been killed without provocation.

Unpredictability is the rule for units of composition beyond the paragraph, as well. However, some authors do offer assistance, such as *unpredictability* following *cannot even be sure*, and *however* in this context (but not in all contexts) suggesting a reversal or change in direction. We must guard against attributing one meaning to any one word, but rather encourage the search for different uses and meanings.

The labels students give their discoveries about cognitive relationships are not important. Nothing could be worse than to spend class time guessing the right answer and quibbling over the right label. What *is* crucial is that students should have a part in developing the concepts they label, and that they study the contribution of structure to comprehension.

EVALUATION AND INTERPRETATION

Evaluation and interpretation have been treated so extensively over the years, in professional textbooks, teachers' manuals, and curriculum materials that they need not be belabored here. They call upon the students' cognitive and affective responses (57). They include the oral reading or at least subvocalization of the passage to express the reader's impression of the author's meaning. They reflect the reader's sensitivity to the author's style (54). They also have to do with the "reading between the lines" that good readers do, and the depth plunges in symbolism and universality which Russell discussed (50).

Four out of five of the questions in the STEP Reading Tests (Educational Testing Service) which were published within the past ten years significantly went beyond what the author said verbatim to what the reader could note and think about the author's inferences, presentation, motivation, and selection of facts.

Students' ability to interpret has been explored by a number of investigators. Hinze (31) observed that "conflict words" interfere, as does affective tone, with the individual's interpretation of a paragraph. Squire (55) used taped interviews with students to note changes in their interpretations of a story at different points in their reading of it. Strang and Rogers (60) found that good eleventh-grade readers more often than poor readers gave symbolic interpretations of a short story. Strang (58) gave a number of techniques for diagnosing the kinds of thinking students do as they read. Of the poor readers she noted that (58:40) "Like leaves drifting down a river, they were moved by random currents of thought. . . . In other words, their personal experiences tended to interfere with their comprehension of the author's thought instead of facilitating it."

One of the major contributions of recent research is the suggestion that the teacher should listen!

Russell (50) pleaded for more than surface study of meaning. (50:16–17) "The story can present these questions if you as the teacher will find a theme, look for symbols, pick out the human values involved, and encourage children to think on these things."

As interpretation is in a sense a harvest of all elements in the reading process, failure in it suggests the need for diagnosis of the entire process, including the student's attitude toward the process, to determine the deficiencies.

The speed at which the student can bring about the harvest continues to be an item of research interest. Studies by impartial investigators seem to come out with findings like those of Wilson and Leavell (73) ten years ago in the comparison of six different kinds of speed training: no conclusive evidence in favor of any one plan. Tinker, reviewing the literature (65), deplores the spread of the erroneous idea that speed begets comprehension. Research continues to reveal (Tinker, 64:111) that "the central processes are the important determinants in reading performance" and that "oculomotor reactions are exceedingly flexible and quickly reflect any change in reading skill and any change in perception and comprehension." In essence he recommends not trying to train the cart to push the horse.

Tinker also noted (65:608–609) that experiments in pacing eye movements usually involve the use of other techniques and are never divorced from increased motivation. While speed may show improvement, there is still no firm evidence that eye-movement training or "elaborate apparatus" has achieved it. The tachistoscope is without value, according to his information, for increasing speed of reading. He rues the emphasis upon oculomotor mechanics which spirits both teacher and students away from the main tasks of reading improvement.

The voice of research in this area has been drowned by the sound of machinery and superb salesmanship.

THE USE OF IDEAS

Ausubel and others (4) stated that "intention to remember facilitates retention by enhancing original learning." We teachers have said this in another way—that when the students were to be held responsible for their learning, they studied harder. The setting of purposes for reading, which became a slogan in the 1940s but which Gates had put into practice much earlier in his reading tests, is one way of forming that intention, whether it is an intention dictated by a situation, a teacher's suggestion, or a student's judgment after reading the first few lines of a passage.

A reader often anticipates the use of ideas as he receives them and as he reacts to them. Use is not always the last thought on something read. "What use can be made of these ideas? Does this information agree with other information I have had? What difference should this idea make to me? What problem will it help me solve? What situation meet?"

Classroom opportunities should be made for group discussion of some of the applications a student or a group of students sees in what has been read. We should be suspicious of the worth of daily reading activities which never offer such opportunity for reconciling the old ideas with the new, for resorting thoughts and seeing some of their personal meanings, for speaking and writing activities in which the student applies his own ideas to a problem, or for the wholesome experience of being challenged by different views on appropriate action.

With the encouragement of reflection and expression, the student will be more likely to invite these same ideas to new uses, and more likely to reflect on whatever he reads on his own thereafter.

* * * * *

In the opinion of this reviewer, we have seen in the past ten years an amazing affirmation of the principle fact of relativity in language. The reader must bring rounded and interrelated concepts, linguistic sophistication, and cognitive versatility to the reading act. All of the elements influence each other and benefit from one another. To insist that any one element should be our first consideration is to deny the dynamics with which we deal. To say that we shall wait for the perfect material before we act is to disavow the subtlety of the process and the importance of our teaching role to the individual student.

For some time it has seemed that the teacher might do better if he could emulate the machine. But the research of the past ten years quite clearly points to the advantages of being human when we deal with the dynamics of language.

REFERENCES

[1] Ames, Wilbur S. "The Development of a Classification Scheme of Contextual Aids," *Reading Research Quarterly*, 2 (Fall 1966) 57–82.

[2] Arbuthnot, May Hill and Shelton Root. *Children and Books* (Chicago: Scott, Foresman and Company, 1968), p. 223.

[3] Ausubel, David P. "How Reversible Are the Cognitive and Motivational Effects of Cultural Deprivation? Implications for Teaching the Culturally Deprived Child," *Urban Education*, 1 (Summer 1964) 24.

[4] Ausubel, David P., Seymour H. Schpoont, and Lillian Cukier. "The In-

fluence of Intention on the Retention of School Materials," *Journal of Educational Psychology*, 48 (February 1957) 87–92.

5 Bailey, Mildred Hart. "The Utility of Phonic Generalizations in Grade One Through Six," *The Reading Teacher*, 20 (February 1967) 413–18.

6 Baranyai, Elizabeth H. "Verbal Comprehension in Hungarian Children of 8–10 Years," *British Journal of Educational Psychology*, 28 (November 1958) 262–65.

7 Bateman, Donald R. and Frank J. Zidonis. *The Effect of a Study of Transformational Grammar on the Writing of Ninth and Tenth Graders*, NCTE Research Report No. 6. (Champaign, Illinois: National Council of Teachers of English, 1966)

8 Beaver, Joseph C. "Transformational Grammar and the Teaching of Reading," mimeographed (Northeastern Illinois State College, 1967).

9 Bloom, Benjamin S., ed. *Taxonomy of Educational Objectives* (New York: David McKay Company, 1956).

10 Bormuth, John R. *Cloze Tests as a Measure of Comprehension Ability and Readability* (Unpublished doctoral dissertation) (Bloomington: Indiana University, 1962).

11 Bormuth, John R. "Mean Word Depth as a Predictor of Comprehension Difficulty," *California Journal of Educational Research*, 15 (November 1964) 226–31.

12 Bormuth, John R. "Readability: A New Approach," *Reading Research Quarterly*, 1 (Spring 1966) 79–132.

13 Bruner, Jerome S. "The Act of Discovery," *Harvard Educational Review*, 31 (Winter 1961) 21–32.

14 Burmeister, Lou E. *An Evaluation of the Inductive and Deductive Group Approaches to Teaching Selected Word Analysis Generalizations to Disabled Readers in Eighth and Ninth Grades* (University of Wisconsin, November 1966).

15 Burmeister, Lou E. "Usefulness of Phonic Generalizations," *The Reading Teacher*, 21 (January 1968) 349–56, 360.

16 Buswell, Guy T. "The Relationship Between Perceptual and Intellectual Processes in Reading," *California Journal of Educational Research*, 8 (May 1957) 99–103.

17 Cassidy, Frederic G. "A Descriptive Approach to the Lexicon," in Irmengard Rauch and Charles T. Scott, eds., *Approaches in Linguistic Methodology* (Madison: University of Wisconsin Press, 1967).

18 Cleland, Donald T. and Isabella Toussaint. "'The Interrelationship of Reading, Listening, Arithmetic Computation, and Intelligence," *The Reading Teacher*, 15 (January 1962) 228–31.

19 Clymer, Theodore. "The Utility of Phonic Generalizations," *The Reading Teacher*, 16 (January 1963) 252–58.

20 Darnell, Donald. "The Relation Between Sentence Order and Comprehension," *Speech Monographs*, 30 (June 1963) 97–100.

21 Deighton, Lee C. "The Flow of Thought Through an English Sentence," in J. Allen Figurel, ed., *Vistas in Reading* (Newark, Delaware: International Reading Association, 1967), pp. 322–6.

22 Edfelt, Ake W. *Silent Speech and Silent Reading* (Stockholm, Sweden: Almquist and Wiksell, 1959).

23 Elkind, David, Ronald R. Koegler, and Elsie Go. "Studies in Perceptual Development: II. Part-Whole Perception," *Child Development*, 35 (March 1964) 81–90.

24 Emans, Robert. "The Usefulness of Phonic Generalizations Above the Primary Grades," *The Reading Teacher*, 20 (February 1967) 419–25.

25 Fries, Charles C. *Linguistics: The Study of Language* (New York: Holt, Rinehart and Winston, Inc., 1962).

26 Fries, Charles C. *The Structure of English* (New York: Harcourt, Brace & World, Inc., 1952).

27 Frostig, Marianne. *Development Test of Visual Perception* (Palo Alto, California: Consulting Psychologists Press, 1961–1964).

28 Guilford, J. P. "The Structure of Intellect," *Psychological Bulletin*, 53 (1956) 267–93.

29 Hafner, Lawrence E. "Research for the Classroom: Cloze Procedure," *Journal of Reading*, 9 (May 1966) 415–21.

30 Hanna, Paul R., Jean S. Hanna, Richard E. Hodges, and E. Hugh Rudorf. "Linguistic Cues for Spelling Improvement," *Elementary English*, 44 (December 1967) 862–65.

31 Hinze, Helen K. "The Individual's Word Associations and His Interpretation of Prose Passages," *Journal of General Psychology*, 64 (January 1961) 193–203.

32 Holmes, Jack A. and Harry Singer. "Theoretical Models and Trends Toward More Basic Research in Reading," *Review of Educational Research*, 34 (April 1964) 131–33.

33 Jenkinson, Marion Dixon. *Selected Processes and Difficulties of Reading Comprehension* (Unpublished doctoral dissertation) (Chicago: University of Chicago, 1957).

34 Karlin, Robert. "Research Results and Classroom Practices," *The Reading Teacher*, 21 (December 1967) 211–26.

35 Labov, William, *Some Sources of Reading Problems for Negro Speakers of Non-Standard English*, ERIC Document Reproduction Service, No. ED 010688. HC: $1.60 (Rockville, Maryland: EDRS, The National Cash Register Company, Box 2206, Zip Code 20852). Published March 5, 1966.

36 Lado, Robert. *Linguistics Across Cultures* (Ann Arbor, Michigan: University of Michigan Press, 1957).

37 LeFevre, Carl. *Linguistics and the Teaching of Reading* (New York: McGraw-Hill Book Company, 1964).

38 Lieberman, Janet E. *The Effect of Direct Instruction in Vocabulary Concepts on Reading Achievement*, February 1967, ERIC Document Reproduction Service, No. ED 010985. HC: $0.56 (Rockville, Maryland: EDRS, The National Cash Register Company, Box 2206, Zip Code 20852).

39 Livingston, Howard F. *The Effect of Instruction in General Semantics on the Critical Reading Ability of Tenth-Grade Students* (Unpublished doctoral dissertation) (New York City: New York University, 1964).

40 Lloyd, D. "Intonation and Reading," *Education,* 85 (1964) 538–41.
41 Loban, Walter. *The Language of Elementary School Children* (Champaign, Illinois: National Council of Teachers of English, 1963).
42 Lorge, Irving. "Reading, Thinking and Learning," in Nancy Larrick, ed., *Reading in Action* (Newark, Delaware: International Reading Association, 1957), pp. 15–18.
43 Lubershane, Melvin. "Can Training in Listening Improve Reading Ability?" *Chicago Schools Journal,* 43 (March 1962) 277–81.
44 MacGinities, Walter H. "Contextual Constraint in English Prose Passages," *Journal of Psychology,* 51 (January 1961) 121–30.
45 McCullough, Constance M. "Implications of Research on Children's Concepts," *The Reading Teacher,* 13 (December 1959) 100–07.
46 O'Donnell, Roy C. "A Study of the Correlation Between Awareness of Structural Relationships in English and Ability in Reading Comprehension," *Journal of Experimental Education,* 31 (March 1963) 313–16.
47 Reedy, John Edward. *A Comparative Study of Two Methods of Teaching the Organization of Expository Writing to Ninth-Grade Pupils* (Unpublished doctoral dissertation) (Boston: Boston University, 1964).
48 Robertson, Jean Elizabeth. *An Investigation of Pupil Understanding of Connectives in Reading* (Unpublished doctoral dissertation) (Edmonton: University of Alberta, 1966).
49 Ruddell, Robert B. "Reading Comprehension and Structural Redundancy in Written Material," in J. Allen Figurel, ed., *Reading and Inquiry* (Newark, Delaware: International Reading Association, 1965), pp. 308–11.
50 Russell, David H. "Reading for Effective Personal Living," in J. Allen Figurel, ed., *Reading for Effective Living* (Newark, Delaware: International Reading Association, 1958), pp. 12–17.
51 Russell, David H. "Research on the Processes of Thinking with Some Applications to Reading," *Elementary English,* 42 (April 1965) 370–78.
52 Russell, David H. and Ibrahim Saadeh. "Qualitative Levels in Children's Vocabularies," *Journal of Educational Psychology,* 53 (August 1962) 170–74.
53 Shuy, Roger, ed. *Social Dialects and Language Learning* (Champaign, Illinois: National Council of Teachers of English, 1964).
54 Smith, Nila Banton, ed. *Development of Taste in Literature,* A Research Bulletin, National Conference on Research in English (Champaign, Illinois: National Council of Teachers of English, 1964).
55 Squire, James R. "From Consciousness, An Important Variable in Teaching Language, Literature, and Composition," *Elementary English,* 42 (April 1965) 379–90.
56 Squire, James R. and Roger K. Applebee. *A Study of English Programs in Selected High Schools Which Consistently Educate Outstanding Students in English,* Cooperative Research Project Number 1994, University of Illinois (Washington, D. C.: U. S. Office of Education, 1966).
57 Stauffer, Russell G., ed. *Language and the Higher Thought Processes,* A

Research Bulletin, National Conference on Research in English (Champaign, Illinois: National Council of Teachers of English, 1965).

58 Strang, Ruth. "Exploration of the Reading Process," *Reading Research Quarterly,* 2 (Spring 1967) 33–45.

59 Strang, Ruth M., C. M. McCullough, and Arthur E. Traxler. *The Improvement of Reading* (New York: McGraw-Hill Book Company, 1967).

60 Strang, Ruth M. and Charlotte Rogers. How Do Students Read a Short Story?" *English Journal,* 54 (December 1965) 819–23, 829.

61 Strickland, Ruth. "The Language of Elementary School Children: Its Relationship to the Language of Reading Textbooks and the Quality of Reading of Selected Children," *Bulletin of School of Education,* Indiana University, 38 (July 1962).

62 Taylor, W. L. "Cloze Readability Scores as Indices of Individual Differences in Comprehension and Aptitude," *Journal of Applied Psychology,* 41 (February 1957) 19–26.

63 Thayer, Lee O. and N. H. Pronko. "Some Psychological Factors in the Reading of Fiction," *Journal of Genetic Psychology,* 93 (September 1958) 113–17.

64 Tinker, Miles A. *Bases for Effective Reading* (Minneapolis: The University of Minnesota Press, 1965).

65 Tinker, Miles A. "Devices To Improve Speed of Reading," *The Reading Teacher,* 20 (April 1967) 605–09.

66 Venezky, Richard L. "English Orthography: Its Graphical Structure and Its Relation to Sound," *Reading Research Quarterly,* 2 (Spring 1967) 75–105.

67 Walker, William Ray. *Factors Influencing Retention of Read English Words* (Unpublished doctoral dissertation) (Madison: University of Wisconsin, 1964).

68 Weaver, W. W. "The Word as the Unit of Language," *Journal of Reading,* 10 (January 1967) 262–68.

69 Weaver, W. W. and Albert J. Kingston. "A Factor Analytic Study of the Cloze Procedure and Other Measures of Reading and Language Ability," *The Journal of Communication,* 13 (December 1963) 252–61.

70 Weir, Ruth H. *Formulation of Grapheme-Phoneme Correspondence Rules to Aid in the Teaching of Reading,* Final Report, Cooperative Research Project No. S–039 (Stanford, California: Stanford University, 1964).

71 Wepman, J. M. *Auditory Discrimination Test* (Chicago: University of Chicago Press, 1958).

72 Whitworth, Richard Cale. *An Appraisal of the Problems Experienced by and the Techniques Used by the English Teachers in Indianapolis, Indiana, Secondary Schools in Improving Student Reading Tastes* (Unpublished doctoral dissertation) (Bloomington: Indiana University, 1964).

73 Wilson, Grace E. and Ullin W. Leavell. "An Experiment with Accelerator Training," *Peabody Journal of Education,* 34 (July 1956) 9–18.

Knowing How to Read Critically

THE PREREQUISITE

DAVID H. RUSSELL

CENSORSHIP USUALLY involves a decision by a person or group about what others should read; ability in critical reading suggests that the individual makes the choice.

We must have competence and established procedures in local districts in dealing with censorship by individuals or in groups, but our first concern is the critical abilities of youth. We want to help young people decide for themselves whether there is communism in *Robin Hood,* pornography in *The Good Earth* or *Drums Along the Mohawk.*

Critical reading does not exist in a vacuum by itself but can be thought of best as closely related to critical thinking.

What is critical thinking? It is best described as essentially a three-factor ability. It includes an attitude factor of questioning and suspended judgment, a conative or functional factor which involves use of methods of logical inquiry and problem solving, and a judgment factor of evaluating in terms of some norm.

The attitude factor, for example, might be represented by, "I'm from Missouri" or "Show me." It means checking on the assumptions of the author—a difficult task, especially in some fiction.

The conative or action factor might include selecting significant words and phrases in a statement, identifying emotion and bias, picking out stereotypes and clichés.

The third, judgment, factor might include distinguishing the relevant

From *Elementary English,* October, 1963, pp. 579–582. Reprinted with the permission of the National Council of Teachers of English.

and irrelevant, assessing literary merit, and looking for evidence in any conclusion drawn by speaker or writer.

These sound like formidable accomplishments. If they sound difficult to us adults, how can they be started with children? They *are* difficult, slow growing, and yet the need to use them is all around us.

There are four reasons why I believe critical thinking must be stressed from kindergarten through college—why I believe teachers and curricullum committees must give development of abilities in critical thinking a continuous place in the curriculum.

1. The mass media of communication influence us to think and act alike. Conformity, not individuality, is stressed in our listening and much of our reading. The effect of our mass culture is to make little bands of conformists—only the home and the school can help children think for themselves, reject the unworthy, resist the blandishments of the "guy with a bill of goods for sale."
2. High performance on an intelligence test does not guarantee high scores on a test of critical thinking. Good mental ability does not guarantee strong critical thinking abilities. The relationship between general intelligence and critical thinking is positive but not high. Critical thinking abilities are not required automatically as a part of general mental growth; specific provisions must be made for their development in all curriculum areas.
3. Attitudes are learned. Youth do not develop a questioning attitude automatically. Teachers and schools have to work to develop the attitude. Such attitudes are learned partly by imitation, for attitudes can be caught as well as taught.
4. Judgment in terms of some norm or standard or consensus implies a background of experience which sometimes the school must supply. Knowledge and experience are prerequisite to critical thinking in the area in which the critical thinking is done. The school must help supply a broad background of experience before problem solving or creative thinking or critical thinking can be attempted. But from the first grade on, let us not stop just with the experience. Teacher and group must discuss, contrast, and compare, and then the teacher moves imperceptibly into questioning and judgment.

NINE PRINCIPLES

Can the 10-year-old or the 15-year old really exercise the judgment necessary for evaluating the newspapers, films, or novels he sees? In partial answer, here are nine statements of things we know or believe which have been at least partly verified by research.

1. Some children have acquired abilities in critical thinking before they enter school. I heard one five-year-old say, "*All* the TV ads say they have the best breakfast cereal."
2. Activities in critical thinking begin in the primary grades—not with the "rational" adult.
3. Critical thinking depends less on specific techniques and more on attitude and experience.
4. Part of the attitude factor in critical thinking is the objectivity which comes from the ability to shift perspective—to see one's own behavior and ideas as they might be viewed by others. (This might be part of developing the self-concept, especially crucial in the junior-high years).
5. The experience factor in critical thinking involves considerable participation in the social and linguistic community. A chance to talk things over or to explore the effects of action produces a validation by consensus which is prerequisite to making sound judgments.
6. Although probably not so important as attitude or experience, there are hundreds of skills in the conative or operational phase of critical thinking. These include the ability to read for exact details, to relate cause and effect in a speaker's statement, and to detect a propaganda device.
7. The evaluation phase of critical thinking is closely related to the ability to check one's own thinking against some norm or consensual validation. This means that the child must know the habits and customs of the group, and the school must be aware of possible differences between home and community values.
8. Irrationality in thinking occurs when the challenge to the individual is too severe, when he does not have the resources to meet the questioning of an idea close to the heart of his own personality or philosophy. If we are threatened by a statement or idea, it is hard to consider it unemotionally and critically.
9. Critical thinking about materials which might be labeled "lewd" or "obscene" or "pornographic" by certain censors is probably related to the reader's standards or tastes. Many teachers report success in raising their students' tastes in literature and in cinema. If this is accomplished, the knowledge and attitude might provide the best bulwark against undesirable material.

These nine principles have been partly validated by research. The need for action is indicated.

ACTION NEEDED

In English and in other curricular areas, we need greater emphasis on thinking abilities. At least six different thinking abilities can be identified, and one of the most important is critical thinking. Most of the influences of modern life are against such skill, and so the school has a peculiar and unique responsibility for developing it, from the first grade onward.

It is not enough to be *against* communism, sadism, hedonism—we must be *for* the development of skills in critical thinking about any "ism." In our pluralistic culture, there are many extreme voices. We must be able to resist some of the statements of a Senator Joseph Mc-Carthy, a Texas oil millionaire, or a high-riding labor boss. We must be able to decide for ourselves that this writer has something to say but that one is merely filthy.

The ability to examine complex community affairs or personal problems begins in childhood and develops slowly over the years. As a product of our schools, we do not want bulging-jawed squirrels crammed with knowledge. We want not sheep but curious, questioning people; not thoughtless conformity but thoughtful appraisal; not parrotting back but reflecting and judging; not prohibiting but evaluating.

"If teachers spend most of their time asking questions, a sure way to improve instruction is to develop the art of questioning."

Questions: An Instructional–Diagnostic Tool

AMELIA MELNIK

A BASIC CONCEPT of reading, which should underlie instruction at all levels, is that reading is a thought-getting process and as a thought-getting process, reading involves comprehension. To comprehend, the reader must judiciously select, organize, and relate the author's pattern of thought. To be selective, the reader must raise significant and appropriate questions relevant to the material as a basis for establishing a purpose for reading. His questions determine what he reads, how he reads, and what he gets out of his reading. In short, questions underlie and guide the reader's quest for understanding as he engages in a dialogue with the author. In this sense, reading is inquiry.

What, then, is the role of questions? And how are they formulated to serve their multiple purposes?

THE ROLE OF QUESTIONS

Questions function in both reading and teaching situations. In reading, questions establish a basis for identifying and clarifying a reader's purpose which influences his method of reading, the degree of comprehension, rate of reading, and the skills employed in reading. More than anything else, a reader's purpose influences what he reads and how he reads.

In instructional situations, the role of questions is by far the most influential single teaching act. According to Taba, "A focus set by the teacher's questions circumscribes the mental operations which students can perform, determine what points they can explore, and what modes

From *Journal of Reading*, 11, April, 1968, pp. 509–512, 578–581. Reprinted with permission of Amelia Melnik and the International Reading Association.

of thought they can learn." (7) Moreover, students' concepts of reading are largely influenced by the types of questions asked by teachers. For these reasons questions play a crucial role in affecting the levels of the teaching and the reading process. Yet there is little evidence to suggest that teachers are well prepared in the formulation and analysis of fruitful questions as a diagnostic and instructional tool.

For example, in examining 17 newly published or recently revised professional reading textbooks, only four of them identified the topic of questions in either the table of contents or the index. Even in these four, however, the treatment of questions was rather brief and superficial, with a four-or-five-paragraph descriptive and prescriptive discussion rather than an analysis with appropriate application. Perhaps in our professional texts too much attention is paid to the content and materials of reading instruction to the neglect of the process of reading instruction.

If teachers are not competently trained in the formulation and use of questions, it is not surprising to find that investigators of teachers' use of questions report that they were found to ask regularly 150 questions per class hour (1). Findings of this kind clearly suggest that the quality of teaching in these situations is at the level of memory of facts and details. Such an emphasis encourages students to read with a mindset to memorize as many isolated details as possible. Unfortunately, even our most able readers reflect a detail-oriented concept of reading, which reflects the types of questions they have encountered in the classroom. In a study of 1500 Harvard and Radcliffe Freshmen, Perry (3) made the following observations:

1. The typical approach of 90 percent of these students was to start at the beginning of the chapter and read straight ahead. No attempt was made to survey the chapter, note marginal headings, or first read the recapitulation paragraph in which the whole structure and summary of the chapter was given. Thus, none of the clues and signals provided as a basis for raising questions were used to identify specific purposes for reading.
2. Their performance on a multiple-choice test on details as far as they were able to read in this manner was impressive. But only one in one hundred—15 in all—were able to write a short statement on what the chapter was about. Perry describes the reading performance of 99 percent of these students "as a demonstration of obedient purposelessness in reading."

Obviously, setting a purpose is a potent influence on reading comprehension. But a purpose for reading can only be defined and established if the reader knows what kinds of questions to ask the author. According to both the Harvard study and the analysis of teachers' questions, it seems evident that students and teachers need to improve the quality of their questions. Perhaps in our teaching we need to shift our emphasis from giving the right answers to raising relevant and significant questions.

THE PURPOSES AND FORMULATION OF QUESTIONS

As a tool in the teaching of reading, questions have two main functions, diagnostic and instructional:

- As a diagnostic tool, they are unstructured, allowing the student to respond in his own fashion, thus giving the teacher opportunity to observe the variety of individual responses in a natural reading situation.
- As an instructional tool, questions are more precisely formulated and logically organized to uncover the author's pattern of thought, develop discussion, and clarify meaning.

Questions also serve to evaluate learning, but in these situations, questions are primarily concerned with the content rather than the process of reading, and for that reason will not be considered at this time.

It is the teacher's responsibility to understand these two separate functions of questions so that he may use them independently and concurrently in appropriate situations to stimulate thinking and help the student increase his awareness of the reading process. To do this, it is essential that the teacher first decide for which of these functions he will be using his questions. His purpose will determine what types of questions to ask and how to formulate them. In each situation, students should also be made aware of the purpose of the questions. Otherwise, they perceive all questioning as testing and the classroom atmosphere is charged with tension as the teacher conducts a threatening inquisition instead of a natural discussion.

DIAGNOSTIC QUESTIONS

As a diagnostic tool, questions are formulated by the teacher to elicit the maximum response from an individual. In analyzing his response, the teacher gains insight into his process of reading, which provides a basis for planning appropriate individual instruction. In obtaining evidence of the student's ability to select, organize, and relate ideas gained from reading, Strang (5) has long advocated the use of the free response. In her study of reading interests and patterns, she used as a stimulus the question, "What did the author say?" This question is purposely somewhat vague in order to leave the subject free to express his habitual response to printed material. From analyzing the responses to this question, she concluded that all aspects of reading are involved in answering it, thus giving the most revealing single picture of the individual's reading ability.

While the formulation of the unstructured question poses no difficulty, the analysis of the response does require the teacher to be skillful in identifying which reading skills appropriate to the material should be noted in the response. Among the insights revealing reading proficiency, the teacher may note evidence of the following:

1. The student's approach to a reading passage;
2. His tendency to relate ideas rather than merely seize on isolated details;
3. His ability to uncover the author's pattern of thought;
4. His ability to organize and show the relation among details;
5. His tendency to let his emotions or prejudices and personal experiences influence his comprehension;
6. His tendency to relate what he reads to other knowledge he has gained;
7. His ability to communicate in writing what he has gained from reading.

Diagnostic questions, then, reveal rather than conceal individual differences.

INSTRUCTIONAL QUESTIONS

As instructional tools, teachers' questions serve the purpose of guiding the reader to select, organize, and relate the author's pattern of thought during or following the reading experience. In these situations, questions are primarily concerned with identifying the types of thought relationship developed to unify the content. In other words, the central purpose of questions at this time is to focus on the process rather than the content of reading.

How is this accomplished? First of all, the teacher must be able to analyze the author's structure of thought to identify the type of relationships around which he has organized his ideas. For example, ideas that are related through comparison will be identified through signals in the text such as: *some-others; either-or; as-so; one-both; all-none; few-many.* In this instance a question may ask for a comparison in which details are related according to likenesses and differences. If a contrast is stressed, then the questions ask for a response in which just the differences are related. Frequently, details are related in a time sequence, as indicated by signals such as *long ago, later, now.* In this case, the question is formulated so that the response relates details to indicate development and/or change. In other thought patterns, sequence according to process rather than time is significant. Here the student reports details logically organized in a specific series of steps. Other types of relationship are cause-effect; problem-solution; main idea-detail. In each case the type of relationship suggests the formulation of a single question which requires the student to select and relate relevant details in his response rather than a series of specific questions which elicit simple yes-no answers or isolated factual detail.

Profitable instructional questions guide and clarify various types of relationships which influence comprehension. Discussion begins with a global question which focuses on the essence of the selection and serves as a point of departure for evolving further related questions which serve to clarify, modify, or illustrate meaning. Challenging questions stimulate students to report relationships among ideas and lead to fruitful discussion in which more time is spent in listening and in supporting or elaborating answers to questions than in asking them.

The following example is presented to concretely illustrate the process of formulating instructional questions and a method of analyzing responses for diagnostic purposes.

Large machines are moving over some cranberry bogs. The machines are picking a bumper cranberry crop. } **INTRODUCTION**

(Long ago,) cranberries were picked one by one. (Later,) pickers used hand scoops. (Now,) machines pick berries on most bogs. Each machine picks thousands of pounds of berries each day. } **MAIN IDEA #1**

(After) the berries are picked, they are stored in large boxes. (Then,) they are put in a machine. The machine blows away leaves and twigs.
   The clean berries then go through another machine. It separates good berries from the bad berries. In the machine, good berries bounce like little balls. (2) } **MAIN IDEA #2**

Analysis of Content	Author's Pattern of Thought (4)	
Cranberry Picking	1. *Main Idea*	SEQUENCE-
hand	detail	TIME
scoop	detail	
machine	detail	

Cranberry Processing	2. *Main Idea*	SEQUENCE-
stored	detail	PROCESS
cleaned	detail	
separated	detail	

Signals: long ago
later
now
after
then

I. Instructional Questions: Two types

A. Isolated Details B. Integrated Thought Relationships

1. How were cranberries first picked?
2. How were cranberries later picked?
3. How are cranberries picked now?

1. How has cranberry picking changed? (Sequence-Time)

4. Where are cranberries stored after they are picked?
5. What happens to cranberries when they are cleaned?

2. How are cranberries prepared for market? (Sequence-Process)

3. What is a "bumper crop?" (Inference-Context Clues)

4. How do machines affect employment? (Conclusion)

II. Diagnostic Question: "What did the author say?"

  A. Scale for Rating Adequacy of Responses (6)

				5
			4	
		3		
	2			
1				A well-organized state-
		One main	Both main	ment of the author's pat-
Vague or		idea and	ideas—time	tern of thought (both
inaccurate	Isolated	some	and process	main ideas and relevant
statements	details	detail	sequence	details)

  B. Examples of Ratings and Responses:

Rating

1 "It is about berry-picking machines."
2 "The author tells us about machines that pick cranberries."
3 "The author tells about picking cranberries—how they used to be picked by hand and now they are picked by machine."
4 "This selection is telling us about the way they used to pick cranberries and how it is done now by machine. It also tells about the cleaning process of cranberries after they are picked."
5 "This selection tells how cranberries have been harvested in the past and how they are now harvested by large machines which do the work of thousands of old-fashioned hand pickers and scoops. The machines also prepare the berries by cleaning them and also separating the good berries from the bad ones."

CONCLUDING STATEMENT

If the effective reader is a questioning reader, more and more opportunity should be given to students to formulate and analyze questions themselves. Perhaps in this changing world of expanding knowledge, it is more important to learn how to formulate significant questions than it is to memorize all the answers.

REFERENCES

[1] Burton, William H. *The Guidance of Learning Activities*, (3rd ed.). New York: Appleton-Century-Crofts, 1962, p. 436.
[2] *My Weekly Reader*. Columbus, Ohio: American Education Publications, 1965.

3 Perry, William G., Jr. "Students Use and Misuse of Reading Skills: A Report to the Faculty," *Harvard Educational Review,* 29 (3), 1959, 193–200.

4 Strang, Ruth and Dorothy Bracken. *Making Better Readers.* Boston: D. C. Heath, 1957, 105–156.

5 Strang, Ruth. *Explorations in Reading Patterns.* Chicago: University of Chicago Press, 1942.

6 Strang, Ruth. *Study-Type of Reading Exercises: High School and College Levels* (with Manual). New York: Teachers College Press, 1960.

7 Taba, Hilda. *Thinking in Elementary School Children.* Cooperative Research Project No. 1574. San Francisco State College, 1964, p. 53.

Teaching the Analysis of Expository Prose

RICHARD L. LARSON

OF THE MANY surprises that a high-school graduate encounters when he becomes a freshman in college (at least at many liberal arts colleges as well as state universities), one of the more perplexing frequently is his instructor's assumption that he is capable of picking up a subtle and complex piece of expository writing and making a rapid, accurate analysis of it. In the first few weeks of his freshman English course, he is likely to meet Aristotle, Forster, Toynbee, James Baldwin, and Thoreau—"On the Duty of Civil Disobedience" was for a long time a standard item in the freshman syllabus—along with well-known but not less demanding writers, and his instructor is likely to assume that he can summarize the content, describe the structure, judge the cogency, and estimate the value of their essays. Class discussion often comprises such activities, and many assignments in the first weeks of the freshman program ask the student to present in clear, well-reasoned prose his interpretations, evaluations, and suggested applications of the essayists' ideas. If he is unable to do so, he must often sit silent during class discussions and fill out his themes with woolly abstractions or ill-conceived predications that bring him grades very different from those that earned him admission to college in the first place.

If freshmen making the transition from secondary school English to college English find themselves in a "muddle" (to use a term once applied to their plight by President Harold Martin of Union College), one important reason is the difference between the work asked of them in many college courses and that required in many secondary school

From *English Journal,* November, 1968, pp. 1156–1162. Reprinted with the permission of the National Council of Teachers of English and Richard L. Larson.

courses in English. In good secondary school courses, the student will learn, perhaps, about the history and dialects of his language; he will study important works of imaginative literature (in paperbound texts as well as in anthologies); and he will write regularly, often about masterworks of literature and sometimes about his personal observations, experiences, and values. What he often will not study, to anything like the extent that college teachers tacitly assume, is expository writing—varied examples of the best of both informal and intellectual prose in English.

I believe that the neglect of expository prose, sometimes the virtual omission of it, in the high school English curriculum is a serious error. It is a culpable error, not merely because it leaves students unprepared for work that their college instructors are going to assume they are competent to perform, but because it leaves them unequipped for what may be one of the most important activities in which an adult human being engages: the collecting and evaluating of information from printed sources. Comparatively few high school students will concentrate in English in college, and still fewer will become professional students of literature or of the English language. But almost all, in college and afterwards, will have to read reports, articles, texts, and other books for information about virtually every subject of concern to them. They will need to know how to identify the principal ideas of professional and amateur writers, how to determine the sources of these ideas, how to judge the conclusions to which these ideas lead, how to discriminate between what a writer promises to give and what he delivers, and how to decide, very broadly, which writers are worth their continued attention. Most colleges do not allocate time in their curricula to help students develop these abilities. One might wish that high school teachers in disciplines other than English would take time to help students acquire skill in appraising the writing in their disciplines. But there is little evidence in the experience of many directors of freshman programs that these instructors do give such help. Therefore, the responsibility for developing such abilities must be added to those already shouldered by the teacher of English. It is an important and humane responsibility, one that can compete vigorously with the teaching about grammar, the teaching of application-writing, and even with research papers, for its place in the curriculum, and one that the teacher of English, by virtue of his concern for the study of how his language is used, is probably best equipped to shoulder.

Teachers may assume that their responsibility for helping students to become good readers (in the broadest sense of the term) is fully discharged by the attention paid to imaginative literature. But the arrangement of materials in discursive prose, informal or intellectual, is not the same as that found in fictional narratives (most of which move chronologically) or in plays (which present the highlights of an action in roughly chronological order). Poems, too, though they are often constructed with the most rigorous logic, employ unique, sophisticated, and concise patterns of language to unfold perceptions and feelings; their success is not judged primarily on the reasonableness of their assumptions, the adequacy of objective evidence, the lucidity of their design, and the reasonableness of substantive conclusions. Even the presence of selections from such authors as Swift, Macaulay, Thoreau, and Arnold in high school anthologies of literature does not usually give adequate opportunity for the study of exposition. The selections are often excerpts from longer pieces by these writers, with the result that teachers are limited to pointing out a few of the main ideas expressd by each writer, or some conspicuous characteristics of his style. In using these selections, the teacher rarely has the chance to encourage students to look at the design and strategy of a complete essay; nor, of course, do the selections help the student to understand the distinctive features of structure and style in contemporary expository pieces. The usual curriculum in literature, then, does not adequately prepare students for the study of exposition that colleges expect of them, or for the extensive reading of exposition that their college work and their adult and professional lives will require of them.

A few years ago it was difficult for the teacher who wanted in his curriculum the small amounts of expository prose offered by anthologies to find appropriate collections of essays that were accessible to students in high school. Happily, with the appearance of such books as *Ideas in Prose* by Oscar Fidell (Prentice-Hall, 1962), *Seach for Perspective* by Richard Beal and Ned Hoopes (Holt, 1965), and *Essay*, Second Edition, by Hans Guth (Wadsworth, 1967), to supplement such collections as *Great English and American Essays* (Holt, 1961), the scarcity of text is no longer an obstacle to prevent teachers from guiding students in the reading and judging of expository essays.

Before they will attempt to add more expository prose to their curricula, however, many teachers (if my experience with composition courses in NDEA institutes and graduate courses in the teaching of composition is a fair indication) feel they need some guidance in what to do with essays and other expository pieces in their classrooms. To provide some suggestions, I present the following outline of questions that can be applied to virtually any piece of exposition, whether written by a professional writer or by a student. Some are directed toward describing prominent features of the essay; others are directed toward evaluating it. Some questions invite both description and evaluation.

The list of questions makes a deliberate attempt to incorporate concepts and insights from both the old and the "new" rhetoric. Users familiar with classical rhetoric will find in it some attention to inventing, arranging, and expressing the three steps in preparing a discourse that organize some instruction in rhetoric today. Walker Gibson's demonstration that there is a "speaking voice" in all prose, an important contribution to the "new" rhetoric, underlies the first few questions. Also underlying these questions are discussions of language and "tone" by I. A. Richards and Reuben Brower, among others. Question V employs concepts brought into focus a couple of years ago by Robert Gorrell; in W, I have applied his theory of commitment and response to one particular kind of promise that writers on controversial subjects often make. I would suggest, therefore, that this model for analysis is reasonably current; teachers should not go far wrong in encouraging students to master these questions and to be ready to apply them, conscientiously, to expository writing, regardless of subject, that proposes to persuade, convince, inform, or even simply to entertain them. (Although the term "essay" is used throughout to designate the work being analyzed, most of the questions apply to other kinds of exposition as well.)

I. THE "DRAMA" OF THE ESSAY: SPEAKER, AUDIENCE, AND OCCASION

A. Who is speaking? How do you know? What sort of person does he "sound like"? What features of his language give you these impressions of him? How much can you infer from his language about his personality or character? (Note: In answering this and the next few questions, never mind the name of the author on the title page. Use evidence within the essay. View the essay as if it were spoken discourse or dramatic utterance, as if the author were assuming a "role," rather than writing in "his own" character. Imagine it being "performed." Although pieces composed for oral delivery and those composed for silent reading may differ in design and sentence structure, these differences should not obscure the value of hearing the essay—in your imagination —as well as reading it.)

B. Who is being addressed in the essay? Is the audience general, or quite specific? What evidence within the essay leads you to your answers?

C. What is the occasion for the writing of the essay? What circumstances (or inner pressures) prompted the writer to speak out? What evidence within the essay leads you to these conclusions?

D. What "tone" is established? By what features of language is it established? (Take "tone" to include the accents, pace, rhythm, vocal inflections, and intonations that you would hear if the piece were indeed spoken aloud. Thus defined, tone is a feature of any discourse, though in some essays the tone is more distinctive than in others. The tone of an essay may give a clue to the speaker's attitude toward his audience and toward his subject. The tone may also help the reader to identify the speaker's social relationship with his audience, and even his feelings about himself.)

II. PURPOSE, THESIS, AND IMPLIED FEELINGS

E. What is the author's purpose in writing (in coming before the reader in his role)? What evidence in the essay leads to your answer?

F. What is the speaker asserting? What is his subject, and what is his major predication about that subject? How do you know?

G. What, if anything, is the speaker recommending or advocating? How do you know?

H. What feelings is the speaker expressing? What doubts, fears, suspicions, confidence, anger, if any, are communicated by the essay? Are these feelings communicated directly (e.g., by overt statement), or are they implied? If they are implied, what features of the essay imply them?

I. What feelings do you think the author wants his reader to have after reading his essay? What evidence leads you to your answer? Do these feelings support, qualify, or contradict what the essay is asserting? How?

III. SUBSTANCE AND REASONING

J. What kinds of data are included in the essay? Do these data seem appropriate to the purpose of the essay?

K. From what sources does the speaker derive his authority for his facts and for the justness of his inferences on his subject?

L. What processes of reasoning are employed by the author? Are they employed soundly?

M. If evidence is required to support the author's assertions, has he offered suitable evidence? Does the evidence consist of facts, opinions, statistics, testimonials, or other material? Are the facts reliably established? Are the opinions those of people whose judgment can be relied on? Are the sources of the statistics or testimonials or other materials dependable? Is the evidence pertinent to the issues under discussion? Does the evidence prove what the author alleges that it proves? Why or why not?

N. Are any generalizations or value judgments taken for granted (assumed) as the reasoning proceeds? If so, are these assumptions reasonable, or are they open to question? If the assumptions are questionable, does their uncertainty cast doubt on the author's major conclusions, or can the conclusions still be accepted even if the underlying assumptions are in doubt?

O. If the author is recommending that someone take a particular action or actions, has he shown that the recommendation promises to achieve the goals the author thinks should be sought? Has he shown that it will solve the problem(s) he believes need(s) to be solved? Has he predicted and evaluated both the beneficial and the harmful results (if any) that may come from following his recommendation? Where necessary, has he shown that what he recommends is preferable to other actions that might be taken?

P. Judging by his language and by the kinds of evidence and reasoning he uses, are you inclined to believe what the speaker says? Or does he impress you as unreliable (because uninformed, biased, excessively emotional, lacking in common sense, or for another reason)? What features of the essay lead you to this judgment?

IV. STRUCTURE

Q. How does the essay begin? Why does the speaker elect to begin in this way? Does he seek to ingratiate himself with his reader, to supply startling information that will require explanation, to introduce a puzzle that invites solution, or to accomplish some other objective? Is the beginning effective?

R. How are the materials arranged? What overall pattern, what principle of order, is followed? Is this principle of order related to the processes of reasoning identified under III, L? Can you identify what each paragraph contributes to the design of the whole?

S. Are the sections of the essay connected? How? Is each connection clear and effective? If not, which connections fail to achieve their goal, and why?

T. How does the author bring his material to a conclusion? Is the conclusion consistent with the data and reasoning presented during the essay? How or how not? Does the conclusion seem effective? Why or why not?

V. STYLE

U. Are there any distinctive syntactic patterns or recurrent kinds of phrases that can be called characteristic of the author's writing? Do his diction and idiom seem in any way distinctive? What figures of speech, if any, does he frequently use? To what kinds of activities does he look for items to use in metaphors and similes? Note enough examples of distinctive syntax, phrasing, diction, idiom, and figures of speech to establish that they are characteristic of the author in this essay.

VI. OVERALL EVALUATION

V. In the introduction to an essay, the speaker makes an implicit commitment to his reader that he will discuss a particular subject from a particular point of view. Has the speaker fulfilled his commitment? What parts, if any, has he failed to fulfill? Is there any explanation for his having ignored these parts of his commitment?

W. In the introduction, does the author assert (or imply) that his views on a particular subject are better than those of another writer, or that his way of handling an issue is superior to that of another man? If so, does the writer substantiate during his essay his claim that his views or his proposals are superior to those of the other writer(s)? Why or why not?

X. Judging from internal evidence, has the author achieved his purpose in addressing his audience? Has he achieved it economically, or is the essay unduly diffuse? Is there undesirable repetition? Are any parts overdeveloped? Is there unnecessary detail? Do the various parts of the essay collaborate harmoniously in achieving the purpose, or does the essay contain material that seems not to fit neatly into the design of the whole? Does each paragraph accomplish *its* purpose efficiently? Is the language (diction, idiom, figures of speech, sentence structure, etc.) on the whole, congruent with the purposes evidently sought by the author? (Are there particular features of the essay that lead to your judgments?) Does the author, in your opinion, lead his readers to feel as he evidently intended them to feel (see II, I)?

Y. Was the author's purpose worth seeking? (Was the essay worth writing?)

Z. If you are familiar with other discussions of the same subject, what special value, if any, does *this* discussion have, in comparison to the others that you know? Does it make a distinctive contribution to your understanding of the subject?

Not all of these questions, of course, will yield equally good results with every essay or expository work. Teachers will need to develop, through practice, skill in recognizing which questions will reveal important features of different pieces. In planning his classes on the reading of exposition, the teacher can make it a practice to check briefly the piece assigned for discussion against each of the questions. He can pass over those questions that seem unlikely to be fruitful, and concentrate on the questions for which he thinks he can point out answers that reveal some noteworthy features of the piece.

All of the questions are suitable for discussion in class; some may also make useful writing assignments. For the teacher who wants his students to write frequently about the essays he reads, here are a few specific suggestions for assignments, some of them familiar, some new. (Once again, not all of the suggestions can apply to every essay.)

1. Summarize the essay—i.e., make a tightly compressed statement of the thesis, supporting conclusions, and principal kinds of evidence used—as if for a reader who does not have access to the essay or does not have time to read it.

2. Again addressing a reader who does not have access to the essay, select what you consider to be an important sentence, explain its meaning (including what is "said" by nouns, adjectives, adverbs, analogies, as well as by the verbs) and demonstrate the importance of that sentence in the thought of the essay.

3. Addressing a reader who is unconvinced by one of the statements (the teacher might stipulate which statement is to be examined), demonstrate how the author has made the statement seem credible.

4. Addressing a reader who believes everything the essay says, demonstrate through analysis of underlying assumptions, evidence used, or other features of reasoning that the essay should not be believed.

5. On a newspaper report of a controversial incident or on a work of history, demonstrate, to a reader who thinks the author neutral in treating his subject, that the author actually favors one side or the other.

6. Addressing one's classmates, demonstrate that the essay is or is not a good example of the successful adaptation of structural design to the thesis advanced.

7. Addressing a reader who thinks that the only interesting thing about it is what the author says in so many words, demonstrate that the feelings expressed through the language and through the apportioning of emphasis contradict or qualify the major thesis the essay seems to assert.

8. Addressing a reader who is indifferent to anything but what the essay says directly, demonstrate that the essay has distinctive characteristics of style and that these characteristics are important to an understanding of the point of the essay.

9. Addressing a reader who is unfamiliar with techniques for identifying the personality of the "speaker," characterize the speaker, explain from what details you draw the characterization, and demonstrate that the speaker's character supports (or does not support) the author's efforts to achieve his purpose with the reader.

10. In the case of an essay that claims to treat its subject more successfully than another essay (or essays), address a reader who does not know how to evaluate this claim, and demonstrate that the author has (or has not) substantiated his claim.

11. Addressing a reader who finds it difficult to make a judgment of the essay, demonstrate why, in your opinion, the essay accomplishes (or fails to accomplish) its purpose with its intended audience.

12. Take two essays on similar themes and demonstrate why one (by its language and reasoning) leads the reader to accept the author's statements of his experiences or convictions more fully than does the other. Address a reader who believes in the superiority of the essay you rate lower.

13. On a subject of your own choosing, compose an essay that follows the same principle of organization used in the essay just studied. Make it evident whom you are addressing, and why.

The practice of analysis recommended in these questions and suggested writing assignments should not be defended simply on the ground that it will make life easier for students when they confront essays in freshman English, although the skill they develop in analyzing exposition should surely bring that reward. Much more important, by learning to analyze exposition students should become much more acute critics of their own writing, much keener judges of whether or not the roles they assume in their essays are ones in which they want to be heard, and of whether or not they themselves have accomplished their purposes with their readers. If the teaching of writing is partly the teaching of revision (it is much more, of course, but teaching students to revise their first drafts is one of the instructor's main jobs), if the goal of the composition course is to help students do for themselves what the teacher has done by his discussion and annotation of themes during the course, then developing our students' skill in the analysis of essays is a step toward improving their writing. And, of course, the familiarity with techniques employed by skilled writers of exposition that will come from such analysis may help guide the students in their own writing and give them some benchmarks for judging what they themselves have written.

But the rewards are even larger than these. Much of college work, outside the laboratory and the field trip, is the study of expository writing. The student who learns best is not the one who memorizes but the one who evaluates data, appraises writers' strategies in the presentation of their views, compares arguments, and chooses the conclusions that convince him. Much of the work of many professions is the evaluation of one or more kinds of expository prose. The man who succeeds is the one who judges wisely the claims and contentions of others, and makes sound choices of what to believe. Many of the student's adult responsibilities can be discharged only after a study of exposition. The effective citizen is one who penetrates specious arguments, recognizes what is misleading in the appeals of those who are superficially ingratiating, chooses his position after careful analysis of issues and evidence, and knows enough about the art of exposition to make his views convincing to others. Early practice in the reading of exposition will not by itself make our students into successful undergraduates, professional men, and citizens, but it will help. And in the process it may shape their tastes so that they can value effective exposition just as we hope they value good plays, stories, and poems.

"A deeply felt conviction, however eccentric, is justification enough for a substitute assignment for that [sincerely objecting] student. But surely it is not justification enough for a major revision in the curriculum."

Book Selection
and Censorship

ROBERT F. HOGAN

FINDING GAPS between the school and the society outside the school is neither novel nor surprising. More often than not, new needs and social forces are first felt on the edges of society. The school, however, is unlikely to stray far from the center of society's gravity, by reason of the local authority which governs the school and measures out its principal support and of teacher recruitment and retention practices. Perhaps this is why impatient architects of recent manpower training programs and youth camps often prefer to operate outside the educational establishment.

We can understand and accept gaps between school and society as a fact of educational life. But we cannot defend taking the same acceptant position when the gaps are within the school itself, when one element of the school draws farther and farther from another. This separation we cannot simply shrug off as part of the "educational condition." And in matters of book selection and censorship, we frequently find such disjuncture.

The issue here is not that some schools exist in community climates that militate against liberal book selection, however true that may be. Neither is it the issue that the school, frequently the pawn in power plays among local groups, may think it best to find the least perilous path toward the next bond issue or millage election. (Some schools with scandalously meager libraries have also lost such elections.) The gap at issue here is not between the school and some external but

From *The Bulletin of the National Association of Secondary School Principals,* 51, April, 1967, pp. 67–77. Reprinted with the permission of the National Association of Secondary School Principals.

148

impinging aspect of society. Rather, *it is the widening gap between the students and the curriculum, between the content of the curriculum and its own goals.* Gaps like these are not closed or made insignificant simply by our sighing over them or trying to shrug them off.

Except when we state them narrowly as intellectual attainments, the goals of any curriculum rightly include the aim of enabling students both to cope effectively with the world they now live in and to meet successfully the demands of an adult society which will soon test their strength. What kinds of worlds are these? Clearly there are social, political, and ethnic worlds. But for adolescents there is also, if we are to be honest, a sexual world. And given this range of issues in classical and contemporary literature, the English teacher then attempts to involve students in all of these worlds. To do this the teacher must be free to select the most effective materials.

LEGALITY OF BOOK BANS

Of particular concern to the English teacher is the recent action taken by the U.S. Supreme Court to spell out the conditions under which the first sales of books may properly be curtailed. In general a book may be banned if (1) its overall theme and appeal are largely to prurient interests; (2) it describes sexual activities in such degree and detail that it outrages public decency; (3) it possesses *no* redeeming social value. If a book does pass the third test—some redeeming social value—it does not matter whether it can pass the first or the second. It was on this ground that books such as *Fanny Hill* and *Tropic of Cancer* were cleared for open sale and distribution.

Local communities and some states may pass and for a time enforce legislation far more strict than this. Yet each such attempt risks judicial review and ultimately the test of constitutionality spelled out by the Court. Of course, some books now in circulation would fail all these criteria; but it is unlikely that anyone is going to go after all these books, one by one. Apart from the effects of local and temporary police action or the varying effects of voluntary boycotts, an open market for books of all kinds seems assured. And the near edge of pornography is banked with virtually unchallenged but pervasively sexual material ranging from cosmetic and lingerie ads to bathing styles to illustrations in "magazines for men."

Whether exposure to sexually oriented materials and, particularly, to salacious books is harmful remains a moot question. A long Puritan tradition and some expert opinion suggest that it is harmful, but other expert opinion and perhaps more evidence say it is not. (For a detailed discussion of this issue, see *Obscenity, the Law, and the English Teacher.*[1])

Granting for the moment that, in the absence of definitive evidence, the administrator must consider the possibility of harm to some students, what position should he take? What alternatives are open to him? Of these alternatives, which is the wisest one? And, for whatever validity resides in analogies, what actions have administrators taken in roughly comparable situations in the past?

PRINCIPAL'S ALTERNATIVES

At least in theory, three alternatives present themselves:

• First, the principal may operate from the most conservative base and permit as basic or collateral text, as library acquisition, or as permissible outside reading nothing that has been challenged. The English curriculum then not only will offend no one in the community; very likely it will excite none of the students and in the long run will encourage the formation of a faculty who prefer an unexciting curriculum.

• Or the principal may neither respond to nor permit any restriction, internal or external, on the individual teacher's selection of texts and collateral reading—perhaps only a theoretical possibility, but possible nevertheless.

• Finally, he may set a climate that directs the staff to devise a program which, while it respects the student's option not to read a book to which he and his parents object on sincerely moral grounds, takes into continuing account that adolescents are maturing sexually as well as intellectually, and that outside of school they are barraged on all sides by sexually oriented materials.

Any realistic discussion of these alternatives will concentrate on the first and third alternatives. No one is going to argue intelligently for long about the unrestricted right of teachers at large to assign any kind of reading they choose, including hardcore pornography. But many will argue—and intelligently—that fear of this possibility has driven some principals too far in the direction of the first and most restrictive alternative.

In at least two other areas schools have recognized the possibility of harm to students and have taken vigorous action. Admittedly, in neither

[1]John Frank and Robert F. Hogan, *Obscenity, the Law, and the English Teacher.* Champaign, Ill.: National Council of Teachers of English, 1966.

instance has the setting been so laced with value judgments and conflicts. Yet this freedom from clouding tensions may point, in the fashion of a controlled laboratory experiment, to productive programs outside the laboratory.

First, it has long been recognized that untutored teen-age drivers are a menace to themselves and to others. Second, it has been recently shown that the level of physical attainment for many students has been well below desirable and normally achievable levels, leaving them weakened and less agile than they should be, far more susceptible to injury and other physical harm. What was the response to these two "clear and present dangers"? The simplest solution would have been to restrict the physical education curriculum and the athletics program and thus reduce to a minimum the possibility of injury, on the school campus at least; and to forbid adolescents to drive cars to and from school. The wreckage in human beings and cars would have mounted, but the schools would have been "in the clear."

The best administrators, of course, saw that neither happened. They responded by stepping up the physical education program and by exerting greater efforts to involve more students in a varied athletics program. And, despite the continuing criticism about "frills," programs in driver education and driver training were instituted or expanded. Schools faced these challenges with vigor and with imagination. They did not settle for playing safe.

SEXUALLY ORIENTED MATERIALS

If we genuinely believe that the maturing but not yet mature mind is possibly in some danger from sexually oriented materials and outrightly pornographic materials, what are we doing about this? Nationally, our first—not brave, but perhaps understandable—urge has been to purify the curriculum. Part of our effort has stemmed from an understandable impulse to make clear that the school as an institution does not condone the exaggerated interest that the larger society demonstrates in sex. But part, too, has been to make sure our hands are clean. So, one by one, books have been removed from library shelves, stricken from required or suggested reading lists, eliminated from the supply of collateral reading in the textbook room: *Catcher in the Rye, A Bell for Adano, To Kill a Mockingbird, Brave New World, 1984, Grapes of Wrath.* Among the books so banished or never allowed admission in the first place are works by some of our best writers—National Book Award winners, Pulitzer Prize winners, Nobel Prize winners.

Even so, it is less useful to condemn the conservative position than to evaluate it. A principal may argue thus: "I don't care if he did win a Pulitzer Prize; this is a dirty book and I don't think young adolescents should read it." This writer thinks that position is usually wrongheaded, but that is not the issue right here. The real issue is how effective is the banishment. If the book is removed from the school library and the text-book room, how dead is it? Publishers are reluctant for a variety of reasons to release sales figures for specific books. But, knowing that the information was to be used in an article on censorship, certain publishing firms released sales figures on some of the most widely controversial books in the curriculum. Here are their reports on sales as of January 1966 of eight books frequently attacked:

Harper & Row estimates that close to 2,500,000 copies of *Brave New World* are now in circulation. For *The Ugly American,* W. W. Norton cites sales of 398,000 in cloth edition; Fawcett, nearly 3,500,000 copies of the same book in paperback, and W. W. Norton has since brought out its own paperback edition. Random House reports that *A Bell for Adano* sold more than 175,000 copies through fall 1965. Viking Press states for *The Grapes of Wrath* continuing sales of 5,000 to 6,000 copies per year of the original Viking trade edition, now 25 years in print, plus additional sales of 500,000 copies per year of the Bantam paperback edition. New American Library published *1984* in two editions, one of which has sold 2,079,439 copies in 23 different printings: the other 2,001,506 copies in 11 printings, for a combined total of 4,080,945 copies.

One of the newest books to be singled out by censors is Harper Lee's *To Kill a Mockingbird,* which as of winter 1965, according to J. B. Lippincott Company, had sold 263,909 copies, with another 11,792,200 copies distributed through book clubs and other sources than the publisher directly. A book which students discovered virtually on their own and which has really made its way into the curriculum is *Catch-22:* Simon and Schuster has sold 40,000 copies in hardback and relays from Dell, the publisher of the paperback edition, a total sales figure of over 1,750,000. Perhaps the most enduring target of the censor and the favorite of the adolescent is *Catcher in the Rye. Time* magazine has reported that sales in all editions are close to 250,000 copies annually since publication 15 years ago, for a total of 3,750,000 copies.

EFFECTS OF BOOK BANNING

If the purpose of the bans is, in complete if misguided sincerity, to protect the child from the book, how effective have they been? It is hypothetical to argue that public banning adds directly to the sales of books, especially books such as these, excellent books which would sell in their own right. But if banning has not promoted the sales of these books, it would be difficult to prove that it has reduced them. Anyone who is really convinced that these books will harm students has a lot to worry about.

It is not enough to say that book banning has not been effective. Even if it has not had the effect intended, nothing so widespread can be without some outcome. One obvious effect lies in the data revealed in the National Study of High School English Programs.[2] In schools carefully chosen from among those known to graduate consistently outstanding English students, the high school library ranks behind the public library and the home library as the source of interesting voluntary reading. Drawing on an earlier study by Robert S. Whitman, the designers of the National Study selected the 35 titles cited most often by outstanding high school graduates over the past four years as providing their most moving, significant reading experience in high school. Of these, the book most frequently cited by students, *Catcher in the Rye*, was found in only half of the libraries, the sixth-ranking book, *Atlas Shrugged*, in only 12 percent of the school libraries.

A comparable study of English programs for slow learners and disadvantaged pupils has not been done. Yet one continuing phenomenon must continue to haunt any educator who cares. Consistently, these students score low on standardized reading tests and often fail to "comprehend" the simplest books in the curriculum. Yet at the legal age—usually 16 and often with a "measured" reading age of 11 or 12—they study a sophisticated and technical pamphlet about driving laws and regulations and pass an equally sophisticated written examination on these laws. The next day they return to school and to the curriculum, and sink to their usual level of performance. For the bright, the slow, and the disadvantaged—and in all likelihood for the average, too—the gap between the curriculum and the student widens almost beyond bridging. If the major offering in tenth-grade English is *Silas Marner* and their free choice is *Brave New World*, the gap is at least impressive.

How does the principal then protect his school against foolish risks and at the same time insure a program that will leave students enriched rather than impoverished? No one has found a panacea yet, but that has not prevented schools from taking intelligent and promising measures.

FRAMING A POLICY

The first step is the framing of a clear, intelligent policy on book selection and its adoption by the Board of Education. In the setting of the

[2]James R. Squire and Roger K. Applebee. *A Study of English Programs in Selected High Schools that Consistently Graduate Outstanding Students in English.* Cooperative Research Report No. 1994. Urbana, Ill.: University of Illinois, 1966.

policy as well as in its presentation to the Board of Education the principal plays a particularly sensitive role. He knows, and many teachers do not, the legal framework for adopting texts, selecting collateral reading books, and acquiring library books. Yet, for the English program at least, it is the teachers who will use the books who ought also to be principally responsible for drawing up the statement. Teachers who are to be entrusted with the teaching of literature to children ought to carry the responsibility for stating the principles on which the literature will be selected. A detailed discussion of such a policy is available in *The Students' Right to Read.*[3]

Whatever form such a policy statement takes, certain principles should be reflected:

- Texts and library books are chosen principally by those professional staff members who will use them.
- Clear procedures are provided in the event that a text or a library book is challenged.
- Those who make the selection initially will be involved in meeting the challenge.
- No one will share in the final disposition who has not read the book challenged—the whole book, not just the excerpts which are alleged to be offensive.

At the same time, the policy ought to respect the rights of the individual parent and student. It ought to guarantee that no child has to read a book to which he and his parents object on principle. Our agony comes in part because the typical institutional response to the individual problem is the establishment of a new policy. If one teacher unwittingly takes the principal's reserved parking space, it is often the occasion for a school-wide memorandum; or, if three or four staff members regularly come late to work, the result sometimes is only a candid conference with the three or four, but more likely the occasion for installing a time clock for everyone. So it is with the books. A deeply felt conviction, however eccentric, is justification enough for a substitute assignment for that student. But surely it is not justification enough for a major revision in the curriculum.

The principal's role, it has already been noted, is a sensitive one. Whether the policy statement is unduly restrictive, loose and vague, or sanely liberal and workable will depend on the specific charge he puts

[3]Edward Gordon *et al. The Students' Right to Read. Champaign,* Ill.: National Council of Teachers of English, 1962.

to his faculty and the climate he sets up in putting this charge. Execution of the policy and the actions of teachers and librarians after a challenge will depend almost wholly on the support the principal gives to it.

A second measure involves the principal's role as instructional leader. A comprehensive literature program usually will include some works to be read by all students, but it will range more broadly than this. If one purpose of the literature program is to build lifetime reading habits, it will probably rely less on "restrictive" or "required" reading lists as a guide to independent reading and more on "suggested" reading lists. Beyond this—and here at once is the riskiest, yet the most fundamental principle of all—it will insure that the student can talk with a sensitive teacher or librarian about *any* book he has read on his own.

THREE-PRONGED PROGRAM

It is inconceivable to me that any harm could come to a student from reading, say, *1984*. But if, with this or any other book, harm were possible for a particular student, how much more danger is there if the reading is secretive and the student left entirely on his own to brood about it and probably to misinterpret what he has read? The principal who looks for a three-pronged literature program—*required texts, suggested supplementary titles,* and *a broadly ranging individual reading program*—is likely to find one or to stimulate an English faculty to creation of one.

No principal will go far in a new direction without support from the community; few will even try it. In this instance, it is not simply a matter of parent education: not all the book lovers are employees of the school system. Whether the parents' organization is the medium of communication and support depends in part on the strength and size of the local chapter. As a first step, a small number of parents, roughly analogous to the Friends of Libraries committees already at work in some communities, probably would suffice. The purpose, as in most sound public relations programs, is to make friends when we do not need them so that we will have them when we do. Often such committees will meet in informal study groups to discuss the very books which have been added to the curriculum or the library and which might be challenged.

A book challenge is by its nature a threat to the intellectual stake of the community; it is right and sensible that the community should share with the schools the defense of that stake. And if, apart from any challenge, the matter of book selection and censorship is to appear on the agenda for a larger parent meeting, how much more effective would it be if that discussion were led in part by parents?

Finally, there are staff relationships—teacher to teacher, teacher to librarian, and both to administrators. Except where team teaching really works, teaching is by its nature a solitary act. Because of the schedule of the school day, the librarian plays an equally solitary role. And from our solitary lives stems much of our grief. Not all the censors are outside the school. There are librarians who, partly because of the role they conceive for themselves and partly because of the knowledge that they will have to stand alone if challenged, refuse to order certain works of literature because, however artistically, they deal with "ugly" themes. And there are librarians who, under pressure, will order a standard illustrated history of art but will remove pictures of nude statues before shelving the book.

ROLE OF THE ENGLISH DEPARTMENT

There are English departments which function more as fiscal or quartermaster units than as instructional teams. They give their energy to rotating books, not to selecting or even discussing them. At the same time it is precisely this climate that impels the eager young teacher, fresh from college, to require a book that good counsel would advise against; and in this solitary climate, good counsel is nowhere to be had.

If an English department reviews and revises its required texts and its collateral reading lists *as a department,* the texts and the lists will range as variously as the collective wisdom of the department permits and the choices will reflect the collective strength of the department. We are not talking here about a chairman's fiat, but consensus. And if the librarian regularly meets with teachers of the department to discuss their common stake in library holdings and new acquisitions, he taps their strength in his role and adds his stature to theirs. Here is an arena for good counsel and for collective wisdom. Here, if anywhere, is where sound textbook selections will be made and where the literature program will gain continually in breadth and depth.

Those who took part in the National Study of High School English Programs found the departmental meetings at times the most exciting and at times the most depressing events of the school visits. In some there was solid rapport, open dialogue, exciting exchange of ideas. In at least some, the school visit at midyear was the occasion for the first department meeting of the year.

Apart from helping to see that departments meet with some regularity and occasionally attending such meetings, the principal can do much to set the climate needed by the charge he puts to the chairman and the department, by the business that he makes clear the department is expected to carry on: textbook rotation (but only if it cannot be handled in a bulletin); selecting and handling works of literature in classrooms; designing and conducting independent reading programs; and planning for and using classroom libraries, the intimate connection between the school library and the English curriculum.

Developing Lifetime Readers

H. ALAN ROBINSON

READING will not be a necessary ability in the foreseeable future is a statement one hears with some frequency today. Programmed instruction through the use of highly competent computer programs is suggested as a replacement for reading material of the traditional kind. Reading for enjoyment will be, according to some sources, discarded for listening and viewing for enjoyment.

It is conceivable that the learners of tomorrow will be skilled viewers and listeners. It is conceivable that computer-assisted instruction will replace reading as we know it today. But, in this writer's opinion, the time is much more distant than rumors would have us believe. Even if instructional programs utilizing other media than reading are perfected in the near future, reading will not be replaced as an activity to be undertaken during leisure time.

Granted the form of reading materials may change and is changing. Granted we may sit at home and punch a button which will permit us to read the book of our choosing on a television-type screen. Granted a library collection may be contained in a small box of microfiche. Nevertheless the potent need and desire to read will still be present. As adults of the future gain more and more leisure time, their need for reading will increase rather than decrease. They will learn many other ways of utilizing and enjoying their leisure too, but many will find it imperative to turn to the solitary, individual act of reading—of choosing their own excursion into the world of yesterday, tomorrow, or even today.

Unfortunately, in the past only a small percentage of those people who know how to read have turned to reading for their own edification and enjoyment beyond the school-required reading tasks. Newspapers,

From *Journal of Reading*, 11, January, 1968, pp. 261–267. Reprinted with permission of H. Alan Robinson and the International Reading Association.

and to some extent, magazines have been read widely even with the competition from other media, but books have been the diet of few. Book sales have increased, but seemingly the minority of lifetime readers read more books.

It seems essential that the secondary school teacher turn his attention to the vital task of developing lifetime readers. High school teachers often bemoan the fact that students do not turn to reading, but the very teachers who do the moaning themselves precipitate the disasters through either inactivity or little activity in this area. Learning *how* to read is a rather fruitless activity if it is not utilized beyond school assignments. This article attempts to bring together a variety of suggestions for developing lifetime readers of secondary school students.

TOTAL SCHOOL INVOLVEMENT

ENVIRONMENT FOR READING

A school building must reflect the importance of reading in each person's life throughout its halls, rooms, and offices. Students and staff members should be able to find out about a new book, a new collection, a new filmstrip. Students should be made acquainted with a variety of kinds of journals, with features of certain newspapers, with new uses for old books. Obviously no one person can make a school building live and breathe reading; displays, notices, information ought to be coordinated by a central, but changing, committee of students, staff members, and parents.

Traditionally, the high school has been amazingly negligent in this vital area. Faculties cannot continue to lament the fact that students do not turn to reading when they themselves do not create the atmosphere for wanting to do so. Particularly the high school principal needs to assume a role in this team effort. If he will spearhead such activity (including serving on the coordinating committee himself), the school environment will become a reading environment. Numerous principals do not realize how significant it is for them to "get the ball rolling," to maintain active interest, and to praise the personnel involved for their efforts.

The school must also attempt to play some role in developing an environment for reading within the home. Without doubt this is a more difficult task, and in many instances a hopeless one. But high schools, generally speaking, have made little effort in this direction. Parents need to be helped to learn that reading materials within the interest and achievement levels of their children ought to be easily accessible in the home and attractively displayed whenever possible. Parents ought to be helped to realize that Aunt Tillie's presents of soberly bound classics which sit on the shelf are not the books which will appeal to many of their youngsters. Parents ought to be helped to understand that in the home, just as in the school, a reading atmosphere is created only with effort, only by providing those reading materials which satisfy adolescent needs and questions.

MODELS TO EMULATE

The thing we teachers do best is talk, preach, tell what to do. We fall short of being examples. Here is an area where adolescents are searching for models and too infrequently do they find them among their teachers or parents. Every teacher must be a reader. He must be a reader of literature above and beyond what has to be read in order for him to function in his role as teacher. There is no acceptable excuse for a teacher "not having the time to read;" he must. The biology teacher is not only a specialist in biology; he is a teacher. He shares equal responsibility with the English teacher and the French teacher for developing lifetime readers. Here too is an area where the physical education teacher should assume a vital role—getting his students to realize that, although the physical education teacher doesn't often teach reading skills, he is nevertheless very much interested in reading and in helping his students to turn to reading.

Each teacher should carry the book he is currently reading for enjoyment or information with him to school daily. He should make it visible to his students. He might try to do some of this kind of reading when he sneaks a minute here and there, rather than grading papers. Probably he ought to plan periods of time in class when students see him turn to his book to finish a page or a chapter. The teacher might sometime share his book with students just as he often expects students to share their books with him. Most important of all is the visible model.

Whenever feasible, teachers ought to chat with parents about their being models to emulate. Too many parents "konk out" before the television set, happy to become just passively involved after a hard day's work. Granted the activity may be pleasant, but if they are concerned about their adolescents' lifetime reading habits, they ought to spend some time making their reading activities visible to their sons and their daughters. They too should share what they are reading—not necessarily the family reading circle—but through a variety of informal techniques which teachers might discuss with parents. More time at PTA meetings and school visits placed on techniques of developing lifetime readers will pay greater dividends in the long run than some of the topics now handled.

KNOWLEDGE OF LITERATURE

Each subject-area teacher needs to be familiar with the adolescent and adult literature related to his particular field and, when possible, with contemporary literature on an even broader base. If students are to become lifetime readers, it's most important to have persons whom they respect available to guide them in selection. The teacher who is well read in terms of adult literature should also be acquainted with adolescent literature (transitional and junior novels, magazines for adolescents, expository and biographical books written particularly for junior and senior high school students). Knowledge of such literature and efforts to chat with adolescents about their literature will very often be a potent force in the development of lifetime readers.

If at all possible, the secondary school teacher ought to take a course in adolescent literature if he hasn't taken one in the past ten years. The books available today are plentiful and often magnificent. Although the teacher will want to review some of the classics, he will also be delighted with contemporary writing by sensitive authors who are conscious of the needs of adolescents. If the secondary school teacher has no time for a course at this point, he should read as widely as he can, and keep up on the book reviews—both in the Sunday editions of newspapers and in numerous other sources where careful annotations of books are available.

SPECIFIC TECHNIQUES

ACCESSIBILITY

Obviously, every high school should have a school library. High schools without libraries should make every effort to engage some type of service that will make books accessible to students. But often books are not accessible to students even when a fine collection of books is kept in a central high school library. Too often high school libraries are occupied all day with study halls or classes in "library science." If we are to encourage students to develop lifetime reading habits, they must have access to a library when they need it. They must be able to meander through many kinds of reading collections. They must have the time to select and evaluate.

The students must also, of course, know school librarians who are not storekeepers of books but active consultants. A student should be able to get from a school librarian, not just assistance in finding information related to a course activity, but assistance in making choices of materials for his personal reading needs. In addition, the librarian should be getting into classrooms and talking about new books related to various subject fields. The librarian ought to visit English classes, for example, to talk about new books related to the problems of adolescents; science, math, and home economics classes to discuss new journals and books related to these areas. Too often the mathematics or home economics departments, for example, are not contacted about books and journals which may very well relate to their areas. Very often students are not informed of the variety available.

Every high school classroom should have its own library collection. These books and related materials should be catalogued and distributed by the central library so that everyone may make use of them; any one collection should not stay in a given classroom more than a few weeks. The librarian and teachers can decide how long they want the collections, and what kinds of materials they want in them. Students should be able to withdraw books from the classroom collection. In a class on Problems of American Democracy, for example, there should be a changing collection related to the ongoing work in the course. In order to have an effective collection, the librarian and the teacher should work with a reading consultant to be certain that the levels of materials are varied enough for the abilities within the class.

DISPLAYS

Along with the classroom collection, a few books should be attractively displayed so that students will be drawn to them. High school classrooms are sometimes rather cold places, and one way of warming them up is to have a small corner devoted to displays of literature related to the subject area. Attractive displays do not necessarily entail a great deal of time and effort. For example, when a dust cover is put on a bulletin board it's possible to mount it on a piece of bright poster paper at an angle, securing a three dimensional effect, by pinning the fly leaves under and pushing the cover up. A shadow box can be made from any cardboard box, decorating and thumbtacking it to the bulletin board, to feature the book of the week.

Such displays are usually most appealing if they feature a specific interest. If the teacher has learned something about the interests of his students, he can put up a short-term display dealing with specific interests of a small group rather than the whole class. Permanent displays are not nearly so effective as short-term displays which focus on specific themes: "for girls only" for a couple of weeks, or "man in a flying machine" for another period of time. Many students remain with a given interest for a long period of time, but others can be weaned away by attractive displays made by teachers who know adolescent interests and literature.

ORAL READING

Oral reading in the secondary classroom has a very slight role to play. It should, of course, not be used for instructional purposes when each student, one after the other, reads a paragraph or two out loud. This technique serves to make reading a rote, mechanical activity rather than an endeavor to unlock meaning. There are times, however, when prepared individuals may read something to the class or a group for their information or enjoyment. At these times the preparation must be excellent so that the reception is excellent. Those who are listening must be well prepared also.

Oral reading by the teacher should be done frequently in high school classrooms. If the teacher is an effective reader, this technique helps students to appreciate the flavor and meaning of good literature. If the teacher is not an effective oral reader, he may ask a colleague to read for him. There are excellent recordings by professional readers which can be used to advantage in many subject-matter classrooms.

DEFEATING LIFETIME READING INTERESTS

There are a number of ways of turning students away from reading. Sometimes it almost appears as though the secondary school attempts to do this. In addition to mechanical oral reading, briefly mentioned above, there are three other ways that teachers can stifle lifetime reading habits.

1. Book Reports. One sure way of encouraging the reluctant reader to remain reluctant is through the use of stereotyped book reports. The mimeographed sheet used every three, four or six weeks, on which the student must record the chief characters, a summary, and his reactions, will certainly work toward defeating lifetime reading interests. High school students ought to be given time and opportunity to read books of their own choosing without reporting to teachers. If reporting must be done, there are a variety of techniques other than the stereotyped book report form. Some students like to tell about their books in class. Some students prefer an individual conference with the teacher. Some students can be drawn out very informally just by a few questions. On the other hand, some students enjoy writing book reports but should be given freedom in the method they choose.

2. *Homework.* Departmentalization makes for hazards in this area. Very often high school students are confronted with hours and hours of homework, primarily because teachers are not able to coordinate their assignments. Thus, they have little opportunity to turn to reading for enjoyment or personal uses. Teachers ought to encourage students at times to read on their own in books that are not required texts; they ought to make the time available. When possible, faculties ought to get together and coordinate their homework efforts. In this present complex society there are so many demands on the teenager that reading often fades into the background unless adults help him to make room for such activtiy.

3. *Literature Program.* Probably the best way of defeating lifetime reading interests is the continuance of an outdated literature program. This is not a plea for the discontinuance of the classics, for there are many students who can enjoy them. It is, however, a plea for faculties to examine literature programs to see if they meet the needs of particular students in today's world. It is possible for students to learn something of the art of literature without requiring all of them to read the same book. Students have various needs at different stages of development and the literature program should be reflective of such needs.

EMPHASIS ON LIFETIME READING HABITS

At the University of Chicago Laboratory School, Coach Sanford Patlak focuses on the development of lifetime readers. He has boys talk about books and talks with them about books. They make informal reports right on the playing field and enjoy it. He has a library collection in a closet near the lockerrooms with a big red and white stop sign to attract the boys' attention. He is constantly on the lookout for suitable books. In addition to Mr. Patlak, there are many teachers at the University of Chicago Laboratory School who, with the help of Miss Ellen Thomas, Reading Consultant, and Miss Blanche Janacek, are constantly striving to develop lifetime readers.

Full staff involvement can't help but aid significantly in the development of lifetime readers. Staff members who make their own reading visible, who make books attractive and accessible to students, who know adolescent literature and relate it to the needs of their students, play a significant role in shaping the leisure-time activities of their adolescent charges.

Evaluation of Development in and through Reading

RUTH STRANG

EVALUATION IS LIKE Tennyson's "flower in the crannied wall"—it reaches out in the whole universe of the reading field. It is concerned with the individual's reading development and the effect of reading on his personal development. Evaluation recognizes that improvement in any reading skill may not only affect the acquisition of subsequent skills but also the individuals' self-confidence and concept of himself. Growth in reading ability may also lead to improved relationships with parents and teachers. As the child grows older he uses reading increasingly as a tool to further intellectual growth. The knowledge obtainable through reading helps him grow socially, educationally, and vocationally. Evaluation, therefore, must be comprehensive and continuous; it must change somewhat with successive stages of development.[1]

The evaluation process begins when we state the goals of teaching reading. Some of these are fairly specific, such as learning to recognize words; others are more intangible, such as enjoyment and appreciation of literature. These goals should be stated as specific abilities, habits, attitudes, appreciations, activities, and interests that can be observed or measured in the teaching-learning situation.

To obtain evidence of these changes—which, if desirable, imply growth—we must select or devise methods and instruments. After we have obtained the evidence, the next step is to evaluate, in the light of

From *Development in and through Reading,* the Sixtieth Yearbook of the National Society for the Study of Education, 1961, pp. 376–397. Reprinted with permission of the National Society for the Study of Education.

[1]*Evaluation of Reading.* Compiled and edited by Helen M. Robinson. Proceedings of the Annual Conference on Reading Held at the University of Chicago, 1958. Supplementary Educational Monographs, No. 88. Chicago: University of Chicago Press, 1958.

our objectives, the adequacy, effectiveness, and worth of the teaching-learning experiences that have been offered. After this has been done, administrators, teachers, and students should apply the results of the evaluation to improve instruction in reading. Thus, evaluation helps produce growth as well as appraise it.

WHY EVALUATE?

Evaluation is essential to learning.[2] It is an incentive to students, an intrinsic part of teaching, and an aid to the administrator and the specialist in improving the program.

For students, evaluation facilitates learning and gives them a sense of direction. Psychological experiments have repeatedly shown that students learn more effectively when they know how well they are doing and what specifically they are doing wrong. Appraisal as a part of teaching helps them identify the reading processes or methods that they can use successfully.

Awareness of one's progress helps build self-confidence. Every student needs the stimulus of success. When the retarded reader sees objective evidence that he can learn to read, he begins to overcome his longstanding sense of failure. Encouraged by evidence of progress, students tend to take more initiative and responsibility for their improvement in reading. "Nothing succeeds like observed success."

Teachers, too, need a sense of progress and the stimulus of success. A comprehensive evaluation process, by broadening and sharpening objectives and highlighting the results that have been achieved, gives teachers an increased sense of the value of their work. On the other hand, an evaluation based on narrow tests of skills is discouraging to the teacher who is broadly concerned with attitudes, new interests, and appreciations.

Evaluation also shows the teacher where to begin. By trying to estimate students' readiness and capacities as well as by measuring their present skills and interests, the teacher can provide the learning experiences that the students need. Evaluation serves as a guide to the choice of procedures and materials.

For the administrator, evaluation may show the strengths and successful features in the program as well as indicate needs for changes in curriculum, instruction, and administrative policy. As it reveals failure in the common effort to attain objectives that have been agreed upon, the administrator asks "why?" Do the students' inadequacies in reading

2Virgil E. Herrick, "Purposes and Needs for an Evaluation Program," in *Evaluation of Reading, ibid.,* pp. 153–58.

stem from an unsuitable curriculum, from poorly prepared teachers, from failure to detect incompetency in the teaching of beginning reading, from lack of suitable reading materials for the wide range of reading ability that is found in most classes, or from homes or communities that are unfavorable to improvement in reading? Naturally, the administrator uses the results of evaluation in explaining the reading program to the community.

To the reading specialist, evaluation reveals strengths and weaknesses in the program. It may show that he has devoted too much time to individual cases and small groups and neglected work with and through the teachers. It may suggest strategic points in the program at which he should concentrate his efforts, such as a developmental reading course for all students or special classes for the gifted.

From the standpoint of research and contributions to the literature in the field of reading, we should have better evaluations of programs and procedures. Future writers should avoid two faults that often occur in the reports now available: (*a*) A program or procedure is merely described without evidence of its effectiveness; (*b*) results are presented statistically with no concrete description of the organization, methods, and materials by which they were achieved. The evaluation process will be described in this chapter, and instruments and methods for obtaining evidence will be suggested.

WHAT IS EVALUATED?

The nature of the evaluative process varies with the accepted concept of reading. Evaluation is a relatively simple matter if reading is conceived as merely pronouncing printed words correctly with little or no regard to their meaning. If reading is broadly defined to include thinking and feeling, the exercise of imagination and character traits, such as determination to overcome difficulties, persistence in practice, and self-confidence in attacking new tasks,[3] then evaluation becomes complex, indeed. In this chapter, the description of evaluation accords with the broad view of reading that is presented in this yearbook.

MAIN GOALS

The goals to be evaluated have been stated in previous chapters, both broadly and as specific behavior that can be observed. In evalu-

[3]Calvin D. Cotterall and Philip Weise, "A Perceptual Approach to Early Reading Difficulties," *California Journal of Educational Research*, X (November, 1959), 212–18.

ating them, we must remember that they are not separate steps; they are interwoven in the reading process from beginning reading to maturity.

HOW TO STATE OBJECTIVES: WITH REFERENCE TO STUDENTS

The stated objectives for development of reading abilities and for personal development through reading should possess those characteristics that are indicated in the following paragraphs.

Be specific.—General goals should be broken down into specific objectives and stated operationally as definite reading skills or behavior. For example, the objective, "acquire skill in word recognition," should be broken down into specific behavior which can be observed or tested, such as: (*a*) shows progress in associating the initial sounds of words with the appropriate letter symbols; (*b*) becomes proficient in identifying sounds in words; (*c*) improves in facility to give words that rhyme with the word presented; and (*d*) year by year becomes more skillful in using various methods to determine the meaning of unknown words —context clues, structural analysis, syllabication, phonic analysis, and use of the dictionary. The stated objectives should also include items relating to the students' personal development; for example, is encouraged by success and evidences of progress in word-recognition skills.

Be realistic and clearly stated.—Objectives should be realistic and precisely rather than vaguely stated. Similarly, we should avoid the use of words that may make the objectives ambiguous or obscure.

Accent growth.—We should try to appraise the student's growth as well as his reading status. Growth is especially difficult to measure. Progress is always relative to the capacity of the student and to his opportunities for learning. As measured by gains on standardized tests, progress should be checked to determine whether it is merely a chance difference or real evidence of growth.

Show relative importance.—It is also necessary to determine the relative importance of each objective at different stages in the child's development. For example, in beginning reading, acquiring a sight vocabulary and word-recognition skills are basic, dominant learnings, although thinking and feeling are also part of the pattern of objectives in the primary grades. In the intermediate grades, learning through reading in new fields becomes increasingly important. During high-school years, still deeper levels of interpretation and critical thinking occupy a central position in the pattern of objectives. Evaluation must take into consideration these changing emphases at different stages in reading development.

Recognize individual differences.—Some objectives are more important and appropriate for certain students than for others. To determine this relative importance, we must have a knowledge of students' interests, abilities, and backgrounds. For example, for a retarded reader in high school, growth in basic vocabulary and word-recognition skills may be the most important evidence of progress to evaluate. For an able student who reads little, an increase of interest in worthwhile reading is most important. Some individuals who are above the test norms for their ages and grades are still achieving below their potential reading ability. On the other hand, a score that is several years below the norm may represent real achievement for a less able learner.

Show progress in patterns.—Ideally, patterns of objectives paralleling the development from beginning reading to mature reading should be described. For example, a pattern of objectives at the developmental level of junior high school, applied to reading a short story, might include: (*a*) show increasing interest in reading short stories; (*b*) comprehend most of the words; (*c*) apply word-meaning skills to unfamiliar words; (*d*) are keen to pick up clues of character and plot from the descriptions of physical appearance, speech, actions, and response of others to a certain character; (*e*) respond in an appropriate manner emotionally to examples of courage, cruelty, and other human qualities; (*f*) communicate more effectively to others their thoughts and feelings about the story; and (*g*) modify their point of view, attiude, and behavior in a desirable direction.

By setting up sequential patterns of reading development, it is possible to see more clearly how children's improvement in reading might progress simultaneously on all fronts through the school years or how a retarded reader, starting with his present pattern of reading development, might make progress.

Consider causes.—If evaluation is to lead to improved practice, it is important to ascertain conditions that may be responsible for the observed growth or lack of growth. Neither teacher nor student can do much to remedy a bad situation or to improve a good one unless he knows what is causing the success or failure. These causes or conditions are complex and can best be recorded and synthesized in a reading case study for each student.

OBJECTIVES: WITH REFERENCE TO STAFF RESPONSIBILITIES

The objectives described thus far have been stated as desirable changes in students. These are the ultimate focus of evaluation. However, an effective reading program may also be evaluated with reference to co-operation, communication, and other constructive attitudes and practices on the part of administrators, supervisors, and teachers.[4,5] An evaluation concerned with students' development should consider how well informed the administrator and supervisory personnel are about the reading program, how effectively they assist teachers in improving instruction in reading, and how adroitly they interpret the reading program to the public and use community resources. It would also be necessary to ascertain how well teachers were combining planning, teaching, and evaluating, and whether they were making appraisal of student progress an intrinsic part of instruction in reading.

GUIDES TO EVALUATION

General procedures for evaluating may be briefly summarized as follows:

1. Evaluation should be continuous rather than periodic.
2. It should be a part of the instructional program, not apart from it.
3. It should obtain evidence on the extent to which the stated objectives have been achieved.
4. In obtaining this evidence, it should use both formal and informal methods.
5. The data collected should be used for the improvement of program and procedures.
6. Increasing emphasis should be placed on self-appraisal as the student grows older.
7. Evaluation of a reading program should be carried on by a team that includes administrators, reading consultants, other specialists, teachers, students, and parents.

INSTRUMENTS AND METHODS FOR OBTAINING EVIDENCE

In describing methods for obtaining evidence of changes in student or staff behavior, we shall relate the method or instrument to the purpose for which it may be used. In actual practice the evaluator should use a combination of methods to obtain a dynamic picture, selecting those most appropriate to each stage of reading development.

[4]Elizabeth Zimmermann Howard, "Appraising Strengths and Weaknesses of the Total Reading Program," in *Evaluation of Reading, op. cit.*, pp. 169–73.
[5]Mildred C. Letton, "Evaluating the Effectiveness of Teaching Reading," in *Evaluation of Reading, op. cit.*, pp. 76–82.

VISUAL AND AUDITORY FACTORS

There are three main ways of obtaining evidence of visual efficiency: (*a*) the teacher may note signs of eyestrain on the part of the pupil; (*b*) students may report symptoms of eyestrain that they have noted in themselves; and (*c*) visual screening tests may be used. Similarly, auditory efficiency may be checked, using an informal listening test and the audiometer.

WORD KNOWLEDGE

Day-by-day teaching-testing.—Classroom procedures play an important role in the appraisal of vocabulary. As the teacher listens to children and asks questions about the meaning of words they read or speak, he obtains evidence about the size and growth of the students' speaking, listening, and reading vocabulary; the kind of words they have learned; and the rapidity with which they learn new words and use them in their conversation. In interviews and class discussion, the teacher may get clues as to why they made certain errors and how they remembered the correct meaning of the words taught.

Scrapbook-type class and individual dictionaries and vocabulary card files of new words made by the students provide objective evidence of growth in word knowledge and a basis for self-appraisal.

Self-appraisal.—If the students analyze the kinds of words they use in their compositions, they will see for themselves how they are progressing in written vocabulary. Somewhat more formal is the method of testing the students systematically on the words they should be learning during the year. If the test requires the student to distinguish the best definition of each word from among four or five choices, each representing a certain type of error, it will be useful for diagnosis of word comprehension. If the test asks the student to write a definition of each word, it requires of him an understanding of the meaning of the word along with the ability to express its meaning clearly in writing. The student's evaluation of his performance on these tasks contributes to growth in self-appraisal.

Vocabulary tests.—A still more formal appraisal may be obtained by use of standardized vocabulary tests. It is, of course, generally understood that effective instruments for all pupils from primary grades through college may be used to measure vocabulary. Simple and effective measures for the primary grades in use at the present time include the *Dolch Picture Cards* of 95 nouns and his longer test of 220 basic sight words. For Grades IV–XVI, the vocabulary section in any modern reading test will give an appraisal of word knowledge. For Grades IX–XVI, the *Inglis Vocabulary Test* is still recommended. For Grades IX–XII, the more recent *Durost-Center Word Mastery Test* is especially effective in emphasizing use of context. For Grades VII–XII, the thirty-minute *New Standard Vocabulary Tests* published by the Educational Department of the *Reader's Digest* from 1955 to 1958 have the advantage of providing six forms.

WORD RECOGNITION SKILLS

Daily performance.—Evaluation of word-recognition skills goes on simultaneously with teaching of meaningful material. For example, in the first grade the teacher may teach such material and at the same time test children's ability to identify sounds in words. Through the elementary grades he will appraise the students' progress as he gives instruction, practice, and informal tests of various word-recognition skills. In beginning reading especially, oral reading is useful in appraising word recognition and phrasing. Later, it also helps develop fluency and ability to communicate the author's thought to others. Tape- or disc-recording of children's oral reading is an excellent way to make them aware of their progress. The teacher may also write dated observations of each individual's performance, compare successive scores on informal tests, and encourage students to keep charts on which the desired skills are listed and checked off as acquired.

Standardized procedures.—Certain individual standardized tests of word-recognition skills are useful for both diagnosis and evaluation. For example, Durrell's "Analysis of Reading Difficulty" includes tests of word recognition, auditory analysis of word elements, and visual memory for word forms under the more comprehensive headings of oral reading, listening comprehension, and silent reading. This is an individual test requiring thirty to ninety minutes. A teacher thoroughly familiar with such a diagnostic procedure could obtain useful information while giving classroom instruction in reading.

COMPREHENSION

Methods for obtaining evidence about students' reading comprehension may be arranged on a continuum from the most informal to the most standardized, beginning with the daily appraisal possible in every classroom.

Appraisal while teaching.—Evidence of comprehension in many fields is best gathered while one is teaching. It can then be acted upon immediately; there is no lapse of time between making an evaluation and doing something about it. For example, in teaching a class how to read a newspaper, the teacher reviewed the purposes of a newspaper, which had been brought out in the previous period: to inform, to persuade, to give opinions, to amuse. The teacher reinforced the students' somewhat tenuous impression by writing these points on the board. Next, the students applied this knowledge: In what three sections of the newspaper would you find facts? Where would you find opinions? In what part would you expect to be persuaded? Amused? Since the group had little difficulty in making this application, they were ready to go ahead with a more detailed study of how to read a news report.

Day by day the teacher should note the accuracy with which students answer factual questions and the acuteness with which they make generalizations and draw inferences from their reading. When they discuss literature or retell a story, he will note evidences of success in character analysis, of ability to see cause-and-effect relations, and of appreciation of the author's purpose and style of writing. Thus, achieving in reading becomes a continuous process of recognizing and overcoming difficulties, of diagnosis and remediation, of appraisal and improvement of instruction.

Analysis of work samples.—At all ages dated samples of the students' responses to reading may be used to show growth. For example, a student may write or make a tape-recording of his first attempt to summarize orally a section of his science book. Then he may appraise this summary according to the accuracy and number of main ideas and important details remembered, the sequence of ideas recognized, and the clarity of his statements. After instruction he may compare his summary of a similar passage with the first according to designated criteria. Similarly, any dated samples of a student's reports on reading or on the discussion of books can be used to show progress in these aspects of comprehension.

The informal group reading inventory.—This group method of appraising students' silent reading can be used in the upper elementary and high school. It employs questions on the use of the index, table of contents, and other study skills. It tests their comprehension of passages taken from the textbooks and charts the types of reading difficulties encountered by each student. To appraise growth, the teacher should repeat the inventory at intervals.

The individual reading inventory.—As one student at a time reads short passages selected from a graded series of reading books, the teacher may gain understanding of the student's·attitudes and approach to reading as well as an indication of his oral and silent reading ability. The construction and use of the individual informal reading inventory has been described in detail by Betts.[6]

Teaching tests.—An educational test of any kind comprises a series of situations which call forth and permit the recording of a special kind of behavior.[7] Teacher-made tests can cover a wide variety of reading situations and outcomes and may take many forms.[8]

Informal tests add more precision and continuity to the teacher's opportunistic but important observation in the classroom. For example, a procedure, *Explore Your Reading*, developed by Melnik[9] for improving the reading of social-studies material in junior high school begins by asking students to state their aims or goals in reading a social-studies assignment. The students are then asked to read a selection from a social-studies book that is typical of the material they will be expected to read in their classes. After reading the passage they answer questions of the "creative response" or "open end" type ("What did the author say?") and a number of multiple-choice questions that are designed to furnish evidence of a student's ability to get the literal meaning, to see relations, to draw inferences, to make generalizations, and to understand the meaning of key words.

As soon as the student has answered the questions, he has data before him for self-appraisal. He marks his own paper. He grades his free response on a ten-point scale, and analyzes the kinds of errors he has made in the multiple-choice questions (each choice represents a certain kind of error). Instruction immediately follows this self-appraisal, while the students are specifically motivated to learn how to get the right answers.

Later, the whole precedure is repeated with another similar selection. After the second exercise is completed and analyzed, the students are able to note the progress they have made. A third repetition of the procedure produces more marked improvement.

After completing the third exercise the students were asked to evaluate their experience by answering such a question as: How did *Explore Your Reading* help you to do better in your social studies? What part of *Explore Your Reading* did you enjoy most? In addition, the students

[6]Emmett Albert Betts, *Foundations of Reading Instruction*, chap. xxi, pp. 438–87. New York: American Book Co., 1957.
[7]Ralph W. Tyler, "What Is Evaluation?" in *Evaluation of Reading, op. cit.*, pp. 4–6.
[8]R. Murray Thomas, *Judging Student Progress*. New York: Longmans, Green & Co., 1956.
[9]Amelia Melnik, "Improvement of Reading through Self-Appraisal." Unpublished Doctor's project, Teachers College, Columbia University, 1960.

rated each of the eleven features of the exercises as to whether it helped them "not at all," "a little," "a good deal," or "very, very much." Of all the features, the students felt that the open-end question, "What did the author say?" had helped them most.

This testing-teaching-evaluating procedure bridges the gap between the hurriedly-made teacher test and the standardized test. It relieves the teacher of some of the burden of making instructional material; at the same time it gives him a concrete model for further testing-teaching-evaluating based on the text or reference books used by his classes.

Publishers' tests.—Some publishers provide, in connection with their basal reading series, tests for the use of the teacher. These tests represent an intermediate level of appraisal, more systematic than most teacher-made tests and less formal than standardized tests.

Standardized tests.—Standardized tests broaden the base of evaluation by extending it beyond the walls of one classroom; they add an authoritative emphasis to appraisal. They supplement but do not supplant the classroom evaluation. Their value depends upon the reliability and validity with which they measure appropriate objectives.

The reading objectives measured by most standardized tests are limited, as shown by Hunt.[10] In an analysis of reading tests he found that the only reading skills measured by the majority of these tests were rate of comprehension, general vocabulary, and paragraph meaning. The results of tests that measure attainment of limited objectives may be misleading. Perry[11] found that many Freshmen at Harvard and Radcliffe who scored above the 85 percentile on a standardized reading test could not give even a vague response to the question, "What is the chapter about?"

More in accord with the broad view of reading are the Educational Testing Service's *Sequential Tests of Educational Progress* (STEP), which cover the whole age range considered in this yearbook; the *Davis Reading Test,* which is for high-school and college students; and the *Iowa Test of Basic Skills.*

An analysis of the kinds of responses made to each test item enables students to examine their errors and to determine kinds of comprehension difficulties. This use of tests as a starting point for reading instruction increases their importance in evaluation. They not only supply a central core of data but, if administered periodically, give a limited but long-range view of growth in reading. However, no test can take the place of the day-by-day teaching-evaluation-improvement process.

[10]J. T. Hunt, "Selecting a High School Reading Test," *High School Journal,* XXXIX (October, 1955), 49–52.
[11]William G. Perry, Jr., "Students' Uses and Misuses of Reading Skills," *Harvard Educational Review,* XXIX (Summer, 1959), 192–200.

It is wise not to spend so much time in testing that there is little time for the daily discovery and application of new evidence.

Self-appraisal.—We must recognize the inadequacy of appraisals that take into account only the product or end result of reading. From the standpoint of learning, it is of prime importance to understand the process by which knowledge is gained and attitudes are changed. Some evidence can be obtained by introspection. Difficult as it is, some students are able to write objective descriptions of their reading methods—telling how they get the main idea of a paragraph, unlock the meaning of unfamiliar words, make accurate generalizations and inferences—and can also describe conditions under which they read and comprehend best.

Each student should keep his own growth record. In his individual record folder, he would put the interpretation of test results, dated samples of his performance, and other evidences of his progress in reading. Evaluation based on this accumulated evidence should motivate him to reinforce his strengths, correct his errors, and move ahead to more mature reading achievement.

ABILITY TO USE READING

Since reading usually leads to some kind of communion with one's self or to communication, it is important to appraise students' ability to communicate ideas gained from reading. Free-response, creative-type or open-end questions, as they are variously called, require independent thinking and develop ability to organize and express ideas in writing. Students need practice of this kind.

The extent to which students use in class discussion the ideas they have gained from reading can be appraised by the group, by the teacher, or by each student individually. The use a student makes of his reading when he writes a term paper can be appraised by comparing successive reports of a similar type. His original plays, stories, dramatizations, and illustrations based on his reading may be partly evaluated by audience reaction. His application of reading to life situations may be observed in his changed behavior.

INTERESTS, FEELING RESPONSES, AND PERSONAL DEVELOPMENT

Many of the important outcomes of education are often the most difficult to measure. In the area of interests, feelings, attitudes, and personal development through reading, changes in individual students can be inferred as we observe their behavior or take at face value the statements they feel free to make to us.

From reading tests some inferences concerning personality development may be made. A gain in rate may indicate less anxiety and fear of failure in reading the material. Improvement in comprehension may result partly from self-confidence which permits a more effective use of intellectual ability. Changes in attitudes and interest in words may contribute to more rapid growth in vocabulary.

Classroom observation has the advantage of being continuous. In many reading situations teachers can sense enthusiasm, interest, absorption, enjoyment—or their opposites—outside of class or in a class discussion. They can learn to read "the language of behavior" and become more alert to the interaction within the class group, which is a potent influence on learning. They may write dated descriptive anecdotes telling what happens when the class is allowed to browse and choose their own reading materials or when books are selected to develop certain qualities such as courage, friendliness, or responsibility. They may obtain evidence of a student's specific reading interests by noting the number of appropriate references he spontaneously makes to books and authors in reporting on a topic, in contributing to a discussion, and in conversing.

Interviews may reveal children's feeling about reading and reasons why they read or do not read. Talking with children and young people about their interests and the books they read last year helps to appraise growth as well as current reading interests and tastes.

Questionnaires have elicited from college students many responses suggesting some influence of reading on their philosophy of life, attitudes, self-concept, and adjustment to college.[12] A questionnaire asking for concrete evidence of appreciation or enjoyment in reading devised as part of the Eight-Year Study[13] included items indicating (*a*) satisfaction in reading; (*b*) desire to read more of the same kind or by the same author; (*c*) desire to know more about what he reads; (*d*) desire to express himself creatively in writing or in one of the other art forms with reference to the books read; (*e*) identification with the persons, places, or situations about which he is reading; (*f*) desire to clarify his thinking about life problems through reading; and (*g*) evaluation of the thing appreciated.

Reading autobiographies, either structured or unstructured, often furnish valuable information about an individual's reading development as he views it. In the reading autobiography, students trace their reading interest and the influence that reading has had on them.

---

[12]Samuel Weingarten, "Developmental Values in Voluntary Reading," *School Review*, LXII (April, 1959), 222–30.
[13]E. R. Smith, R. W. Tyler, and the Evaluation Staff, *Appraising and Recording Student Progress*, pp. 251–52. New York: Harper & Bros., 1942.

Check lists or interest inventories suggest interests to the student as well as give him the opportunity to indicate his present interests.

Incomplete sentences, such as "Reading is ———," "I would rather read than ———," give evidence on students' attitudes and interests.

Real problems, which encourage students' evaluation of books, can be posed: "Which books shall we order for our class library? Which story shall we make into a radio or puppet play?"

Librarians and parents may furnish additional information about the nature and extent of children's voluntary reading.

Students' written free responses about the effect of books on themselves are of special significance. Such compositions, of course, are worthless unless the students are interested and co-operative. In a class where there is mutual respect and trust among teacher and students, much may be learned from unstructured compositions. The author has obtained many students' written responses to the following directions: "Sometimes we wonder what reading does to people— what effect reading has on their points of view, attitudes, and behavior. Will you help us find out? This is what you can do: Think back over the books you have read. Try to remember how any of the books influenced you. Did you think differently or feel differently or act differently after you had read the book or part of the book? Just write whatever you remember about how any book changed your way of thinking or feeling or acting."

Some of the replies from ninth-grade students were definitely discouraging:

> I have never read a book that changed me.
> Most books have no influence on me but *White Fang* was one book I enjoyed. It has adventure from beginning to end and makes me want to read more.
> In general, I hate to read books. But I do like car magazines which make me want to have a car so I can do what the guys in the book did to their cars.

The following report is representative of many of the responses received:

> Sue Barton's *Senior Nurse* changed my way of thinking very much. I used to think that nurses had to do horrible things. After reading Sue Barton's books my ideas of nursing changed completely. If I weren't so headstrong on becoming a teacher, I would like to become a nurse after reading Sue Barton's books. It seems wonderful to help ill people and new mothers.

The following statement is an unusual analysis and summary of the influence of books of different kinds on an impressionable young adolescent:

Some books make you feel you're a different person and you are living at the period of time or the kind of place the book is based on. Some books such as *Johnny Tremain* and other stories of the United States during war time make you feel very patriotic. Other books about simple American families such as *Little Women* and *Our Town* make you feel very sentimental and more aware of your own home life. Different kinds of religious books give you many ideas about what you really believe and start you thinking on many different trains of thought. Science fiction stories start you thinking about the future and the world to come. I especially like stories of people who find out what their career is going to be. Stories of people such as *Florence Nightingale* and *The Life and Thought of Albert Schweitzer* get you to thinking and wondering about jobs in the field of medicine. Books that show a great deal of hard work and courage make you want to be more like that. Stories of Lincoln, Jefferson, Jackson and other great American leaders influence your ideas about what makes the United States so great. Some books make you want to work harder and do a better job at what you're doing. Many books of adventure stories such as *Mrs. Mike* and *Drums along the Mohawk* help to relax you and get you away from the world you live in. Books that make you happy and make you laugh are very good to read when you feel downcast or afraid. These books can cheer you up and lift your spirits and make you less afraid. Books of inspiration about simple everyday boys and girls in this country and other countries abroad make you feel that you are not different from other young people all over the world and help to promote international friendship, which is very important for World Peace.

SUMMARY

Several main methods for obtaining evidence of development in and through reading have been briefly described:

1. Questioning-observing-appraising as an intrinsic part of teaching
2. Recording dated observations over a period of time
3. Analyzing students' oral and written responses to reading and other work samples
4. Using informal teacher-made tests and questionnaires
5. Preparing and using testing-teaching-self-appraisal exercises in each subject
6. Administering standardized tests of intelligence and reading achievement
7. Studying introspective evaluative reports by teachers and students

Which of these seven methods the evaluator will select depends upon many factors, such as the age and ability of the students and the amount of skill and time that are available for making the evaluation.

For evaluation purposes, each of these methods should be used repeatedly over a period of time. Some evidence obtained, such as day-by-day observations, can be charted to show continuous growth. Some, acquired through standardized tests, questionnaires, personal documents, and the like, may be obtained at the beginning and at the end of the year and used to show changes that have taken place in the more subtle aspects of development through reading.

EVALUATION OF GROWTH IN INDIVIDUAL STUDENTS

The evidence on each of the several aspects of reading development should be evaluated against a background knowledge of the situation and the students. The real test of an individual's potential reading ability is the progress that he, through the best possible instruction, is able to make. The "best possible instruction" would, of course, vary with the individual's age, interest, and reasons for his reading difficulties.

Appraising a student's progress with reference to his capacity presents many difficulties. In estimating potential reading ability, it is important to study all the available evidence about a student: his scores on standardized intelligence tests and listening comprehension tests, observations of his mental alertness in everyday situations, family background, and early school experiences. A discrepancy between the student's potential ability and his present achievement may be caused by poor teaching, lack of purpose or persistence, negative parental attitudes toward education, too much pressure or indifference on the part of parents, and a great variety of emotional disturbances.

The case study should bring together information about the interrelated aspects of home background, health, school and social conditions; results of individual tests of mental ability, listening comprehension, and reading achievement; and observations of interests and personality. It relates changes in reading development and personal development through reading to causative conditions. The case-study approach emphasizes simultaneous growth in all aspects of reading important for an individual. At every point, it takes into account his ability and learning opportunities.

A well-designed reading program stands or falls on the basis of desirable changes in student development, both with respect to personality traits and advancement in reading skills. In working with an emotionally disturbed girl changes were noted, not only in test results but also in subjective impressions of her improvement in reading and personal development. Her reactions were described as a more relaxed attitude, less anxiety, less self-depreciation, more pleasure in reading, extended areas in which she could concentrate, increased awareness of reading methods she could use most successfully, and day-by-day improvement in comprehension of different kinds of material.

Evaluation of these more subtle aspects of development may be made by noting evidences of changes in a pupil's attitude toward reading, toward school, toward himself, and toward his family, as in the case of Donald. The quotations are from tape-recorded interviews and are given in the order of their occurrence from the beginning of the first to the end of the twenty-seventh interview:

Donald's chronological age, on November 10, was 13 years 3 months; mental age on the *Stanford-Binet Test*, 14.2; I.Q., 108; 68 percentile; reading expectation, seventh grade. *Gray's Oral Reading Paragraphs*, given at about the same time, indicated that he was reading on about the 1.8 level. Also significant was his mastery of the Dolch basic vocabulary, his ability to read many signs and directions, and his efforts to get some ideas out of his eighth-grade social-studies books.

Although there was definite improvement in Donald's reading during the time he was coming to the Reading Center, the most important change was his attitude toward himself and to reading. He came to the Center with a negative attitude toward reading and anything pertaining to it. But even in the first interview he showed a ray of hope. In response to the question, "Did you want to come to the Reading Center?" he said, "Nothing to lose. Everything to gain." He expected to fail but hoped there was some magic that would make it possible for him to read better.

Even during these first interviews he made some positive comments: "I could do the tests if I could read them." When told he was reading much better one week, he said, "I know."

Although he resisted word study on certain days, he showed interest in reading the names on the subway map and names of airplanes and engines. In the sixth interview, when given words in an envelope to make into sentences, Donald said, "This is like TV. 'Beat the Clock.' It's fun. . . . It's easy to do when you know the words."

After the seventh interview, comments like the following became more frequent: "Don't you have a little harder vocabulary cards?" "Could I have some homework to take home?" "I came by myself today. My father wrote down the directions." "I want to read. I want to read a book. I want to read some hard books—hard-cover books."

At home the father, too, noted progress. At the end of the series of interviews, the father wrote, "I realize there has been an improvement. . . . You're the first teacher he really respected."

The study of movement in a series of verbatim interviews can be made more scientific by making a content analysis, charting changes in the number of comments the client volunteers, the attitudes which he states or which can be inferred, and the kind of responses he makes to certain teaching techniques.

Similarly, changes in parents' perception of and attitude toward the child with reading difficulties can be traced over a period of five group-discussion sessions which have been tape-recorded. Changes in the expressed attitudes of one mother were as follows:

Session I. My son is just plain lazy. The guidance director told us he was below average in intelligence and this seemed to fit in with what we thought of him.

Session II. I still think it is a form of laziness or maybe impatience. Possibly my child has as much intelligence as an average child, but he is not using it.

Session III. I'm letting up on the pressure now and have stopped criticizing him constantly.

Session IV. I am taking it easier with him; maybe it's working. He doesn't seem to be any worse anyway.

Session V. Well, I am relaxed for the first time, sitting back and letting things go by for a little while and, believe it or not, the child seems to be much better.[14]

APPRAISAL OF THE READING PROGRAM AS A WHOLE

Instead of attempting to evaluate a given method of teaching reading by making inconclusive experimental control-group studies, it would appear to be more rewarding to recognize the complexity of the problem and to describe the combination of methods and materials that result in reading growth of many individuals and groups of different ages, abilities, and backgrounds. It might then be possible to vary one method with the same group of individuals and measure subsequent improvement or note lack of improvement.

To appraise reading material, well-known formulas such as the Gray-Leary, and Dale-Chall, and the Lorge may be used to estimate the structural difficulty of a given piece of material. But other aspects of readability should also be taken into account—organization and the interrelation of ideas, interest, difficulty of concepts, unnecessary technical words, vividness of expression, originality, imagination, and personal references. In appraising reading material we should also consider its contribution to solving personal problems, lightening one's burdens

[14]Janice MacDonald Studholme, "Changes in Attitudes of Mothers of Retarded Readers during Group Guidance Sessions," Unpublished Doctor's project, Teachers College, Columbia University, 1960.

through laughter, furthering ethical development, understanding one's self and associates, and studying the nature of the world.

Numerous descriptions of school and college reading programs have been published, most of which have been presented with practically no evaluation. The only evaluation in the majority of the other reports is based on differences between initial and final scores on standardized reading tests. Very few of these reports consider the standard error of measurement with respect to the test scores and the standard error of the difference between the initial and final scores. Still fewer observers have attempted to measure the persistence of gains made after the experimental period. Rarely does any investigator report the frequent use of short, informal tests charted to show students' progress. Evaluations of reading programs are still seriously lacking in reliability and in valid appraisal of reading, broadly conceived.

Only brief references may be made to several different patterns of the evaluation procedures reported. Durrell and others obtained evidence of the effectiveness of their beginning reading program from group and individual tests, including standardized and informal types, tests of word-recognition abilities, and others pertaining to oral reading and paragraph reading.[15] Quite a different approach to evaluation is directed toward administrative provision and teacher behavior, e.g., "Is a definite time set aside in the school program for the teaching of reading skills in each grade?" Tormey and Patterson[16] depended largely on student statements and suggestions for evidence of the effectiveness of a developmental reading program. Baron and Bernard[17] emphasized the use of informal evaluation techniques in the classroom. Applying the analysis of co-variance technique, McDonald and Paul[18] evaluated the Cornell University reading program with respect to increase in vocabulary, speed of comprehension, and three measures of academic achievement. In the evaluation of the reading and study program at the University of Missouri, Ranson[19] obtained evidence on the progress and the superiority of those enrolled in the reading course from grade-point averages, re-

[15]Donald D. Durrell, Alice Nicholson, Arthur V. Olson, Sylvia R. Gavel, and Eleanor B. Linehan, "Success in First Grade Reading," *Journal of Education,* CXL (February, 1958), 1–48.

[16]Mary K. Tormey and Walter G. Patterson, "Developmental Reading and Student Evaluation," *Journal of Developmental Reading,* II (Winter, 1959), 30–43.

[17]Denis Baron and Harold W. Bernard, *Evaluation Techniques for Classroom Teachers.* New York: McGraw-Hill Book Co., 1958.

[18]Arthur S. McDonald and Walter Paul, "Teaching College Freshmen To Read," *Phi Delta Kappan,* XXXVIII (December, 1956), 104–9.

[19]Kathleen M. Ranson, "An Evaluation of Certain Aspects of the Reading and Study Program at the University of Missouri," *Journal of Educational Research,* XLVIII (February, 1955), 443–54.

sults of reading rate and comprehension tests converted to *t* scores, and subjective appraisal by students. The effect of one group-therapy session per week in a college reading program was evaluated by means of an elaborate battery which included the *Wechsler Adult Intelligence Scale*, the *Diagnostic Reading Test Battery*, *McDonald-Byrne Reading Versatility Inventory*, *Michigan Vocabulary Test*, several personality tests, and a semistructured diagnostic interview.[20]

CONCLUDING STATEMENT

Evaluation of reading programs is not an end in itself; it is a means to better reading. Consequently, it should be closely associated with instruction. Moreover, evaluative techniques are more likely to be used immediately if evaluation is an intrinsic part of the teaching-learning process. Data should include evidence not only of acquired knowledge and skills but also of the conditions favorable or unfavorable for learning. Probably few teachers view instruction and evaluation as inseparable.

In-service education is needed to help teachers learn convenient ways of evaluating student growth in reading. As the student progresses through school he becomes an active participant in the evaluation process. He should have a clear and concrete conception of his reading goals or purposes and assist in gathering evidence of his progress toward these goals. With the help of the teacher and the stimulus of his fellow students he should overcome difficulties that are hindering his improvement.

We have a long way to go in reaching a scientific, experimental type of evaluation. Progress will be made as standardized tests measure the attainment of broader objectives; informal methods become more precise; and evidence from various sources is analyzed, interpreted, and synthesized more expertly.

The present emphasis of evaluation of reading seems to be on continuity of appraisal and instruction, co-operation or the team approach, and complexity, which recognizes the broad view of reading instruction presented in this yearbook.

[20]Arthur S. McDonald, Edwin S. Zolik, and James A. Byrne, "Reading Deficiencies and Personality Factors: A Comprehensive Treatment," in *Starting and Improving Reading Programs*, pp. 89–98. Edited by Oscar S. Causey and William Eller. Eighth Yearbook of the National Reading Conference. Fort Worth: Texas Christian University Press, April, 1959.

PART THREE

REMEDIAL ENGLISH: READING AND WRITING FOR DISADVANTAGED HIGH SCHOOL AND COLLEGE STUDENTS

As local communities become more and more vocal in demanding that the drop-out rate in high schools be decreased and as demands grow for more liberal open-door admissions policies on the part of community and junior colleges, the need for remedial English, that is, the need for improving reading and writing skills of students, will increase proportionately. Unfortunately the majority of teachers now being assigned to this mushrooming area of instruction are unprepared to teach such a course, and generally they are given little assistance by people in authority who may be ignorant, indifferent, or naive about an area of instruction they find distasteful. As a result, there is a void between progressive social forces operating on the school on the one hand and generally conservative unprepared teachers and administrators unable to respond properly to these forces on the other hand. The selections in this section are meant to help fill that void by giving the educator a clearer picture of what is involved in this critical area of instruction.

Corrective and Remedial Instruction by Robinson, although mainly concerned with reading, serves as a good introduction to this section because it defines terms and problems peculiar to this area and discusses general principles, methods, and materials suitable for this kind of instruction.

Two subsequent articles by Weingartner and Bossone focus on this area of instruction at the high school and junior college levels respectively. Each asks the reader to reconsider the objectives, methods, and content of this course if it is to be a more relevant and successful experience for the remedial student who is compelled to take it.

Knowledge of key issues in this area of instruction will indeed help the teacher be better prepared to teach, but this is not enough; before he can hope to resolve the issues and develop techniques for instruction, the teacher certainly needs information regarding good mental health practices and the development of optimum personality characteristics among remedial English teachers. Klausner provides such information and firmly establishes the dictum that a teacher's personality traits strongly affect the success of a remedial program.

The remainder of the articles in Part Three deal primarily with teaching techniques. Rauch's article establishes some general guidelines and suggests materials for the teacher to utilize in teaching the disadvantaged, in particular the student with reading problems.

Strang reinforces and extends Rauch's thinking by demonstrating how his objectives can be put into practice. She describes specific and effective procedures for teaching reading to adolescents who enter high school "burdened with the weight of six to nine years of failure."

Lighthall emphasizes in her essay, "Procedures and Materials for the Culturally Disadvantaged Reader: In Grades Nine through Fourteen," that the majority of students in these grades are living in what their teachers would consider an "intellectual vacuum" because they have practically no formal background information, as we know it, from which to draw. As a result, she concludes, the teacher has the difficult task of selecting materials that are both fast-moving and adult in content as well as easy to read. Also, the teacher must give an introduction to assignments which includes enough background information so that the assigned material will make sense; and, finally, the teacher must skillfully lead a discussion which points students toward meaningful interpretation and appreciation of the material.

Lighthall's article serves as a bridge to the remainder of the essays in this section, which are concerned primarily with the two-year college remedial student.

Ford's article, *Improving Reading and Writing Skills of Disadvantaged College Freshmen,* points towards implementation of many of the ideas advanced by previous writers. He reports on the success of a three-year project which had as its objectives "(1) to determine whether or not specially selected reading materials and experiences and specially devised methodology can motivate culturally disadvantaged students to improve their reading and writing skills more readily and thoroughly than the normal experiences of a typical Freshman English course; and (2) to determine whether or not culturally disadvantaged students who have improved their reading and writing skills because of effective motivation in the Freshman English course will likewise achieve at a higher level in other academic subjects involving these skills."

The two remaining articles, dealing primarily with remedial writing problems of two-year college students, represent two different approaches to the problem: one highly structured, the other relatively unstructured. Roth and Altshuler argue that, because most remedial students do not know how they are expected to perform, the teacher must assist the student in the pre-writing process, that is, he must "break down the writing process into a series of structured steps." Rubenstein, on the other hand, argues that, because most remedial students "fear and hate English" and have suffered "defeat, discouragement, or at the least boredom," in previous English classes, they should be taught in a relaxed and informal atmosphere which encourages self-expression.

Corrective and Remedial Instruction

HELEN M. ROBINSON

CORRECTIVE or remedial reading is needed whenever the progress of a learner is interrupted or blocked so that his level of reading remains almost static. As a result, his development through reading is also impaired. As the student falls further and further behind his reading potential, he becomes increasingly frustrated in academic areas which require reading, and, as a rule, comes to dislike reading. Consequently he does not rely on reading either for information or for pleasure. Without practice in the use of his reading skills and abilities such a student may actually regress rather than progress. Thus begins the circle of lack of progress, frustration, dislike for reading, and avoidance of reading tasks which, in turn, leads to failure in related areas.

Reading progress may be interrupted at any stage in the sequence of development. The early stages of acquiring sight vocabulary and effective methods of unlocking unfamiliar words are particularly troublesome. However, while word recognition may be learned, the meanings of the words glibly pronounced may not be known. Furthermore, recognition and knowledge of meaning of words do not insure adequate understanding of the text. Some students learn to read but do so laboriously and form immature habits so that they read quite slowly and often read everything at the same pace. It is possible that no difficulties have appeared in any of the foregoing areas but that reading has never become a satisfying experience and is avoided whenever possible. Also, some students learn to read narrative materials but fail to acquire skill in reading materials in the various content areas.

Retardation may be found in one or even all of the foregoing areas; it may be slight or serious. Bond and Tinker categorize retarded readers

From *Development in and through Reading,* the Sixtieth Yearbook of the National Society for the Study of Education, 1961, pp. 357–375. Reprinted with the permission of the National Society for the Study of Education.

as having: *simple retardation* (lacking general maturity); *specific retardation* (deficient in a particular skill or ability); *limiting disability* (deficient in most basic skills which limit over-all progress); and *complex disability* (severely retarded with complicating factors).[1] All groups need special instruction to correct their difficulties. When appropriate help is given early to those in the first three categories, severe retardation, with all of its complications, may be avoided. Instruction given to students with mild and uncomplicated problems is often called "corrective reading." When the difficulty in reading persists and retardation is serious, instruction is usually described as "remedial." However, in the literature, the terms are often interchanged and used to refer to the same types of problems. Regardless of the designation, the aim of instruction is to help the student increase his reading skills and abilities so that he may profit from the developmental program in the classroom which is now his level of expectancy.

Because "corrective" instruction has not been clearly differentiated from "remedial" instruction except possibly by the degree of retardation involved, the remainder of the chapter does not consider the two separately. It will be understood, of course, that the greater amount of retardation requires more extensive diagnosis, more individual instruction, better adapted or especially prepared materials of instruction than do the milder forms of retardation. It is obvious that highly specialized teachers will be involved in these services.

IDENTIFYING RETARDED READERS

The retarded reader, as the term is used in this chapter, is one whose achievement is significantly below his capacity. Studies have shown that many retarded readers have I.Q.'s above 90 when the intelligence test used did not require reading. Based on the writer's experience, the I.Q.'s of retarded readers may range from 70 to more than 180.

The major problem in identifying the retarded reader is to properly assess his capacity for learning to read. Obviously, he can score no better on a group intelligence test requiring reading than he can on a reading achievement test. Yet, nonverbal aspects of intelligence tests are known to have relatively low relationships to reading achievement. Such tests as the *Stanford-Binet Tests of Intelligence* (Houghton-Mifflin, 1937) or the *Wechsler-Bellevue Intelligence Scale for Children* (Psychological Corporation) are among the most dependable. Where neither the time nor trained examiners are available, reading capacity is often estimated

[1] Guy L. Bond and Miles A. Tinker, *Reading Difficulties: Their Diagnosis and Correction,* p. 81. New York: Appleton-Century-Crofts, 1957.

by a listening-comprehension test. Students whose reading scores are significantly lower than their listening scores are most likely to profit from remedial instruction. Those who rank low on both tests probably should be referred for individual psychological examinations.

Achievement in areas which do not require reading, such as arithmetic computation, has often been considered in identifying retarded readers.[2] Good teachers can identify through observation students whose mental alertness and oral insights are of a significantly higher order than are their responses to printed materials.

At the secondary and college levels it becomes increasingly difficult to determine capacity for improvement in reading. Students who are highly motivated are known to compensate for deficiencies and to make some progress in reading. Whenever there is reasonable doubt, the student should be given an opportunity to participate in a reading-improvement program.

A combination of standardized and informal tests, teachers' observations, examination of cumulative records, and an interview with the student should identify the retarded reader with a fair degree of accuracy.

DIAGNOSING DIFFICULTIES IN READING

According to Harris, "diagnosis of reading is a process of systematic exploration of the characteristics and causes of a difficulty in functioning . . ."[3] carried on by a well-informed person who knows the right questions to ask and how to approximate or obtain answers. Bond and Tinker properly advise that a diagnosis should proceed only as far as is necessary to formulate the required remedial programs.[4] They suggest three levels: general diagnosis, analytical diagnosis, and case-study diagnosis. If the first diagnosis does not determine the pupil's needs, the second should be initiated and, if necessary, the third type should be used.

A general diagnosis is usually made by the classroom teacher, assisted by others as necessary. It aims to determine the reading-achievement levels of all pupils, to compare their achievement in reading with that in other areas and with their own capabilities. This step permits the teacher to assess the range of reading achievement, the amount of retar-

[2]Mary C. Austin, "Identifying Readers Who Need Corrective Instruction," in *Corrective Reading in Classroom and Clinic*, chap. iii. Supplementary Educational Monographs, No. 79. Chicago: University of Chicago Press, 1953.
[3]Albert J. Harris, "Diagnosis of Reading Disabilities," in *Corrective Reading in Classroom and Clinic, op. cit.*, p. 81.
[4]Bond and Tinker, *op. cit.*, p. 128.

dation among individuals, and to identify those learners who need ana-lytical diagnosis. There are many instructional problems common to groups within classes and among selected individuals that can be iden-tified by this procedure. General plans for remedial instruction may also be formulated.

Analytic diagnosis requires an understanding of general and specific types of reading problems. A broad framework might include: word recognition, word meaning, comprehension, rates of reading, study skills, and reading interests. A detailed analysis of a retarded reader implies the need for more specific information within each of the foregoing broad areas.

When the difficulty is primarily one of word recognition, range of sight vocabulary and efficiency in various word-attack skills should be explored. When word recognition is adequate, knowledge of the mean-ings of words must be assessed. Retarded readers who recognize words readily and know the meanings may be unable to comprehend larger units. The simplest level of comprehension is that of understanding the literal meaning–understanding the details, the stated main ideas, the conclusions presented by the author, the stated cause-and-effect rela-tionships, and the like. A more advanced level of comprehension in-volves the nonliteral aspects, such as getting implied meanings, deter-mining the tone, mood, and intent of the author, evaluating for accu-racy and adequacy of statements, interpreting the point of view, and comparing the materials presented with other sources.

Reading rates may be rapid for easy and familiar materials read for the general idea, or relatively slow for unfamiliar materials read for depth of meaning or for critical evaluation. Flexibility of rates of read-ing is far more important than single rates, but, to determine the range within which the learner can be flexible, the two extremes need to be ascertained.

Study skills obviously embrace more than reading. Nevertheless, study skills may be needed when a learner plans to make specific use of con-tent materials.[5] Therefore, in addition to the abilities that have been described, the teacher should appraise a student's ability to select and evaluate, to organize, to recall, to locate information, and to follow directions.

Reading interest should never be overlooked because of its relation to reading improvement. Among retarded readers it is necessary to deter-mine the extent of their interest in reading and to develop it system-atically.

[5]Nila Banton Smith, "Teaching Study Skills in Reading, *Elementary School Journal,* LX (December, 1959), 158–62.

The brief description of a general and specific framework for analytic diagnosis should provide for systematic and planned identification of the level of performance in word recognition and meaning, in comprehension, in rates of reading, and in reading-study skills. Furthermore, the detailed analysis within each area enables the teacher to determine specific reading skills and abilities which should be taught. The sequential development of these skills and abilities is essential in correcting any reading difficulty.

Case-study diagnosis is reserved for the more severely retarded readers and those who do not respond to correction. Usually it is made by a remedial reading teacher or in a child-guidance or reading clinic. However, with the assistance of special school personnel, teachers may learn to do limited case studies. A diagnostic plan, which has proved effective for retarded readers from the lower elementary grades to adulthood, includes seven steps: first, compiling a case history from as many dependable sources as possible; second, obtaining objective data concerning the probable capacity of the learner and interpreting the data in the light of observation to secure the best possible estimate; third, appraising the level of oral and silent reading achievement with some estimate of strengths and weaknesses in general areas (it is important to ascertain that the subject is really a retarded reader and not a slow learner); fourth, analyzing the reading problem; fifth, identifying the factors that appear to be interfering with learning to read; sixth, collating and interpreting the data; and seventh, arriving at sound recommendations for remediation.[6]

In this type of diagnosis, appropriate techniques and tests may be selected, depending on the level of attainment in reading and the areas of difficulty in the reading process which are unique to each learner. It is important to continue diagnosis throughout the period of remediation so that plans can be adjusted as the need arises.

The final goal of diagnosis is to point up the best steps to follow in remedial therapy. The diagnostic examination should identify inhibiting factors which should be eliminated if possible. It should determine the stage, in the sequence of each of many reading skills and abilities, at which instruction should begin. Diagnosis should point to appropriate methods and materials for remedial instruction. Armed with the foregoing insights, the good remedial teacher continues diagnosis with each instructional period, making necessary adjustments as new insights are secured.

[6]Helen M. Robinson, "Clinical Procedures in Diagnosing Seriously Retarded Readers," in *Better Readers for Our Times*, pp. 152–56. Edited by William S. Gray and Nancy Larrick. New York: Scholastic Magazine, 1956.

FACTORS THAT INHIBIT READING PROGRESS

During the diagnosis, an effort is made to identify factors which might interfere with progress in reading. Scores of studies have been made of the causes of reading retardation. For the most part, these studies have dealt with learners, from age seven upward, after they have become retarded in reading. While it is quite possible to determine the status of retarded readers at any age and while the anomalies found may, indeed, be interfering with learning at the time of the examination, they may or may not have been present at the time the learner first failed to make progress in reading. Therefore, such anomalies might more appropriately be called inhibiting factors, rather than causes of reading retardation. Among the most prominent factors are: school practices, emotional disturbances, family and peer relationships, visual difficulties, dominance, brain damage, hearing, and general physical or health problems.

School practices.—Reading retardation is often attributed to failure to adjust instruction to the learner, poor teaching, overemphasis on oral or silent reading, too much or too little phonics or other skills, and the like. Teachers' failure to identify and correct particular confusions and to note sequential steps not yet mastered often block further progress in reading. Lack of emphasis on the meaning of what is read and on practice to develop independence are further examples of contributors to reading difficulty. Pupils who change schools frequently and who experience different methods of teaching, those who are frequently absent without help to catch up, and older students who have had no recent instruction may become retarded in reading. Social promotion far beyond reading achievement places a pupil in his age group but does not always make him a part of it. Continuous frustration in using reading as a tool for learning characterizes these retarded readers.

It is especially difficult to assess the relative importance of school practices on groups of retarded readers or on individuals. Cumulative records, case histories, and interviews yield illuminating but inconclusive evidence.

Emotional disturbances.—Both research and experience reveal that many retarded readers show some evidence of emotional disturbance. There is considerable evidence to support the conclusion that emotionally maladjusted pupils make less rapid progress than those who seem to be well adjusted. Furthermore, experience reveals that the smaller the group in which they are taught, the greater the likelihood that the emotionally maladjusted pupil will learn to read. In fact, individual instruction seems to be essential for the maladjusted, and, although it is not intended as psychotherapy, reduction of tension and frustration and better adjustment often result from improved reading.

Of special interest is the fact that, as learners advance in school, the symptoms of maladjustment change. However, each pattern of the learner's reactions is unique, and no general description applies to all.

Research has been reported making use of the projective techniques, paper-and-pencil tests, questionnaires, interviews, and observation. Except in clinics with especially trained personnel, the last two methods appear to be most useful. Harris suggests twelve questions that may serve as a guide to interviews.[7] Strang and others have suggested the use of the incomplete sentence.[8] Probably the best evaluation of emotional problems of retarded readers is made by a sensitive teacher, clinician, or psychologist who observes learners in many situations, wins their confidence and lends a sympathetic ear, and looks beneath surface behavior for motives.

Family and peer relations.—Closely related to personal maladjustment is the problem of home and family status and interrelationships among them. Social class appears to be related to the values placed on reading. Most case study outlines include guides for securing information on the home and interfamily relationships. *The Minnesota Scale of Parents Opinions* (University of Minnesota, Institute of Child Welfare) is an example. Although little research has been done on peer relations, many experts now point to the attitude of young people toward others who enjoy reading. In some instances they are called "squares" or bear other uncomplimentary titles. The effects of these attitudes remain unappraised.

Vision.—Conclusions concerning the relation of visual status to reading success and failure have been conflicting. Most agree that good readers tend to be nearsighted and that poor readers are more likely to be farsighted. Furthermore, lack of co-ordination of the two eyes as measured by tests of phoria, ductions, and binocular reading often characterize the poor reader.[9] Those who find no relationships between groups having visual and reading difficulties suggest that individual learners may be handicapped by vision problems.

To identify vision difficulties, visual screening tests and teacher observations are recommended. The *Keystone Visual Survey Test* with

[7]Harris, *op. cit.*, pp. 272–73.
[8]Ruth Strang, Constance M. McCullough, and Arthur S. Traxler, *Problems in the Improvement of Reading*, p. 245. New York: McGraw-Hill Book Co., 1955.
[9]Helen M. Robinson and Charles B. Huelsman, Jr., "Visual Efficiency and Progress in Learning To Read," in *Clinical Studies in Reading*, II, pp. 31–63. Supplementary Educational Monographs, No. 79. Chicago: University of Chicago Press, 1953.

the Telebinocular (Meadville, Pennsylvania), the Ortho-Rater (Bausch and Lomb, Rochester, New York), the *Massachusetts Vision Test* (Welch-Allen, Auburn, New York), and the *Eames Eye Test* (World Book Company) are examples of commercial visual screening tests.

Observations of symptoms of visual problems necessitate some training of observers. A list of symptoms may be particularly useful.[10]

Hearing.—Loss in auditory acuity, unless severe and binaural, may not be a potent factor in reading retardation. However, high-frequency losses among retarded readers may be undetected and may limit skill in phonetic analysis of words. Deficiencies in both auditory discrimination and memory span may limit reading progress. The degree of these relationships is still under investigation. Experience reveals that retarded readers in upper grades and high school profit by training in auditory discrimination given prior to phonetic instruction.

An audiometer is the most accurate means for identifying loss of auditory acuity. A carefully constructed test of auditory discrimination has been published by Wepman.[11] Others, such as those included in reading readiness tests are rather gross measures.

Dominance.—Intermittently for several decades, association between left or inconsistent hand, foot, and eye preference and reversals in reading has been reported. Neurologists frequently attribute reading difficulty to the lack of a dominant hemisphere in the brain. Considerable disagreement concerning this problem is found in the literature. At least two studies between 1955 and 1960 again point up the frequency of mixed preference[12] and lack of unilateral bodily organization.[13] However, except in seriously retarded readers with difficulty in recognizing words, dominance is probably of less importance than other factors discussed.

Dominance is usually inferred from tests of laterality or preference for hand, foot, ear, and eye. Simple tests of sighting, throwing, kicking, and the like are most frequently used. The *Harris Tests of Lateral Dominance* (Psychological Corporation, New York) is standardized.

Brain damage.—Slow maturation in establishing laterality is often associated with minimal brain damage. While gross neurological difficultes are accompanied by observable physical handicaps, it is difficult to identify minimal damage, even when a specialist examines the

[10]Gertrude Knox, "Classroom Symptoms of Visual Difficulty," in *Clinical Studies in Reading*, II, *op. cit.*, pp. 97–101.
[11]Joseph M. Wepman, "The Relationship between Auditory Discrimination, Speech, and Reading," *Elementary School Journal*, LX (March, 1960), 325–33.
[12]Albert J. Harris, "Lateral Dominance, Directional Confusion, and Reading Disability," *Journal of Psychology*, XLIV (1957), 283–94.
[13]Carl H. Delacato, *The Treatment and Prevention of Reading Problems.* Springfield, Illinois: Charles C. Thomas, 1959.

learner. Special tests, such as those used by Halstead[14] appear to be promising but no such tests are available to teachers for identifying learners with minimal brain damage. Only a reading clinic is prepared to study such severe problems.

Other physical problems.—Smith and Carrigan[15] suggest three dimensions as the cause of reading disability: the presence of a chemical imbalance affecting synaptic transmission in the cortex of the brain, a low concentration level of the two substances, and anxiety. Medical treatment appropriate to each of the three types is recommended. Further research is needed before these factors are considered by remedial teachers.

Multiple factors.—It is generally agreed that no single anomaly is responsible for reading difficulties. This conclusion is supported by studies at the primary-grade level.[16] and of older, severely retarded readers.[17] Unique patterns or constellations of inhibiting factors may be anticipated in dealing with each learner. Identification and correction of inhibiting factors usually prepare the child to learn to read more readily with proper remedial instruction.

REMEDIAL INSTRUCTION

Children and young people with mild retardation in reading usually profit from instruction given in small groups either in the classroom or in a special room, while those who are severely retarded frequently require individual tutoring. Instruction given in the group situation is usually adapted to each individual.

ORGANIZATION OF REMEDIAL CLASSES

At the elementary level.—Different patterns of grouping[18] should permit the classroom teacher to instruct several retarded readers. However, grouping by reading achievement may combine slow learners

14Ward C. Halstead, *Brain and Intelligence: A Quantitative Study of the Frontal Lobes.* Chicago: University of Chicago Press, 1947.
15Donald E. P. Smith and Patricia M. Carrigan, *The Nature of Reading Disability.* New York: Harcourt, Brace & Co., 1959.
16Eve Malmquist, *Factors Related to Reading Disabilities in the First Grade of the Elementary School,* p. 390. ACTA Universitatis Stockholmiensis, Stockholm Studies in Educational Psychology II. Stockholm: Almquist and Wiksell, 1958.
17Helen M. Robinson, *Why Pupils Fail in Reading.* Chicago: University of Chicago Press, 1946.
18John M. Bahner, "Planning for Teaching Different Groups," in *Reading Instruction in Various Patterns of Grouping,* p. 97. Edited by Helen M. Robinson. Supplementary Educational Monographs, No. 89. Chicago: University of Chicago Press, 1959.

with retarded readers. The instructional needs of the two groups are likely to be quite different.

When a remedial teacher is available, small groups of three to eight pupils from different classrooms may be organized according to instructional needs.[19] The classes meet three to five times each week, often at the same time that reading is taught in the classroom. When one pupil progresses so that he can succeed in a classroom group, another is scheduled in his place. Only a few schools report the assignment of 15 or more pupils to a remedial teacher regularly for half-days for a semester.

Summer sessions offering special instruction for retarded readers are being reported increasingly.

At the secondary level.—A few English teachers provide remedial instruction in reading in the classroom, but the most common pattern is assignment of retarded readers to special sections of English or to special reading classes.[20] Credit may or may not be offered for the classes that meet two to five times per week. A reading laboratory, reading center, or reading clinic[21] may offer both group and individual instruction.

At the college level.—As a rule, either the English or the guidance department organizes special classes known as "reading improvement," "basic reading," or "reading laboratory" courses in a room where appropriate materials are available. Attendance may be required or voluntary, and credit in English may be offered. Usually the classes vary from 10 to 20 members; and instruction is provided two or three times each week with added periods when students may come for individual assignments. Severely retarded readers are infrequntly assigned to classes. Referral to reading clinics in the school system or in a college or university is a common practice.

MATERIALS FOR INSTRUCTION

Many types of materials of different levels of difficulty should include basal readers, workbooks, textbooks, special remedial materials, tradebooks, magazines, newspapers, pamphlets, teacher-constructed materials, and instruments.

Some criteria for the selection of materials are:

[19]Mary Lou Austin, "Schedules and Procedures Effective in Teaching Several Groups: In Corrective and Remedial Classes," in *Reading Instruction in Various Patterns of Grouping, op. cit.,* pp. 106–9.
[20]Glenn Myers Blair, *Diagnostic and Remedial Reading,* p. 150. New York: Macmillan Co., 1956 (revised).
[21]*Ibid.,* pp. 161–62.

1. At the beginning of instruction, it is essential that materials be at an appropriate level of difficulty. Since most retarded readers have experienced failure, the material should be sufficiently simple to permit success in order to motivate further efforts.
2. Subsequent materials should increase in difficulty but not too rapidly. It is essential to maintain a delicate balance between success and stimulation to attain higher levels of efficiency.
3. Materials should always be interesting to the reader. Genuine interest generates effort. Frequently materials which satisfy a current need on the part of the learner will be more effective than those related to ultimate goals. For example, one young man made rapid strides in learning to read menus from different restaurants because he wanted to take his girl-friend out to dinner.
4. Materials should provide for sequential development of the skills and abilities shown by the diagnosis to be most deficient and essential for further progress. Frequently the teacher must examine the materials critically rather than rely on the statements made by the publisher. For example, many materials designed to improve comprehension use only questions calling for details. Such materials will have little value if the comprehension difficulty lies in drawing conclusions or in getting implied meanings, for example.
5. Materials should vary in length. Short selections are often more appropriate for initial instruction in how to use particular skills and abilities. Other skills require selections of considerable length. Students should learn to read a whole chapter and a book effectively for different purposes.
6. Materials presenting different approaches to, or views on, a single topic are essential to critical reading, or to organizing reports from different sources.
7. Practice materials should be appropriate to the purpose for which they are used. Furthermore since understanding the author's message is the ultimate goal, it is most helpful if the skills and abilities are practiced in a meaningful setting.
8. For recreational reading, books and magazines with mature interests dealing with characters of ages equal to or older than the learner and having relatively easy vocabularies are needed. Books preferred by retarded readers are often characterized by humor, action, a minimum of description, and a good plot.[22] Science and science fiction have considerable appeal to boys.

[22]Sidney Holmes, "The Selection and Use of Trade Books with Poor Readers," in *Clinical Studies in Reading*, II, *op. cit.*, pp. 112–18.

Basal readers and their accompanying workbooks, other than those previously used, are appropriate for elementary pupils with mild retardation. A wealth of published instructional materials prepared especially for retarded readers at all levels is available,[23] and new ones appear with increasing frequency. The remedial teacher should be familiar with a variety of special materials and should choose the most interesting ones and those best suited to the needs of groups or individuals. Some teachers obtain a large number of single copies of practice materials, then separate, classify, and file the different types of exercises for students' use.

Books and newspapers for recreational purposes may be identified from prepared lists,[24] but it is also important that the teacher be familiar with as many books as possible. The school librarian has an important role in assisting teachers as well as in guiding retarded readers.

Audio-visual instructional materials and mechanical devices can be helpful when they are wisely chosen and properly used.

INSTRUCTIONAL TECHNIQUES

Individuals or groups with mild retardation usually respond well to the techniques used in the classroom developmental reading program if they are adapted to the level at which the student can succeed. Adaptations of classroom methods or special methods may be needed for severely retarded readers.

A prime requisite is the establishment of a climate in which students may feel comfortable. For severely retarded readers especially, errors should be recognized as evidence of needs rather than of failure. At all times the good remedial teacher suggests ways to eliminate errors and appropriate practice for mastering needed skills and abilities. Patience, enthusiasm, and confidence help materially in creating a satisfactory atmosphere for learning.[25]

Principles for teaching.—Several general principles should guide remedial reading instruction:

---

[23]See George D. Spache, *Good Reading for Poor Readers* (Champaign, Illinois: Garrard Press, 1958); Blair, *op. cit.*, chap. viii; and Ruth Strang and Dorothy Bracken, *Making Better Readers*, pp. 348–50 (Boston: D.C. Heath & Co., 1957).
[24]See Spache, *op. cit.*, and Harris, *How To Increase Reading Ability*, *op. cit.*, pp. 592–619.
[25]Russell G. Stauffer, "Basic Problems in Correcting Reading Difficulties," in *Corrective Reading in Classroom and Clinic, op. cit.*, chap. x.

1. Begin at the level at which the student can be successful. Regardless of his age or grade placement, the nonreader must begin at the beginning, both in materials and skills. The junior high school student whose level of development is only at fourth grade must begin at that level.

2. Since the levels of development of different skills and abilities are likely to be uneven in a given individual, emphasis should be placed on those skills and abilities which are most essential to immediate success, seeking always to maintain a balanced program.

3. Diagnosis continues with instruction. Continuous appraisal of progress is essential in order to place proper emphasis on particular skills or abilities. It also enables the teacher to identify areas in which re-teaching is needed. Finally, continuous appraisal enables the remedial teacher to determine when each student is ready to profit from classroom instruction.

4. Compensations should be made for uncorrected, inhibiting difficulties. If possible, such difficulties should be corrected before or in connection with remedial instruction. Otherwise an instructional method would be chosen which permits maximal learning. Thus, a child with uncorrected visual difficulties may need shorter periods of near-point work. Those with emotional problems may require greater amounts of success and encouragement.

5. Success must be demonstrated as early and as consistently as possible. Therefore, every known means for developing successful performance is used by good remedial teachers. Direct assistance is appropriate in the teaching situation to avoid further practice of inefficient skills and abilities. Gradually, as children learn to use the necessary skills, the guidance is diminished.

6. Meaningful practice is essential in improving reading abilities just as it is in learning to swim or to drive a car. The practice must be sufficient to insure smooth and easy performance of the essential skills. For this purpose, much easy reading of the proper type is often used. But study-type reading is also required in many instances. Particularly at the high-school and college levels, laboratory periods are set aside for practice purposes.

7. Records of progress should be kept by both the teacher and the student. Tape-recorded selections of oral reading, charts showing the number of new words recognized, notebooks or card files of a new vocabulary, scores on comprehension questions answered correctly, records of books read, and students' reports on their use of reading in other classes are examples of records that may be used to encourage pupils toward further progress.

8. Independence in using the skills taught should be attained. Teachers

often mistake the pupil's ability to cite the rules for phonetic analysis of words for his facility in the use of the rules. Critical analysis of short articles does not automatically guarantee ability to handle longer selections. Rapid reading of easy, familiar prose does not insure adaptability of rate to purpose and to unfamiliar materials. The ability to complete one carefully selected book may make the learner ready to accept another, while inability to locate a second one may block further reading. Thus, gradually, students must be guided to independence in all reading activities appropriate to the classroom level to which they will return.

9. In choosing methods for teaching retarded readers those most likely to result in successful experiences with reading are most appropriate.

Thus, overemphasis on analysis of words, sentences, paragraphs, or stories may develop power while sacrificing satisfaction. Such learners may never choose to read except when they are with the teacher. Hence, the ability to learn through reading may never be achieved.

In addition to application of the general principles, instruction in particular areas requires specific techniques. Attention is called to the fact that several areas may require instruction at a given time.

Word recognition.—Most learners whose reading scores on standardized or informal tests are below grade 4.0 need instruction to improve sight vocabulary and/or word-attack skills. Regardless of the age of the student, he may need readiness experiences, particularly in auditory and visual discrimination.

Although there are two divergent points of view on whether to begin by building readiness in weak areas or to teach word recognition through avenues of strength, most would agree on attempting to do both simultaneously. However, both the teacher and the student should understand the purpose and goal of each type of instruction.

Three common methods of teaching word recognition are sight, phonic, and kinaesthetic methods. A study by Mills[26] revealed that retarded readers, especially those with different levels of intelligence, learn more effectively by different methods. However, any method which proves to be effective in the initial stages should be supplemented[27] by others to keep the program in proper balance. Furthermore, meaning should be emphasized at all times. Isolated word-study

[26]Robert E. Mills, "An Evaluation of Techniques for Teaching Word Recognition," *Elementary School Journal,* LVI (January, 1956), 221–25.

[27]Helen M. Robinson, "Appraisal of Methods of Teaching Nonreaders and Pupils Who Make Slow Progress in Learning To Read in the Primary Grades," in *The Appraisal of Current Practices in Reading,* pp. 130–36. Edited by William S. Gray. Supplementary Educational Monographs, No. 61. Chicago: University of Chicago Press, 1945.

is meaningless unless the words are taken from context and returned to the same setting.

Meaning vocabulary.—Recognition of words for which students have no meaning concepts fails to increase power of understanding. To develop word meanings, direct experiences are preferable. However, vicarious experiences acquired through the use of films, filmstrips, pictures, and discusison are of value. Frequent opportunities to use the words in reading, speaking, and writing and in many settings are needed. Knowledge of common prefixes and suffixes often permits rapid expansion of meanings. Informal checking of the efficiency of use of the dictionary and instruction as needed is suggested. Experience shows that small group instruction is valuable when each learner stimulates others to understand and correctly use a large variety of word meanings.

Comprehension.—When word recognition and meaning are adequate for what is read, instruction should be directed toward obtaining the literal meanings. As soon as students can recall details, identify stated main ideas, and see their relationships, other literal meanings along with implied meanings may become the focus of instruction.

Guiding questions often serve to direct the students' attention to meaning. The type of question used should be appropriate to the comprehension skill being developed. After the selection is read and the questions are answered, discussion of the answers and how they were secured leads to improved power. The practice of marking wrong answers, without helping students go through the necessary steps to secure correct answers, accomplishes little and is discouraging to the student.

Early selections should be short and appropriate to the types of questions used. Gradually, selections may increase in length, difficulty, or complexity.

Rates of reading.—Only when the foregoing abilities are considerably superior to rate of reading should it be given specific attention. Pupils who have made recent gains in these areas need time and practice before pressures for speed are applied.

Those who habitually read too slowly beyond the primary grades may be motivated to increase their reading speeds through the use of timed exercises, reading "against" the clock, pacing instruments, and films. Easy, interesting materials read for the general ideas or to follow the thread of the story are suggested to develop the most rapid rate. Considerable practice in rapid reading of easy materials is essential if the gains are to be retained. In addition, frequent short periods of reading study-type materials for different purposes, especially for detail and thoughtful reaction, provide practice for acquiring flexibility. The ability to adjust rate to the reader's purpose and the difficulty of the materials presupposes that he has command of a wide range of rates to apply in different situations.

Instruction in any of the four foregoing areas may result in gains in the others, because, as Holmes[28] revealed, certain skills are common to several areas.

Interest in reading.—Few retarded readers enjoy and use reading. Consequently, methods of instruction must be selected with a view to developing this interest. Successful attainment of increased competence in all skills and abilities permits the student to read materials more nearly in harmony with his age and intellectual level, and enables him to pursue topics which are interesting to him.

Frequently the first book must be thin and filled with action or humor. One technique may be to read aloud enough of the story to acquaint the students with the characters (pronounce their names) and the setting. At an exciting part of the story, the teacher may close the book and expect one or several to continue on their own. Careful guidance in the selection of books and informal oral, rather than formal written, reports lead to continued success and pleasure in reading. When a student chooses to read for pleasure, his difficulties are at least partially overcome.

EVALUATION OF PROGRESS

Satisfactory progress for a retarded reader must be evaluated in terms of his reading problems and the stage of his progress. Frequently those who begin with word recognition move slowly at first, but more rapidly later. Students who have difficulty with vocabulary must learn the meanings of many words before a standardized test will reveal measurable progress. However, retarded readers should show more than average progress if they are to be returned to the developmental program.

The methods of evaluation are the same as those for the developmental program and are described in detail in the next chapter. Students who are in special classes should demonstrate sufficient progress to profit by classroom instruction before they are released to the regular classroom. In some instances, it is wise to reduce the number of periods out of the classroom gradually, unless the student is eager to close his special instruction.

[28]Jack A. Holmes, "Factors underlying Major Reading Disabilities at the College Level," *Genetic Psychology Monographs*, XLIX (February, 1954), 1–94.

READING CLINICS

Students who do not profit from remedial instruction in schools, or whose problems are persistent, may be referred to reading clinics. The clinic should have well-trained personnel who can do analytic diagnosis and experiment with a variety of techniques for individual therapy. Furthermore, the reading clinic may call upon trained personnel in allied fields to assist in identifying complicated inhibiting factors.

When the diagnosis is completed and the individual instruction is resulting in rapid progress, the student is usually ready to return to a remedial class in the school.

CONCLUDING STATEMENT

Corrective and remedial reading are seen as one part of the total reading program. Insights gained by the remedial or clinic teacher should be available to the classroom teachers who also deal with related problems. Furthermore, improved classroom practices resulting from co-operative efforts of remedial and classroom teachers should reduce the number of retarded readers. Certainly classroom or subject teachers at all levels should become increasingly adept in discovering those who need diagnosis and remedial instruction before retardation results in loss of interest in reading and concomitant personal problems.

English for What?

CHARLES WEINGARTNER

AS MONTAIGNE put it (quoting Cicero), "Most commonly the authorities of them that teach, hinders them that would learne."[1] If anything, this observation is more appropriate today than it was when first made. It is, also, most suitable as a comment on the teaching of English. The demands of the times have affected the teaching of other subjects in high school in ways that have yet to reach English.

When viewed from this perspective, the problems of disadvantaged youth in the English class are not different in kind from those of other students; they are different in degree, and so they are more visible. Might it be that the problem is less with the students than with "English"? Might it be that the form and substance of the subject need to be examined from the point of view of its ostensible purposes and how, or even whether, these purposes are achieved?

Long before "disadvantaged youth" came to be regarded as a special problem, such an examination produced the following report:

> The pupils could parse and construe sentences and point out the various parts of speech with great facility, repeating the rules of grammar applicable in each case, yet were utterly unable to put this theoretical knowledge to any practical use, as they showed when called upon to write an ordinary English letter. . . .[2]

Colonel Francis Wayland Parker, as a member of the school board in Quincy, Massachusetts, wrote this report in 1873. In *Slums and Suburbs*, James Conant notes that Col. Parker went on to develop procedures which were revolutionary and successful. His innovations led John Dewey to refer to him as "the father of progressive education." Today, "progressive education" is an epithet.

From *Teachers College Record*, December, 1965, pp. 201–206. Reprinted with the permission of *Teachers College Record*.

At the same time, Francis Keppel, United States Commissioner of Education, notes:

> Those who cheer, with good cause, the new problem-solving approach to physics by Dr. Jerrold Zacharias or the new approaches to learning by Dr. Jerome Bruner often fail to realize that they have brilliantly developed what John Dewey conceived a generation ago.[3]

SYMPTOMS AND CAUSES

It is curious that so much of the dialogue about what must be done in English consists of just so much dead rhetoric. It makes about as much sense as talking of new ways to refurbish a steamboat for a trip to the moon.

Since Col. Parker reported what he observed about the lack of relationship between the "naming of the parts" approach to the study of our language and the ability of students to write it, hundreds of studies have been made which simply reaffirmed his conclusions. The *Encyclopedia of Educational Research* reports virtually nothing else. Yet, right at the present moment, the kind of sterile ventriloquizing of rules Col. Parker succeeded in eliminating in 1873 in Quincy consumes an inordinate portion of time in English classes. It is not uncommon to find, in the face of alarm about student deficiencies in writing, an increase in the amount of time spent in this manner in an attempt to solve the problem. We fail, when we do this, to distinguish between symptoms and causes. How much we *fail to realize.*

We fail to realize that we need not just more old answers to old questions, but, rather, some new questions which will permit new answers and, so, new solutions. It may be that the emergence of a concern for disadvantaged youth can help to further the search for a new English, relevant to our times, by making ways of helping students to learn the focus of attention. It is, alas, quite common to hear English teachers refer to disadvantaged youth in the following terms: "They just don't want to learn." "They just aren't interested." "They just don't have the IQ." "They just don't have the verbal ability." "They don't learn it no matter how many times I teach it."

Notice that the onus is always on the student. *What* is it that they do not want to learn? *What* is it that they are not interested in? How can something be *taught* if no one learns it? Might some of the causes of the problem reside in the fact that much of what passes for "English" is simply irrelevant?

Might it be said that we should be asking how a subject concerned primarily with the role of language and literature in human affairs can best be approached to permit student interest to play a role so that learning, useful learning, can occur? Plato noted that ". . . education can accomplish its goal only if reason has an adequate emotional base."[4] The adequacy of such an emotional base must be judged from student response. To date, such a mode of judgment is rare. The rarity with which such student response is included in determining the *what* and *how* of English is in no small measure a result of the fact that readers of English are largely uninformed about:

1. the psychology of learning,
2. the psychology of communication,
3. the significance of scientific knowledge about language, and
4. the significance of cultural changes consequent to technological change.

Such awareness, however acquired, could produce the changes in attitude toward and about the teaching of English that are needed before such teaching can become relevant. One change which might help would be for teachers of English to hold less "moral" attitudes about language. In particular, they might hold a more flexible position reflected in less rigid adherence to unrealistic and unreasonable standards which they, the teachers, characteristically insist upon. Commonly ignored is the fact that students do use language effectively in various ways during virtually every waking moment, and that students are members of a culture. It is merely not the culture of the teacher. Adolescents, and particularly the disadvantaged, may seem to lack verbal ability in the English class because just about every attempt to speak or write is made in the face of the threat of correction commonly made in a manner intended to disparage or ridicule rather than to help.

The most usual kind of attention that student writing, for example, gets from the English teacher is sharply negative: the red pencil is used to slash away at "errors" with a vengeance appropriate to the Old Testament. In this process, we fail to realize that a useful distinction can be made between writing and editing, and that while it is the students' editing ability that is being evaluated (rather than, as is supposed, their writing ability), students have little or no training in editing. The distinction between these two quite different abilities is obscured by what is called composition.

Beyond this is the fact that students seldom have an opportunity to engage in an attempt at real communication by writing about something of significance to themselves for some real purpose to someone whose response they seriously wish to affect. They are doomed to "writing writing," usually, for its own sake, which turns out to mean for a grade. In the face of all this, their lack of writing ability should come as no surprise.

SELF-FULFILLING PREDICTIONS

Much has been said and written about the difference between the middle-class culture of teachers, on the one hand, and the, apparently, nonmiddle-class culture of students, particularly the disadvantaged, on the other. The most critical difference seems to lie in the teachers' perception of and attitude toward these students.[5] To put it simply, the teacher's lot is not a happy one. The English teacher especially seems condemned to chronic frustration as a consequence of adherence to expectations which cannot reasonably be realized. The teacher, as is well known, responds most favorably to students who are neatly dressed, obedient, and who are not noticeably "different." Since most English teachers are women, girls are generally favored over boys. Girls like English much more than boys do. Disadvantaged students, especially boys, most commonly fail to meet these expectations of the teacher, and so they are vulnerable to her disfavor. They are used as "whipping boys," on whom the teacher works out the accumulated frustrations of the job. They have little defense except to drop out of school, and about 1,000,000 a year do just that. Indications are that the English class triggers the drop-out.[6] As Edgar Z. Friedenberg points out, "The most tragic thing that happens to lower-class youngsters in school is that they learn to accept the prevailing judgment of their worth."[7]

INDIVIDUAL DIFFERENCES AND
ASSEMBLY-LINE PROCEDURES

With all the talk about individual differences, a careful look at the school as a process quickly reveals that the premium is much more on making students alike than it is on helping them to make the most of their individuality. They are all expected to learn the same thing in the same way at the same time. The pressure is great to make them into standardized, interchangeable parts. The idea of standardized parts permitted a tremendous breakthrough in assembly-line production, but when it is used as a basic metaphor for dealing with human beings it leaves much to be desired. Indeed, as experiments with the ungraded high school suggests, the egg-crate or lock-step arrangement found in most high schools may be one of the major causes of the "problem of disadvantaged youth."

But to illustrate again that the problem is not peculiar to the disadvantaged, and that it may lie more in the structure of the school and the curriculum than in the student, it is worth noting that there are various indications of student discomfort in the face of increasingly dehumanized and mechanized approaches to schooling. The protests of university students about this are increasingly audible. And there is the emergence of the "nego."

It was the boys at Exeter who gave the name "negoism" to the most virulent form of . . . [student] pessimism. This is not crackpot thinking nor is it isolated. It is a fair sample of a deep pessimism prevalent among boys at some of America's finest prep schools. "You don't want to become just a man without a thought—refusing to realize why you are desperate," said a 17 year old at Exeter. "If you face the tough part, and question, and hurt with the questioning, maybe you become someone able to think deeply and clearly. . . . Perhaps my only real doubt is for the survival of sweetness—the survival of warmth and feeling. Is that disallowed nowadays?"[8]

The disadvantaged find Holden Caulfield[9] no less a spokesman for themselves than do the boys at Exeter. They are engaged, just as Holden was, in a search for meaning, and they do not know how to search. We may need something other than a Horn Book approach to "inculcating values." The question is, "What changes in the purposes, functions, and procedures of the school, and particularly in the teaching of English, might be made to help these youth come to grips with their most immediate concerns in ways that permit some resolution?"

AN ECUMENICAL SPIRIT IN EDUCATION

That there needs to be a kind of ecumenical spirit, a willingness to reassess the relevance of English to the world in which we are all attempting to live, generated among those charged with the responsibility for deciding the what and how of it, is coming to be recognized. George H. Henry suggests the need for a "sociology of English." He notes:

Many mathematicians and scientists . . . are perceiving the sociology of their educational task. From Woods Hole, in late 1959, at the Conference on Fundamental Processes in Education sponsored by the National Academy of Science, comes this report: "The processes of education involve, then, four components: a curriculum, the methods of teaching, the context in which the teaching occurs, and, centrally, the teacher.' The word "context" here means the forces in the culture that play upon the teaching of mathematics and science—something that few English departments now seriously study or even recognize. What irony that science must remind English departments that English is not an island! In contrast to the scientists, the Modern Language Association has not yet come to this realization.[10]

One cannot help but wonder how it was that our scientific colleagues omitted the learner from their list of ingredients in the processes of instruction. Still, the NAS conference signals an ecumenical spirit in education, even if it is not yet shared by those concerned with the teaching of English.

REASSESSING PURPOSES AND PROCEDURES IN THE TEACHING OF ENGLISH

This, however, is not to say that pleas have not been made for reassessing the *raison d'etre* of English. In his presidential address to the National Council of Teachers of English in 1962, G. Robert Carlsen[11] called for a substantive shift away from the teaching of English as facts to be memorized to the active involvement of students in the processes of inquiry. His concern was the student and what happens to the student. It seems clear that Carlsen's remarks were provoked by his awareness of the fact that traditional objectives for the teaching of English were not and are not being achieved. Beyond that, he clearly articulated an awareness of the need to include the student in decisions being made about the teaching of English.

One of the most significant attempts ever made to assess ways of teaching literature in high school was in a book by George W. Norvell,[12] while he was supervisor of English for the State of New York. His purpose was to identify better means of dealing with literature. It is well worth the time it might take for an English teacher to read. In it, Norvell states:

It is the well-nigh universal practice in American public schools for a part, at least, of the program in literature to consist of selections studied in common . . . this plan has been vigorously assailed, particularly on the grounds that the reading materials used [selected by teachers and course-of-study makers] were frequently seriously disliked by a considerable percentage of the pupils. The result, it was pointed out, was a disgust with the literature rather than a love for it.[13]

. . . the differences between the interest scores of superior, average, and weak pupils in the same school grades is so small as to be negligible.[14]

Norvell, too, points to the fact that the student must be carefully considered when someone is planning educational activities intended to affect him. It seems that Plato was right all along.

Norvell's report includes a variety of interesting speculations as to what might be done to minimize alienating students while ostensibly teaching them literature. Could it be that the *what* of a subject is inseparable from the *how* of its being taught? Could it be that all of the strident talk about *content* on the one hand and *methods* on the other obscures the issue by trying to separate the dancer from the dance? In his recommendations, for example, Norvell states: "It may well be that . . . the teacher's knowledge of what to *refrain* from recommending is more important than his actual recommendations . . . in view of the high standing both artistically and in children's favor of many modern selections, the use of a large portion of modern literature seems justified."[15]

In the same direction, Frank G. Jennings candidly suggests, "We may have to scuttle some of the shabbily genteel lesson plans we have built . . ."[16] Dora V. Smith and Paul Witty, reviewing studies relating to the effects of the teaching of literature, report, ". . . investigation reveals the need for recognizing the interests of students and attempting to provide a more suitable and varied reading program."[17]

As was previously mentioned, we must note that this problem of the irrelevance of the *content* of English is not peculiar to the disadvantaged. That English has been "out of joint" for some time, and is increasingly so, can hardly be gainsaid.

With the urgings for including modern literature which interests students in a course in English, it should be recognized that the primary literary experience for them, as well as for our society at large, is through television and film, rather than through print. We can ill afford to ignore this fact. Marshall McLuhan,[18] professor of English at St. Michael's College, University of Toronto, refers to the schools as "the first line of defense against media fall-out." It would be naive of English teachers to dismiss too quickly the possibility that he may be right.

For better or for worse (it may depend on whether we attend to McLuhan), the electronic media comprise the essential vicarious experience of adolescents, disadvantaged or not. The Beatles, lest we forget, were recently knighted, much to the dismay of some whose values most closely parallel those of teachers of English.

THE HEART OF THE MATTER

The central problem for all of us is that of developing strategies for survival. This accrues from the central fact of our time: change— massive, rapid, unceasing, accelerating change. As a central strategy, we need to develop ways of assigning viable meanings to the products of the change we constantly confront.

The theater of our time is the "theater of the absurd." Why absurd? What is absurd? It is that to which it is difficult, or impossible, to assign a rational meaning. The theater of the absurd, along with the literature of the absurd, reflects the world of the absurd in which we are all try- ing, with increasing difficulty, to survive. What could be more absurd than the mosaic of incongruously juxtaposed reports in a daily news- paper? We have difficulty developing a posture from which to view the world about us with some equilibrium, for we lack strategies for assigning meanings to the unceasing swirl of happenings about us. And this problem, too, is by no means confined to the disadvantaged.

A ROLE FOR THE SCHOOL

Edgar Z. Friedenberg suggests a role for the school in dealing with this problem:

> The school exists fundamentally to provide the young people of a com- munity . . . with a fairly tough and firmly fixed philosophical apparatus for making a certain kind of sense out of their lives, and communicating with other people who may be assumed to have basically similar apparatus . . . [the school's] lack of philosophical structure I should judge to be the chief obstacle to the development of high-school curricula which would use our best cultural resources to help students to make sense out of the lives they actually lead.[19]

What better cultural resources could we use for this purpose than language and literature? Yet, in no quarter of the school "box" is a philosophy (compare with George H. Henry's sociology) for this pur- pose more lacking than in the teaching of English. In a discipline cen- trally concerned with the study of language, the philosophy would most appropriately have at its core strategies for assigning meaning, since nothing is more critical to our survival as individuals and as a group than this.

A ROLE FOR ENGLISH

The seeds of such philosophy can be found, perhaps, in the comments above. Indeed, they may already have begun to sprout. In a recent observation, G. Robert Carlsen wrote:

We all know that a minor revolution has taken place in the teaching of science and mathematics in American schools. Those of us in English suddenly find ourselves faced with a desperate need to catch up. But our attempts to imitate the revolutions in science and math have been based on inadequate understanding of the changes in those fields. While these two areas have changed their content to some extent, they have changed their methodology to a greater extent. The mathematicians and scientists saw clearly that the way a student studies in the subject is fundamental if he is to learn to think within the subject. In English most of our efforts have been in the area of content to be taught. It is time that methods of teaching English again become a major concern within our profession. . . . Methods can usually be described as a choice of one of three roles the teacher selects for himself and his students. . . . Role I: The Teacher Tells —The Student Memorizes and Stores. . . . Role II: The Teacher Molds— The Student Conforms. . . . Role III: The Teacher Stimulates—The Student Teaches Himself. . . . Plato defines the teacher as an "intellectual midwife." . . . My feeling is strong that English at present is structured to use *telling* and *molding* about 95 percent of the time. We have not really learned as yet how to set up situations in which our students are stimulated and permitted to make discoveries on their own. . . . Inquiry and discovery are the very essence of the reading of literature, yet here too, we as teachers have substituted didacticism and molding.[20]

For reasons that are clear and reasonable, the disadvantaged simply resist this didacticism and molding. The nondisadvantaged merely acquiesce.

Anticipating Carlsen's concern, Arthur W. Foshay reminded us:

Any discipline is a way of knowing—a way of grasping reality. Disciplines differ from one another according to the phenomena they purport to deal with and according to the rules of evidence they employ. By using the rules of a discipline, one may make meaning out of the phenomena it deals with. . . . It is in the making of knowledge that a discipline comes to life, and it is therefore central to the quality of good teaching that the student be drawn into the making of knowledge, according to the nature and rules of the discipline he is trying to learn. In brief, the purpose of studying . . . any discipline is to learn to think the way people in the discipline do

. . . the whole tendency of the pedagogic tradition is toward following the book. We have tried to remove all uncertainty from subject matter. In doing so, we have repeatedly taken the life out of it. In the name of teaching a corpus, we have taught a corpse, and called it a course.[21]

ENGLISH FOR NOW

As was noted at the outset, talking about the problem of disadvantaged youth may be a less fruitful way of getting at needed changes in the teaching of English than talking about the problem of making English relevant. What we have before us is the prospect of restructuring English in a manner which permits the student—disadvantaged or otherwise—to enter with *his* emotional and intellectual experience to participate in inquiries into how language works and what differences it makes, as well as into the literature of the world around him, whether it is in print or some other medium, and in the process discover ways to assign viable meanings to the otherwise meaningless.

It is probably apparent that an attempt is being made here to translate some of the suggestions made by Jerome Bruner into procedures that can be useful in the teaching of English. Neil Postman and Charles Weingartner[22] have described briefly, but with some illustrations, how students can participate and have participated fruitfully in English classes conducted primarily in an inductive manner. The students are not only permitted but encouraged to bring to the inquiry their experience and their meaning as the most essential part of the enterprise. Pursuing inquiries into language, they behave as linguists behave. Inquiring into literature, they behave as literary critics behave. In this latter dimension, the work of I. A. Richards[23] is heavily drawn upon.

This is not studying language and literature for its own sake. As I. A. Richards points out:

. . . all the questions that matter in literary history and criticism take on a new interest and a wider relevance to human needs. In asking how language works we ask about how thought and feeling and all the other modes of the mind's activity proceed, about how we are to learn to live and how that greatest thing of all, "a command of metaphor"—which is great only because it is a command of life—may best, in spite of Aristotle, "be imparted to another." But to profit we must remember with Hobbes that "the scope of all speculation is the performance of some action or thing to be done," and, with Kant, that "We can by no means require of the pure practical reason to be subordinated to the speculative, and thus to reverse the order, since every interest is at last practical, and even that of the speculative reason is but conditional, and is complete only in its practical use."[24]

It might be said about disadvantaged youth that they agree with Hobbes and Kant. They have no taste for what is not clearly relevant and practical. We might learn something from them.

SUMMARY

In sum, then, what is suggested here is that:

1. the "problem of disadvantaged youth" may reside more in the what and how of English than in the student;
2. there are alternatives to placing the onus on the student;
3. one alternative is to reexamine the reasons given for including English in the curriculum in the first place;
4. such a reexamination may suggest the need for increasing the relevance of English;
5. one possible way to do this is to shift from a closed body of content to be covered, to an open inquiry into language and literature through which students can address themselves to cogent questions with some prospect of developing their own answers;
6. in such a process they can learn how to learn, which is to say that they can learn strategies for assigning viable meanings to the otherwise meaningless.

It is possible to do this. The longer we wait, the longer the disadvantaged, along with everyone else, will be without means of making sense out of their lives.

REFERENCES

[1] Quoted in Arthur W. Foshay, "What Is the Message?" *Saturday Review*, February 13, 1960, p. 60.
[2] Quoted in Percival M. Symonds, *What Education Has to Learn from Psychology*, Bureau of Publications (Teachers College, Columbia University, 1961), p. 42, from *Francis Wayland Parker: His Life and Educational Reform Work* (New York: E. L. Kellogg and Company, 1900), p. 18.
[3] *New York Times*, October 25, 1964, p. E9.
[4] The Republic, 536–537.

5 Frank Riessman, *The Culturally Deprived Child* (New York: Harper and Row, 1962), p. 81.
6 Carl L. Byerly, "Pupils Who Do Not Respond," *Educational Leadership*, February 1963, p. 312.
7 Edgar Z. Friedenberg, *The Vanishing Adolescent* (New York: Dell Publishing Co., 1959), p. 117.
8 "The Voice of the Nego," *Life*, Vol. 52, No. 21, May 25, 1962, p. 8.
9 J. D. Salinger, *The Catcher in the Rye* (Boston: Little, Brown and Co., 1951).
10 George H. Henry, "English, the Life of English, and Life," *English Journal*, February 1963, p. 84.
11 G. Robert Carlsen, "The Way of the Spirit and the Way of the Mind," *English Journal*, February 1963.
12 George W. Norvell, *The Reading Interests of Young People* (Boston: D.C. Heath, 1950).
13 George W. Norvell, *ibid.*, p. 83.
14 George W. Norvell, *ibid.*, p. 48.
15 George W. Norvell, *ibid.*, p. 85.
16 Frank G. Jennings, "Literature for Adolescents—Pap or Protein," *English Journal*, December 1956, p. 530.
17 Dora V. Smith and Paul Witty, *NSSE 47th Yearbook*, Part 2 (1948), p. 20.
18 Marshall McLuhan, *The Gutenberg Galaxy* (University of Toronto Press, 1962), and *Understanding Media* (New York: McGraw-Hill, 1964).
19 Edgar Z. Friedenberg, *op, cit.*, p. 75.
20 G. Robert Carlsen, *"How Do We Teach?"* *English Journal*, May 1965, p. 364.
21 Arthur W. Foshay, *op. cit.*, p. 58.
22 Neil Postman and Charles Weingartner, "The New English—A Forward Look," (pamphlet, New York: Holt, Rinehart, and Winston, Inc., 1965).
23 I. A. Richards, *Practical Criticism, Principles of Literary Criticism, Interpretation in Teaching*.
24 I. A. Richards, *The Philosophy of Rhetoric* (New York: Oxford University Press, Galaxy Book, 1965), p. 95.

Remedial English in Junior Colleges

AN UNRESOLVED PROBLEM

RICHARD M. BOSSONE

THE JUNIOR COLLEGE, the stepchild of education in the past, is rapidly becoming the favorite son. It has grown in number of institutions from 18 in 1904 to approximately 800 today and currently enrolls more than one million students. It is continuing to grow and multiply and by 1970 should become the largest member of the academic family. However, its growth is not without the usual growing pains. Like an adolescent it is struggling to find its true identity, and like most adolescents it is discovering that this is a confusing, contradictory process.

The junior college is a relatively new kind of institution that is neither secondary nor higher education—it is between them with a foot in each camp. One foot stands firmly on ground labeled "less than college-grade programs" and the other foot on ground labeled "lower division work for students who expect to transfer to higher institutions." Such a comprehensive objective, offering two major curriculums (terminal and transfer) plus myriad community services, is not without problems and headaches. The fault is not so much that the junior college offers two major curricular selections but that, first, the students are usually unrealistic about their curricular preference (on the average, two-thirds profess to be transfer students, yet only one-third do transfer) and, second, the teachers are usually more partial to the transfer program than to the terminal program.

Many of these students who are unrealistic about their curricular

From *College Composition and Communication,* May, 1967, pp. 88–93. Reprinted with the permission of the National Council of Teachers of English.

217

preference are attracted to the junior college by its open-door policy and through their own desire for status, coupled with immature fantasies about college being a lot of fun. This situation is further complicated by the carry-over of immature high school attitudes, by half-hearted class attendance, and by the naive belief on the part of the students that they can hold a full-time job and have time and energy left to study. In addition to this, approximately 70 percent of these students reflect academic and linguistic deficiencies which they optimistically believe will be remedied immediately. Unfortunately, there is no magic or panacea to resolve their problems or deficiencies. There is only the unguided, haphazard remedial treadmill, which offers few remedies and many failures.

Add to this the large number of disoriented teachers who must instruct these students: teachers whose professional training is usually limited to the study of literature, not the fundamentals of English which they must teach; teachers who do not feel it is important to offer remedial work; teachers who are generally more in sympathy with the transfer students, who are not representative of the majority of students; teachers who, because of the large size of classes, are unable to give students the individual help they need. And add to this, administrative indifference in an institution which operates primarily for expediency in dealing with masses of students and which does little to encourage research and experimentation in the area of remedial English.

The end result of all this is an unresolved problem, an academic ulcer if you will, which threatens to grow worse and make all of those involved more uncomfortable as enrollments increase and as the four-year institutions tend to leave the problem more and more with the junior colleges.

That this is often an unresolved problem in the junior colleges is borne out in a recent study by the author entitled *Remedial English Instruction in California Public Junior Colleges: An Analysis and Evaluation of Current Practices.*[1] The objectives of the study were as follows:

1. To discover on what basis junior college students are being classified as remedial English students and what the institution's general policy is regarding remedial English.
2. To discover what junior college remedial English teachers are doing in their classes, what their attitudes are regarding the subject, and what they know about their students' abilities, interests, and problems.

[1] (Sacramento, 1966).

3. To discover what junior college remedial English students' attitudes are toward English and what they consider to be their interests and problems in English.
4. To make recommendations for improving the effectiveness of junior college remedial English classes.

Though many California public junior colleges have more than one level of remedial English, this study was concerned only with the remedial English class which the student must take if he fails the English placement examination and which he must pass to be admitted to English 1A (or equivalent transfer course).

To obtain data needed to accomplish the first three objectives, the investigator chose twelve out of the seventy-five California public junior colleges which were representative of various factors (rural-urban, geographical location, size, age, socio-economic) to insure an adequate sample and cross-section of personnel and students.

The investigator visited these junior colleges during the Fall semester, 1965, to talk with personnel and students connected with the remedial English program, to obtain course outlines and samples of students' writings, and to administer three questionnaires: the first was administered to the chairmen of English departments, the second to at least four teachers of remedial English on each campus, and the third to at least 100 day students currently enrolled in remedial English classes on each campus. Where a class had fewer than 25 students because of absences or withdrawals, the investigator visited additional classes on that campus to insure involving the maximum number of people. The total number of people involved was as follows: 12 chairmen of English departments, 56 teachers of remedial English, and 1239 students.

Generally the data in this study indicate that remedial English classes in California public junior colleges are not very effective and are in need of reappraisal by all concerned with improving the teaching of English in the two-year college. Undoubtedly there are many contributing factors that make these classes ineffectual, and this study has noted only a limited number of these factors; however, they are important and must be considered if we are to rectify this unpleasant state of affairs. The factors noted in this study are as follows:

1. Questionable placement procedures
2. Lack of communication between those involved in testing or counseling and guidance and those involved in the teaching of remedial English.

3. Oversized classes and overworked teachers
4. Inadequately trained teachers and generally unenthusiastic teachers
5. Outdated and superficial course outlines
6. Vague objectives
7. Lack of agreement about what should be emphasized in the course
8. Lack of suitable instructional materials
9. Confusion about methodology
10. Lack of knowledge about students' reading and writing abilities and interests
11. Lack of knowledge about students' personal problems, limitations, and preferences for methods and materials
12. Variety of subjective grading standards
13. High percentage of student failures
14. Insufficient experimentation.

No doubt there are other contributing factors but the above should be enough to make one realize it is imperative that we set our dimensions of thought regarding this problem of improving remedial English instruction on a research basis rather than on an intuitive basis.

Every year the problem of what to do about remedial English cries out louder for attention; and yet, in our period of the "Great Society," when education beyond high school is becoming a right, not a privilege, and when by 1970, seventy-five percent of all students who first encounter higher education will do so through a junior college, this problem continues to be met with apathy, withdrawal or disdain. In short, it is left unresolved.

Such a serious problem has been left unresolved simply because the organization and composition of the academic world insures that the onus of failure falls on the student and not on the institution or teacher. However, if administrators and teachers were to organize remedial instruction to insure learning, this might not be the case; that is, if teaching became less of a self-hypnotic affair concerned only with what teachers feel students must learn and became equally concerned with what students want to learn and can learn, we might begin to resolve the problem. As a step in this direction educators might do well to consider some of the following suggestions for working with remedial English students.

First, educators must intelligently and comprehensively identify the remedial student, that is, evaluate his present development in each of the major language skills through standardized and informal tests so that each student's needs can be properly determined. Remediation must not precede adequate diagnosis. If the chief function of remediation is to insure proper learning, then it becomes increasingly important that plans for remediation be thoughtfully conceived and executed, and this cannot be done without a diagnosis of the individual's problems and needs.

Through records and reports, as well as interviews, the instructor should learn as much as he can about the student—biologically, psychologically, and environmentally. Granted the instructor may not have the opportunity to learn all he should about the student from such a vantage point, but he should be knowledgeable about the general language characteristics of such a student. Instructors cannot excuse their ignorance here, for this is clearly their job. Unfortunately, too many instructors are ignorant of the general language characteristics of the remedial student and, as a result, they fail to engage in teaching that recognizes and accepts the limitations of such a student or is geared to his level of ability. The end result is frustration and failure for both parties.

Often the remedial student already has too long a history of failure and cannot afford to have another similar experience. Instructors should recognize that the reason these students generally tend to be less motivated is simply because they have a long record of failure and that they need an opportunity to succeed. These students generally cannot be motivated or made receptive to learning unless they experience some success; therefore, it is imperative that a teacher insure this. In short, the teacher is the mediator who must see that diagnostic and motivation complement each other; for diagnosis makes possible effective teaching, and motivation makes possible efficient learning.

To insure success or sustained motivation it is essential to formulate specific objectives and to employ methods and materials that are appropriate for such linguistically handicapped students. And the instructor cannot do this without being knowledgeable about the following general language skills of these remedial students, as well as being knowledgeable about general principles for remedial teaching. For sake of convenience let us divide these language skills into four areas: listening, speaking, reading and writing.

In the area of listening, the junior college remedial English student has a short attention span. He tends to lose the gist of long lectures, to be unable to select important details from what he hears, and to forget what he hears.

The teacher needs to vary classroom activities and assist the student in taking notes, not only encouraging him to listen attentively but also outlining on the blackboard the key ideas being presented. This student needs to have his listening experiences reinforced by visual experiences whenever it is possible. Further, the teacher needs to remember that his own rate of speech and presentation should be determined by the rate of the student's listening ability.

In the area of speaking, although the junior college remedial English student depends almost entirely upon oral communication, he is not fluent; generally this student has an impoverished vocabulary, repeats phrases and expressions, speaks in elliptical phrases, employs simple or immature sentence structure, enunciates poorly, and reflects a lack of social poise.

The teacher should provide many varied opportunities for the student to explain and discuss his ideas so that the student may have an opportunity to grow in speaking power and the teacher may have an opportunity to continually diagnose and evaluate the student's oral work. Tape recording of class discussions and individual presentations should be utilized during the semester in order that the individual's progress can be noted.

In the area of reading, the junior college remedial English student tends to have an inadequate vocabulary, as well as the inability to grasp the central idea of long passages and supporting ideas. This is also complicated by the fact that he cannot concentrate very well.

The teacher needs to introduce carefully new words to the student before a selection is read by presenting them in context on the blackboard. This student needs help in not only grasping the meaning of the word but also perceiving and retaining the visual image of the word. Comprehension skills also need to be taught by building a background for the selection to be read and by directing the student's thinking via questions to be answered and points to be understood. This student cannot engage in much abstract reasoning; therefore, he needs a great deal of guidance in conceptualizing, whereby main ideas and subordinate ideas are noted and proper conclusions are drawn. Above all else, the teacher should assign selections that are short and of high interest to the student. No pressure should be made to increase the student's rate of reading speed, for he can only read as fast as he can think.

In the area of writing, the junior college remedial English student has problems with correct usage, avoiding gross errors (such as sentence fragments, lack of agreement between subject and verb and noun and pronoun, and inconsistency in verb tense), mechanics (particularly spelling), organizing ideas, and maintaining interest in the kind of writing assigned to him.

The teacher needs to give this student an opportunity through imitation and action to develop effective and acceptable patterns of usage.

(It is highly doubtful that traditional instruction in traditional grammar will do this kind of student any good.) Pattern drills used by foreign language teachers might serve as examples of the kind of work in which the student might engage. Oral practice of correct usage and the avoidance of gross errors should precede written drills.

Rules involving mechanics should be sparingly used and should be carefully selected, and, most important, they need to be illustrated and demonstrated repeatedly in meaningful contexts. Spelling should be taught on an individual basis with each student being encouraged to perceive, understand, and pronounce accurately those words he needs to write. Long spelling lists and complicated spelling rules should be avoided.

The teacher needs to help this kind of student devise sentences which reflect clear thinking and paragraphs which reflect unity, coherence, and adequate development. Teaching the five basic sentence patterns and the rhetoric of the paragraph as set forth by the transformational-generative grammarians may prove to be helpful.

The teacher needs to help the student organize his writing assignments by giving him models to follow; the teacher initially needs to outline the work for him, suggesting main ideas and subordinate ideas to be expressed which will serve as topic sentences for the paragraphs. Writing assignments should be kept short, frequent, and suitable. The student should not be rushed too early into writing expository essays; before he is asked to engage in abstracting about someone else's complex abstractions, he should be made ready by the writing of personal letters and by the writing of his own experiences and thoughts.

To become more familiar with the learning principles that are applicable to remedial English students, teachers would do well to borrow basic tenets of programmed learning: (1) The pursuit of knowledge is an activity. If the student is to learn the material, he should respond to, participate in, or interact with it at every step. (2) Efficient learning requires that the student respond correctly, being guided towards proficiency by every technique and trick available to the teacher. Errors never indicate progress. They are merely a sign of inadequate teaching. (3) The material must be presented in a rational and cumulative manner, dependent on both the structure of the subject matter and the ability of the student to grasp it. (4) For effective learning, the student must be able to evaluate his own progress by being provided with knowledge of results immediately after each response.

If the public junior college were to be judged by a student persistence rate, we would be alarmed—indeed shocked—by the great percentage of students who drop by the wayside. Although it may be true that a junior college student withdraws for many reasons, we must still ask if one of the major reasons for his withdrawal may not be ineffectual or unsuitable instruction. In the case of the remedial English student, one could well wager after reading the above study that the answer is "yes." Quite simply the public junior college does not appear to be achieving one of its major objectives: to offer effective remediation to those students who come from a limiting environment with linguistic handicaps.

And yet, ironically enough, the junior college prides itself on being an open-door college which emphasizes good teaching. If this is so, then it has a definite responsibility to provide the best instruction to all those it admits. And further, if the junior college, the largest member of the academic family, is to achieve its goal of good teaching, it must develop the courage to admit what is ineffectual, the courage to invite analysis and evaluation, and the courage to seek new means of resolving its problems. For if it does not, it will become as enervated as other members of the academic family suffering from hardening of the educational arteries.

Screening and Development of the Remedial Reading Teacher

DOROTHY CHENOWETH KLAUSNER

WHY DID JOHNNY gain three years in a remedial reading course from Miss X and then lose one and one-half years in a second course from Miss Y—both teachers using the same methods? The next ten years will certainly include research on the causes of this recurring problem of varying success of different teachers of remedial reading.[22]

Attention may well be directed both to the fact that the teacher's personality is important to her success in teaching remedial reading and to the specific personality traits which are helpful. Methods of developing such desirable personality traits—both in teacher-training and in teachers already serving—will surely follow.

Relatively few reading teachers have had the personality screening required by such programs as Columbia's[3] for the Diploma of Reading Specialist, which states that "The Diploma is granted only to those who do a high quality of work, *and possess personal and professional aptitudes essential for success in this field.*" Many are English teachers or elementary classroom teachers who have been assigned to teach remedial reading without special training or personality qualifications. Others are teachers who have had some instruction in the teaching of remedial reading, varying from in-service sessions to correspondence, extension, and university courses. But almost none have had an opportunity to consider their own personalities in relation to effective reading improvement.

From *Journal of Reading*, 10, May, 1967, pp. 552–559. Reprinted with permission of Dorothy Chenoweth Klausner and the International Reading Association.

What personality traits are considered important? Mackie and Engle[20] list the following:

1. Sympathetic and understanding attitude
2. Warm, approachable, and friendly manner
3. Spirit of cooperation and helpfulness
4. Genuine love of and interest in people
5. Faith in the dignity and worth of a person regardless of social position or handicap
6. Enthusiasm
7. Optimistic, idealistic, yet practical attitude
8. Keen-thinking, intellectually alert mind
9. Emotional maturity
10. Tolerance, kindness, patience, and tact

To which experienced teachers would add a sense of humor, perseverance, courtesy, and a strong stomach. Certainly these personality traits would be helpful to any teacher. Why are they especially needed by teachers of reading improvement?

First, because it's harder to develop the necessary good relationship with most disabled readers than with the average student. Each is different, of course, but more than 70 percent of disabled readers show some degree of personality maladjustment.[26] The remedial reading student usually has a history of failure. He is discouraged, apathetic, or hostile, according to *his* personality. He thinks the teacher doesn't want to and/or can't help him, or that he himself doesn't want or need help. His pride has suffered, not only from failure, but from being put into this special classification. He is afraid—that maybe he really is "dumb," or of the new situation, new teacher, reading machines, diagnostic tests.[7, 28] He is under pressure from himself, his family, his teachers. He often has physical and neurological problems which affect his behavior and his appearance. His personality may be thorny and unpleasant. Habits of wiggling and squirming, spitting when he speaks, picking off scabs and pulling out his hair, neglected runny nose, frequent belching, and rude or sarcastic remarks may make him very difficult to like.[23]

Spache[26] described "five patterns among elementary retarded readers —the hostile, adjustive, defensive, solution-seeking, and autistic or withdrawn. For each of these groups he suggested logical adjustments of the teacher-pupil relationship and the climate of the remedial reading program." Obviously the teacher needs to be emotionally mature, and to have a warm, cooperative, sympathetic, tolerant, yet enthusiastic attitude to get through the wall created by such disabled readers. If, as Roswell[23] says, developing a good relationship is achieved through "total acceptance of the child as a human being worthy of respect" and "encompasses a collaborative spirit within a planned structure, compassion without overinvolvement, understanding without indulgence, and above all, a genuine concern for the child's development," then the teacher needs a personality strong in such traits as those listed by Harris[13]: optimism, enthusiasm, good cheer, creation of a calm, relaxed atmosphere, kindness, praise, sensitivity to emotional needs, appreciation, respect, friendly interest, building up of self-confidence and self-respect. "Appearance, dress, age, speech, theoretical knowledge, experience—all these are less important than a genuine fondness for children as they are, complete with their faults and annoying habits." Just as "reading cannot be regarded as separate from the behavior of the individual,"[7] so success in the teaching of reading improvement cannot be regarded as separate from the personality of the teacher.

Causes of reading problems may be neurophysiological (inferior learning capacity, defective vision or hearing, speech difficulties, deficiency in language and motor functions, poor health), psychological (lack of interest, instability of temperament interfering with attention, passive or antagonistic attitude toward learning), educational (inadequate habit formation in the mechanics of reading, insufficient practice), sociological (inadequate background, foreign-language background, poor home training, population mobility),[17] or a combination of these. The teacher may attempt remediation with methods based on the phonics approach,[2, 14, 15, 27, 30] kinesthetic tracing,[9] visual-perceptual-motor training,[10] language experience approach,[1] neuropsychological principles,[4, 29] basic sight word vocabulary,[6] or a combination of these and others. Neither diagnosis nor remediation methods, however, but the teacher's personality will get over to the disabled reader the essential message, "I like you. I *can* help you," which is basic to success in remedial reading.[23]

Second, the remedial reading student must often follow procedures which at best are strange to him, and may often strike him as babyish or useless, unrelated to reading. And again it is the teacher's personality traits of understanding, enthusiasm, cooperation, and faith in the student's dignity and worth rather than his knowledge of procedure that makes the difference in the student's effort and cooperation. If he is to practice drawing lines from left to right,[19] tracing words with his finger while saying the word aloud,[9] sounding out nonsense syllables,[30] or trying to read words flashed on a tachistoscope,[21] he must believe that it will help him and that it is not some incomprehensible busywork which will demean him.

Third, the development of good work habits and the ability to persevere, never easy to teach, is doubly difficult and doubly necessary with the disabled reader. He has been cajoled, reprimanded, subjected to all sorts of training methods, and gotten progressively more frustrated. The reading teacher's real interest in him as an individual, understanding, patience, enthusiasm, and emotional maturity in acceptance of his slips and starts will be more effective in helping him develop acceptable work habits than will knowledge of the underlying causes or methods of remediation. As Roswell[23] says: "A teacher needs to have confidence that she can help, but she needs to realize also that she is not personally responsible for lack of progress. She must understand that . . . it is simply a reality to be remedied. When . . . her own status is not threatened . . . she can then recognize the child's ultimate potentialities, not his present achievement."

And fourth, tests of all kinds are administered much more frequently by the reading improvement teacher than by subject teachers. Diagnostic tests and progress tests are an integral part of the reading improvement program. Validity of the tests may depend on the teacher's personality traits—understanding the student and his fears, recognizing the peripheral influences affecting him and his day-to-day progress, securing his confidence and trust so that his test performances reflect his reading skills as accurately as possible.

Diagnostic testing may be done outside the classroom,[26] but there are still progress tests and the informal testing of teacher observation. If the reading teacher has established good rapport with the student, such informal testing will yield much helpful information about his attitudes, working habits, reading skills, and reading needs. His interests, distractibility, speed, dependence on listening for a substitute become a part of the sum total which helps the teacher help him. "Each adds another tentative bit of information about the child's present reading behaviors, his progress, and his future," says Spache.[26] But if the teacher's lack of warmth, sincerity, and faith in the individual have prevented development of a good relationship, if the student is still afraid or apathetic or hostile, test results may very well lack validity.

Besides the relationships with the student, the reading improvement teacher is more closely involved with parents, with administrators and other teachers, and with the community in relation to her work than is the average classroom teacher. And personality traits will strongly influence the success or failure of these relationships. Widespread interest in reading and equally widespread lack of information about methods and techniques of improving reading create the situation where reading teachers "find themselves required constantly to defend the modern reading program rather than being engaged in explaining it,"[26] or, as Schick and Schmidt[24] put it: "Whether he wishes it or not, the teacher of reading is forced into the role of publicist, advocate, and explicator of reading instruction."

Parents who are worried, critical, hostile, or uncooperative, well-intentioned administrators who become critical of what seems to them to be slow progress,[23] fellow teachers who feel that reading is not their concern nor related to their subjects, and community organizations and representatives who believe that reading problems wouldn't exist if only the "good old-fashioned methods" had been used—how does the reading improvement teacher affect these people? With knowledge, certainly, of causes of disability and techniques of remediation—but for that knowledge to affect others, with personality traits of tact and diplomacy, patience and understanding, willingness to listen and cooperate, and enthusiastic belief.[5, 28]

If we accept the dictum that personality traits strongly affect the success of the reading improvement teacher, what can we do about it? Personality improvement courses and personality screening may be provided as part of teacher-training for new teachers. But what of teachers now in the field?

"To prescribe 'maturity,' 'serenity,' or 'interest' as requirements for good teaching, without helping teachers to remove their inner impediments to these healthy and desirable states of mind, is to burden them with assignments for which they have no adequate preparation."[7] Personality tests? The questions are often not effective and sample only certain facets of personality. It is doubtful that persons respond truthfully and objectively. And they are usually complex in scoring and interpretation, requiring extensive training of the examiner.[26]

Assessing one's own personality in relation to the traits listed might be a first step. Most teachers possess these traits in some degree, or they would not be teachers. But with thoughtful analysis most of us could discern a need to develop more tact, or real belief in the fundamental dignity and worth of every person, or more patience, or a better understanding of other people's motives, etc. At the same time, a realistic appraisal of one's personality strengths and the types of pupils with whom these would be most successful would be helpful. Gates[12] says, "The fact is that teachers, like pupils, have specialized abilities and disabilities. . . . Thus the ideal remedial program involves a teacher-pupil-method totality."

Using the basic principles of mental health as a second check might follow. "The majority can improve their relationships with children greatly, by studying principles of mental hygiene and trying to incorporate them into their everyday relations with children," according to Harris.[13] Such books as *Mental Hygiene—A Manual for Teachers*,[11] *Mental Hygiene in School Practice*,[8] *The Psychology of Adjustment*,[25] *The Psychology of Personal Adjustment*,[16] and *Psychology in the High School*[18] are among the many that offer helpful information and bibliographies leading to other reading in this field.

In-service training related to mental health and personality development would be valuable not only to reading improvement teachers but to all teachers. With recent recognition that reading is taught by "*every teacher, at every level, from the early grades throughout college and adult classes*,"[24] in-service training has greatly increased. It has been designed to acquaint subject-teachers with the reading improvement program and techniques, as well as to convince them that good reading habits will make their students more effective, require less of their time in drill and repetition, and in effect help them to do a better job of teaching their subjects.

Perhaps such in-service training might equally well offer help in personality improvement to all teachers. In many schools, the in-service training program is developed by the reading improvement teacher. According to Schick and Schmidt,[24] as he passes on to his colleagues the knowledge and skills he has acquired, he "learns more and more about theory and practice and results. . . . He enlarges his own stature while assisting his fellow-teachers." By the same token, if the reading improvement teacher were to include information on good mental health practices and development of optimal personality characteristics in a program of in-service training, he might very well at the same time learn how to improve his own personality.

Until the next decade's research and methods of personality screening and development are available, perhaps we can make a start with informal methods such as these.

REFERENCES

[1] Anderson, Irving H., and Walter F. Dearborn. *The Psychology of Teaching Reading* (N.Y.: The Ronald Press Co., 1952), pp. 259–266.

[2] Bond, Guy L. and Miles A. Tinker. *Reading Difficulties: Their Diagnosis and Correction* (N.Y.: Appleton-Century-Crofts, 1957), pp. 420-422.

[3] Columbia University. *Programs for Reading Specialists and Supervisors* (N.Y.: Teachers College, Columbia University, 1957), p. 1.

4 Delacato, Carl H. *The Treatment and Prevention of Reading Problems* (Springfield, Ill.: Charles C. Thomas, 1961).

5 D'Evelyn, Katherine. *Individual Parent-Teacher Conferences* (N.Y.: Teachers College, Columbia University, 1958).

6 Dolch, Edward E. *Helping the Educationally Handicapped* (Champaign, Ill.: Garrard Press, 1950); and *A Manual for Remedial Reading* (Champaign, Ill.: Garrard Press, 1945).

7 Ephron, Beulah Kanter. *Emotional Difficulties in Reading* (N.Y.: The Julian Press, 1953), pp. 7, 27, 275.

8 Fenton, Norman. *Mental Hygiene in School Practice* (Palo Alto, Calif.: Stanford University Press, 1943).

9 Fernald, Grace M. *Remedial Techniques in Basic School Subjects* (N.Y.: McGraw-Hill, 1943), pp. 35–55.

10 Fostig, Marianne. "Corrective Reading in the Classroom," *The Reading Teacher* (April, 1965); and *The Fostig Program for the Development of Visual Perception* (Chicago, Ill.: Follett Co., 1964).

11 Griffin, Laycock, and Line. *Mental Hygiene—A Manual for Teachers* (N.Y.: American Book Co., 1940).

12 Gates, Arthur I. *The Improvement of Reading* (N.Y.: Macmillan, 1955), pp. 132, 486–487.

13 Harris, Albert J. *How to Increase Reading Ability* (N.Y.: Longmans Green, 1954), pp. 250, 249, 250.

14 Hay and Wingo. *Reading with Phonics*, rev. (Chicago, Ill.: J. P. Lippincott, 1954).

15 Heilman, Arthur W. *Phonics in Proper Perspective* (Columbus, Ohio: Charles E. Merrill, 1964).

16 Heyns, Roger W. *Psychology of Personal Adjustment* (N.Y.: Dryden Press, 1958).

17 Hildreth, Gertrude and B. C. Wadell. *Identifying Reading Difficulties* (N.Y.: World Book Co., 1959), pp. 3–4.

18 Jersild, Arthur T. and Kenneth Helfant. *Psychology in the High School* (N.Y.: Teachers College, Columbia University, 1953).

19 Kephart, Newell C. *The Slow Learner in the Classroom* (Columbus, Ohio: Charles E. Merrill, 1962).

20 Mackie and Engle. *Directors and Supervisors of Special Education in Local School Systems* (Washington, D.C.: U.S. Government Printing Office), pp. 40–41.

21 Pollack, M. F. W. and Josephine Piekarz. *Reading Problems and Problem Readers* (N.Y.: Van Rees Press, 1963).

22 Albert J. Harris[12] says: "A few people seem to be naturally endowed with warmth, tact, and sympathetic understanding. Such people usually get good results, even if the methods they employ are far from the best." Arthur Gates[12] insists that "It is imperative that first meetings develop in the pupil a feeling that the teacher is a good sort and will surely help him." Ruth Strang[28] adds: "Emotional relations in the classroom affect learning" and "There is no substitute for an adequate understanding of

the individual (and) a sensitivity to his needs." George Spache[26] concurs: "In our opinion, the reason for the moderate success that almost any remedial approaches achieve lies in the type of interpersonal relationship established between the pupil and the remedial teacher."

[23] Roswell, Florence C. and Gladys Natchez. *Reading Disability: Diagnosis and Treatment* (N.Y.: Basic Books, 1964), pp. 142, 65, 66, 178–79.

[24] Schick, George B. and Bernard Schmidt. *Guidebook for the Teaching of Reading* (Psychotechnics Press, 1966), pp. 44, 43, 47.

[25] Shaffer and Shoben. *Psychology of Adjustment* (N.Y.: Houghton Mifflin Co., 1956).

[26] Spache, George D. *Toward Better Reading* (Champaign, Ill.: Garrard, 1963), pp. 298, 120, 299, 263, 204, 121; and *Good Reading for Poor Readers* (Champaign, Ill.: Garrard, 1966), p. 4.

[27] Spalding, Romalda Bishop and T. Walter. *The Writing Road to Reading* (Whiteside Inc. and William Morrow, 1957).

[28] Strang, Ruth. *Reporting to Parents* (N.Y.: Teachers College, Columbia University, 1957); *Understanding and Helping the Retarded Reader* (Tuscon, Arizona: University of Arizona Press, 1965); Strang, McCullough, and Traxler. *Problems in the Improvement of Reading* (N.Y.: McGraw-Hill, 1955), p. 70.

[29] Stuart, Marion Fenwick. *Neurophysiological Insights into Teaching* (Palo Alto, Calif.: Pacific Books, 1963).

[30] Terman, Sibyl and Charles S. Walcutt. *Reading: Chaos and Cure* (N.Y.: McGraw-Hill, 1958).

ADDITIONAL SOURCES

Abraham, Willard. *A New Look at Reading—A Guide to the Language Arts* (Boston, Mass.: Porter Sargent, 1956).

Blair, Glenn M. *Diagnostic and Remedial Teaching in Secondary Schools* (New York: The Macmillan Company, 1946).

Blumfield, Leonard and Clarence L. Barnhart. *Reading, A Linguistic Approach* (Detroit: Wayne State University Press, 1961).

Bond, G. L. and Eva Bond Wagner. *Teaching the Child to Read*, 3rd edition (New York: The Macmillan Company, 1960).

Brogan, Peggy and Lorene K. Fox. *Helping Children Read* (Holt, Rinehart, & Winston, Inc., 1961).

Cleary, Florence Damon. *Blueprints for Better Reading* (New York: H. W. Wilson Company, 1957).

Durkin, Dolores. *Phonics and the Teaching of Reading* (New York: Teachers College, Columbia University, 1962).

Haring, Norris G. and E. Laken Phillips. *Educating Emotionally Disturbed Children* (New York: McGraw-Hill Book Co., Inc., 1962).

Hovious, Carol. *Following Printed Trails* (Boston, Mass.: D. C. Heath and Co., 1936).

Kottmeyer, William. *Handbook for Remedial Reading* (St. Louis, Missouri: Webster Publishing Company, 1947).

Miller, Helen R. and John DeBoer. *Creative Reading* (Graessle-Mercer Company, 1951).

Scheifele, Marian. *The Gifted Child in the Regular Classroom* (New York: Teachers College, Columbia University, 1953).

Stagner, Ross. *Psychology of Personality* (New York: McGraw-Hill Book Company, 1961).

Witty, Paul. *Helping Children Read Better* (Chicago, Ill.: SRA, 1950); *Streamline Your Reading* (Chicago: SRA, 1949); *How to Become a Better Reader* (Chicago: SRA, 1953); *How to Improve Your Reading* (Chicago: SRA, 1956).

Ten Guidelines for
Teaching the Disadvantaged

SIDNEY J. RAUCH

IT IS NOT MY PURPOSE to identify, define, or describe the characteristics and behavior patterns of the culturally disadvantaged student. This has been done in scholarly fashion by Conant,[1] Riessman,[2] Clark,[3] Passow,[4] Strom,[5] and others equally perceptive. I am not going to question or analyze educators' and sociologists' reasons for labeling such individuals as "handicapped," "underprivileged," "culturally deprived," "culturally disadvantaged," "environmentally limited" or plain "disadvantaged." What most teachers clearly recognize is that the great majority of disadvantaged students have reading disabilities. No matter how we define "remedial" (either in terms of intellectual capacity or grade placement), many of these youngsters fall into this category. It is the purpose of this paper to develop guidelines and suggest materials to help teachers overcome these reading problems.

GUIDELINES

1. Proceed on the assumption that your students are capable of reading improvement. Don't be misled by the results of group intelligence tests or standardized reading tests. Don't underestimate your students' levels of comprehension and ability to express ideas. John Niemeyer, President of Bank Street College of New York City, has succinctly described this attitude: "A major reason for low achievement among children in poor neighborhoods is the low expectation as to their

From *Journal of Reading*, 10, May, 1967, pp. 536–541. Reprinted with permission of Sidney J. Rauch and the International Reading Association.

learning capacity held by teachers."[6] If you want to get a reasonably good estimate of their powers of comprehension and verbal ability, discuss a popular movie, sporting event, or incidents of local interest. During these discussions, see how they respond to questions relating to main ideas, significant details, inferences, and vocabulary and concept meanings. Above all, remember that intelligence and creative thinking are communicated in ways other than verbal expression.

2. Your students should have a reasonable chance for understanding the printed materials with which they are faced. Thus, the materials used should be at or slightly below their "instructional" level. The concepts of "instructional level," "frustration level," "independent level," and "capacity level" should be clearly understood by the teacher as he selects materials appropriate to his students' interests and abilities. (See Chapter VII of *Guiding the Reading Program* by Robinson and Rauch for a discussion of these concepts as an outgrowth of informal reading inventories.[7])

3. Reading assignments should be brief, concrete, and well-motivated. If possible, selections should deal with people and specific situations your students can identify and relate to. It would be best to keep some specific record of daily assignments to reinforce a feeling of accomplishment. A record of daily progress on a chart or graph, or a collection of mimeographed worksheets, provides concrete evidence of achievement. One of the reasons for the success of the Follett Publishing Company's *Basic Learning Series* is the development of well-organized, brief, easy-to-read selections that assure success.[8]

4. Be alert and sensitive to the reading needs of your group. Since "motivation" is a basic factor in attracting these pupils to the printed page, it is important to know "why" and "what" they want to read. Whether these disadvantaged youngsters prefer the "how-to-do-it" type of book, stories about minority group heroes, sports, science-fiction, or war adventures, it is part of the teacher's job to know sources of information that will enable him to match the right book with the right pupil at the proper psychological moment. Become familiar with such helpful booklists as *Reading Ladders for Human Relations*, Fourth Edition,[9] *Books About Negro Life for Children*,[10] *Good Books for Poor Readers*, 1964 Revision,[11] *Good Reading for Children*, 1962 Revision,[12] *A Place to Start*, 1965 Revision,[13] and *About 100 Books—A Gateway to Better Intergroup Understanding*.[14]

5. When possible, avoid standardized reading tests. In all probability, these pupils have been tested year after year with the same results—i.e., scores three or more years below grade level. The results come as no sur-

prise to them. They know it, their teachers know it, and the administration knows it. These pupils have had their fill of testing. As Dr. Robert W. Edgar, Director of BRIDGE project (Queens College, N.Y.C.), reported: "During our Project we discovered that the very tests which we used to evaluate the growth of the children such as the Metropolitan Achievement Tests, were viewed by many of the pupils simply as efforts on our part to demonstrate once again how stupid they were."[15]

6. Word and concept meanings are a major block to reading in the content areas. These meanings must be clarified in preparation for reading. To do this, make ample use of firsthand experiences, audio-visual devices, concrete illustrations, and repetition of the word in various situations. In all cases, promote semantic sensitivity, i.e., a word has more than one meaning, and meaning varies with context. Don't be afraid to teach affixes and stems. Many teachers have reported success and interest in this form of structural analysis.

7. At the same time, make sure that your reading program involves more than word recognition exercises. This is only the first step, though a vital one. Reading is more than word recognition. It requires an understanding of the relationship among words and sentences. The reader should also be able to react critically and even emotionally to the content, and finally to use the ideas gained to modify his own thinking.

8. Use a variety of approaches and vary your daily program. Remember students can learn from media other than the printed page. Make use of trips, television, radio, films, recordings, overhead projectors, transparencies, cartoons, filmstrips, magazine and newspaper illustrations, etc. There is a place for experimentation in reading methodology. Programmed materials, the language-experience approach, linguistic-oriented texts—all have their adherents. However, it is best to evaluate innovations realistically. As Walter Barbe has aptly stated,

> It is a strange but very real fact that all new programs in reading seem to be successful. Started with careful planning and based upon an understanding of the goals to be accomplished, every report in the literature of different methods reports more success with the new procedure than with the old. Almost amusing is the fact that those trying one method report better success, while others, rejecting that method but trying the different method, report better success. Is this not perhaps the best indication that like everything else, too much doing of the same thing makes it become routine and often sterile? And when teaching becomes routine, it is both more difficult for the teacher and less effective for the children. In discussing one particular program, Olson observed that "change in itself

appeared to be beneficial." And so, perhaps a plea for flexibility, if not for change itself, is in order.[16]

9. In all probability, content area teachers can contribute most of the improvement of reading by emphasizing the reading-study skills. These skills may be categorized as follows:

a. *Skills of locating information*
    (1) Using parts of the book (author's organization of materials, preface, introduction, table of contents, index, glossary, etc.)
    (2) Use of dictionary skills
    (3) Use of encyclopedias, almanacs, atlases and other references
    (4) Reading maps, charts, graphs, diagrams, etc.
    (5) Use of library techniques
b. *Skills of evaluating information*
    (1) Reading with a critical attitude
    (2) Using several sources to evaluate materials
    (3) Judging author's competency
    (4) Distinguishing between fact and opinion
    (5) Learning propaganda techniques
    (6) Evaluating relevancy of information to topic being studied
c. *Skills of organizing information*
    (1) Note-taking
    (2) Classifying facts and ideas
    (3) Arranging ideas in sequence
    (4) Knowing outline format
    (5) Knowing how to outline
    (6) Techniques of summarizing
d. *Skills of retaining information*
    (1) Use of Survey Q3R[17]
    (2) Systematic study vs. cramming
    (3) The need for re-reading
    (4) Note-making vs. note-taking as a memory aid
e. *Adjusting rate to purpose and to the difficulty of the reading selection*
    (1) There is no such thing as rate in isolation. It must always be considered as *rate of comprehension.*
    (2) A good reader must have at least four basic rates of reading:
        (a) Skimming (skipping with judgment)
        (b) Rapid reading (timed reading exercises—no skipping of material)

(c) Intensive reading (the art and necessity of re-reading)
(d) Recreational reading rate

10. Finally, remember that the psychology of the learning process can be distilled into the following four steps:

a. Motivation (creating the desire and purpose, and providing readiness)
b. Clarification (the teaching process: furnishing information and developing understandings)
c. Application (the necessary drill and application to other areas)
d. Satisfaction (the feeling of accomplishment on the part of the student)

While these steps are essential to any learning process, they have even greater implications for the teaching of the disadvantaged. Each step is a *must* as you prepare your lessons.

RECOMMENDED MATERIALS

WORD RECOGNITION

EDL Word Clues Series, Grades 7-13, Educational Developmental Laboratories, Huntington, N. Y.
Phonics We Use, Books E, F, G, Lyons and Carnahan, 1966.
Tactics in Reading, Books I and II, Scott, Foresman and Company.
Using the Context, Books E and F, Barnell Loft Ltd., Rockville Centre, N. Y.
Vocabulary Development (Macmillan Reading Spectrum), The Macmillan Co.
Word Analysis (Macmillan Reading Spectrum), The Macmillan Co.
Word Attack: A Way to Better Reading, Harcourt, Brace and World, Inc.

COMPREHENSION SKILLS

Advanced Skills in Reading, Books 1, 2, 3, Macmillan Publishing Co.
Be a Better Reader, Second Edition, Books I-V, Prentice-Hall.
Better Reading, 3rd Edition, Globe Book Co.
Building Reading Power (Programmed Instructional Kit), Charles E. Merrill Books, Inc.
Follett Basic Learnings Series (English, Social Studies), Follett Publishing Co.

Follett Vocational Reading Series, Follett Publishing Co.
New Rochester Occupational Reading Series, Science Research Associates, Inc.
Reading for Meaning, Grades 7-12, J. B. Lippincott Co.
Reading for Understanding, Grades 5-12, Science Research Associates, Inc.
Springboards, Portal Press Publishers, New York City.
S.R.A. Reading Laboratories (junior and senior high school levels), Science Research Associates, Inc.
Tactics in Reading, Books I and II, Scott, Foresman and Co.
Teen-Age Tales, Books I-VI, D. C. Heath & Co.
Turner-Livingstone Reading Series, Follett Publishing Co.

READING-STUDY SKILLS

Advanced Skills in Reading, Books 1, 2, 3, Macmillan Publishing Co.
Be a Better Reader, Second Edition, Books I-V, Prentice-Hall.
Better Reading, 3rd Edition, Globe Book Co.
Better Work Habits, Scott, Foresman and Co.
Building Reading Power (Programmed Instructional Kit), Charles E. Merrill Books, Inc.
EDL Study Skills Library (Reference), Grades 4-9, Educational Developmental Laboratories, Huntington, N.Y.
EDL Study Skills Library (Science), Grades 4-9, Educational Developmental Laboratories, Huntington, N.Y.
EDL Study Skills Library (Social Studies), Grades, 4-9, Educational Developmental Laboratories, Huntington, N.Y.
Graph and Picture Study Skills Kit, Science Research Associates, Inc.
Tactics in Reading, Books I and II, Scott, Foresman and Co.

TEXTS FOR TEACHERS

Crosby, Muriel (ed.). *Reading Ladders for Human Relations,* Fourth Edition (Washington, D.C.: American Council on Education, 1964).
Heilman, Arthur W. *Phonics in Proper Perspective* (Columbus, Ohio: Charles E. Merrill, 1964).
Reading: Grades 7-8-9—A Teacher's Guide to Curriculum Planning, Curriculum Bulletin No. 11, 1957-58 Series (Board of Education of the City of New York, 1959).
Reading in the Subject Areas, Grades 7-8-9, Curriculum Bulletin No. 6, 1963-64 Series (Board of Education of the City of New York, 1964).
Robinson, H. Alan and Sidney J. Rauch, *Guiding the Reading Program:*

A Reading Consultant's Handbook (Chicago: Science Research Associates, 1965).

Spache, George D. *Reading in the Elementary School* (Boston: Allyn and Bacon, 1964).

Strang, Ruth, *Diagnostic Teaching of Reading* (New York: McGraw-Hill, 1964).

REFERENCES

[1] Conant, James B. *Slums and Suburbs* (New York: McGraw-Hill, 1961).

[2] Riessman, Frank, *The Culturally Deprived Child* (New York: Harper and Row, 1962).

[3] Clark, Kenneth B. *Dark Ghetto: Dilemmas of Social Power* (New York: Harper and Row, 1965).

[4] Passow, A. Harry (ed.). *Education in Depressed Areas* (New York: Bureau of Publications, Columbia University, 1963).

[5] Strom, Robert D. *Teaching in the Slum School* (Columbus, Ohio: Charles E. Merrill, 1965).

[6] *Ibid.*, p. 33.

[7] Robinson, H. Alan and Sidney J. Rauch. *Guiding the Reading Program: A Reading Consultant's Handbook* (Chicago: Science Research Associates, 1965).

[8] *Follett Basic Learning Series* (English, Social Studies) (Chicago: Follett, Publishing Co.).

[9] Crosby, Muriel (ed.). *Reading Ladders for Human Relations*, 4th ed. (Washington, D.C.: American Council on Education, 1964).

[10] Baker, Augusta (ed.). *Books about Negro Life for Children* (New York: New York Public Library, 1965).

[11] Spache, George D. *Good Books for Poor Readers*, rev. (Champaign, Illinois: Garrard Press, 1966).

[12] Eakin, Mary K. (ed.). *Good Reading for Children*, rev. (Chicago: University of Chicago Press, 1962).

[13] *A Place to Start*, rev. (Syracuse, N.Y.: Language Arts Center, Syracuse University, 1965).

[14] Wolfe, Ann G. *About 100 Books*, 5th ed. (New York: The American Jewish Committee Institute of Human Relations, 1965).

[15] Edgar, Robert W. "History, Reading, and Human Relations: an Integrated Approach," *Social Education*, 29 (March, 1965).

[16] Barbe, Walter B. *Educator's Guide to Personalized Reading Instruction* (Englewood Cliffs, N.J.: Prentice-Hall, 1961), p. 6.

[17] Spache, George D. *Toward Better Reading* (Champaign, Illinois: Garrard Press, 1963), pp. 345–346.

Teaching Reading to the Culturally Disadvantaged in Secondary Schools

RUTH STRANG

THE TEACHING OF reading to culturally disadvantaged adolescents is difficult for a number of reasons. During their pre-school years they have not been encouraged to talk, to think things out for themselves, to be curious. They are more often told to "be quiet" than given a reason for being quiet. This kind of family atmosphere develops "modes for dealing with stimuli and with problems which are impulsive rather than reflective, which deal with the immediate rather than the future, and which are disconnected rather than sequential."[1] Moreover, this type of arbitrary family control—"Do this because I say so"—plus a tendency on the part of parents to disparage rather than to encourage the child's effort, also tends to develop certain characteristics that are unfavorable to success in reading.

However, disadvantaged children are not necessarily poor children.[2] Children from well-to-do homes may be psychologically disadvantaged. They may have been deprived of the psychological vitamins that would have promoted their best development.

On the other hand, some children from very poor families prove not to be psychologically deprived. They have received a wealth of genuine affection and a strong sense of family stability. Each member of the family has been expected to assume some responsibility for the welfare of all; each has real work to do. Instead of patronizing expensive spectator sports, they enjoy family games, baseball in a vacant lot, trips

From *Journal of Reading*, 10, May, 1967, pp. 527–535. Reprinted with the permission of the International Reading Association.

to the museum, zoo, and public parks. The parents appreciate the value of good educational opportunities for their children. In some of these homes the Bible is still the most important book.

The adolescents with whom we are concerned in this article are those who have been deprived of the pre-reading experiences and other advantages that children from more privileged homes enjoy. These disadvantaged children often fail to learn to read in the first grade. From then on their reading difficulties snowball, especially as they come to accept the concept of themselves as persons who can't learn to read. They enter high school burdened with the weight of six to nine years of failure.

ANTIDOTES TO APATHY

Yet "hope springs eternal"; underneath their apparent apathy and their surface indifference to school success, many of these youngsters feel both a need and a desire to learn to read better. An unruly girl in the ninth grade who was reading at the second-grade level begged her teacher, "Please, Mr. G., teach me to read. I want to be a nurse when I grow up. You have to know how to read." When a social worker told a 15-year-old juvenile delinquent that she would help him get a job, he answered, "Nobody, including you, can get me a job. Don't you know I can't read? Not one word." An older boy who realized that he could not accept the promotion his boss offered him because he couldn't read well enough to meet the new responsibilities was strongly motivated to learn to read better. Many others realize that they cannot get the kinds of jobs they want without further training and they cannot get further training without a certain level of reading efficiency.

Desire to pass the test for a driver's license motivates many to acquire the necessary reading skill. Others have social motivations—to be able to read a girl friend's letters when one is away at camp, to order a meal at a restaurant, to read movie captions.

One intelligent Mexican-American boy, who had made no progress in reading in the ninth grade, confided to his teacher that he felt no future was possible for a person of his status, and thus there was no incentive for him to learn. The teacher told him that times were changing and that people of his nationality were becoming more prominent in American society and politics. A few days later she put on his desk a clipping about a Mexican-American who had recently been appointed to an important local government position. From then on the boy began to apply himself; he made marked progress in his reading.

It is important for the teacher to recognize and exploit any underlying incentives a student may have to put forth the effort that reading improvement requires. She should inquire: How might reading be personally rewarding to this student?

DIAGNOSIS WHILE TEACHING[3]

In light of the foregoing considerations, it is important to begin reading instruction not with a standardized test, but rather with material that has immediate meaning, use, and purpose for the individual pupil. A standardized test often intensifies the retarded reader's sense of failure and inadequacy. More immediately useful diagnostic information can be obtained from an informal test based on road signs and directions, titles of popular records, a paragraph from a driver's manual, ads in the newspaper, a menu, a recipe, or directions for making a dress or a model plane. As the pupil reads the selection aloud, he reveals his difficulties in word recognition. As he tries to give a summary of the author's thought or answer directive questions, he displays his ability, or lack of ability, to comprehend the author's meaning and to interpret, generalize, and apply what he has read. This is the "teachable moment"— the time to give instruction in the reading skills for which the pupil has and feels an immediate need.

SOME EFFECTIVE PROCEDURES

It is difficult for teachers to bridge the gap between theory and practice, between knowing what to do and knowing how to do it. One way of bridging this gap for the teacher is to describe procedures that are theoretically sound and that have seemed to be effective with certain disadvantaged groups or individuals.

The groups of disadvantaged pupils who were the subjects of this study have certain common characteristics: their performance IQ is in the normal range and is usually higher than their verbal IQ; they are reading three or more years below their grade placement. Since they were deprived of the pre-school prereading experiences that more privileged children have, their verbal communication is restricted and their language habits are different from those used in school. They also have poor habits of looking, listening, and paying attention in class; these are both a cause and a result of a history of failure and fear of failure. Of central significance is the fact that they lack the positive self-concept that is vital to learning. This lack of self-esteem, which is fostered in many disadvantaged homes, is too often reinforced by school experiences.

The following descriptions of procedures that have been successful in certain situations can be adapted to other situations.

1. INSTRUCTION GROWING OUT OF AN INFORMAL TEST

Non-readers may be asked merely to read their names and addresses and some familiar road signs. Others may be given a first-, second-, or third-grade paragraph from *My Weekly Reader* on some topic of adult interest, such as rockets. The more able readers are given a short selection—informational, humorous, or inspirational—for example, the following paragraph:

> Each young person has resources within himself to improve himself. He should think of his strengths, not his faults. Many years ago a young lawyer was very discouraged. He wrote, "I am now the most miserable man living. Whether I shall ever be better, I cannot tell; I awfully forebode I shall not." He was wrong. He gained strength and health through work that needed to be done. His name—Abraham Lincoln.

The pupil reads this silently and answers the unstructured question, "What did the author say?" This can be followed by questions on vocabulary, the main idea, and the most important details. Then, with the teacher's help, the pupils discuss their answers and appraise their own reading ability. Did they get the message of this paragraph? How was the paragraph built? (A main idea and an illustration). What was the purpose of this paragraph? How can they apply it to their own lives? Which of the difficult words did they know? How did they learn? Which unfamiliar words were they able to pronounce? After pronouncing them, did they know their meanings? From his individual study of his responses to this paragraph, each pupil may find some aspects of reading that he needs to work on by himself or in a group. Each can set certain goals for himself.

2. INSTRUCTION AND PRACTICE IN WORD RECOGNITION

In their individual efforts to read something that is of real interest to them, some pupils may discover that they are blocked by lack of word-recognition skills. The teacher may begin with some interesting exercises on context clues, the first ones involving meanings that are easily inferred—the word is defined in the sentence, a synonym is given, the meaning is made clear by a contrast, familiar expression, a summary or an association with a common mood. The pupils will bring in other sentences with the word omitted to see if their classmates can supply it.

They will discover that some sentences give no clues. These call for other methods of word recognition—structural analysis, phonics, and the dictionary. In reviewing phonics, the phono-visual charts are useful: the scientific basis on which the sound-letter associations are grouped distinguishes this approach from primary-grade methods. With high school pupils discovery and reasoning should replace simple associations as the essence of instruction in word-recognition skills.

3. TO FIX WORDS IN MIND

Some pupils may have difficulty in remembering the words they have newly acquired. In this case they can make a vocabulary card for each new word as they learn it: one side shows the word as a whole and as divided into accented and unaccented syllables; on the other side are the definition of the word and a sentence using it correctly. If they review these words from time to time, they can see objective evidence of growth in their meaningful vocabulary.

4. PROGRESS IN WORD KNOWLEDGE

Pupils who have extreme difficulty in remembering words can often master them by the Fernald finger-tracing, or kinesthetic, method. To avoid an unfavorable initial reaction to this method, the teacher introduces it by explaining that the mind receives impressions from all five senses; the more sense impressions, the more effective the learning. This brief excursion into psychology prevents high school pupils from rejecting the method as "babyish." After writing the word in large letters on a card for each pupil, the teacher demonstrates the process of looking at the word, pronouncing it, and tracing it with the finger, syllable by syllable. As the pupils trace the word, the teacher makes sure they are doing it correctly. When they feel that they know the word, they try to write it without looking at the model. If they make any errors, they do not try to correct them; they repeat the tracing process and then try again to write it correctly. When they have written it correctly three times, they add it to their card catalogue of words that they have especially wanted to learn or that have given them difficulty.

5. HOW TO READ A SENTENCE

Disadvantaged children, who have not become familiar with the "sound of sentences" through hearing correctly spoken English at home, are in special need of instruction in sentence structure. In one lesson with a group of disadvantaged pupils, Mrs. Barbara Dean, a core teacher in Rincon High School, Tucson, Arizona, combined instruction on the role of imagination in reading, the selection of accurate and vivid words to describe what one sees, the construction of sentences, and the use of sentences in writing paragraphs and in writing a story.

The stimulus was a picture of warlike Arabian horses and riders. Today the pupils were to describe this picture so vividly that another person would be able to see it in his imagination. The teacher first developed some vocabulary by listing on the board a number of nouns representing items the pupils found in the picture—*horses, men, rifles;* then words describing the action—*trot, gallop, fight.*

To encourage them to give descriptive words and phrases, the teacher suggested sentences for them to complete—"The horse runs _____," to which the pupils responded with adverbs and phrases such as *steadily, swiftly, like the wind.* From these several classes of words the pupil began building sentences, starting with a basic pattern—*the horse runs*—and elaborating it by using descriptive words and phrases —*the white horse runs fast, like the wind.* After sample sentences had been written on the board and the pupils knew exactly what to do, they divided into groups. Each group chose one noun that it wanted to write about. As the groups worked diligently, the teacher made helpful and encouraging comments. Finally the class chose the best sentences to form a story, which was mimeographed for them to read the next day.

The high interest that was maintained throughout this period might be attributed to several factors, primarily to the teacher's very clear, very precise directions and explanations, and her continued encouragement and approval of the pupils' earnest effort. They also appreciated the opportunity to work as a team on a concrete rather than on an abstract task. They felt successful and had objective evidence of their success.

6. INSTRUCTION IN PARAGRAPH COMPREHENSION

Practice in constructing clear paragraphs is a good prelude to improving paragraph comprehension. We have already mentioned the desirability of studying different kinds of paragraphs and diagramming their structure.[4] It is also important to consider the purpose a given paragraph serves and the chain of logic that underlies its organization. To get a sense of the sequential development of a paragraph, pupils enjoy reconstructing paragraphs from sentences which have been typed separately. Their methods of locating the main idea or ideas may make more sense to their classmates than the instructions the teacher gives:

"Well, if the idea isn't interesting. I don't think it is important."

"You read and what it says mostly I think would be the main idea."
"I just read the sentences in the paragraph and which to me makes
the most sense, I pick it."

To become proficient in paragraph reading, these pupils need to go
through the process with the teacher again and again with different
kinds of paragraphs on various subjects that they want to read about.

7. ACCENT ON SPEECH

Since these pupils are especially weak in verbal communication and
many of them come from non-English-speaking homes, much practice in
oral language is a prerequisite to effective reading. Mrs. Betty Frey, a
most successful teacher in a Tucson, Arizona, junior high school and a
Laubach trainer of volunteer workers, has developed several successful
and helpful methods. One method involves dialogues on various subjects, written by the pupils or by her. First she reads the dialogue to
the group with natural intonation, rhythm, and stress. Then the class
repeats it with her as in choral speaking. When the class has become
familiar with the sound of the sentences, the boys read one part, the
girls the other. Finally, pairs of individuals volunteer to read sections of
the dialogue aloud.

Another popular procedure is a current events assignment. Each
pupil finds a newspaper paragraph that interests him. He reads his
paragraph to the class, writes the topic sentence on the board (if there
is one), and underlines the phrases that tell *what, why, when,* and
how. This approach combines instruction in skimming, oral reading,
paragraph comprehension, and sentence structure.

8. OPERANT CONDITIONING

Because disadvantaged adolescents have such a need for immediate
satisfactions, the procedure of rewarding specific desired behavior has
proved successful with both individuals and groups. This technique may
be illustrated by an individual case reported by Staats and Butterfield.[5]
A 14-year-old Mexican-American delinquent boy, with a long history of
school failure and misbehavior, had achieved only second-grade reading
ability. His Verbal IQ was 77, Performance IQ 106, and Full Scale, 90.
Over a period of four and one-half months he was given 40 hours of
instruction and practice on the Science Research Associates Reading
Laboratory booklets. He was given tokens of three different values—
1/10, 1/5, and 1/2 of a cent—for correct responses: e.g., when he correctly pronounced the new words in a story, when he correctly read a
paragraph aloud, when he was apparently attentive while silently read-

ing the selection, and when he answered a question correctly. The tokens were plotted on a chart so that he always had visual evidence of his progress. He could use the tokens to purchase a variety of items that he chose. During the four and one-half months he received a total of $20.31 while maintaining a high level of attention and participation, learning and remembering 430 new words, and advancing his reading achievement to the 4.3 grade level. For the first time he passed all his courses and decreased his misbehavior to zero. (Other kinds of rewards may of course be used where appropriate.)

The same psychological principle of reinforcement was applied in a group of disadvantaged high school pupils. They were given a check mark on a wall chart every time they came to class on time, finished their homework, and did other specific tasks that were conducive to, or made them accessible to, reading instruction. Instead of money, they were given certain privileges, such as attending the afternoon movie, in return for a certain number of check marks. This group also benefited from this aproach: they became more receptive to learning.

The results in both instances were probably due not only to the immediate rewarding of specific desirable acts, but also to the social reinforcement that was given by the experimenter, to the stimulating effect of being in an experiment, and possibly to other extra-experimental factors.

9. OTHER METHODS

A number of other methods and materials have also been used successfully with disadvantaged adolescents. In a youth camp, students were assigned for daily sessions in the SRA Reading Laboratories. They also regularly used the Pilot Library for work in vocabulary development, reading and discussing books they themselves selected, and writing at least one book report on self-assigned reading in fiction or nonfiction. The library became "an oasis of silence and calm" where students began to come voluntarily.[6]

Auto-instructional and programmed materials and methods have also been used to reduce these pupils' passivity. They gain a greater sense of achievement and reward by seeing the value of their own responses than by having them judged by the teacher.[7]

10. READING MATERIALS

The success of all reading procedures and methods depends upon the suitability and attractiveness of the reading materials; this is where instruction starts. The first step is to let the student select something that he really wants to read. Then he has the incentive to acquire whatever skills the reading or the dramatization of the stories requires. It is helpful to have on hand multi-level materials such as the SRA Laboratories; the Educational Development sets also contain interesting short articles; trade books and series of high interest and low difficulty can be found on all subjects.[8] A number of magazines and newspapers that are simply written and yet capitalize on genuine adolescent interests are now available: for example, *Scope,* published by Scholastic Magazines; and *News for You,* published by Robert S. Laubach (Laubach Literacy, Inc., Box 131, Syracuse, N.Y. 13210).

Regardless of what specific procedures or reading materials are used, teachers and administrators must take an attitude of "positive expectancy" toward these pupils, must focus on their assets rather than on their faults. Instruction must be personalized. Each pupil must see its purpose and must feel rewarded by objective evidence that he is making progress toward becoming the kind of person he wants to be.

REFERENCES

[1] Hess, Robert D. and Virginia Shipman. "Early Experience and the Socialization of Cognitive Modes in Children," *Child Development,* 36 (December, 1965), 870–871.

[2] Congreve, Willard J. "Not all the Disadvantaged are Poor," *The P.T.A. Magazine,* 60 (February, 1966), 15–17.

[3] For more detail see Strang, Ruth. *Diagnostic Teaching of Reading* (New York: McGraw-Hill Book Company, 1965).

[4] Strang, Ruth and Dorothy Bracken. *Making Better Readers* (Boston: D.C. Heath and Company, 1957), pp. 125–129.

[5] Staats, Arthur W. and William H. Butterfield. "Treatment of Nonreading in a Culturally Deprived Juvenile Delinquent: an Application of Reinforcement Principles," *Child Development,* 36 (December, 1965), 925–942.

[6] Rivera, Emilio. "The Disadvantaged and the University Camp," *Teachers College Record,* 67 (May, 1966), 557–563.

[7] Deutsch, Martin. "Some Psychological Aspects of Learning in the Disadvantaged," *Teachers College Record,* 67 (January, 1966), 260–265.

[8] Strang, Ruth, Ethlyne Phelps, and Dorothy Withrow. *Gateways to Readable Books,* 4th ed. (New York: H.W. Wilson Company, 1966).

Procedures and Materials for the Culturally Disadvantaged Reader

IN GRADES NINE THROUGH FOURTEEN

NANCY LIGHTHALL

THE ACADEMIC achievement of culturally disadvantaged students in grades nine through fourteen is likely to be closer to a fifth- or sixth-grade level; at the same time, because of having been held back or because of having been temporary dropouts along the way, they may well be several years older than the average student. The situation confronting the teacher of such a group, then, is this: in interest, experience, motivation, maturity, and general wisdom about the ways of the world, the class is an adult one; but in achievement (including reading achievement) and, equally important, in the realm of general information, the class is a slow, incredibly childlike one.

No matter what his age, there are certain bits of background information that the severely culturally disadvantaged student can be depended upon not to possess. For example, he probably will not know what Congress is, even though he may already be of voting age. He may have heard of the Civil War, but he won't know what it was about or when it occurred. It is possible that he will have heard of the United Nations, but the chances are that he will not have the slightest idea as to what its functions are. And at least one student of the writer's

From *Meeting Individual Differences in Reading*, Supplementary Educational Monographs, No. 94, pp. 155–159, by permission of The University of Chicago Press. Copyright 1964, by the University of Chicago Press.

acquaintance did not know, until the matter came up in class, that the earth is round.

In short, then, the level of reading achievement of such a class requires not only that the teacher provide material which, though mature in content, is readable in terms of vocabulary and sentence structure but, in addition, that the presentation of the material must be made with care. If, for example, the class is to read a story dealing with a group of soldiers stationed somewhere in England in 1944, the teacher must first be absolutely sure that the class knows why these men were where they were in this particular year. He cannot take it for granted that they will read the opening lines and immediately know that this is a World War II story.

Why this intellectual vacuum exists is not the subject for discussion in this paper. But it does exist, and this fact is of extreme pertinence to the work of the teacher of culturally disadvantaged students. If he does not recognize and appreciate this sad fact, he is beaten before he starts.

The task confronting him, then, is basically twofold. First, he must select his material with care, making sure that it is both fast-moving and adult in content but not unreasonably taxing to the reading skills of the class. And, second, he must be sure that his introduction of the material includes enough background information so that the assignment will make sense; and after the reading, he must fill in with a skilful discussion which will lead the students to a meaningful interpretation and appreciation of the material.

SUGGESTED READINGS IN LITERATURE

Much of Hemingway is ideal material for such a group, and some of his early short stories, dealing with the adventures of Nick Adams, a thinly disguised, youthful Hemingway, make an excellent starting point. Short, with simple sentences, an easy vocabulary, and familiar situations, these stories move swiftly from opening scene to climax. Violence, though rarely described, is often suggested, frequently hovering just below the surface and lending an air of intangible excitement to the story. Most famous among the Nick Adams stories is, of course, "The Killers,"[1] a story which moves with incredible swiftness from the initial exposure of the hired gunmen to the tragic despair of the Swede who lies in his room facing a violent, inevitable death. In class, the students can be encouraged to look more deeply into the story. Why was the

[1] M. Edmund Speare, ed., *A Pocket Book of Short Stories* (New York: Washington Square Press, Inc., 1959), pp. 1–10.

Swede to be killed? Was there any chance that he might escape death? What about men who kill for money? What effect might his own involvement in this tragedy have in the life of young Nick Adams? Other Hemingway stories popular with such a group include "Indian Camp,"[2] in which a much younger Nick is introduced simultaneously to the horrors of a primitive birth and a violent death, and "The Battler,"[3] in which Nick becomes briefly involved in a strange, but somewhat touching, relationship between an ex-fighter and his companion.

Although not so easy to read, James Michener's story "The Cave"[4] is well worth the extra effort. This story concerns a group of navy men stationed on a little island in the Pacific during the height of World War II. On this island, some of the men have found a cave where they go whenever there is a moment of quiet to drink, to talk, or just to forget; and from these brief retreats to the cave, the men find a new courage which helps them to face battle. Near. the end of the story, Michener spells out his symbolism with meticulous care. Each of us, he says, has a cave within us to which we retreat and from which we get courage whenever the going gets tough. Some sort of a goal is the thing which keeps us together, which helps us meet our day-to-day experiences. No student will miss the point of this story. For each one of them, there is a "cave," a dream of respectability, of education, of being someone; and it is this cave within him which brings him to school and which, if it is strong enough, will keep him coming. Months after they have read it, I have had students refer to and want to discuss this story again.

"Impulse," by Conrad Aiken, concerns a young, middle-class man who impulsively decides to try to shoplift a razor in a drugstore.[5] When he gets caught and sentenced to jail, his wife, who was not too happy with him anyway, decides that this is an excellent opportunity for her to leave him. A story like this, which deals sympathetically with the plight of a shoplifter, is virtually always successful in a class of culturally disadvantaged students. For those who, at one time or another, have themselves succumbed to such a temptation (and there may be several in such a class), it is apparently a perfect description of the mental processes which precede and follow a sudden impulse to shop-

[2]Ernest Hemingway, *In Our Time* (New York: Charles Scribner's Sons, 1958), pp. 15–21.
[3]*Ibid.*, pp. 65–79.
[4]Orville Prescott, ed., *Mid-Century: An Anthology of Distinguished Contemporary American Short Stories* (New York: Pocket Books, Inc., 1958), pp. 289–320.
[5]Robert Penn Warren and Albert Erskine, eds., *Short Story Masterpieces* (New York: Dell Publishing Co., 1954), pp. 15–28.

lift. For those who have been caught, the wife's behavior afterward is sadly typical of those on whom one should have been able to depend.

Ring Lardner is always appealing to such a class, although sometimes his tongue-in-cheek style is a little difficult for them to grasp. However, a careful discussion of Jim, Lardner's antihero in "Haircut,"[6] will bring the class to the realization that the author must have intended us to look beyond the superficial analysis given by the dim-witted barber. "Champion,"[7] another Lardner story written in the same vein and also concerning a scoundrel, is always popular, partially, at least, because it deals with a boxing, a favorite sport among many members of such a class.

So far our discussion has centered around the assignment of short stories, which most students can complete in an hour or so of careful reading. It is also possible, however, for the class to tackle longer works, such as novels and plays, providing that the selections are chosen with care and the teacher is prepared to devote a number of class sessions to each work. Lorraine Hansberry's play *A Raisin in the Sun*,[8] for example, is a fast-moving, absorbing study of some of the problems besetting a Negro family in today's urban culture. Arthur Miller's *Death of a Salesman*,[9] though dealing with problems less familiar to the culturally disadvantaged student, has enough universality in its tragic theme to cut across social class lines. John Steinbeck, who writes with sympathy and understanding of the problems of the underdog, is a favorite with these students. In spite of its length, *The Grapes of Wrath*[10] is always worth the many weeks it takes a class to complete it; the students will become completely absorbed in the Joad family's familiar struggle with poverty, discrimination, and exploitation. Considerably shorter but almost as popular is *Of Mice and Men*,[11] Steinbeck's moving story of two homeless men. Ernest Hemingway's *The Old Man and the Sea*,[12] with its short sentences, simple vocabulary, and totally masculine theme, is also a popular selection.

In the field of poetry, two poems by Carl Sandberg come to mind. One of them is "Chicago," and the other "The Hangman at Home."[13] Although both will be well received, the latter can be depended on to

[6]Speare, *op. cit.*, pp. 165–176.
[7]Philip Van Doren Stern, ed., *The Pocket Book of Modern American Short Stories* (New York: Washington Square Press, Inc., 1954), pp. 95–116.
[8]New York: New American Library, 1959.
[9]New York: Viking Press, 1958.
[10]New York: Viking Press, 1958.
[11]New York: Bantam Books, 1958.
[12]New York: Charles Scribner's Sons, 1952.
[13]Gerald D. Sanders and John H. Nelson, eds., *Chief Modern Poets of England and America* (New York: Macmillan Co., 1950), pp. 596, 608–609.

stimulate discussion. The identity of the hangman, the part of his guilt we share, Sandburg's real feelings about capital punishment, and the students' real feelings about capital punishment are some of the topics which will arise during discussion of this controversial poem. Robert Frost is always popular with such a class, and good starting points for Frost are "Stopping by Woods on a Snowy Evening" and "The Road Not Taken."[14] Later, the class may want to tackle one of Frost's longer poems, such as "Birches."[15] "Richard Cory,"[16] by Edwin Arlington Robinson, often makes good reading. Its unexpected twist at the end and its implicit suggestion that money and happiness do not always go together can be depended on to arouse interest and discussion.

SUGGESTED PAMPHLETS AND PERIODICALS

In addition to literary selections, there are other sources of materials one should consider. For example, well-chosen pamphlets often made interesting and informative reading for this kind of class. In Chicago, the police department puts out a pamphlet entitled *Know the Law*. This pamphlet describes types of crimes, laws regarding automobiles, and reasons for arrest. Other pamphlets which made good reading are some of those put out by banks describing their services and those put out by the Social Security Administration describing some of the benefits of Social Security. All of these pamphlets are available in quantity to the teacher without charge.

In the field of periodicals, there are two which bear mentioning. One of these is *Consumers' Reports*, with its unique evaluation of products as well as its introduction to the idea of co-operatives. The other is *Time,* each issue of which will contain some sections of interest. It goes without saying, however, that selection of reading assignments in either of these magazines must be made with care because there will be large parts which will be beyond the reading comprehension of students. Both magazines are available at classroom rates.

Newspapers offer good reading practice. However, since a newspaper becomes obsolete so quickly, it can be used with real effectiveness only if the reading assignments are made and carried out within the classroom situation.

For the teacher who wishes to supplement his program with a more structured type of material, there are a few fairly good workbooks

[14]*The Pocket Book of Robert Frost's Poems* (New York: Washington Square Press, 1956), pp. 194, 223.
[15]*Ibid.,* p. 89.
[16]Sanders and Nelson, *op, cit.,* p. 494.

available. The main problem with workbooks, of course, is to find material at a low enough academic level that is also sufficiently mature in content to be interesting. Good examples of such workbooks are *How To Read Better* and *Progress in Reading,*[17] which, although written at the fifth- and seventh-grade levels, respectively, both contain material that will be of interest to the older student.

Surprisingly enough, the Bill of Rights makes an excellent classroom reading assignment. That there are actually some rights which are guaranteed to each citizen of the United States is a new and intriguing idea for these students, and as they get into those amendments which are particularly pertinent to their lives, most of them will read and begin to interpret with lively enthusiasm.

Finally, there is the material produced by the students themselves. One of my own favorite assignments is to have each student write an autobiography. This is a long-term assignment providing practice not only in writing skills but also in outlining and planning a longer paper. Behind every culturally disadvantaged student, there is, inevitably, a story; and for those who feel like sharing it, it can be a fascinating one. The teacher who is looking ahead will hold on to the best of these, copy them, correct the spelling and grammar, disguise the identity of the writer, type the polished version on stencils, and use them for reading in next year's classes.

[17]Harley A. Smith and Ida Lee King, *How To Read Better* (Austin, Texas: Steck Co., 1956); Ullin W. Leavell and William Leonard Gardner, *Progress in Reading* (Austin, Texas: Steck Co., 1957).

Improving Reading and Writing Skills of Disadvantaged College Freshmen

NICK AARON FORD

IN THE SPRING of 1964 my colleague, Professor Waters Turpin, and I were notified by the U.S. Commissioner of Education that we had been awarded a research grant of $49,842 to conduct a three-year experiment in improving the reading and writing skills of culturally disadvantaged college freshmen. Our application for the grant contained the following introductory statement:

> The problem to be attacked is the lack of success in developing satisfactory reading and writing skills by the majority of college freshmen from poor cultural backgrounds. It is important and significant to the field of education for three major reasons:
>
> (1) At present more than one-third of the students in the public schools of America's fifteen largest cities are products of and continue to live in poor cultural environments. It is reliably reported that by 1970 more than 50 percent of the pupils in the public schools of the fifteen largest cities will come from culturally disadvantaged backgrounds.
>
> (2) Although many of these culturally disadvantaged students are graduated from high school and manage to enter college, they are dropped for poor scholarship largely because they do not develop sufficient skills in reading and writing to master academic subjects required for graduation. This unfortunate situation results in a great loss of potentially skilled manpower from active participation in the Amer-

From *College Composition and Communication*, May, 1967, pp. 99–105. Reprinted with the permission of the National Council of Teachers of English and Nick Aaron Ford.

ican economy. In addition, it adds unnecessarily a large body of frustrated citizens to the urban centers.

(3) Most of the culturally disadvantaged students who, because of unusual talent or industry, are finally graduated from college are denied the opportunity to pursue graduate or professional studies because they cannot satisfactorily pass Graduate Record Examinations or other professional tests which are heavily weighted with cultural items. These students, though talented, remain culturally disadvantaged because they have never developed the skill to read with ease and pleasure, nor to express themselves effectively in speech or writing.

We stated the two major objectives of our proposed project in the following manner: (1) to determine whether or not specially selected reading materials and experiences and specially devised methodology can motivate culturally disadvantaged students to improve their reading and writing skills more readily and thoroughly than the normal experiences of a typical Freshman English course; and (2) to determine whether or not culturally disadvantaged students who have improved their reading and writing skills because of effective motivation in the Freshman English course will likewise achieve at a higher level in other academic subjects involving these skills.

The Educational Policies Commision has identified the five main streams of the culturally disadvantaged as Negroes from the rural South, "Hill Whites" from the Appalachian upland, Puerto Ricans, Mexican-Americans, and Reservation Indians. The students involved in this experiment were selected from the predominantly Negro student body of Morgan State College, Baltimore, Maryland, who received their secondary education in the schools of the Middle Atlantic region of the upper South; the majority were natives of Maryland, largely of urban origin.

We started the project July 1, 1964, by devoting the first two months to selecting, editing, and mimeographing text materials. At the beginning of the fall semester in September, we created two experimental sections of Freshman English consisting of twenty-five students each, randomly selected from a segment of the incoming freshman class whose scores on the various entrance tests confirmed their eligibility for possible selection. Each student in the experimental sections was matched with a student from the remaining segment of eligibles (approximately 400 from a class of 1,000). The criteria used for matching were scores on two standardized English tests (A.C.T. and Cooperative English Expression), a standardized reading test (Cooperative Reading Comprehension), an over-all aptitude test (A. C. T. Composite), and a personality-type test (Edwards Personal Preference Schedule) to obtain information on non-intellective factors which possibly affect the development of reading and writing skills. The fifty matching students, who were designated as the control group, were randomly scattered among a dozen sections of Freshmen English taught by eight different teachers.

METHODOLOGY

The next day after a news release on our large research grant was carried by the local newspapers, my colleague and I were visited by the branch manager from one of the largest audio-visual manufacturing companies in the nation. He informed us that he had just read the news about our research project concerned with seeking methods to improve the reading and writing skills of disadvantaged college freshmen and that he had the answer to all of our problems. His answer was a new machine his company had developed which would cost less than a thousand dollars. If we bought his machine, he joyfully confided, we would accomplish our purpose and still have $49,000 left to use to our own advantage. We told him, of course, that no machine could achieve the goals we had in mind, for our philosophy is that the development of reading and writing skills is a matter of motivation rather than mechanical stimulation, and that we would not be interested in using a machine even if it were a free gift. Naturally, he was bitterly disappointed and focused upon us such a look of nightmarish disbelief that he stumbled over two chairs before he could realize that he was not in a world of fantasy.

My colleague, Professor Turpin, and I believe that the development of skills in reading and writing is primarily a psychological process and that once a reader has been sufficiently motivated to *want to read* articles and books because they reveal information and points of view that are interesting, challenging, and significant *to him,* there are few, if any, barriers strong enough to prevent his mastery of the art of reading. This truth is also applicable to the art of writing. Our major task, therefore, as we envisioned it, was to select, organize, and present a collection of readings in such a way as to stimulate the kind of interest necessary to motivate culturally disadvantaged students to *want* to read and write.

It is our belief that these freshmen who now are so woefully deficient in reading and writing skills were never motivated in elementary and high school *to want* to read and write because reading and writing were never made relevant to their poverty-stricken, slum-ridden lives. In the *Saturday Review,* September 11, 1965, Nancy Larrick, former president of the International Reading Association, begins an article entitled "The All-White World of Children's Books" with the question "Why are they always *white* children?" raised by a five-year-old Negro girl, who was looking at a picture book at the Manhattanville Nursery School in New York. Miss Larrick comments, "With a child's uncanny wisdom, she singled out one of the most critical issues in American education today: the almost complete omission of Negroes from books for children. . . . Yet in Cleveland, 53 per cent of the children in kindergarten through high school are Negro. In St. Louis, the figure is 56.9 per cent. In the District of Columbia, 70 per cent are Negro. Across the country, 6,340,000 nonwhite children are learning to read and understand the American way of life in books which either omit them entirely or scracely mention them."

We approached our task with two major objectives insofar as methodology is concerned: (1) to compile a collection of readings that would be concerned with the personal needs, drives, and interests of the culturally disadvantaged; and (2) to devise ways of presenting these readings that would encourage the students to want to talk about and write about their reactions, and to want their responses to be in standard English. We began the first year with a mimeographed anthology of approximately 500 pages, organized around the following themes:

Unit   I: Understanding the Nature and Uses of Language
Unit II: Understanding One's Self
Unit III: Understanding Limitations and Opportunities of Minorities in the United States
Unit IV: Understanding Global Problems
Unit V: Understanding Race and Democracy: Exploring Philosophic Perspectives

It was our intention to capture the student's interest by first focusing on readings that were pertinent to his personal problems and situations and gradually, step by step, to widen his horizon from the personal to the community, from the community to the nation, and from the nation to the world. As teachers, we felt it was our responsibility to help the student to see how his personal problems and situation were similar to those of other groups in the community, in the nation, and in the world. We felt that if we could, by our method of presentation, help the student to identify with the various races and nationalities of man, we would be motivating him to want to learn about, think about, talk about, and write about ideas and experiences that had meaning for him. For instance, here are the titles of some of the readings in the unit on Understanding Limitations and Opportunities of Minorities in the United States:

"Why We Can't Wait" by Martin Luther King
"Black Muslims: Asset or Liability to Negro Protest" by Phyllis Barber
"Thurgood Marshall: Counselor at Law" by Saunders Redding
"Everybody Knows His Name (James Baldwin)" by Marvin Elkhoff
"Ivy League Negro" by William Melvin Kelley
"The Puerto Ricans" by Nathan Glazer
"Let the Indian Be the Hero" by Stanley Walker
"Types of Anti-Catholicism" by Robert McAfee Brown
"On Being Irish in America" by Charles Keenan
"What is a Jew?" by Morris Adler

Each article was followed by questions for study and discussion, including tests for comprehension, opportunity for examining rhetorical effectiveness, vocabulary study, and writing assignments. In other words, reading, discussion, and writing in this experiment are the heart of the learning experience, while grammar and English usage are important in making these experiences more understandable and meaningful.

ASSUMPTIONS

Three major assumptions underlay our methodolgy:

ASSUMPTION NO. 1

We assume that disadvantaged students do not learn to read and write effectively because the learning experiences generally furnished by the school are irrelevant to much of contemporary life. One simple example of this irrelevance, other than the failure of textbooks to be concerned with the lives and problems of minorities, can be seen in a recent experience I had in visiting a slum high school English class in a large city, taught by a teacher who had been highly praised as the best in the all-Negro school. The major objective of the lesson was to develop effective expression by having students view or recall a familiar sight or sensory experience and describe in vivid language their reactions to it. The teacher had spent much time in preparing the lesson by clipping from magazines interesting advertisements calculated to stimulate student reaction. The first clipping exhibited was a colorful advertisement of a beautiful girl luxuriating in a spectacular circular bathtub of sparkling baby blue suds in an elegant bathroom of ceramic tile furnished with every kind of luxury imaginable. Pointing to this picture, the teacher asked for volunteers to describe the feelings of the girl in the bathtub. When no hands were raised the teacher was disgusted with the lack of response and told me afterwards that she found it almost impossible to motivate her students to express themselves. Evidently she did not realize that none of her students had ever been exposed to luxury of any kind, that some had never seen a bathroom, and that many had no bathrooms or even private toilet facilities in their homes.

ASSUMPTION NO. 2

We assume that the American school and college are obligated to teach all native students *standard English* as the acceptable means of communication. We mean by *standard English* the dialect generally admitted by the majority of speakers to be superior to all the other dialects in the language. Since standard English is the system of communication used in "carrying on the affairs" of the American society, it is necessary for the schools to insist on its mastery by its native students, if the schools accept the responsibility of helping to prepare all students to participate on an equal basis in the affairs of the nation. This assumption rejects the practice that is becoming popular in some important centers of instruction to teach standard English as a second language to the culturally disadvantaged. For to promote this "second language" theory is to forge a new chain of segregation and discrimination which national civil rights laws are intended to destroy.

ASSUMPTION NO. 3

We assume that culturally disadvantaged students not only *can* learn to master standard English as a primary language but that the majority of them *want* to do so. We deny the doctrine of Dr. Frank Riessman, Professor of Educational Sociology at New York University, who says in an article in the *Saturday Review*, September 17, 1966:

> The key ground rule of the Dialect Game—for both teacher and teaching situation—is acceptance of the students' nonstandard primary language. The instructor who makes clear to his pupils that their primary language is not something to be denied or suppressed, but is in fact a linguistic entree to that other language which, in more formal circumstances, can produce more effective results, is building firmly on positive grounds.

We believe a teacher who is guided by this doctrine will not be building on positive grounds, but rather on sinking sand, on the sand of condescension and denial of the ability of the disadvantaged student to master the predominant dialect of his native land, a dialect that he and more than fifteen generations of his forefathers have intimately lived with from birth. It is the duty of the teacher to demand that disadvantaged students discard their substandard dialect as the first step in the process of discarding the ghetto and second class citizenship. To say that the Negro child believes the teacher who rejects his substandard dialect rejects him is nonsense, for the average Negro child, who certainly knows the meaning of picket lines and civil rights demonstrations, knows that his substandard dialect is a part of the substandard living conditions that he and his parents are trying so desperately to escape. In fact, he is more likely to believe that those who are satisfied to have him think of standard English as a second language may be expressing a subconscious satisfaction at having him remain a second class citizen in a land where the users of standard English dispense the rewards of job opportunities and social approval.

Two years ago Professor Turpin and I prepared a questionnaire on this subject and requested 1,000 freshmen, 98% Negro, from more than 25 states to fill in the answers with a check mark without signing their names. The results were as follows: To the question: "Should high school English teachers discourage non-standard language usage by minority group students whose families and neighbors continually use such patterns?" 73% said yes. To the question: "Do the parents of minority group students approve their children's use of standard English?" 82% said yes. To the question: "Do associates of minority group students discourage the students' use of standard English?" 73% said no. To the question: "Do minority group students resent teachers who reject their dialect?" 59% said no.

EVALUATION

Unfortunately, English teachers are seldom knowledgeable about the intricacies of objective testing. Consequently, we included an expert in tests and measurement as the third member of our team. Dr. Otis D. Froe, Director of Research and Evaluation at our college, is officially designated as statistician for our project and is concerned only with the objective evaluation of our efforts. I shall not attempt to reproduce for you the seven tables, bristling with technical terminology, which he used in his report on our first year's progress; I shall be content to quote those pertinent parts in which he summarizes his findings in a language suitable for laymen.

He explains that January and May post-testings were administered to both the experimental and control groups after one and two semesters of instruction. Since the two groups were comparable in the beginning, success of the special treatment was measured in terms of the size of the gain made by each group after "experimental" and "control" instruction. In the analysis of the results, the part scores were considered as well as the total score.

In terms of the skills involved in "effectiveness of written expression," both groups made mean gains (statistically significant at the .05 level) after the first semester of instruction. Neither group made significant mean gains from the second testing (beginning of the second semester) to the third testing (end of the second semester). On the "Mechanics of Expression" part of the test, the experimental group made statistically significant gains (.01 level) after the first semester of special treatment. The control group made no significant gain in this area after one (the first) semester of instruction. This is indicated by a critical ratio of 1.35. After the second semester of instruction, the experimental group still made further statistically significant gains (.01 level of confidence), while for the control group the gain made was not significant in terms of a .01 level of confidence. The gain for this latter group was significant at a little better than the .05 level of confidence. When the total test is considered, the data indicate that the experimenal group made gains in communication skills, for both periods of instruction (first and second semesters), which are significant at the .01 level of confidence. For the control group, there has been no significant gain (total test) for either period. Only for the first period of instruction was the gain significant at better than the .05 level. If we look at the results in another way, it can be said that the experimental group has a mean gain that is twice that of the control group. The critical ratio of the difference in mean gains for the two groups is significant at the .01 level of confidence. Also of importance is the fact that from the pretest to the post-test in English at the end of the first semester a number of cases were noted in which there was a decrease in raw score. Among the control group, there were twice as many cases of this type as among the experimental group. The number of cases of a decrease in raw score for these two groups was 15 (28.8 percent) for the control group and only 7 (13.4 percent) for the experimental group.

The three aspects of reading achievement measured by this test are vocabulary, level of comprehension, and speed of comprehension. When the total groups are considered (experimental and control), it is seen that the experimental has made gains significant at the .05 level of confidence in the areas of "level of comprehension," and "speed of comprehension." The gain for the experimental groups on the vocabulary section of the test is not significant. The control group has not made statistically significant gains (either at the .01 or .05 levels of confidence) in either area of the reading test. In summary, although no phenomenal gains were made by either group on the reading test, the gains made by the experimental group in the areas of comprehension and speed seem to surpass those of the control group in these same two areas. The nature of this test is, perhaps, such that phenomenal gains in vocabulary and level of comprehension skills cannot be expected among culturally deprived students after only two semesters of special treatment. Then, too, the experiences provided in this special treatment were not aimed directly at these particular skills. The emphasis seemed to be concerned with a change in reading and writing interests of students. Tests aimed at this non-intellective-type behavior will be administered at the end of the sophomore year for those participants who are still enrolled in the college.

Other criteria considered in assessing the effectiveness of the special treatment provided the experimental group were grades assigned in the Reading and Writing courses (English 101 and English 102), and the disposition of those cases where the student did not complete the course or received a grade indicating unsatisfactory completion of the course during the first attempt. It was decided to use grades as a criterion since the bases for assigning grades in the Department of English have been more objectively formulated than is the case with many other academic departments in the college. Objective-type "keys" have been prepared which teachers use in evaluating themes and other work done by the student. When the total experimental and control groups are considered, it seems that overall the experimental group has received a more favorable pattern of teacher ratings (grades) than the control group. This is true both in English 101 and 102. For example, over 34 percent of the experimental group has received the grade of "B" in English 101. Only 15 percent of the control group received this grade. While the percentage of students receiving the grade "C" in English 101 was the same for both groups, twenty-one percent of the control group received some type of "W" (withdrawal) grade in English 101, as against 4 percent of the experimental group. In English 102, the percent receiving the grade of "U" among the control group is twice that of the experimental group.

In summary, the data collected seem to indicate that the special treatment given to the experimental group, in the way of specially selected reading materials and experiences and specially devised methodology, has promise of motivating culturally disadvantaged students to improve their reading and writing skills to a greater extent than the typical kind of experiences found in similar Freshman English courses.

In conclusion, I must say that my colleague and I do not yet know whether or not the final evaluation of our experiment, due to be completed at the end of the summer, 1967, will be favorable. If in the end it is judged to be a success, we will be the first to admit that it is not *the* answer to the problem, but only *one* answer. Regardless of the result of this effort, we have pledged to ourselves never to be satsified with *one* new insight or *one* new answer, but to continue in the spirit of Tennyson's Ulysses: "to strive, to seek, to find, and not to yield."

Ending the Teacher-Student Mystery

STRUCTURED ASSIGNMENTS

AUDREY J. ROTH AND THELMA C. ALTSHULER

TEACHERS CAN BE mysterious creatures to remedial students in a junior college writing class. They stand in the position of authority, in front of the room. They are arbiters of rules, dispensers of grades.

The student knows that his future depends in part on the way a teacher views him; yet he often finds it hard to break through the mystery of what he is expected to do.

At the begining of each course, "The Great Guessing Game" is played. "What does he want?" wonders the student. This worry reaches its high point the day a theme assignment is made. Already worried about the ability to write anything which can elicit enthusiasm from his instructor, the student's concern is deepened by the assignment to "Discuss . . ." What? How?

A PLAN

Instructors who care about good teaching in the junior college do not want students to play the guessing game. The solution is to take the mystery out of what is expected on a writing assignment.

An assignment sometimes given to English students is "Write an

From *Junior College Journal*, December-January, 1968–1969, pp. 33–34, 36, 38. Reprinted with the permission of the American Association of Junior Colleges. The exercise in this article is adapted from Chapter 5 of the book *Writing Step By Step* by Audrey J. Roth and Thelma C. Altshuler (Boston: Houghton Mifflin Company, 1969).

essay about a strong emotion you have felt." A good student has no difficulty with the assignment; he has confidence in himself and in his ability to write the assigned essay. He realizes that any one of a great many possible essays would fit that rather open assignment.

But the remedial student needs more help. Instead of presenting him with what seems a vague and mysterious assignment, his teacher must do some of the prewriting work for him.

The teacher should know why the assignment is being made, make it as clear as possible, and then do something which only the experienced writer can do—*break down the writing process* into a series of structured steps which will inevitably require the student to do the assignment successfully by meeting the teacher's expectations.

The parallel can be found in modern business, especially in the market research questionnaire. There would be a smaller response from consumers if people were asked simply "What do you think of our product?" and then given a blank page for an essay. Few would take the time to think about the subject, and even those who did would probably not come up with a good essay. Instead, the research organization does the breakdown beforehand and makes it easy for the consumer to respond.

The structured assignment gives useful assistance. In a sense, it borrows from questionnaires and coupons with their explicit directions "Check which one is wanted," or "Circle one of the following."

The following example of a structured assignment shows how a remedial student can be directed to describe a personal emotion. It contains many aids and explicit details which may gradually be lessened as student writing ability increases. Thus, like the training wheels removed from a child's bicycle, some of the steps which serve as writing props can be removed.

WRITING ABOUT A PERSONAL EMOTION

PART A. CHOOSING THE TOPIC

STEP 1. There are many different kinds of emotions. Here are some common ones. As you read this list, think of those you have experienced. Use the spaces to add other emotions you can think of.

fear	confidence	shyness	eagerness
excitement	indifference	happiness	jealousy
anger	sympathy	enthusiasm	shock
embarrassment	boredom	nostalgia	_____
_____	_____	_____	_____

STEP 2. An emotion is caused by a variety of situations, and many situations may cause the same kind of emotion. For example: You are the player during a crucial part of a game. You drop the ball; your team loses the game.

From the following situations, select at least four you have experienced. Then, in the space next to those you select, write an emotion from the list in STEP 1 which tells how you felt.

Example: You are one of the contestants waiting for the winners to be announced in an important contest. Response: Eagerness

Situation	*Emotional Response*
1. You are walking toward a person to whom you intend to apologize.	
2. You are called to the telephone to speak to someone you never expected to hear from again.	
3. You reach for your wallet to pay for some tickets and discover you left your money at home.	
4. You are saying goodbye to someone who means a great deal to you.	
5. You have been overcharged in a restaurant, and the waiter has his hand out for a tip.	

There are no "correct" answers. People respond differently and what would cause intense anger in one person might cause bewildered retreat in another.

More than one emotion is possible in response to a situation, of course. But mixed feelings are harder to describe than a single one;

therefore, for this assignment choose *one* dominant emotion for the situation.

PART B. GATHERING INFORMATION

STEP 3. In the space below, write a situation you would like to use in order to tell about a personal emotion. It may be one from the list in STEP 2, or you may choose a completely different situation Then, on the line to the right, record the one dominant emotion you felt regarding that experience. Choose from the list of words in STEP 1. Be brief; use the example in STEP 2 as a model.

Situation   Emotion

_____

_____

_____   _____

STEP 4. [Students are here given examples of the physical manifestations of certain emotions and of how the same emotion can be shown in a variety of ways.]

Select one of the situations in STEP 2 next to which you have written an emotional response. Then list the physical way you felt. [An example is given.]

Physical manifestations: (Use as many ways as possible to show the emotion. The example is a guide; you may add others.) List the physical manifestations of the emotion you have selected as your essay topic.

Head: _____

Throat: _____

Hands: _____

Heart: _____

Skin: _____

Knees: _____

PART C. ORGANIZING THE THEME

STEP 5. You are now ready to make your final plan for writing an essay about an emotion. Fill in the following:

I remember an emotion which made me feel _____

_____.

The situation was _____

_____.

(The above information comes from STEP 3.)
Other details a reader would want to know about the situation:

Time: _____

Place: _____

Other people involved: _____
The emotion made me feel this way physically:

_____

_____

_____

(Information comes from STEP 4.)

STEP 6. You are ready to write about a personal emotion. Use the information recorded in STEP 5. Write in standard essay form. Give the essay a title before you begin.

PROOF TO THE STUDENT

By following the instructions and noting the examples, the student will have written an essay on a subject of his choice and out of his own experience. Instead of being left with the multiple mysteries of "Write an essay about a strong emotion you have felt," he has had part of the mystery cleared up.

He knows that any one of the choices he makes is the right one. He has been given the names of a good many emotions he has probably experienced but would not have been able to name. He has had common situations suggested to him, and yet with few enough details so he can make each one his own. He is being helped to gather the information he will need and to label where appropriate as he goes along. Then he is helped to observe his own reactions in specific detail. Finally, he is shown how to mention the time, place, and other people involved in the situation—and how to put all this information together.

The student must write a successful theme when he follows a structured exercise because the organization has been worked out in advance. Yet the experience and the feelings belong to the student writer himself. No one has told him what he should be saying. He is his own boss, in subject matter as well as in time and place. The assignment, therefore, has the extra advantages of showing that his feelings are important and that he can write about them successfully.

True, the theme was written with assistance, but the essay is a completed assignment and its organization is correct. It satisfies the teacher, and, it proves to the student that he is capable of writing an acceptable essay.

As he develops the specific skills required on this assignment, he will gradually be able to apply them to other assignments.

DEBT TO PROGRAMING

The student gets needed help from a structured assignment whether he realizes it or not. If he were to write an essay, even under supervision, on the original assignment "Write an essay about a strong emotion you have felt," he would probably not realize how much he had to say.

The technique of structured writing owes a great deal to programing. It is the kind of assignment which takes the mystery out of writing because the person making the assignment has thought through in advance the many elements of an essay and has broken them down into individual, understandable, readily performed actions.

The standard, nonstructured assignment "Write a personal essay . . ." implicitly says to the student: "You have had a great many experiences and as a result have many ideas and feelings worth writing about. I want you to choose one from among all these possibilities as your subject. If you are good at choosing the subject, you are likely to get a better grade than if you choose one which is too vague or too general. Then you will have to decide on what you want to accomplish in this paper, explore the many possibilities inherent in the subject you choose, and select those ideas best suited to your purpose. After you gather the information, you will have to organize it according to a particular, predetermined method best suited to this material. Finally, you have to write an essay demonstrating your ability to put all your ideas into grammatically correct language and effective sentence structure and style." A structured assignment says all this to the student, but it says it explicitly, clearly, concisely.

CLUES FOR CLARITY

1. Like programing, the structured assignment has limited objectives. An essay assignment may be designed to demonstrate the student's

abilities in any of the following areas: originality, memory, observation, organization, reading comprehension, mechanics, grammar, etc. The teacher who knows in advance which of the many choices he wants to emphasize is making both teaching and learning less frustrating.

2. The assignment must be chosen to allow a student to demonstrate what the teacher wants him to show. If the purpose of an assignment is to show evidence of close observation on the part of the student, the teacher would make an assignment different from one whose purpose is to show originality of thought.

   An assignment emphasizing recall may need to be only a list turned in by the student; sentence structure may not be important. But one requiring evidence of a student's ability to explain an opinion hinges first on comprehension of the idea upon which to base the opinion; the assignment then has two parts rather than just one.

3. The teacher must determine what steps are required in order to complete successfully the assignment he plans. Sometimes there are several sequential requirements in one assignment: understanding a quotation given by the teacher, remembering material read for homework, relating the ideas of these two sources, and finally writing.

4. The teacher must make it possible for the student to follow these same steps by being as explicit as possible. If all he is interested in is mechanical accuracy, then he ought to let the student know in advance. In that case, even the accuracy of content may not matter. But if he wants to encourage the student to express himself and to believe he has worthwhile ideas and feelings, then the assignment should contain assistance for him to do this.

5. The assignment should have brief, clear examples. Remedial students require the guidance that an example gives. It also aids understanding by showing what is expected, thus removing some of the mystery about following instructions.

6. The assignment has to be made so that the student can work on his own, without close supervision. If the next step is there for him to see, he can proceed at his own pace The structured assignment then becomes adaptable for those who work at varying speeds.

SUMMARY

All remedial writing problems cannot be solved by any one method. The structured writing assignment does not necessarily improve spelling, punctuation, or such perennial grammatical problems as subject-verb agreement, dangling modifier, pronoun case, and pronoun reference. But it does help to reduce those errors by providing parts of some sentences and by focusing student attention on the subject itself, rather than on editing.

It will not work for all teachers and all students. Teachers may object to the idea of offering so much to students who ought to be able to write better after having been in school at least twelve years already. They may be shocked to realize that students require such "spoon feeding of bite-sized pieces." Some students may be impatient at the necessity of thinking and planning so much before actually writing the complete theme. In part, it is a matter of temperament. Some personalities resent any request for preparation. They want to plunge abruptly into an essay and take a chance on success, even though past experience indicates the greater likelihood of failure. However, most of the students in experimental sections at Miami-Dade Junior College who tried structured writing were delighted to be offered so much individual help on the printed page.

The advantages seem to outweigh the disadvantages. For the student, the structured assignment offers reassurance, confidence, support, and the chance for success through a positive activity. He can look forward to the time when he will be able to write well on his own, as he becomes accustomed to an orderly selection of topics, gathering of information, and organization of theme. And he no longer needs to regard his teacher as a mysterious figure of authority who must be pleased in some unknown way before the coveted grade is awarded.

For the teacher there are also advantages. He can do a better job of diagnosing the cause of student error and he can then work to eliminate a specific problem. He spends less time grading papers because he can often look at the first steps, before the essay is written, and know whether the aims of a particular assignment are being fulfilled.

As a result, the teacher's morale is improved. He can be his best self. He is not a drill master, boring everyone with repetitious instructions; nor a detective, searching out dishonesty; nor a misunderstood genius, forced to waste his time with dolts. When his assignments speak clearly for themselves, irritation and mystery disappear. Both teachers and students benefit in the new atmosphere of understanding.

Say Something in English

BONNIE RUBINSTEIN

ONE WARM DAY in spring a few years ago, I was working at my desk in a portable office on the school grounds of Merritt College. The office was poorly ventilated, so the doors were propped open with desk chairs. I heard voices approaching, voices too young to be part of the regular college population. I looked up to find three little girls, ages ranging somewhere between eight and ten, peering in at me through the doorway.

"You a secretary here?" one asked.

"No, I'm a teacher here," I replied. I could see I didn't fit their frame quite right. The girls registered surprise and another of them now more interested and bold ventured:

"What do you teach?"

"English," I offered, expecting some form of groan to rise up from my new friends. But they only looked puzzled and the third one, unable to contain her curiosity, concluded the interview with the most marvelous suggestion:

"You teach English? Say something to us in English."

Each time I recall this incident, I smile to myself, because I feel that these children in their charming naiveté revealed what so many students of somewhat more advanced vintage and supposed seasoning really feel about English. That is to say, it is basically a foreign tongue which they as college students still have not managed to master. Many of them are convinced that if they can just learn those rules which have "bugged" them for a decade or more in the lower grades, they can pass out of English, forget it and its nasty old grammar and proceed with the business of their respective worlds.

From *Junior College Journal*, October, 1967, pp. 7–13. Reprinted with the permission of the American Association of Junior Colleges.

Rarely do any of my students think of English as something they are all, in a sense, experts at, something they use and have used every day for years to think and listen in, read and write in. English is to many a body of exhortations, wrapped in a winding sheet, presented to them year after year in an increasingly mummified state, and eventually accorded proper entombment somewhere in the catacombs of the psyche. English is not something alive, their language, their bridge to the past, a grip on the present and possibly their gift to the future, but rather something quite divorced from the parts of their experience that matter.

The incident that spring with the three girls stuck in my mind and began to send out roots. I am certain that it was this experience, in large part, which moved me to open my remedial English class last spring at Laney College with a little free association test. I read off ten words and asked them to jot down the first word which popped into their minds in connection with each.

It was their response to only one of these words which really concerned me and this was "English." When the class and I put their reactions to this word on the board after the test, we needed no psychometrist to interpret the results. Words such as "trouble," "hate," "fear," "help!" "ugh," "joke" predominated; other words such as "grammar," "spelling," "verbs," "nouns," and "test" figured prominently in their feedback. Only a few responses, "language," "reading," "speak," hinted that the testee might cherish some idea of English as a living medium of communication, rather than a bag of labels or a remembrance of past disasters.

FEAR OF ENGLISH

Using this little free association test as a springboard to discussion, we stopped and considered together why students should "fear" and "hate" English. It developed, not surprisingly, that most of their previous experiences in classes devoted to this subject had been associated with defeat, discouragement, or, at the least, boredom. Despite their admission slips to college, their new notebooks, their shiny morning faces, many of them, I was certain, thoroughly expected to continue this syndrome of dislike and failure.

When asked why they were taking this course, many indicated quite openly their feelings about remedial English in particular: "I'm too dumb to take any other English." "I have always disliked English." "My chances are slim . . . I figured it would be easier with a woman than a strict old man." "If I could get out of taking English I probably would, for I don't find it that interesting." "I'm taking this course because I have to take it; I don't wish to take it."

Perhaps I may seem to be belaboring the obvious, but I have found that it is the obvious that sometimes escapes unseen. Being a student of English, and a very good student at that, in a college or university does not necessarily equip one to be an effective teacher, particularly in what may be the alien field of remedial English. Confronted by several such sections of this type of class with its reluctant population, teaching two or three other courses involving different preparation, grading mountains of compositions weekly, it is remarkable that we in junior college English do as well as we do. But so little time remains to reflect on the process we are engaged in and to search for the meaning of what we are trying to do—at least this has been my experience. So if much of what is being said here is elementary, I must beg your kind indulgence; perhaps I am what is known as a late bloomer. But what one discovers for himself always seems fresh and exciting.

I cannot help but marvel at how I, conscientious and well intentioned as are so many English teachers, had for so many semesters labored diligently to cure ills without having the vaguest notion of their etiology. In this search, I have found it extremely valuable, particularly with remedial students, to start the semester by bringing some of these fears and dislikes out in the open. For many of these people, beginning an English class is like returning to the scene of the crime. They have come, seen, and failed on too many occasions already. The teacher of sociology or anthropology, for instance, may not encounter this hostility to his subject matter, although a student may carry his low self-esteem wherever he goes, which brings me to another important matter facing many an English instructor.

DANIEL SANCHEZ

I have never read anywhere that fear and dislike of what one is doing coupled with low self-esteem generally lead to success. I have already quoted some of the students' feelings about English. Here is a response to the question, "Who am I and why am I here?"

Daniel Sanchez is not a very intelligent person, nor does he have confidence in himself. Lack of education is the goal which pushes him forward, and the want to get ahead. To be a commercial artist is his goal, but to succeed he has to go through many years of strenuous college life. Between his goal and his future is a desire to have a more active part in family life. Now is the time in his life when he wants to paint, remodel, dine and do those hobbies which he enjoys.

Daniel Sanchez, a frail boy of Mexican background with artistic ability was so inaccurate in his estimation of himself as to dramatize in the extreme the critical barriers in my class. Very quickly, I became aware of what I believed to be a striking disparity between his intelligence, sensitivity, actual performance and his view of himself and I set out to do whatever was within my power to recondition this self-image, at least where English was concerned. I asked him directly after I had worked with him in class for some time, why he lacked confidence. He gave the standard reply. He had done poorly in grammar in high school, had shifted schools, and had lacked interest.

It was this same fear-ridden, self-deprecating student who was able to write in the final month of the semester the following critique of a visit to the Kinetic Sculpture Exhibit at the University of California. It is printed here in full just as it was written by him. It so happened that Daniel Sanchez turned out the most proficient prose in his class.

Kinetic Sculpture Exhibit
Tuesday, April 26, 1966, at University of California
Chosen by personal interest

By kinetic sculpture the artists refer to sculpture that is in motion. The exhibit was a mass of moving objects made of different moving objects made of different metals combined with electrical, gravitational, and magnetic forces, which were the stimulants of motion. The exhibit was held in a small auditorium. The sculptures were mounted on walls, placed on the floor, and suspended from the ceilings. While in motion the objects (sculptures) made noise and had some kind of optical effect. For example, one particular sculpture which had an audiovisual effect was a small table model radio, which by the way had no shell, but was built into a wire and metal frame that had a rotating feather on the top of it that played while the radio stations were constantly changing.

The sculpture which particularly caught my eye was a large replica of a human lower leg and foot which stood about four feet high, made of a wire construction with turning wheels and discs driven by belts and motors. The symbolism of the leg sculpture was the most interesting thing to me. The turning motors and wheels with the leg reminded me how complex an organism is the human body and how easy it is for something to go wrong. To take this symbolism one step further and combine it with moral beliefs, I found that within each rotation of the wheels a flexible piece of tin would strike eight different spokes with a pause between the first and last spoke, thus symbolizing the days of the week, Sunday a day of rest not being honored by men of today, so he works constantly with a pause to reassure himself that just a few more days and he will be finished; or the common laborer of today who works eight hours, pauses for a coffee break, and then struggles for another eight hours.

The sculptures which I did not like nor consider kinetic sculpture were a picture of a man with superimposed eyes that were greatly enlarged and another of the Eiffel Tower gradually crumbling. The pictures did not move, they produced no sound nor were they three dimensional like the rest of the sculptures. Another aspect of the exhibit which I did not like was that the sculptures competed with each other; the exhibit sounded like a small mechanical factory. It was difficult to focus my attention on one sculpture for any length of time without being attracted by the sound of another. By having the exhibit in a larger building, I think this could have been corrected.

I strongly recommend the exhibit to all, especially the grade school, college, and art students. There is a lot to be seen that is beneficial. The imagination that the artist put into his sculpture is beneficial to the young (grade school), since they may see the possibilities of what can be done with gravitational, electrical, and magnetic forces. The art students may benefit from what can be done with these forces too, but design and color are more significant to them. The human replica of a leg was greatly enlarged which is an "attention getter" used by commercial artists which is an example of design. The spinning wheel which made one feel he was dropping through an endless tunnel is an example of how color creates an optical effect and stunning design.

The sculptures in motion exhibited could very well be the basis of ideas for the young viewers in his understanding of "forces" and a good stimulant of the imagination, or to the artist who gets to see what others in his field are doing to express themselves. The spectator viewing the Kinetic Sculpture Exhibit may see symbolism, which is significant to him and others around him, as I did in the larger than life wire structure of the human leg.

The teacher's job as I conceive it with a student like this is primarily to help him see what is *there* in its already articulate form, to get him to recognize how proficient he already is in English.

ALVIN JOHNSON

Another response was made by a Negro student, Alvin Johnson, recently discharged from the army. The corrections are mine:

I am put in the vale (fail) catigorie. I have a spiritual feeling with live (life) inside of me know to me and call by man as a soul. I am able to feel a variation of feeling and emotions. But in material cost and productions, chemically I am worth northing, but one sixth of a dolar. But to me and mines, their is no price the world could put up for me. I am taking this course for two reasons. One for my major and the other reason to broaden my outlook on life and its surrounding.

Truthfully, I must admit to feeling a chill every time I read these words, incorrectly spelled as they are. I felt, from the moment I first read these lines, privileged to be made party to such a communication. Here, unlike Daniel Sanchez, is someone who says he is worth something. But one senses, nonetheless, the fierce fight for dignity and worth waged every moment. Here too is the awareness of the external judgment of failure which he is struggling not to accept, at least in its entirety.

Unlike Daniel Sanchez, Alvin Johnson did have real problems in spelling, punctuation, and grammar to which we devoted attention in the course of the semester and which were, of course, not wholly eradicated. But with support and encouragement and a growing awareness that he had a great deal to communicate and the essentials to say what he honestly felt, he wrote many pieces which delighted and informed his classmates, me, and, most important, himself. Here is an example of this writing:

Negro Servicemen in Vietnam
Darkness is beginning to lift on this new day. I've been dug in this foxhole all night. Ever since my patrol got pinned down, I haven't had any sleep, Lord knows how long.

Since I've been in this hole, I have begun to think for the first time, why? Why am I here fighting? I know they said for freedom, but freedom for who? A people I know nothing about? I am sent here to wage a contest with death; yet I haven't freedom myself back home.

Sure I'm patted on the back and given a few medals and spoken to, "That's a good job boy, keep it up." But when this is all over and I get out, okay, I will be the same Nigger, as I fall into the ranks of our society, rejected and abused, because of my skin color; yet I am looked for and called on to fight for this land called Vietnam, or be courtmartialed and go to jail.

No, this is not me, nor my experience but this is what's running in the minds of American Negro fighting men. "Why am I here? Should I fight for a people, for their freedom, and I don't have freedom myself?" I say: "No!" This is not a war that the Negro should participate in.

I think all the Negroes should be at home trying to get freedom for ourselves, our people, in the Northern cities and behind the cotton curtain, wishing for one thing, freedom; to do what we want and feel that it's right, to have a say in the government, go to a school of our choice.

I will go along with war which will threaten the United States opposition, and fight just as hard as the next man. If we were to go to war with Russia or Red China, I'll join tomorrow. But this war is none of ours.

By no means is the Negro a coward, for our record of valor has been displayed down through history. No, we're not cowards, but we are tired of being used!

At the risk of overstating my point and losing my audience, I would like to quote from a letter I received from another student:

I came to your class a reject from another class of higher qualification. The feeling of rejection really hurt my pride. . . . You really gave me confidents when you said to the class that your spelling isn't superior. . . . Mrs. Rubinstein, there is something I think you never realized about me from my participation in the class discussion and that is I haven't very much confidents in myself. For doing anything well. I have always felt subordinate to others. I must say at this time that I feel equal and some-times a little above average in things I do now.

And these words were written by one of the most poised and orally facile members of the class.

As an English teacher of some five years duration, I am only now beginning to understand and define what I feel to be my correct function in the classroom. And I am not demanding that all English teachers must follow suit. But I know there are many like myself, uneasy with the role of glorified proofreader and teacher primarily of rules—descriptive, prescriptive, or transformational—who see the inadequacy of this stance dramatized with low achievers. So it has been my intent to discover ways and means of touching lost chords in students and reconditioning association with English and reversing, whenever possible, the negative self-fulfilling prophesy so many carry with them into class. This approach should not be construed as an attempt to preempt the psychoanalyst's couch, by any means. One can teach skills and increase human power in many ways. Certainly this is what Hughes Mearnes, John Holt, Sylvia Ashton-Warner, and many others struggled for.

10-MINUTE WRITING

One project which did some unlocking of barred gates and seemed to profit student and teacher alike was something we can call, for lack of a more swinging name, the "10-Minute Writing." Many of you may be doing something similar in your classes. But it developed in particu-larly interesting ways in our class last year. The initial ideas for this exercise emerged from several sources; primarily my own feeling that the method involving single sentence refinements is not appropriate, at least initially, with this group. These students, plagued with what I jokingly refer to as "verbal constipation" (in written forms) need to write freely on a variety of subjects without fear of reprisal by red pencil. Further, S. I. Hayakawa enthusiastically described a similar exercise and, finally, an observation of a technique used at Synanon impressed me greatly.

Synanon, the organization devoted to reorganizing the lives of drug addicts and others with "acting out character disorders," uses talk to combat drugs. Talk is a way of life. For example, after lunch every noon and on some evenings, a Synanon is held which involves throwing an idea on the board and letting members and visitors react to it. Or in some sessions, they declare a free choice and anybody can go to the platform and talk on whatever subject interests him. The audience then offers criticism or commendations. Many of these addicts had been frightened, withdrawn people all their lives, yet they got up, faced the group and talked fluently.

Thus, I decided to throw an idea on the board, bring in a painting, an interesting object or play music for the first ten minutes of each class meeting. But instead of talking, which many remedial students do quite well, the class members were asked to write their reactions. They were encouraged to write as much as possible in the time allotted without stopping to worry about spelling, punctuation or grammar. They were instructed *not* to use the dictionary and interrupt their flow of words. If they could not spell a word, they were told *not* to try to replace it with another, which many, I learned, tend to do, but to approximate it on paper, circling to let the reader know the writer was unsure here.

Sometimes a quote was used such as the one from Thoreau: "It takes two to speak truth—one to speak and one to listen" or their own words, "I know what I mean but I can't explain it" or a parable, a children's story, a Zen tale, a bit of news: "McNamara announces 20,000 more men will be sent to Vietnam. What is your reaction?" A painting such as "Christina's World" by Andrew Wyeth, something provocative by Magritte, a phrase such as "culturally deprived"—these and many other bits and pieces from life afforded material for writing.

THINKING ON PAPER

Initially, some people wrote very little and sat hunched self-consciously in their seats. But as this became a kind of class ritual, more

and more students engaged themselves until everyone was writing
something and many could cover a page or more in the time. Those
who explained that they were not writing bcause they were "thinking"
were urged to get down what they were thinking on paper—to think
on paper, as it were, even if it meant writing, "I don't get this" or "This
means nothing to me; I don't dig."

At first, I did not pick up their responses every day but let several
weeks elapse before reading them as a group. I returned this first batch
with ideas scattered here and there, no technical corrections. When I
read something particularly exciting or curious, as became more and
more the case, I would suggest that the student develop the idea in
longer form. And some very good essays did grow from these seedlings.

Then, the class and I stumbled onto a preferable approach to this
exercise. A student in my class had suggested the class take a field
trip but we did not know what would most interest the class as a whole.
One morning, I arrived in the classroom after the students had assembled, and this man informed me that *he* had given the 10-minute for
the day, "What do you do for entertainment?" He then picked up the
writings, commented on them and gave them back to me to read at
the next class meeting. It was from this point on that I used, on most
occasions, student offerings, taking my turn only when I wanted to get
some specific information or utilize the writing for some classwork
during the period. The student responsible for the assignment also
assumed responsibility for commenting on these papers which I too
read and remarked on if I felt so inclined. The new approach involved
students more directly and guaranteed more interchange among students and more direct feedback. Most of the time, there was no problem getting volunteers who knew a class meeting in advance that their
contribution was due.

DIRECT STUDENT QUESTIONS

The students asked much more direct, often personal questions of
each other than I would have dared to have asked them. "Why study
etymology? Isn't it a bore?" "Some things happen in life to shatter your
confidence and leave your personality out of tune. Discuss." "As a
child, what dreams did you have and what happened to them?" "If
you can communicate, why take English classes anyway?" And their
comments to each other on these papers were also delightful to read,
often thoughtful and sympathetic but, at times, much harder hitting
and direct than what a teacher in his position might chance to say.

Sometimes the 10-minute contribution marked the entrance of a student into the classroom family from which he had remained estranged. This was the case with one large, ungainly, epileptic boy who had generally sat self-consciously over in the back corner of the room, a green beret pulled over his eyes. He brought in a print of Picasso's "Guernica." That day everyone read aloud his writing, because we were discussing differing perceptions as a problem in communication. He saw his contribution occupy fifty minutes of class time After this, he wrote much more, his spelling which had been hideous, spontaneously improved, and he participated in class discussions.

Electronic music, jazz, newspaper ads, Biblical quotes, a poem from *Black Dialogue,* an original poem by a student—these and many more experiences students introduced to each other and enriched the class thereby in these 10-minute beginnings.

TEACHER WRITES, TOO

Then, it occurred to me that since the students wrote for me when I put forth a 10-minute idea, I should reciprocate and write for the student when he was the contributor. So, on most occasions when I did not have to use those ten minutes for some desperate last minute prep, I too wrote, grappling as diligently with the problem before us as did the students and I too was subjected to the scrutiny of the reader's eye, which, I must say was often kind, although I was informed by several that my handwriting was fairly unreadable.

Many of the students found reading the teacher's views interesting and many registered surprise that a teacher should think the way a student sometimes does. I feel I became less a stock type and more a human being. Some wrote back what fun it was for them to have a chance to comment on a teacher's paper for a change.

ONE STIMULUS, MANY RESPONSES

In sum then, the 10-minute experiences were very exciting for teacher and most students alike. These writings served to dramatize how one idea, one visual or aural stimulus can arouse so very many different, yet equally valid responses in people. We discussed how no two people, like no two fingerprints, were identical and that this makes life exciting but is often the source of communication difficulties; i.e., we forget this and assume the other guy's reactions are just like ours. These writings brought this home as little else I have tried ever did.

Also, the students got to know each other better and became more curious about each other. They wondered why Mr. Jones said this while Miss Brown said that. And they sincerely wanted to know what their classmates felt about some of the quests that have puzzled men through the ages. "What is happiness?" for instance. One Negro student who entered the class with downcast eyes and sat uncomfortably twisted together in a back row seat in fear and trembling of being called upon, was the only class member to have two shots at this exercise; it was with his question that we terminated the semester: "What does life mean to you?"

Perhaps I should mention here how more can be done with this project in terms of longer essays. One day, I put the symbol "H₂O" on the board. The initial reaction was surprise but by this time the students were becoming conditioned to expect anything. Only one student, educated in Mexico, did not recognize this as the chemical sign for water but, was, nevertheless, able to write at length on this problem of nonmeaning of symbols. We spent the entire class period utilizing their responses to show how very much they have to say potentially about so many subjects. As they watched me transcribe their associations with water on the board, many laughed to see how many obvious ideas they had left out of their own papers.

These ideas included the chemical properties, water's uses, its relation to biology, geography, its place in sports, hospitals, health, cooking, social problems of water shortage as in New York, the California battle, fluoridation, personal experiences, references in books and films such as *Moby Dick, Mr. Roberts, The Ship of Fools,* military uses of water and so on. Then we focused our attention on one of these categories, set up a problem and, in one class wrote a rough draft of an essay on the use of water in hospitals and, in another class, water as a recreational playground.

At the end of the course, I passed out a questionnaire about the relative value of various activities conducted in class that semester. The students were asked: "What single experience stands out in your mind?" I received such replies as the following:

"The most exciting experience was mostly the 10-minute writings. They were fun to write on and it was fun looking at the different ways of communicating."

"Writing without having any concern about if its right or not helped release the brake on my inner feelings."

"The most helpful I found was the way you made us write those 10-minute writings. This forces us to write more and think harder."

"The response to my 10-minute idea, being able to read everyones."

Then, on another page where all the class projects were listed and students were asked to check degrees of value, almost all checked very interesting and very helpful for the 10-minute writings. The few who lacked enthusiasm were largely students who rarely attended and, therefore, did not quite get with it, so to speak.

At the end of the course, I read the students the Scandinavian folk tale *Nail Soup* which tells of the man who comes to an old woman's house asking for a meal. She is ungiving and unwilling to help him out, pleading her own poverty as an excuse. But he persists and says he has a nail for making soup, if she will only provide the water. Then he requests a few vegetables, meat, etc. and the woman, by now curious, begins to volunteer ingredients from what proves to be a well-stocked larder. The soup, in short, is a great success, tasty and full-bodied and the two go their separate ways the next morning great friends with full stomachs. The story's relevance to themselves the students readily see. The English course is in them, not out there somewhere in the wild blue yonder and the problem is tapping their own natural resources and then refining and sharing these. The 10-minute writing project was one of these nails in the soup and it was, in part, through this that the class was fed.

CHANGING THE EQUATION

I do not mean by this article to appear as some kind of swami or faith healer, nor do I mean to suggest that all souls were saved that semester or that this single experiment managed to solve all manner of difficulties experienced by my students. But a portmanteau filled with such untraditional approaches can, I believe, be of great value to the teaching of English, particularly when the bulk of students have not achieved with more traditional methods. This could be a step in the right direction.

The right direction, as far as I personally am concerned is the direction of *salvage*, which is supposedly one of the junior college's prime functions. Yet we either do not have a clear notion of how to salvage or we are not really committed to the idea in the first place, as most of us know who teach the large numbers who revolve out of our doors assisted in their exit by the math and English departments in particular.

If, in fact, the purpose of remedial courses is not to remedy but to eliminate, let us not deceive ourselves with euphemisms. If, on the other hand, we are really there to harness human power, then the areas for fresh thinking and experimentation are vast and very exciting. Certainly Richard Bossone's recently published report on remedial students in twelve California junior colleges points out confusions and inadequacies of current programs and registers the need for revisions.

By placing spelling, punctuation, and grammar concerns in their proper perspective as part of a much larger picture of human communication, and by allowing the students more exploration of the territories of their own minds and those of their classmates, perhaps it is possible to change the equation: English equals hate, fear, and "ugh."

Say something in English? Gladly.

PART FOUR

TERMINAL ENGLISH IN THE JUNIOR COLLEGE: UNANSWERED QUESTIONS

Most students (approximately 75 percent, according to some estimates) who attend a public two-year college do not transfer to a four-year college; they either drop out before obtaining an Associate in Arts degree or they obtain it and use it to qualify for better jobs than they would have been able to obtain without some college preparation. It is therefore ironic that most two-year colleges have virtually ignored the problem of terminal English courses for this vast majority of students. The striking absence of articles on this topic in the professional journals is strong evidence that this is the case; as a result, the two commentaries presented here are offered as a feast in a famine.

Both writers tend to raise more questions than they answer, but this is only normal when we consider that not only a portion of the English profession but also many of the two-year colleges themselves have been basically resistant or hesitant about awarding such courses a legitimate place in the college program.

Leidlich's article illustrates a division within the college English world centering around this area and the reluctance of the English profession to devote massive attention to terminal English courses. But, more important, the author raises major questions that need to be answered at once if the public two-year college is to sustain a truly open–door policy as opposed to a revolving-door policy.

McPherson's often-quoted essay compliments Leidlich's by attempting to answer two of his major questions: Who are the terminal students and what are the objectives of the terminal English course? Within this area of English teaching, which she characterizes as essentially neglected and ill-defined, McPherson presents an optimistic note in the face of so many unanswered questions by explaining what these questions mean. "The questions mean that the junior college has an opportunity to develop a meaningful course of its own, independent of what high schools have done or the senior colleges insist that we do."

Undoubtedly, most readers of this section will emerge with the hope that the two-year colleges will get on with the job immediately.

Reflections on the State of Our Knowledge of Terminal English

RAYMOND D. LIEDLICH

ROBERT BENCHLEY USED TO TAKE great delight in harassing his acquaintances by sending them disconcerting telegrams. One of his favorite messages read simply: "Please ignore previous wire." There had been, of course, no previous wire. The tale is also told that Benchley went to Italy's famed city of Venice for the first time and when he got there he sent a telegram to his travel agent, saying "Streets flooded. Please advise."

I think junior college teachers of English are in an analogous, although considerably less than humorous, situation: Our streets are flooded, and we're not certain if this is a normal state or a state of emergency. (Or perhaps the normal state for junior colleges today is a state of emergency.)

Edmund J. Gleazer, Jr., executive director of the American Association of Junior Colleges, pointed out recently that there are now 780 two-year colleges in the United States, enrolling between 1,250,000 and 1,300,000 students. He went on to say:

> During the 1964–65 school year alone, . . . some 50 entirely new community colleges sprang up across the country, maintaining a steady 20% growth of the junior college population for the past few years. Furthermore, one out of every three students entering college for the first time is going to a two-year institution, while about 13% of the entire college and university enrollment in this country . . . is in a two-year college. . . .[1]

From *College Composition and Communication,* December, 1966, pp. 237–240. Reprinted with the permission of the National Council of Teachers of English and Raymond D. Liedlich.

[1]Quoted in "The Deprived Student in the Two-Year College: New Breed with a New Need," *Publisher's Weekly,* January 3, 1966, p. 26. (A report on a con-

It is evident that we are indeed facing—and will continue to face—a flood of students. This in itself is an enormous problem. But even more disturbing is the knowledge of what happens to these students once they are in college. In his 1963 report, *The Two-Year College and the Teaching of English,* Albert R. Kitzhaber says:

> Because of the prestige that we as a nation have placed on "college education" (almost regardless of the kind or quality of college), about two-thirds of the young people who enter junior colleges declare that they are planning to move as juniors to a four-year institution, and they accordingly enroll in the academic curriculum intended for "transfer" students. The results often are unhappy all around. Only a third survive the two years and actually transfer to a four-year college.[2]

Assuming that a large share of the two-thirds who drop out do so because of limited transfer potential, we must ask ourselves if we are satisfied to let this great a percentage of our students simply fade out of the educational picture or if we should try to channel as many as possible into a program more consistent with their needs and abilities. Dr. Gleazer had something to say about this too:

> The concept that higher education is exclusively for the elite is changing. Education beyond high school is becoming a right not a privilege, and it's becoming a matter of national policy to demand this right. Everyone wants his place in the sun. Many students have gaps in their education; many represent new pools of talent. Not so many years ago they would not have thought about going to college. Now college is open to them. . . . If these students are accepted, the institution that accepts them has the responsibility to provide the education, materials and curriculum they need. Junior colleges are entering a new day—opening the door to a new society and a new economy, complementing the other kinds of educational institutions. . . .[3]

One of the central issues that CCCC study groups have dealt with over the years is implicit in these remarks: the question of whether or not we should provide separate programs for terminal and transfer students. It is interesting and—I think—revealing to follow the statements on this issue in the annual CCCC reports. If my information is

---

ference on The Teaching of the Remedial Student in English and Mathematics sponsored by the College Section of the American Textbook Publishers Institute in cooperation with the American Association of Junior Colleges, held December 7, 1965, at the Hotel Plaza, New York City.)

[2]Albert R. Kitzhaber, *The Two-Year College and the Teaching of English,* November, 1963, pp. 3–4.

[3]"The Deprived Student," p. 26.

correct, the first workshop on teaching composition and communication in the junior college was held in Chicago in 1957, and, of course, this question was one of the several raised. It has been debated with varying results at most of the subsequent meetings, as the following summary shows:

1957 (Chicago) The question of two separate curricula . . . is not ready for settlement, and in the absence of agreement there appears to be no need of a separate English class for terminal students.

1958 (Philadelphia) [No conclusion on the question was reached.]

1959 (San Francisco) [Nothing pertinent to the issue was voted, although the report indicates that terminal programs were in evidence.]

1960 (Cincinnati) Separate transfer and terminal programs are not necessary.

1961 (Washington, D. C.) The basic difference in philosophy between East and West/Mid-West noted in . . . 1960 seemed to be apparent again. The junior college as a basic two-year transfer institution and the community college offering something for everyone beyond high school seem to be the two philosophies. Nevertheless, the general feeling was that "we give them the chance," and that if by the end of the first term, the student has not come up to requirements he must leave. [I interpret these remarks as another vote against separate programs.]

1962 (Chicago) [The question was not raised.]

1963 (Los Angeles) There was almost consensus that clarity in the purpose of the course is essential, that clearer demarcation between terminal and transfer students is desirable, and that terminal courses should be further studied and strengthened.

1964 (New York) The workshop reached agreement on the following points (1) That terminal students should take the regular courses in English. (2) That the English program should be varied enough to provide course work for a complex student body.

1965 (St. Louis) The consensus . . . was that communications programs must be designed to fit the needs of the individual student and the community. Programs will vary, therefore, from college to college.

After hearing this last item we are likely to have mixed emotions. We don't know whether to wring our hands in frustration or clap them in applause. But as we look at the dates and places of the meetings, particularly in the present decade, I think a pattern may be discernible. Consider the relationship between the locations and the conclusions:

Cincinnati (1960)—Separate . . . programs are not necessary.

Washington, D. C. (1961)—We give them the chance and if they don't come up to requirements they leave.

Los Angeles (1963)—Clearer demarcation is desirable. Terminal courses should be studied and strengthened.

New York (1964)—Terminal students should take the regular courses.

St. Louis (1965)—Communications program must be designed to fit the needs of the community. Programs will vary from college to college.

Doesn't it seem that, generally speaking, when the ball is in the Eastern court, the terminal course is out of the game, and when the ball is returned to the Western court, terminal English gets the recognition some of us believe it deserves? When, as in 1965, it moves to a relatively midway point, we come up with a compromise. I'm not much of a tennis player, but to paraphrase Theodore Roethke—a fine poet who was also a fine tennis player—perhaps we do learn by going where we have to go.

In other words, I believe that last year's recommendation was not only sensible but inevitable. Given the nature of the public junior college as a community institution, this question has been answered the only way it could be.

I would not wish to see future CCCC panels or workshops constantly reopen this question. I hope we are ready now not to praise Caesar but to bury him. For while we continue to look over this problem, we continue to overlook the problems we *should* be dealing with:

1. What are the characteristics of terminal English students?
2. How are students placed in these courses?
3. What are the course objectives?
4. What should the course content be?
5. How much composition should be taught and what kind? How should it be approached?
6. What is the role of literature in these courses? How much should be taught and what kinds? How should it be approached?
7. What teaching methods are particularly effective?
8. What instructional materials are available? What materials are needed?
9. How do we evaluate terminal students?
10. How do we train instructors to teach these courses?
11. How can we make these courses more appealing and more worthwhile for both students and teachers?

How many of us are prepared to offer sound, substantiated answers to questions such as these? The fact is that in the face of a knowledge explosion, teachers of terminal English are faced with a knowledge vacuum. We know little enough about both the regular and the remedial programs in junior college English. But we do have the Kitzhaber report mentioned earlier; we do have the report of last year's Tempe conference on *Research and the Development of English Programs in the Junior College*,[4] and we do have the Weingarten-Kroeger report, *English in the Two-year College*.[5] Yet, note how little attention most of these reports give to the terminal program. I certainly do not mean to belittle any of the persons responsible for these reports, nor do I wish to demean their accomplishments All of us should be grateful for what these reports have contributed to our knowledge of junior college English. What we see in their omissions is only further evidence of this enormous vacuum we face when we consider the *real* problems of terminal English.

And now *is* indeed the time to address ourselves to such problems. I believe that we are presently witnessing a significant increase of interest in terminal English.

The CCCC-NCTE has sponsored for the first time a series of regional conferences on English in the Two-Year College. All of these conferences apparently scheduled panels and/or study groups on terminal English. I attended the conference at San Bernardino Valley College last March, where the terminal English panel and study group drew the largest attendance and held the longest meetings. (Incidentally, as further evidence of our lack of knowledge, ours was the only one of five groups that failed to come up with any specific conclusions or recommendations.)

A month later, NDEA sponsored for Southern California Junior Colleges a one-day workshop in English, wholly devoted to the non-transfer program. It was held at Cerritos College on, appropriately enough, April 1st.

And when have we ever seen in one spring the publication of five texts specifically intended for terminal courses? Last spring offered *A Search for Awareness* by Bens (Holt, Rinehart and Winston), *Plain English Please* by Cowan and McPherson (Random House), *Design for a Composition* by Hackett and Williamson (Harcourt, Brace and World), *A Various Collection* by Wilkinson and Blatt (Aegus), and *Writing Practical English* by Wylder and Johnson (Macmillan).

"To be or not to be" is no longer the question. Terminal English is an established part of numerous junior college programs. The question now is: What is it going to become? We may have nothing to look backward to with pride, but we can have something to look forward to with hope.

---

[4]Jerome W. Archer and Wilfred A. Ferrell (eds.) *Research and the Development of English Programs in the Junior College* (Champaign, Ill.: NCTE, 1965).
[5]Samuel Weingarten and Frederick P. Kroeger, *English in the Two-Year College* (Champaign, Ill.: NCTE, 1965).

Will the Real Terminal Student Please Stand Up?

ELISABETH McPHERSON

PROBABLY NO AREA in the field of English teaching, from kindergarten's show-and-tell period through the doctoral dissertation, is more amorphous and ill-defined than the course known in some junior colleges as "terminal English." This paper offers no bibliography because there is precious little information available. Such mention of terminal English as occurs in recent NCTE publications, even those devoted to junior colleges, suggests merely that there is great opportunity here, and rather wistfully points out that the need for research is desperate. In addition to the NCTE publications and an occasional article in the *Junior College Journal*, recent CCCC conventions have devoted one workshop to terminal English. The chances are that no discussion will get far until two very important questions are answered: Who are the terminal students? What should the terminal course try to accomplish?

Because two-year colleges differ, the answer to the first question is not as obvious as it may seem. In some technical schools, all students are terminal; in a few feeder schools for four-year colleges, the terminal student is anybody who fails the college-level courses. In comprehensive community colleges, however, where the student body ranges from the half-reformed high school drop-out to last year's valedictorian, and may include the grandmother of both of them, deciding who is a terminal student and who isn't becomes highly important. So who decides? Is the terminal student to be self-identified or school-identified?

If we let terminal students identify themselves—that is, if we place all those who say they mean to take a two-year technical course in

From *College Composition and Communication*, May, 1967, pp. 93–98. Reprinted with the permission of the National Council of Teachers of English and Elisabeth McPherson.

terminal English and all those who announce their intention of seeking a B.A. in transfer English, what will we gain? One gain may be that the self-defined terminal students will be better motivated if they think there is a direct relationship between the papers they write and the job they are training for; they will approach such classes in a better spirit than if they think they are being forced to deal with irrelevant rhapsodies about beautiful, beautiful sunsets.

Some of the vocational-technical faculty join their students in distrusting the content of general English courses; they tend to regard what goes on in the regular freshman course as extraordinarily esoteric, a kind of pledging ceremony for Master's candidates in the higher criticism, and they transpose some of this uneasiness into a suspicion that any English course not specifically designed for their own students is likely to be useless to any ordinary human being planning to lead a normal life. Further, some of them are quite frank about wanting courses that all their students will be sure to pass.

If separating students according to declared aims keeps both students and faculty happy, why not do it? The first and most cogent argument against it is that, whether or not they care now, the students themselves are being short-changed. Rigidly utilitarian English courses, restricted to the kind of reports these students will have to write once they become draftsmen or nurses, offer them no chance at the liberalizing and humanizing elements most of us believe necessary for satisfying lives.

Let's take a moment at this point to get straight what we *don't* mean by "liberalizing and humanizing elements." Although an occasional rhapsodist does slip into our ranks, very few English teachers really believe that the purpose of any college writing class is to describe sunsets or refer to Burns's poetic images as "ethereal birds flitting against a sunlight wall, who knows whither-from or whence-to." Unfortunately, there are just enough rhapsodists around to give some substance to the myth, and an occasional junior college administrator who sees himself as a "practical man" seems to get as much comfort and security from this misconceived hasty generalization as Linus does from his blanket. By liberalizing and humanizing, we mean developing attitudes that, although they may not contribute to an immediate increase in salary, can at least keep the student from being duped now and then and at best can contribute to a richer and fuller life. Terminal students certainly don't need to gush about sunsets, but they do need to develop habits of clear, orderly expression that will apply equally well to a draftsman's report or an argument to the planning commission. They have no need for esoteric literary criticism, but they will have a continuing need for some critical ability to help them separate sense from illogical nonsense in union proposals and political campaigns.

Secondly, even if we were to concede that vocational students would be temporarily better off in courses specifically tailored to fit their particular trades, have we any right to offer such narrow training when technology is changing so fast that many trades are obsolete before the ink dries on the vocational certificates? When retraining becomes necessary, the student who has had a broader, more flexible English course will surely have an advantage.

Equally important, perhaps, is the question of where such specialization stops. Already many schools offer English for secretaries and English for engineers. Do we need English for nurses? English for automotive mechanics? English for cooks? Such proliferation of courses can lead only to proliferation of jargon: shall we offer English for elementary teachers, in which the eager students are taught to write that Johnny "suffers from malfunctioning of the ego due to compulsive obesity" when they mean that Johnny would be better off if he weren't so greedy?

There are several serious drawbacks to the program that lets the terminal student identify himself and then develops specialized courses catering to his supposedly special needs. A more sensible alternative is for the college to identify terminal students on the basis of their present ability in reading and writing. Clearly we need some measuring instruments better refined than the standardized tests or thirty-minute diagnostic themes now available to us, but a consideration of sectioning materials is beyond the scope of this paper. Whatever method we use, when we make a realistic identification of terminal students based on their present English ability, what we are saying is not that one *student* is terminal and another transfer, but that the English *course* he begins with is terminal; that is, the course is not intended to transfer to a four-year college. A program that groups students according to present achievement, rather than vocational intentions, assumes that all segments of the population, from data processors to potential doctors, need training in clear expression and logical thinking. The student who continues to regard himself as a transfer student can move from the terminal course into regular freshman English whenever he demonstrates a reasonable chance of succeeding there, and the capable technical student will have been given a writing course as challenging as his abilities deserve. He has been protected against the "dead end course" that worried Eley when he prepared his report on terminal English for the Tempe conference. Moreover, the technical student will have stored up some transfer credit if, two years or ten years from now, he changes his mind about going on to college.

Some schools offer a three-track system: terminal English for the terminal student, transfer English for the well-prepared, and remedial English for the self-identified transfer-hopeful who wants one more chance to do in a quarter what he has failed to accomplish in the last twelve years. The student in remedial English may not know the statistical odds against such attempts, but most of his teachers do. If he is one of the eighty percent who fail the one-shot remedial course, what becomes of him? Does he move back into the terminal program where plenty of writing at his own level might have given him much needed practice in organization and coherence, or does he "terminate" in the fullest sense of the word? Many four-year schools have abandoned remedial programs, partly because they weren't getting anywhere with them and partly in the comfortable belief that the junior colleges will take up the burden. Might junior colleges also be justified in relegating conventional remedial courses to the night program and concentrating on more practical approaches to reading and writing in the general terminal course? Where such approaches have been tried, at least as much remedying seems to take place in them as occurs in one last dogged attack on rules for punctuation and the identification of prepositions.

Thus we arrive at the second and more difficult question: what should the terminal course try to accomplish? Some of its aims are implicit in the discussion of who the students will be. More explicitly stated, however, the main aims are these: (1) to help the student get more understanding from what he reads and to approach his reading matter, whatever it is, with increased critical skill; (2) to persuade the student that good expository writing, whatever its subject may be, is clear, definite, logical, and orderly, and to help him put some logic and order in his own writing, even though mechanical perfection may remain beyond his reach. In other words, a good terminal program should lift the really valuable elements from the regular freshman course and offer them on a simpler level, using language and materials that these students can understand.

The first step in setting up such a program is a genuine agreement among those who will teach it that choice usage is not necessarily a prerequisite for orderly thinking and clear expression. Unless such a conviction exists, and unless it is periodically reiterated, most overworked teachers are likely to take the easy way out and grade for mechanics instead of content. But the minute the student's writing is judged primarily on spelling errors and comma splices, the terminal program is in danger of becoming just one more bonehead course. The successful terminal teacher must be prepared to forgive weak spelling, fragmentary punctuation, and awkward sentences. He must concentrate instead on the underlying idea that redeems them. Even if the teacher has trouble finding a redeeming idea, he must still keep reminding both himself and the student that the absence of an idea is a fault more grievous than the absence of a predicating verb.

Once we have found teachers willing to overlook their own natural predilection for choice written English, what can we do to eliminate student prejudice against what they consider a sub-standard course? Getting into transfer English becomes a status symbol, and the student assigned to the terminal course arrives for the first session feeling demeaned or belligerent or both. Probably not much can be done to combat these defensive attitudes. For generations students have unerringly labeled as "bonehead" the lower part of any ability-sectioned program, no matter what euphemistic term the college has devised for it: remedial, technical, terminal, nontransfer, or, most recently, "repair English." But students are usually pretty good judges of the quality of the material offered to them; their defensiveness will relax if they can be convinced that what they are being asked to do in this English class is realistic and meaningful. Defensiveness may disappear altogether in those students who discover that for the first time they are being given a real chance to succeed in an English class.

Another sticky question that follows on the decision to emphasize ideas rather than mechanical correctness is how standards are to be maintained. If "anything goes," what is left to grade on? Should we automatically pass all the students sleeping comfortably in the back row, regardless of the quality of their work (if any)? Clearly not. Terminal English concentrates on essentials and, without belittling the value of standard usage, treats it as an incidental grace. Such a course creates its own integrity. First, the writing assignments must be completed and the directions followed. Second, the student's writing should be realistically evaluated, with most of the attention given to how well he has found the purpose of his writing, and whether he has stated his point clearly and supported it rationally.

Not all students will or should pass this course. Some will fail because they don't do the work. Others will fail because they cannot organize or express even the most elementary ideas. But the same attitudes and abilities that cause them to fail this course would prevent them from writing a coherent report or filling out an accurate order. Even though terminal courses take students where they find them, unless we take them some place from there, such courses will become no more than empty gestures—a way of salving our itching notion that everybody's transcript should show credit in something called "English."

When we do insist on standards, even though those standards are different from those of the transfer courses, we must convince our colleagues in other areas that the standards we use are reasonable, realistic, necessary, and fair rather than just another device by which the English department serves as axeman to keep their favorite students from graduating. We can convince our colleagues more easily if the terminal course results, as it should, in improved work in other courses.

How much time will be needed to improve the student's writing? Because his skills are less, he should spend at least as much time on English as his friend in the transfer section. We can't hope to do much for these students if we offer them less than three class hours extending through the whole year, and more would be better. If many of them are vocational or technical students, however, their programs may already be filled with time-consuming laboratory courses, and the suggestion that they set aside even more time for a writing course will bring vigorous howls from all directions. This scarcity of student time probably accounts for the integrated communications courses that try to combine reading, listening, writing, and sometimes literature in a single one-year course.

Undoubtedly these terminal students need reading help somewhere in the program, if for no other reason than that reading and writing skills are closely intertwined. In addition, nearly all of these students need a wide range of help in reading for its own sake. Some need enough knowledge of elementary phonetics to cope with unknown words; others need to accelerate beyond a hundred words a minute on easy material. The question is not whether the terminal English course should include reading but only how the reading is to be handled. Shall time be taken from the writing course, where it is badly needed, and given to reading, or should special reading courses or laboratories be set up?

And how much literature should the course include? If we insist that English deserves attention because it is a liberalizing and humanizing discipline on any level of achievement, we certainly can not ignore literature. Again, however, if we really mean to make some realistic alteration in thinking and writing habits, we need the whole year for writing. Surely it is not unreasonable to require some literature in the second year. Do the literature courses too need to be sectioned according to ability? Many schools get along with a single introductory course serving both terminal and transfer students. Other schools are experimenting with non-transfer humanities courses, in which they combine and relate introductions to literature, music, painting, and drama. The rationale here seems to be that, even though nobody has time for everything, the terminal student should be given at least a taste of the arts.

If student time is a major consideration, staff time presents an even greater problem. Just as these students need more time and more practice to improve their writing, so they need more individual attention. If maximum class size for regular composition is 25, with no teacher having more than three writing sections, as the Weingarten report recommends, maximum class size for these terminal courses should be 20 (15 is better), with no teacher having more than two sections. These figures mean money for extra staff; a properly taught terminal program is expensive. There is, of course, no way of knowing how many promising programs have been scuttled by the college budget.

Suppose, however, the money is available from an enlightened administration which insists that junior college graduates must read and write competently, how shall the staff be chosen? Will these courses be better taught by finding—or at least, seeking—specialists in terminal English? (Aside from the self-styled ones, are there any?) Or can we offer an adequate program by asking most of the teachers in the department to diversify their approach and keep themselves flexible by dividing their time between transfer and terminal English?

Once the staff has been recruited, what teaching materials do they use? Certainly not a drill program that runs the student around and around the same old treadmill that made him dizzy long before. Four years ago there was little to choose from; the teacher could select either material that defeated the student because it was unrealistically sophisticated or material that bored the student with hopeless juvenility. Within the last year, however, national publishers have brought out four books written especially for terminal courses, and doubtless next year will see even more. But even though texts are available, the department must still decide to what extent English should be a tool subject, not in the special sense of helping draftsmen write the kind of reports the local industries want but in the more general sense of helping students read the texts assigned in their other courses or write the kind of essay exams that will convince their other teachers that they have understood the material of the course. The teacher must also decide to what extent he will supplement the text with current material from local newspapers or national magazines.

All these questions demand our attention, and there is at least one more: should credit for terminal English apply toward an AA degree, or should that degree be limited to those who can complete the first two years of a transfer program? Although this may seem a decision for the entire college, in a very real sense the recommendation made by the English department about credit for its own courses may influence the policy the whole college adopts.

In one way it is encouraging to be faced with so many unanswered questions. The questions mean that the junior college has an opportunity to develop a meaningful course of its own, independent of what the high schools have done or the senior colleges insist that we do. Whether the course we develop is really meaningful, however, will depend on the way we answer the two really important questions: Who are the terminal students? What should the terminal program try to do for them?

PART FIVE

COMPOSITION: IN HIGH SCHOOL AND COLLEGE

Upon examination of the professional literature on the subject of composition in high school and college, one soon has the feeling of being a salvage diver, dropped into a sea of words and looking desperately for some concrete matter to which he can cling. The search is indeed desperate, for it often seems that all we can discover is that composition tends to be poorly taught and that there is exceedingly little agreement on how it ought to be taught. Nevertheless, in this sea of words, the following commentaries may be worth considering for they at least shed light on the problem and offer the reader hope for future direction.

Lacampagne's analysis of major trends in composition not only gives an overview of the teaching of composition in high school but also presents new theories and methods that should soon supplant the traditional and inaccurate assumptions underlying many of the problems in this field.

The report by the Executive Committee of the Conference on College Composition and Communication contains an extensive survey and summary of the status of present freshman composition courses. Maintaining that the nature and future of the freshman composition course are unclear, the document, as stated in its introduction, "aims to clarify the situation by sketching several alternative approaches and displaying some fundamental considerations for the shaping of an effective course." The concluding section of the

303

report offering recommendations for the preparation of teachers of composition
is instructive especially for its implied criticism of the view that one needs
only desire and benevolence in order to teach basic composition.

The next three articles explore the scope and content of the composition
course in high school and college and present logical rationales for what
most writers regard as an ill-structured teaching area.

Hach, basing his thinking on both Skinner's and Bruner's ideas, sees not
"a sequence in composition" (as he did in 1960) but rather two "sequences
in composition" for two groups of pupils, "Better-Average and Honors" and
"Lower-Average." Although Hach presents in skeletal outline the types of
composition required for the two above groups in grades 9–12 only, he does
point up the need for an articulated program in composition from K through
12. He also makes clear that "these sequential programs mean nothing unless
they are translated into action in the classroom."

Guth defines the heart of the rhetoric program as appropriate materials
and criteria that make for forceful and significant prose. He maintains that
"a writing course cannot miraculously widen and enrich the student's experience, but neither can it teach skill in a vacuum. What it can at least
start to do is to teach disciplined self-expression, responsible interpretation
of experience, articulate participation in the public dialogue."

Jernigan presents six minimum expectations entitled "Basic Proficiency
Guidelines" as drawn up by the Michigan College Association's ad hoc Committee on English Proficiency and he uses these guidelines in slightly modified form as basic objectives toward which a freshman composition program
should be directed: Fluency, Unity, Development, Diction, Syntax, and
Mechanics. He also offers suggestions on the implementation of these objectives. Like the other writers, Jernigan's analysis of objectives and structure
in composition is his means of arriving at what constitutes proficiency in
English composition.

The next two articles deal mainly with specific methods for teaching composition and offer the reader relatively distinct points of view. Bossone, like
Jernigan, advances a more highly structured situation with concentration on
expository prose. Murray, on the other hand, tends to favor a less structured
situation in which students, with a sense of responsibility for their own
learning, are left to explore any form and any topic. Taken together, these
two articles reflect some of the surface differences so prevalent at the 1966
Dartmouth Anglo–American Seminar on the teaching of English, between
those who teach writing on a relatively impersonal level as opposed to those
who teach it on a more personal level or, more specifically, those who would
pursue a more logical or subject-matter approach as opposed to those who
would emphasize a more psychological or student-centered approach. But
more careful reading will reveal that both writers consider each approach as
the basis of the other. If this is understood, it should help to eliminate the
dead-end "either-or" approach.

The remaining four articles deal with specific problems the teacher will
encounter while teaching composition. Farrell discusses the problem of com-

position assignments: what kind of assignments should be avoided and what kind should be developed. He suggests that "if assignments are composed carefully so as to assist students to produce appropriate voices or 'selves' in their writing, if students are not asked to do what the teacher would not want to do, if they are given a choice of assignments as well as the opportunity to create their own, then their writing should be more pleasurable to read and much easier to evaluate."

Christensen discusses the problem of how the new grammar might be brought to bear on composition. In the belief that students write poorly because teachers do not know how to teach writing, Christensen develops the notion that composition should be taught through principles of the generative rhetoric of the sentence: what he calls the writing of "cumulative" sentences through a process which makes the modifier "the essential part of any sentence." Christensen illustrates lucidly the four principles of his generative rhetoric of the sentence: addition, direction of modification or movement, levels of generality or abstraction, and texture. In so doing he argues that teaching the student via this method will not only make the student a better writer but also a better reader of literature and that he will also gain "insight into the elusive thing we call style."

Diederich treats the problem of grading and measuring writing ability by advancing a rating scale and by describing a scientific way to measure growth in writing ability. Based upon a major research study conducted with two colleagues in the Research Division of Educational Testing Service, Diederich's findings represent a landmark in the no-man's-land of evaluating students' writing performances.

In a related essay, Larson engages the problem of writing comments on themes. He argues that a teacher of composition should be taught how to write effective marginal and final comments on students' themes not only to insure fairness and consistency but also to enable teachers to serve as models and guides for improving student writing. Any reader should find Larson's guidelines helpful when engaged in a severe test of his own power to communicate, a test to demonstrate the skill he teaches.

Major Trends in the Teaching of Composition

ROBERT J. LACAMPAGNE

THE LEAD ARTICLE in the first issue of the *English Journal,* published in 1912, was titled "Can Good Composition Teaching Be Done Under Present Conditions?"[1] The first paragraph was. succinct in its answer— "No." If the same title were used in a similar article today, the answer would undoubtedly be, "Yes, but. . . ." Yes, through research, experimentation, and new methods and materials, the profession has at present the knowledge and ability to teach composition well, certainly better than it has been taught before. But no, despite such promising conditions, composition is not taught well in most schools.

Much of the profession's recent concern over the teaching of composition has been a reaction to widespread criticism of student writing at all grade levels. "They can't write!" cry employers of recent high school graduates, professors working with doctoral candidates, and English teachers themselves. Whether or not students today are writing better or worse than those of yesterday is beside the point. What is important is that there is general dissatisfaction with students' writing, and this has resulted in some important shifts in professional thinking on how to teach writing. As a consequence, the teaching of composition today shows signs of a renaissance, with the emergence of promising new trends and developments.

IMPLICATIONS FROM RESEARCH

Teacher assumptions about writing instruction have been seriously challenged. Current research has negated many widely held assump-

Written especially for this volume.

tions, causing considerable reevaluation of the teaching of composition. Three of these assumptions, as well as an illuminating research study of what happens in high school English classes, bear special examination.

The notion that a knowledge of traditional or formal grammar will improve writing has probably been the most firmly held assumption among English teachers Yet there is virtually no support for such a position. In fact Braddock, Lloyd-Jones, and Schoer in their important book *Research in Written Composition* conclude, ". . . the teaching of formal grammar has a negligible or, because it usually displaces some instruction and practice in composition, even a harmful effect on the improvement of writing."[2] While a few recent studies in structural and transformational grammar have shown more positive results, almost no one in the profession today sees intensive work in grammar as leading to major improvements in writing.

Another popularly held assumption is that writing frequency—one learns to write by writing—will improve writing. But Robert Hunting in reviewing five studies of writing frequency concludes, ". . . it isn't so."[3] It may seem logical that "the more you write the better you write," but present evidence does not support this premise. According to this assumption, it would be reasonable to expect that a writer's second and third novel, play, or short story would be better than his first. Any English major, however, could recall offhand dozens of examples of the opposite being true.

Teachers who spend weekends carefully correcting and annotating student papers presumably assume some dividend in terms of improvement of their students' writing. Again, research has not upheld this assumption. Studies by Arnold,[4] Burton and Arnold,[5] Stiff,[6] and Sutton and Allen[7] suggest that written comments and corrections have little if any effect on the improvement of writing. On the other hand Lynch[8] found that personal conferences exert a positive influence on writing achievement and on student attitudes toward writing. Unfortunately, Lacampagne[9] found that students are seldom if ever given opportunities for such conferences.

While English teachers should be aware of the findings of the above studies, they should also learn to analyze such research critically. No one in the profession advocates having students write infrequently, nor would many (at least in the upper grade levels) suggest that no corrections and comments ever be made on papers. But teachers should not expect that these methods *per se* will improve writing. Hopefully, these procedures, used in an individualized, developmental writing program, will be helpful to students. The act of writing "more of the same" or the reading of teacher comments, however, is not likely to be productive.

To view major issues in composition in proper perspective, it is helpful to know as much as one can about how composition is currently being taught. Squire and Applebee's *High School English Instruction Today*[10] describes a massive research study of high school English programs in which observers visited schools in forty-five states. Although schools were selected primarily because of the excellence of their English programs, the magnitude of the study suggests that its findings may well constitute a national report on the current state of English teaching. The most surprising finding was that only 15.7 percent of class time was spent in composition and that most of it was spent in "after-the-fact" teaching, namely the correction of papers and their subsequent revision. Virtually no time was spent in teaching students *how* to write. What is particularly discouraging was that schools visited were reputed to have superior English programs. (Isolated studies of individual school situations indicate an even smaller percentage of English class time being spent in composition.) It is sobering to note that the majority of teachers in the study said they spent nine to twelve hours a week correcting papers, considerably more time than the five to eight hours they said they spent in preparing for their classes. The most important result of the Squire and Applebee study is that English departments are reevaluating not only their methods of teaching composition but the amount of class time spent in this important aspect of English instruction.

Unfortunately, most research in composition has uncovered what does *not* work. Although there are some encouraging studies on pre-writing activities, the profession lacks a substantial body of studies indicating what composition practices *do* work. Nevertheless, certain trends and developments, based on new assumptions about teaching writing, are being increasingly integrated into the new English curriculum.

THE NEW PRE-WRITING, WRITING, AND POST-WRITING PROCEDURES

Partly as a response to research findings, English teachers today are acknowledging that students need to know more about the process of writing than that "Every paragraph must have a topic sentence" (an oversimplification and inaccurate statement at best) or that every composition must have "an introduction, body, and conclusion." Proposals have been made to teach students more about the writing process and, perhaps more important, to encourage and motivate them to write. The following approaches are suggestive of an important trend to emphasize the pre-through-actual writing experience as opposed to the more common write-then-correct approach.

Leavitt and Sohn's *Stop, Look, and Write!*[11] and Leavitt's *The Writer's Eye*[12] are attempts to develop a writing program in which photographs and pictures are used to teach such writing skills as using comparison and contrast, expressing ideas, developing characterizations, and detailing the specific. The approach rests on the premise that ". . . all effective writing depends primarily on accurate, insightful observation" and that too much emphasis has been placed on learning rules with too little stress on students finding "something lively and meaningful to write about." The Leavitt-Sohn approach emphasizes the use of pictures to promote observation, use of the senses, and use of the imagination, which may in turn produce better and more vivid writing.

One promising trend is the increasing rejection by English teachers of artificial forms of writing. For example, the assignment to write a single developed and coherent paragraph on a given topic (often given on the junior high level) represents a difficult task—as any teacher trying it will find. Except for the "Talk of the Town" column in *The New Yorker*, it is a form of writing seldom practiced outside the classroom. The so-called "five paragraph composition" appears to be losing favor as the basis of writing instruction in the upper school grades, as is the "term" or "research" paper that so seldom involved a term's work or true research. In the place of these predominantly sterile exercises in writing, the trend is toward using a wide variety of writing experiences reflecting the types of writing that are more relevant to the student and his society. Moffett's *A Student-Centered Language Arts Curriculum Grades K-13: A Handbook for Teachers*[13] contains excellent discussion of such writing experiences, describing such possibilities as dramatic and Socratic dialogue, the short play, the public journal and the private diary, writing based on interviews or observations, spontaneous reflections, and profile writing. But whatever the assignment, current opinion is that it should reflect an actual literary or practical form of writing.

An increasing number of teachers report remarkable success with deeply personal student writing often partly based on or initiated by students' informal speech or speech activities. A classroom atmosphere that is open, free, and conducive to creative work is essential for this approach. Of several books stressing this approach, the two pamphlet-sized works that are most readable are Langdon's *Let the Children Write*[14] and Kohl's *Teaching the "Unteachables."*[15] Both describe actual classroom experiences and contain numerous examples of student writing. Langdon, in her explanation of what she terms "intensive writing," was struck by the difference between the dullness of the students' written work and the excitement of their speech which was ". . . the very stuff of life, pulsating and vibrating with vigour and individuality." Langdon's book outlines her program for transferring the enthusiasm of the spoken word to the written word. Kohl too emphasizes the personal, asking children to write about ". . . what their homes were like, whom they liked, where they came from," concluding that, given a non-threatening class situation, children write directly and honestly.

Those who have worked with disadvantaged students of all ages are aware of the numerous mechanical errors in their writing; a teacher could easily spend all his time correcting these errors. Kohl's response to this difficulty reflects yet another trend in composition, particularly in work with students below the high school level.

> If a child asked me to comment on the substance of his work, I did not talk of the sentence structure. There is no more deadly thing a teacher can do than ignore what a child is trying to express in his writing and comment merely upon the form, neatness, and heading. Yet there is nothing safer if the teacher is afraid to become involved. It is not that I never taught grammar or spelling; it is rather that the teaching of grammar and spelling is not the same as the teaching of writing. Once children care about writing and see it as important to themselves they want to write well.

Many classroom teachers share Kohl's impression that when students are vitally involved and interested in their writing mechanical errors decrease.

The kinds of imaginative writing experiences suggested above are at present most widely accepted as appropriate for students below the high school level. A different approach suggests that one critical aspect in working with older students is a diagnosis of their writing difficulties, followed by a program of corrective and remedial instruction. Illustrative of the position is Bossone's study, "The Writing Problems of Remedial English Students in Community Colleges of The City University of New York,"[16] in which a major finding was that

> . . . the most serious writing problems of these remedial English students . . . center around "organization," "ideas," and "sentence structure" which unfortunately do not receive as much attention (judging by number and extent of teachers' comments) as punctuation, mechanics, and spelling.

Other writers such as Hach and Jernigan suggest the need for greater organization, sequence, and structure within writing programs.

Use of computers makes possible the sorting out of student writing errors with direct feedback of information to students and teacher. With the increasing availability of computers in schools it is interesting to theorize over their possible use in the English classroom.

Recent catalogues of the National Council of Teachers of English list such titles as *Emerging Outlines of a New Rhetoric, Rhetoric and School Programs, Toward a New Rhetoric,* and *Rhetoric: Theories for Application,* testifying to the renewed interest in rhetoric which has grown in recent years. The term *rhetoric* still has as its basis the Aristotelian concept of techniques by which one can convince or persuade an audience to think or act in a certain way. Evans and Walker note, however, that there are major differences between the classical and the "new" rhetoric.

> Gone is the old notion that rhetoric consists of a bag of tricks with which the writer or speaker persuades his audience to take his point of view. The new rhetoric is conceived as thought unfolding in the search of truth, however tentative. While traditional rhetoric was concerned with skill in expressing pre-conceived arguments and points of view, the new rhetoric is concerned with the exploration of ideas. While traditional rhetoric was based on established patterns of discourse, the new rhetoric is based on the assumption that organization grows out of the subject being treated.[17]

In teaching students to write effectively using rhetorical techniques, audience, evidence and argument, and use of comparison and contrast are commonly stressed. In addition the tools of rhetoric provide students with a way of analyzing writing so as to understand how a writer achieves the effects desired—a most important lesson for a writer.

Murray's *A Writer Teaches Writing: A Practical Method of Teaching Composition*[18] describes methods of teaching writing based on the experiences of professional writers. The author, a professional writer and professor of English, was asked by the New England School Development Council, representing over three hundred school systems, to develop a new approach to composition. He states that as teachers

> . . . we cannot discover how the writer works merely by studying what he has left on the page. We must observe the act of writing itself to expose to our students the process of writing as it is performed by the successful writer.

Murray's method is based on an examination of what writers do when they write, followed by a duplication of that process by students. Of particular interest to teachers is his discussion of the skills needed by a writing teacher. According to Murray, he himself listens, coaches, diagnoses, writes with students, hones creativity with discipline, keeps his distance, and is flexible. One of the most important aspects of the book is its specific description of the pre-writing experience, that vital process known to be lacking in most English programs.

THE TEACHER AS WRITER

Murray's contention that teachers of writing should write is provocative. Teachers who delude themselves in telling their students that writing is fun, that it is not hard "once you get started," probably do not write themselves except for a string of abbreviations, as *sp., punct., cap.,* and *awk.* (hardly a recognized literary genre). Numerous concerns of the writing teacher—whether they be unity, coherence, and emphasis; finding an audience or voice; or limiting a topic—can best be understood by one who is often frustrated by these very problems.

The concern with the English teacher as writer may well have started in the middle 1960's by English teacher institutes sponsored through funds of the National Defense Education Act. Institute directors were astonished to find that many of those teachers who complained of their students' inability to write could not write themselves. It was a traumatic experience for all, particularly for those teachers who found their papers filled with red pencil marks.

No one expects any but a few English teachers to have the competence to write professionally. However, many other options are available. For example, a teacher can attempt the writing assignment he gives his students (just this very act has caused teachers to alter their assignments drastically); the more intrepid may distribute his paper with the rest of the class's for a class evaluation of the anonomously written assignments.

An excellent composition lesson recently seen by the writer was the reading of a paper written by the teacher for a college course. The students, an able group of high school juniors, analyzed and then attacked the paper's structure, particularly its logical development, with little mercy but with obvious delight. After the dissection, the students inquired as to the grade it had received. "A-", replied the teacher. "Would you have given any of us that high a grade on such a paper?" asked another student. The students, of course, roared when the teacher blushingly admitted that he wouldn't have!

THE USOE ENGLISH PROGRAM

Another important force in initiating and implementing new developments in English was "Project English," later known as the English

Program of the U. S. Office of Education. This federal project, initiated in 1961, funded over twenty Curriculum Study and Demonstration Centers throughout the country. The Centers were charged with developing innovative English curriculums and study units on local and statewide levels. Butler and O'Donnell's[19] description of each Center and the material available from it is instructive, especially to those charged with developing a total English curriculum. Fourteen of the Centers developed curriculum materials which reflect current interest in rhetoric for teaching composition in grades 7-12. Materials developed by the University of Georgia, Northwestern University, and the University of Oregon are among the most useful to the classroom teacher.

THE DARTMOUTH SEMINAR

The 1966 Anglo-American Seminar at Dartmouth College brought together fifty educators from the United Kingdom and the United States who were concerned with the teaching of English. Two books describe the proceedings: Muller's *The Uses of English*,[20] written for the public, and Dixon's *Growth through English*,[21] written for the profession. Without question this month-long meeting has had a significant influence on the future direction of English teaching in this country. While concerned with all aspects of English, participants at the Seminar recognized particularly serious deficiencies in the teaching of writing and sought to recommend more promising approaches.

Foremost in the thinking of participants was the necessity of engaging students in the writing process. British participants saw what they termed "talk" and "drama" as integral to writing. Dixon suggests that ". . . writing-assignments without a background of discussion and shared experience are unlikely to elicit much response from many children and young people," and he urges, "let exploratory talk precede writing."

The question of audience was another concern of Seminar participants. Traditionally, American students have written for an audience of one—the teacher. Occasionally schools have provided a broader forum for student writers through a creative writing magazine or school newspaper, but these have invariably restricted publication to students who write well already. Participants felt that by limiting his audience one limits a writer's options—that the teacher, in fact, should simply be one person in a large audience. An audience, it was pointed out, can be expanded in many ways. For example, students can share their writing with each other through class magazines containing a writing sample from everyone in the class.

Participants split, usually along national lines, on the type of writing that should be emphasized in the English classroom. A number of Americans suggested that, since expository writing is the kind of writing most often done in adult life, it should rate prime consideration in the classroom. The British were nearly unanimous in feeling that imaginative, personal writing was more important. As it turned out, more discussion centered on aspects of creativity and imaginative writing than on exposition, with an underlying agreement that the former might be most appropriate during the early school years, the latter in the upper levels.

One result of the Seminar was the American's discovery that much of what is done across the Atlantic may be applicable to our schools. This has encouraged increased examination of British approaches to the teaching of English.

AMERICAN vs. BRITISH APPROACHES

American teachers tend to regard the teaching of writing in a mechanistic manner with most instruction consisting of correcting student errors. The British teacher of English, in contrast, appears more apt to view writing from a psychological rather than mechanistic stance, with writing seen as an integral part of the student's growth and development. As Muller describes this, writing should teach children ". . how to order and shape their experience, thereby learning more about life and themselves." While American teachers often express interest in "involving" students in written assignments, the British take an even stronger position, contending that writing can literally "shape" the student's psyche. The previously mentioned work of Kohl and Langdon suggests practical applications of such a philosophy. Another work, Holbrook's *English for the Rejected*,[22] is particularly persuasive in this vein and is highly recommended for teachers working with the disadvantaged child. While using writing to "order and shape their experience," Holbrook nevertheless cautions against the temptation for classroom teachers to play analyst in their interpretations of student writing, particularly writing of an intensely personal nature.

Partly as the result of the Dartmouth Seminar, Squire and Applebee decided to do a counterpart of their National Study by visiting British and Scottish schools. In a speech drawing upon findings of the international study,[23] Squire noted a sharp cleavage between American and United Kingdom views on the correction of student papers.

The writing [of British students] is read, shared, pinned on bulletin boards, published in school magazines, but it is seldom criticized in detail by the teachers and almost never corrected. In almost no instance in our visits to forty-two schools did we find a child rewriting a paper after the teacher had offered detailed suggestions; in only a few cases did we find more than an overall mark, a spelling error, or a single teacher comment on papers returned to the students!

To American conservatives like myself, the most striking discovery about this approach to writing is that it actually works. By the time young people enter the upper years of secondary school—whether in selective or unselective institutions—they are clearly writing as well as, although no better than, American students of similar age. And they write with a zest of enthusiasm and freshness that most American teachers would envy. Moreover, writing for them involves neither drudgery nor hard work. Writing is not a punishment inflicted by the teacher. Writing is an interesting, non-threatening experience in self-expression. Nor do the British teachers suffer under the staggering paper loads which age and tire their American colleagues well before their time.

The British writing programs observed tended to stress personal or imaginative writing, to emphasize talk and drama as initial steps toward writing, and in general to provide students with an open classroom situation which allowed and encouraged the free flow of ideas and words.

CONCLUSION

The major trends in the teaching of composition discussed in this article are only suggestive of the numerous innovations in the field. Articles to follow will explore additional and sometimes conflicting approaches to teaching writing. It will be interesting for readers to compare the various positions advocated. In a country without a national school curriculum, such differences of opinion are to be expected and should no doubt be encouraged. Certainly it is only through experimentation with new ideas that teachers can develop better educational programs.

REFERENCES

[1] Hopkins, Edwin M. "Can Good Composition Teaching Be Done Under Present Conditions?", *The English Journal*, I (1912).

[2] Braddock, Richard; Lloyd-Jones, Richard; and Schoer, Lowell. *Research in Written Composition*. Champaign, Illinois: National Council of Teachers of English, 1963, p. 37.

[3] Hunting, Robert. "Recent Studies of Writing Frequency," *Research in the Teaching of English*, I (Spring, 1967), p. 30.

[4] Arnold, Lois V. "Writer's Cramp and Eyestrain—Are They Paying Off?" *The English Journal*, LIII (January, 1964), pp. 10–15.

5 Burton, Dwight L., and Arnold, Lois V. *The Effects of Frequency of Writing and Intensity of Teacher Evaluation Upon High School Students' Performance in Written Composition.* USOE Cooperative Project No. 1523, 1963.

6 Stiff, Robert. "The Effect upon Student Composition of Particular Correction Techniques," *Research in the Teaching of English,* I (Spring, 1967), 54–75.

7 Sutton, J. T., and Allen, E. D. *The Effect of Practice and Evaluation on Improvement in Written Composition.* USOE Cooperative Research Project No. 1993, 1964.

8 Lynch, James J. "The Conference as a Method in the Teaching of English Composition in the Junior-Senior High School." Unpublished Ph.D. dissertation, New York University, 1963.

9 Lacampagne, Robert J. "A National Study of Selected Attitudes and Approaches to Writing of Twelfth Grade Students with Superior Writing Performance Versus Those with Average Writing Performance." Unpublished Ph.D. dissertation, University of Illinois, 1968.

10 Squire, James R., and Applebee, Roger K. *High School English Instruction Today.* New York: Appleton-Century-Crofts, 1968.

11 Leavitt, Hart Day, and Sohn, David A. *Stop, Look, and Write!* New York: Bantam Books, 1964.

12 Leavitt, Hart Day. *The Writer's Eye.* New York: Bantam Books, 1968.

13 Moffett, James. *A Student-Centered Language Arts Curriculum, Grades K-13: A Handbook for Teachers.* Boston: Houghton Mifflin Company, 1968.

14 Langdon, Margaret. *Let the Children Write.* London: Longmans, Green and Co. Ltd., 1961. (Available through the National Council of Teachers of English.)

15 Kohl, Herbert R. *Teaching the "Unteachable."* New York: The New York Review, 1967.

16 Bossone, Richard M. *The Writing Problems of Remedial English Students in Community Colleges of The City University of New York.* New York: City University Research and Evaluation Unit, 1969.

17 Evans, William H. and Walker, Jerry L. *New Trends in the Teaching of English in Secondary Schools.* Chicago: Rand McNally & Company, 1966, p. 53.

18 Murray, Donald M. *A Writer Teaches Writing: A Practical Method of Teaching Composition.* Boston: Houghton Mifflin Company, 1968.

19 Butler, Donna, and O'Donnell, Bernard. *A Guide to Available Project English Materials.* Champaign, Illinois: National Council of Teachers of English, 1968.

20 Muller, Herbert J. *The Uses of English.* New York: Holt, Rinehart and Winston, Inc., 1967.

21 Dixon, John. *Growth through English.* Reading, England: National Association for the Teaching of English, 1967. (Available through the National Council of Teachers of English.)

²² Holbrook, David. *English for the Rejected.* Cambridge, England: Cambridge University Press, 1964.

²³ Squire, James R., and Applebee, Roger K. *A Study of the Teaching of English in Selected British Secondary Schools.* USOE Project No. 6–1849, Champaign, Illinois, 1968.

This statement has been developed from the deliberations of the 1966 convention in Denver and refined at the 1967 "Scholar's Seminar" in Louisville, both sponsore[d] by the Conference on College Composition and Communication, whose Executive Committee endorsed its publication in CCC. Contributors to the statement include Jerome Archer, Arizona State University; Richard Braddock, University of Iowa; Wallace Douglas, Northwestern University; Walker Gibson, University of Massachusetts at Amherst; Robert Gorrell, University of Nevada; Patrick Hogan, University of Houston; Harold Kelling, University of Colorado; Richard Lloyd-Jones, University of Iowa; and Bain Stewart, University of Tennessee.

The Status of Freshman Composition

Executive Committee, Conference on College Composition and Communication

THE NATURE and the future of the freshman composition course are unclear. The very expression, "*the* freshman composition course," is misleading, for it covers many approaches, some good and some bad. One hears of this college or that reducing or even abandoning its freshman composition requirement, but one wonders who is abandoning what—or whom. This document aims to clarify the situation by sketching several alternative approaches and displaying some fundamental considerations for the shaping of an effective course. The document concludes with a review of the preparation an instructor needs in order to teach the fundamental considerations effectively.

A considerable portion of the four-year and two-year college freshmen in our country have home backgrounds in which little premium has been placed on a rich experience with language, little emphasis given to a precision with words. In some elementary and secondary school

From *College Composition and Communication*, February, 1968, pp. 81–85. Reprinted with the permission of the National Council of Teachers of English.

systems, students still do almost no writing; they merely fill out workbooks and take short-answer tests. In many schools and in some high school honors courses, students write frequently but have little or no organized program of instruction in composition. Numerous other schools teach a few formulas for writing paragraphs, focus instruction and practice heavily on achieving mechanical correctness and, with the mistaken notion that it will improve sentence structure, on reviewing the concepts of traditional grammar. Still other schools, however, have carefully designed courses of study which lead the students from simpler to more complex aspects of a range of types of writing for various kinds of readers and situations.

Obviously, colleges and universities need placement procedures and several different freshman courses when they admit students whose home and school backgrounds vary widely. On what basis placement can best be made necessarily varies according to the students and the desired end results of the freshman composition program. More study is needed of what is involved in various types of writing for different types of readers in different situations and of how various students learn to do these different things well. Until these considerations are better understood, detailed course models and accompanying placement procedures cannot be suggested. But surely more is involved in effective placement than merely a "general level of writing ability," which may not even exist.

Hypotheses on the teaching of composition abound, yet little is really known about processes of composing, and a comprehensive theory of modern rhetoric is still suffering the pangs of birth. Too many college instructors, their graduate study devoted almost entirely to literature, have made no advanced study of composition, display little more than average competence in their own writing, and see their professional advancement associated with literary or linguistic scholarship. It is no wonder that study and research in the deeper aspects of composing have not traditionally received the sustained attention of our best minds. Nor should it be surprising to find conflicting evidence on whether or not freshmen typically improve their writing as a result of their composition instruction.

Certain recent developments hold promise of clarification and improvement. The Head Start program offers a way to enrich the language backgrounds children bring to school. NDEA institutes in English have exposed thousands of practicing teachers to advanced work in composition, more and more undergraduate English majors are taking advanced courses in composition as a part of their preparation for teaching, and graduate English departments have begun to add advanced courses in rhetoric and in the teaching of freshman composition. Stimulated in part by federal grants, research in written composition is investigating problems barely recognized before, and new tools of research are being devised in the process. In the light of these promising developments—many of them barely initiated—it seems precipitous to abandon freshman composition without careful consideration.

ALTERNATIVE APPROACHES

When a college sees no desirable alternative, it may well drop the freshman requirement. That is, if it conceives of freshman composition merely as a means of insuring that its students achieve "minimal literacy" and if it carefully selects for admission only students who have already achieved that minimum level, there is no point in requiring a course which teaches what the students already know. For such an approach to be a responsible one, not an abdication, it should include several features:

1. Unless all the freshmen come from high schools—and transfer students from junior colleges—known to have well designed writing programs taught by effective teachers, the college needs to include among its selection procedures not merely objective testing but the screening of a writing sample from each student, conducted by a faculty committee familiar with the college standard and willing to apply it.[1]
2. To help students maintain the abilities they have developed in their previous schooling, the college should insure that several of the liberal education courses (not special composition courses) include some planned instruction in the kinds of problems faced by writers in those fields. This may be much more difficult to do in some institutions than it would be in a small, excellent liberal arts college with a highly literate and dedicated faculty, for some instructors in more typical institutions may act merely as proofreaders or do nothing at all, in either case overlooking the intellectual aspects of writing. For this reason, when a faculty does undertake such a program it should evaluate it after several years to determine whether or not its objectives are being achieved after the initial enthusiasm has worn off.
3. Because the writing done in liberal arts courses as described above

[1]For a more thorough discussion of testing in composition, see the terminal report of the Committee on Testing, *College Composition and Communication*, XVII (December, 1966), 269–272.

will doubtless be academic in nature, the college should also offer an elective course or a variety of elective courses in writing which emphasizes perception and imagination more than criticism and argument.

If the composition requirement is maintained, what shape might it take?

One approach is to offer a "skills" course—emphasizing a review of grammar and the marking of errors in grammar, usage, and mechanics in student papers. Faculties should realize, however, that after years of such experience in the elementary and secondary grades, students in college usually do not improve their composing with the same approach.[2] If the approach is not effective, it is understandable that some colleges make such courses as inexpensive and easy as possible, herding large numbers of students into lecture halls or televised classrooms and marching them through the pages of programmed textbooks dealing with old-fashioned grammar to the neglect of the intellectual aspects of the composing process. No brief can be held for the set of prescriptions familiar to the conventional offering—an offering repeating the least admirable practices of high school teaching. If a college does have such a course, the catalog and transcripts should label it for what it is —remedial, subcollege work.

Are there courses in composition that are not simply remedial, do not repeat earlier training, and can take a respected place in the education of a college undergraduate? We believe there are. But we also believe that there are several varieties of such courses and that even these varieties may well vary in details from one campus to another. At the risk of being vague, we undertake here to suggest what some of the varieties are and what fundamental considerations underlie them all.

FUNDAMENTAL CONSIDERATIONS

The essential feature of these courses is their insistence on regarding every act of composing as an act of choice among various approaches and means of expression. The purpose of the courses we here propose is simply this: to increase and refine the student's awareness of his available choices and to prepare him to anticipate the effects of such choices.

The subjects traditionally associted with composition courses—litera-

2For an evaluation of the "skills" course at the peak of its popularity, see Porter G. Perrin's "Maximum Essentials in Composition," *College English*, VIII (April, 1947), 352–359.

ture, language, rhetoric, and mass communication—pertain to a study of choices in two ways: (1) they may stimulate rhetorical invention or (2) they may contribute knowledge directly by clarifying methods of choice. That is, in the first way, a poem or story may excite or annoy the student enough to provide a topic, generalizations, arguments, support for his writing. In the second way, a poem or story may exemplify an approach to a matter like organization, adding to a student's stock of approaches and means of expression by illustrating one or more of them.

It is in these two ways—by stimulating writing and by contributing to a study of writing choices—that subjects like literature, language, rhetoric, and mass communication have a place in the composition course. If these subjects themselves become the focuses or organizing principles of the course, it loses its justification as a writing course, and a title like "composition course" becomes merely an inaccurate label.

If a course is described largely in terms of the literary selections it employs or is organized by literary types or chronology, it certainly does not seem to be a composition course. If it is a course in "composition and literature," it should also be organized according to the nature of composing, and this organization should be equally wedded to the organization of the literature employed as a means of teaching composition. If the student writing is merely analysis of literature without deliberate attention to available approaches or means of expression in composition, it is essentially a literature course. If literature is used as a springboard for writing—to afford students and instructor a common basis in experience for writing and discussion, it is essentially a composition course.

Similarly, the study of language may serve a composition course if it helps the student explore the ways in which language has changed in the past and the dialects and styles in which it occurs today, helps him by liberating him from the notion that language is a single, pure, unchanging thing—a notion which confines him rather than opening up for him the various means available for writing. Some instruction and practice in the manipulation of complex sentence elements may be useful in helping a student increase his control over a variety of sentence structures he has not been writing, but this aspect of a college-level composition course should never degenerate into a study of syntax with application in the rudiments of usage.

These same principles apply in composition courses with other subject matters. The distinction must be drawn between *learning about* the history of rhetoric or various rhetorical approaches (or memorizing figures of speech!) and *using* in the student's actual composing the insights gained from studying the rhetorical principles and practices of others. In a mass communication-oriented composition course, the student is led to increase his own writing power by applying in it what he learns from analyzing the forms and limitations of various types of communications for various large, dispersed, unseen audiences. He may well compare the styles of articles on the same subject in a learned journal and a popular magazine, for example, for an awareness (which he should apply in his own writing) of the approaches and means of expression which some find appropriate for different kinds of readers. But if the course emphasizes the history of mass communication or the application of certain given principles in the preparation of scripts or articles, it is an introductory course in mass communication or a course in trade writing, not freshman composition.

In the courses we propose, then, the student is not so much analyzing style or learning about rhetoric; he is *doing* it, by being encouraged to speak for himself and his experience in more than one way. It is the student, his experience and his expressing of it, that provides the true material for these courses. This experience need not always be written down in the earliest stages. What is it like sitting in this room, here and now? How many different people can you make of yourself as you answer that question from different points of view, for different readers, in different styles, and in different acts of communicating? What effects can be anticipated of these alternate forms?

As the student increases his control of his language, he learns to extend his perceptions to other people's experiences and points of view, at first those close to him and then those more removed in time, space, and point of view. Consequently, the student is led to understand their experiences and values from books and other media and to seek a wider range of means for analyzing other people and their concerns, for clarifying his and their points of view, and for resolving the problems that come between them. But the emphasis always remains on the choices among the available approaches and means of expression in writing, and the test of success is ultimately the effect of the writing on its intended readers.

There is finally a matter of responsibility for what one writes and how he writes it. Just as a student cannot responsibly take a position on a controversial question unless he is familiar in detail with its background and various possible positions on it, a student can hardly choose responsibly among competing approaches and means of expression until he has actually developed some experience in using the alternatives. Another way of putting it is this: the student cannot choose responsibly among several selves unless he knows what those selves are.—It may be too much for the composition instructor to promise that a student may "find himself" through the expression of many selves. But the implication is strong that this training can be valuable beyond its application in writing for practical purposes.

PREPARATION FOR COLLEGE COMPOSITION INSTRUCTION

Our unhesitating contention is that much of the disarray of the present situation in freshman composition is the inevitable result of the incompetent practitioner, the "instructor" who uses the course to pursue his own interests in narrowly conceived ways rather than to help his students increase and refine their own awareness of approaches and means of expression from which they may choose.

The composition instructor must be able to write in a variety of ways and be able to analyze various kinds of writing, for he must be able to recognize merit when he sees it and to perceive the problems of the student writer and help him solve those problems. Although an occasional instructor will develop his understanding and proficiency through his own study and writing, most should prepare for their profession by formal study. Since composition is a central concern of the field, certainly everyone entering college English teaching should have these five essential features in his preparation:

1. He must have had the experience of writing at a level beyond the freshman composition course, either by taking a course in advanced composition or by writing for formal publication or for the scrutiny of other critical audiences.
2. He must have developed an understanding of how English vocabulary, grammar, and style have changed through the years and how they vary at the present from place to place and from situation to situation. He should have a knowledge of the modern grammars but should not conclude that such knowledge should be directly transmitted to the students in his composition courses nor that this knowledge provides him with an easy tool for the improvement of much of his students' composition.
3. He must understand various theories of rhetoric, not so that he will have his students memorize the topics or lists of figures of speech but so that he may draw from rhetorical theory in helping students improve their composing.
4. He must have read a wide variety of writing, have developed a sensibility to the ways in which a variety of forms and styles have been and are used with varying effects on different readers, and he must

be able to select passages from his reading to help students improve their composing.

5. He should have preparation for the practical problems of his class-room teaching, including such matters as planning lessons, designing assignments, reading papers, evaluating textbooks, and discovering the resources available from professional organizations.

Needed: Sequences in Composition

CLARENCE W. HACH

IN NOVEMBER 1960, the *English Journal* published an article of mine titled "Needed: A Sequential Program in Composition." Now, seven years later, many school systems have a sequence in composition. Sequence probably characterizes more courses of study in composition than it does any other area of English, though sequence, Kindergarten —Grade 12, is also needed in language and literature, as well as in such other facets of English as speech, library references, and, today, even the film.

I'm not sure, however, that sequence has improved the quality of composition in our schools as much as it should have. In fact, it may well have failed. There are many reasons to which I can attribute such failure. One is that schools have only a sequence in composition when what is needed is *sequences*. Ideally, we should have as many sequences as we have pupils because all of us know that pupils have various needs and they progress at various rates. This heterogeneity is evident no matter how refined an ability grouping system a school has. We all know that even in a very select honors class, for example, there is a top and a bottom with many rungs in between. If we are truly to have individualized instruction and meet the needs of each pupil in that class, we really cannot put everybody through the same steps in the same way at the same time. Yet that is what most of us are forced to do because of the way pupils are scheduled and because of the kinds of teaching schedules we teachers have.

All of us who have taught for awhile know that deep in the structure of any class lie factors which hinder effective learning and teaching. Ole Sand, Director of NEA's Center for the Study of Instruction, recently cited a number that pertain to elementary classrooms but which

From *English Journal*, 57, January, 1968, pp. 69–78. Reprinted with the permission of the National Council of Teachers of English and Clarence W. Hach.

also, I think, characterize many in the secondary school. One factor he cited is that only about one-fifth of the pupils in a typical classroom are actually on the grade level at which they belong. The rest have capacities and skills which would place them in grades above or below the level at which they find themselves. And Dr. Sand reminds us that no amount of grouping by age or by mental ability can correct that. Another factor is that any class of twenty to thirty students represents, in effect, a mythical group, and the teacher too often tries to achieve mythical "oneness" for the class. Still another is that too many classes are so organized that pupils are forced to learn the same thing at the same time for the same length of time. In the majority of elementary classrooms, Dr. Sand says that some of the pupils need to spend 40 per cent of the day on reading; others not more than 10 per cent. Yet most elementary classrooms compel all children to spend a flat 20 per cent of the day on this subject. Dr. Sand also cites the factor that nearly every classroom in the country contains gifted children who are locked in the rigid schedule of the instruction which does not permit them to develop their individual talents.

I think that these same factors can be applied to high school classes in a somewhat different way, of course, because in most secondary schools, unlike elementary schools, we do have some degree of ability grouping and therefore the "oneness" of instruction is at least a little more related to the needs and abilities of all the pupils in a class. I really think that many of our problems in the secondary school stem from the factors that Ole Sand says pertain to the elementary school and that it is time something is done about them. If, as Ole Sand says, only one-fifth of the pupils in a typical elementary classroom are in the grade at which they belong, what can one teacher in a self-contained classroom really do about that kind of heterogeneity? And if an elementary teacher, also as Ole Sand says, tries to achieve mythical "oneness" for that class, think of how many pupils are being neglected. Probably every single person in that class is being neglected in some way, not just those at the extremes in terms of ability and/or achievement.

How many elementary self-contained teachers can spend 40 per cent of a day on reading for those who need it? How many can spend 40 per cent of a day on other related language arts activities, such as oral English, both speaking and listening, which we know are extremely important in creating the background necessary later to develop facility in writing composition? The answer to these problems lies in restructuring of the elementary school, of course, and that is being done in more and more school systems by the introduction of team teaching and ungradedness. As a result students can be grouped and regrouped according to their needs, so that it is possible for a pupil to spend 40 per cent of a day on reading if there is that need.

The job of teaching English effectively in the high school is, as we all know, dependent on what happens in the elementary and junior high schools. Sequence, therefore, should be a Kindergarten—Grade 12 concern for us in all areas of the language arts. I think Ole Sand's factors point up the need for a school system to be concerned with sequence K–12. It is not enough to evolve sequential programs for Grades 9–12 or even Grades 7–12. If sequence is really to work, there must be sequence K–12. And it is not enough to have sequential programs on paper. These sequential programs mean nothing unless they are translated into action in the classroom; therefore, restructuring of the traditional classroom kind of teaching in all grades is important to implementing a meaningful sequential program.

Fortunately, there are glimmers of hope on the horizon for secondary schools to meet more adequately the needs of all of our students. Several high schools have already been restructured as ungraded schools so that students can progress at their own rate. The days are numbered for teachers teaching four or five classes of 100–150 or more students every day in boxed-in classrooms, with everyone in a particular kind of class getting pretty much the same kind of instruction in the same way. "It is time for us to discontinue 2 x 4 x 6 teaching," Dr. Sand explains, "teaching that is carried on between the two covers of a textbook, the four walls of a classroom, and the six periods of a school day."

In English we are beginning to think of the kinds of activities we need to teach our subject most effectively—to get away from "2 x 4 x 6 teaching." There are some activities, for example, for which large groups are most effective, especially if a teacher plans his presentation exceedingly well and makes use of visuals and other new media. There are other activities for which perhaps a normal-sized class is efficient. There are still others when seminar-sized groups ranging from eight to fifteen are essential. And there are many, including much of composition, when a one-to-one relationship is necessary. And there are also some, including again much of composition, when a pupil must work completely on his own in so-called independent study, or independent learning.

Of course, to carry out this kind of program we need certain kinds of physical facilities which many schools are begining to get, and we need a different kind of time schedule. We do need physical areas for large-group instruction, for average-sized classes, for seminars, for independent learning. We need a flexible time schedule that will permit us to have pupils for whatever amount of time seems best for the kind of activity we're going to have. We need to think through how to make maximum use of both teacher and pupil time. There is so much wasted potential learning time in our schools today that I wonder how long a corporation would stay in business if the same amount of potential productive time were wasted. I think of the many classroom periods when really very little teaching and therefore very little learning takes place, just a lot of teacher talk. I think, too, of how many teaching hours, for example, teachers waste showing a film to a number of classes when under more ideal conditions a segment of a film could be shown throughout a day and pupils could go to the film during some of their free time, thus making possible more efficient use of teacher time. In most of our schools now we teachers sit in our classrooms or auditoriums, passively watching two, three, or more times a day Hamlet stabbing Polonius through the tapestry or Lady Macbeth taunting Macbeth with

"O proper stuff!
This is the very painting of your fear.
This is the air-drawn dagger which, you said,
Led you to Duncan."

And no matter how much we may love *Hamlet* or *Macbeth* as literary works of art, we get bored observing the same sequence of events with the same actors and actresses several times a day at least once every year. And I think of the conflict in my pupils' schedules and in mine, too, that make it almost impossible for a pupil and me to get together for a conference during the day and how next to impossible it is to have a worthwhile conference before school begins in the morning and also how virtually impossible it is to have the needed number of conferences after school. When we really stop to think about the conditions under which teachers have taught these many years and under which we ourselves have been students, it's rather amazing that as much teaching and learning have taken place as have.

But in this day and age with the cost of education what it is, and becoming increasingly expensive, and with the amount of learning necessary also growing by the hour, the teaching-learning process is going to have to improve and improve rather rapidly, I believe. That's why I think that our teaching and therefore students' learning are going to have to be restructured, in fact, are being restructured, as I've said, in many places . . . I believe that the restructuring of the teaching of English along the lines of large-group instruction, seminar discussion, individual student-teacher conferences, and independent learning will do much not only to enhance the teaching-learning process in all areas of English but certainly in the area of composition. It will make possible a more individualized writing program than we now can have because teachers will have more open time during the school day when they and pupils can get together for individual conferences. Students will also have more open time to work independently under teacher direction in the areas of their needs and strengths. Schools are beginning to have well-equipped resource centers and flexible schedules to make possible all of what I've said.

With changes in the teaching-learning process will come *sequences* in composition in which students really progress on the basis of successful achievement. The next step in a sequence will not be performed until a student demonstrates a degree of success in a previous step. Teachers of English will have to recognize that learning is a gradual growth process, and they will need to make it possible for students to succeed rather than fail, as is so often the story now in the way in which composition is handled in our schools. As teachers of composition we are going to have to recognize that undergirding progress in composition is success, not failure, and that therefore the reason so many of our students really don't learn how to write is that they are moved along through writing assignments, without acquiring the skill that they should and therefore not experiencing very much success. Too often undergirding a student's composition work is failure, failure which we teachers continue to perpetuate. Perhaps eventually, however, with restructuring of the teaching-learning process and sequences in composition we will reach the Utopian goal of having all of our graduating seniors, except our slowest learners, with the ability to write a single expository paragraph that is well developed and practically free from error. I say Utopian goal because I think that most of our schools have not reached it yet. I should hope that in time we can say that our goal for all graduating seniors is for them to have the ability to write a simple five-paragraph expository theme that is well structured and developed, but there is no point in setting that as a goal until we first reach a more attainable one.

Until such time as we can restructure our entire teaching of English along the lines of varied group sizes and flexible schedules, however, there are some things that we can do to improve our teaching of composition. We can create realistic sequences for various ability groups and undergird our sequences with the philosophy that progress in composition depends upon pupils' experiencing success in writing, not failure.

In the guest editorial in the May 1966 *NEA Journal,* Harold Howe, the U. S. Commissioner of Education, says that in the novel *War and Peace,* "Leo Tolstoy deprecates the importance of generals and strategy in deciding battles, saying that victory depends on the unpredictable responses of individual soldiers who, at some instance of personal challenge, decide whether to take one step forward or one step back."

Learning to write is like victory in battle because it, too, depends on responses of individuals, not soldiers to be sure, but pupils, often also unpredictable, but who at an instance of personal challenge do decide to take one step forward or one step back. It is our job to see that they take this one step forward, and it is for this reason that we must have a sequence for each pupil that represents a forward step in learning to write and that a pupil is likely to go forward rather than backward if he experiences success in this sentence.

What would be realistic sequences that would make possible forward steps undergirded with success for the various kinds of pupils we have in our high schools? In Evanston we are currently experimenting with two that we think offer some hope for various degrees of success for two different groups of pupils in each grade, one for those of flower-average ability and one for those of better-average or honors ability. Though for this present school year (1967–68) we have moved into less rigid classroom grouping and a degree of flexible sheduling that will eventually, we hope, make possible a sequence for each pupil because we will have less rigidly structured days for both teachers and pupils, we still think that it is necessary this year to have the varied grade-level sequences that are based on structural aspects of writing and that provide for pupils having a variety of composition experiences during their four years of high school work.

By now most teachers are familiar with B. F. Skinner's theories that have contributed much to programmed learning in which knowledge is broken into parts and in which pupils learn by making responses and getting responses reinforced immediately. And most teachers are familiar, too, with the theories of Jerome Bruner in which he emphasizes the importance in teaching the structure of a subject, saying that learning can be enhanced if we emphasize the structure of a subject in such a way that it gives a pupil a sense of the fundamental ideas of that subject.

Our sequences are based upon both Skinner's and Bruner's ideas. Following is a skeletal outline showing the types of composition required for the two groups of pupils. The sequence for the lower-average pupils is adapted for basic or slower learning pupils. Teachers of these classes are told to attempt to accomplish as much of that outline as possible. The outlines are still grade-level oriented because we are still not an ungraded school. We think, however, that the sequences are more realistic than if we had only one sequence for a grade level. Our sequences are still tentative, but we hope with independent study and teacher-pupil conference time as a part of each English course that we can adapt the sequences for most pupils in those tracks. We probably will need to provide some kind of writing laboratory for those who do not meet what we are going to call performance criteria for the various tracks. Pupils will be assigned to this laboratory to remain until they can fit into the regular stream of composition for the track to which they have been assigned.

Better-Average and Honors Freshmen

I. The expository paragraph

We believe that the first writing experiences of freshmen should generally be limited to the expository paragraph to serve as a review of principles studied in Grades 7 and 8 and because competence in writing the single expository paragraph is essential for all later writing. The idea of this review in Brunerian terms is reinforcement, a dipping back via the spiral curriculum to enable pupils to regain the skills they had in writing expository paragraphs at the end of the eighth grade. In reviewing the expository paragraph, students study again the following aspects of paragraph writing: unity, the topic sentence, the position of the topic sentence, the order of details (chronological, importance, and the like), and coherence.

II. Types of expository paragraphs

In reviewing the expository paragraph pupils are expected to be given assignments calling for developments of a paragraph by facts, examples, incidents, and reasons.

III. The descriptive paragraph

Because the paragraph of description is first taught in Grade 8, including it in the freshman program is also for review purposes. But since the emphasis is first on exposition, assignments in writing paragraphs of description are usually not given until late in the first semester.

IV. Paragraph answers in essay exams

Because of many essay exams, freshmen are given formal instruction in writing the paragraph answer to an essay question, a form of expository writing, of course.

V. The three- and five-paragraph expository theme

The maximum goals for better-average and honors freshmen are to achieve competence in writing, first, the paragraph, next the three-paragraph theme, and finally the five-paragraph theme. The three-paragraph theme is taught only when pupils have demonstrated a degree of competency in writing the various kinds of expository paragraphs. They then are taught how the three-paragraph theme is an expansion of the single paragraph: the topic sentence becoming the opening paragraph; the body of the paragraph becoming the body of the three-paragraph theme, probably with a new topic sentence to serve as a transition from the opening paragraph; and the clincher sentence of the paragraph becoming the final or concluding paragraph of the three-paragraph theme.

After much practice in writing the three-paragraph theme competently, hopefully by March, though for many it will come earlier, instruction is given in writing the five-paragraph theme. In this connection pupils review principles of topical outlining. By June it is hoped that all better-average and honors freshmen will have written a number of five-paragraph themes and become quite proficient in writing them.

Other aspects of the better-average and honors freshman composition course of study include effective titles, emphasis on specificity of paragraph development, and writing based on reference reading, part of the strand that will culminate for them as juniors and seniors in a source theme. The course of study also calls for teachers giving pupils much practice in writing about books (not book reports) to help them become discerning readers. Writing on books is related to the types of composition being taught.

Lower-Average Freshmen

The composition course of study for this track is exactly the same as for the better group with exception of the five-paragraph theme. It is felt that if teachers will concentrate only on paragraph writing and move to the three-paragraph theme, perhaps by March, that more writing competency will be achieved by these pupils than if the five-paragraph theme is also introduced. Of course, if a teacher has pupils who demonstrate competence in the paragraph and in the three-paragraph theme, it is expected that he will handle these pupils individually or in small groups and introduce them to the five-paragraph theme. This procedure is expected particularly if a teacher is going to recommend that some of these pupils be placed in better-average classes for the next school year.

Better-Average and Honors Sophomores

I. Review of the three-paragraph expository theme

Before pupils are assigned the writing of five-paragraph themes, they are expected to have as much practice as necessary in writing the three-paragraph theme again in order to demonstrate (1) that they have a reasonable understanding of its structure, (2) that they have facility in writing opening and concluding paragraphs, (3) that they have reasonable competence in writing a variety of paragraphs as suggested by their developing adequately the middle paragraph or the body of the three-paragraph theme, and (4) that they understand the need for each paragraph to relate to the preceding one—that they understand transitions.

II. Review of the five-paragraph expository theme

When students have demonstrated some competence in writing the three-paragraph theme, then they are assigned five-paragraph themes for which they also again review the topical outline. Emphasis is placed on developing the paragraphs of the body specifically and adequately.

III. Paragraph of persuasion

This type of paragraph is introduced to give teachers an opportunity to teach principles of critical thinking. Since the paragraph of persuasion is normally developed by reasons, it is a good type to assign along with the theme of persuasion, since it is a very easy way for students to see how a paragraph can be expanded into a theme: a paragraph of persuasion, for example, with three reasons would be a theme of persuasion of five paragraphs. The topic sentence would be expanded to the opening paragraph, each of the reasons would become a topic sentence for the paragraphs of the body to be developed with concrete detail, and the clincher sentence would become the concluding paragraph.

IV. Theme of persuasion

V. Paragraph of comparison

VI. Theme of comparison

When a student demonstrates some competence in writing paragraphs of comparison, he is ready to handle a comparison in a more sustained form.

VII. Narration

Students learn to write simple narration in the seventh and eighth grades, mostly limited to one paragraph. In Grade 10 they begin to write longer narrative pieces and consider various aspects of narrative writing.

VIII. Narration and description in exposition

So that pupils will not get the idea that writing is straight exposition, narration, or description, some work is given to show them that the three types can be combined, in fact, often are, in the personal narrative, the character sketch, the informal essay, and the book review.

IX. The paraphrase

The paraphrase is taught as a study skill to help pupils get the thought from the printed page and to rephrase it in simpler form. Because there are so many opportunities for using the paraphrase in sophomore English—in Shakespeare, poetry, and the like— teachers teach its technique early in the year and require many paraphrases throughout the year.

X. Investigative report

As preparation for writing a short formal research paper in Grade 11, better-average and honors sophomores have several opportunities during the year to write short reports based on reference reading. Such assignments are important to give students practice in notetaking and synthesizing information in their own words. The investigative report also gives teachers an opportunity to teach some of the library references designated for Grade 10 and to teach informal documentation within the text of the paper, not with formal footnotes which students learn in Grade 11.

There are other aspects of composition for better-average and honors sophomores, but the preceding outline suggests most of the types of composition required.

Lower-Average Sophomores

The course of study for this group starts with a review of the expository paragraph again, just as it did for them at the beginning of the freshman year. Since the paragraph is really a composition in miniature, it is reasonably wise, we believe, to expect lower-average sophomores to demonstrate some competence in it before they compound writing weaknesses in longer compositions. As pupils demonstrate some semblance of competence, they may move to the three-paragraph theme, which, you will recall, is the maximum length theme most of these pupils wrote as freshmen. In reviewing the three-paragraph theme, teachers emphasize such writing principles as good opening and concluding paragraphs, bridging the gaps between paragraphs, and adequate and specific development of paragraphs.

When lower-average sophomores have achieved some competence again in the three-paragraph theme, they are introduced to the five-paragraph theme, which, you will remember, is taught to better-average and honors freshmen. The rest of the composition course of study for lower-average sophomores is the same as for the better group with the exception of the investigative report, which they learn to do as juniors.

Better-Average and Honors Juniors

The junior year for better-average and honors pupils begins in spiral fashion with a review of the five-paragraph theme which serves as a diagnostic instrument. In its writing, students will reveal weaknesses in writing opening and concluding paragraphs, well-developed paragraphs in the body of the theme, and transitions between paragraphs, as well, of course, as other writing problems. Remedial instruction can then be planned. There is little point in moving ahead in the composition course of study, we believe, until most of a class has demonstrated competence in writing the five-paragraph theme or provisions have been made for those who haven't.

Once the simple five-paragraph theme has again been "mastered," teachers introduce students to themes of definition; the informational essay, which may or may not be based on reference reading; and the research paper, which for better-average and honors juniors is short—1,500–2,000 words. The emphasis is on teaching students techniques of preparing a research paper. These juniors also learn how to write the job and college application letter and the essay on college application blanks.

Lower-Average Juniors

Lower-average juniors once more review the single expository paragraph and then the three- and five-paragraph expository theme. They are likely to stay with themes of this length for most of the first semester or for some most of the year. Other writing activities for this track include the paraphrase and the précis, the informal informational essay, which substitutes for them as a research paper and therefore is based to some extent on some reference reading, and the job and application letters and the essay on college application blanks. They are not taught the theme of definition until the senior year.

Better-Average and Honors Seniors

The better-average and honors seniors start the year with a review again of the five-paragraph theme, but, of course, most of them can move on to more complicated writing rather quickly, such as themes of explanation developed by analogy or cause to effect or vice versa; the essay of opinion; the theme of analysis; some writing of criticism; and a research paper in which the emphasis is on polishing the techniques learned in the junior year.

Lower-Average Seniors

Lower-average seniors review again the expository paragraph and the five-paragraph theme and then learn to write themes of definition, the process theme, the essay of opinion, and a short formal research paper. Sometimes some classes do a little critical writing.

We are aware that some professional writers and some teachers, too, are critical of restricting students to writing three- or five-paragraph themes on the basis that they are artificial. We admit that they are pedagogical devices but important ones, we think, because pupils do need to learn how to write structured papers. Creating assignments that lend themselves to three or five paragraphs is not difficult. Once students see that an idea dictates a particular form, a particular structure, we believe that we have helped pupils to become writers who know how to organize their thoughts and who see that form and idea are interrelated. Too many high school students write pages in disorganized form because they have never been taught that writing has structure. If the three- and five-paragraph themes are somewhat forced, they are no more so than the exercises most musicians perform before they become masters and can introduce variations on a theme that even then have form.

Some of you will recall that in 1961 George B. Leonard, Jr., in an article in *Look* (June 20) charged that writing is the disgrace of American education. That charge went to 15,000,000 readers. That fact bothered me then, and it bothers me now, because I don't like being associated with failure, and I dislike having the dirty linen of my profession aired in public. The fact that writing is the disgrace of American education does not make me proud to be an English teacher. I would much rather be associated with something more successful. It also concerns me, too, that the author of that article in *Look* said afterward that never in his experience as a staff writer had he encountered such unanimously favorable response to a single story.

In an article published some time ago in *Elementary English,* an article titled "The Teaching of Writing and Composition in Today's Schools," Dr. James Squire, [then] executive secretary of NCTE, reviews what all of us have heard many times as to the reasons for pupils not learning to write—teaching loads, the lack of preparation of teachers by the colleges and universities to teach composition, and the like. He also refers to the research report done by Richard Braddock at the University of Iowa in which he indicates that there is little solid research evidence to indicate that children learn to write better when teaching loads are reduced. And he mentions the study done by Frank Heys in Massachusetts in which he demonstrates that frequency of writing does not necessarily lead students to proficiency, though it does demonstrate clearly that writing cannot be taught without much reading and discussion.

Squire says in his article that "under-prepared and overloaded teachers surely account for many of the problems, yet it is not primarily of these that I write. As important perhaps in contributing to present chaotic conditions has been the absence of a consistent point of view, the failure to plan progressive, incremental and developmental programs, and articulated programs in writing and composition which move progressively from the primary experiences with teacher-dictated sentences to the personal stories of the intermediate grades; from the personal writing of the junior high school to the increasingly rigorous and disciplined practice of high school and college."

That statement points up the need for an articulated program in composition from K–12. I know that such a program is not easily come by because of vested interests, of teachers resenting courses of study because they say that they are a violation of their freedom as professional people, and of opinionated administrators, supervisors, and teachers, too, who are not well-qualified in composition and do not understand the writing process. And even in school districts where there are carefully articulated programs on paper, there is not the implementation in the classroom for a variety of reasons.

I think that the report of the State Citizens' Committee (*The English Language Arts in Kentucky,* State Department of Education, 1961) really has the answer to our dilemma. This Kentucky report is from a group which spent nine months visiting schools, studying courses of study, and interviewing teachers and administrators. Few states in recent years have done more to improve the standard of English instruction than Kentucky. Here is the statement from the citizens's report that I think provides our answer:

> The lack of articulation, of a carefully worked out sequence of study from grade to grade, was evident in almost all systems. If a junior high school was part of the arrangement, there was little correlation with the efforts of either the elementary or the senior high schools involved. If the seventh and eighth grades were departmentalized units of an elementary school, the break was likely to be as great. . . . Whatever the organization . . . however, the problem for vertical articulation remains and can be solved only by the following of fairly detailed guide lines in English, close relationships among the supervisors involved, and a systematic getting together of the teachers in sequentially related grades both within and between individual schools. The Committee was amazed to discover on many occasions that teachers knew nothing of what was going on in the next classroom, let alone the next grade or the next school.

I agree with Squire that more than anything else this lack of coordination is our basic problem. There must be a K–12 program. Somehow our administrations must make this kind of program development possible. Once evolved, the program must be implemented in every classroom. Unless it is, we are really not being very serious about this business of education; we are wasting taxpayers' money; and we are cheating our young people.

Rhetoric and the
Quest for Certainty

HANS P. GUTH

FRESHMAN ENGLISH has long had the reputation of lacking reliable procedures and concrete results. Recently, there have been numerous proposals to remedy its uncertainties by modeling it on presumably more respectable academic disciplines. According to such proposals, the teacher should have a more or less clearly defined specialty. His area of study and teaching should have an identifiable subject-matter. Expert knowledge would result from concentrated work in a limited area. Such knowledge would be authoritative as the result of a rigorous methodolgy. It would be pursued because of its intrinsic interest or fascination. Teaching in this area would produce results that could be objectively measured and statistically evaluated.

Such proposals are attractive because they promise a clear rationale for an otherwise confusing field. Nevertheless it is possible to question their plausibility both on general theoretical grounds and in the light of specific alternatives. In the framework of liberal education, the more rigorously limited the subject-matter of a course is, the less significant it may be and the less enjoyable it may be to teach. The area of literary studies, for instance, is blurred at the edges and unavoidably impinges on psychology, philosophy, economics, anthropology. Literary study becomes meaningful, and becomes a liberal and human pursuit, in proportion as it refuses to dwindle into narrowly specialized activity. Similarly, history is a meaningful and liberalizing discipline in proportion as it attempts to work factual data into a perspective not rigorously limited and not subject to rigorous tests of verification.

From *College Engish*, November, 1962, pp. 131–136. Reprinted with the permission of the National Council of Teachers of English and Hans P. Guth.

It is true that the current search for tangible subject-matter in freshman English stems in part from a legitimate fear that programs designed to be broadly significant may turn out to be merely miscellaneous and shallow. Freshman English has sometimes been a freshman's digest of otherwise respectable academic disciplines. It has introduced the student in the course of six weeks to sociology (Riesman) and aesthetics (Langer), physics (Eddington) and anthropology (Mead), nuclear fission (Laurence) and psychoanalysis (Freud). The instructor has had to pretend to the knowledge of the specialist, and to the skill of the popularizer, in a wide variety of subjects.

Fortunately, our choice does not have to be one between narrow specialization and taking all knowledge for our province. The opposition of the expert and of the genial but ineffectual amateur is only another one of the false dilemmas that has produced in the teaching of freshman English the present age of anxiety. Even an expert must be knowledgeable about fields beyond his immediate professional competence. Even the most ardent generalist tends to return to the topics that his experience equips him to discuss with confidence and authority. The subject-matter of freshman English is a clearly identifiable discipline in the general framework of liberal education, taught preferably by a teacher competent in the discipline and liberally educated at the same time. That discipline, traditionally known as rhetoric, borders on the one side on those branches of applied linguistics that go up to but not beyond the sentence, and on the other side on the study of imaginative literature. The art of rhetoric concerns itself with meaningful, responsible, effective expository or non-fiction prose. The specialist in this area is someone who gives concentrated attention and a major share of his time to the study and practice of effective writing. He should be reasonably competent in both of the two sister disciplines, that is, in both linguistics and literature, to prevent the kind of lopsidedness that results when either the linguistic or the imaginative elements in rhetoric are treated out of context.

Within the discipline of rhetoric, the writing of the expert as expert plays a respectable but minor role. His presentation of factual material and systematic analysis of relationships provide the model for "technical" writing ranging from the theme on "How My Refrigerator Works" to the research paper on the variations of sentence structure in Jonathan Swift's prose. The student can learn much from the expert's respect for facts (and ability to distinguish them from inference and hearsay), his patience when confronted with knotty problems of classification, his skill in marshalling complex materials. At the same time, the teacher of rhetoric remembers that some of the worst and most uncommunicative writing that he sees is produced by experts writing about their fields. He also remembers that some of the most naive polemics are produced by experts writing about matters outside their immediate professional competence. The transfer of the scholar's and expert's accuracy and patience and sustained thought, first to effective communication in his field, and then to general verbal ability, is often disappointing.

The heart of a rhetoric program, therefore, is in an area where its special contribution as a discipline and its general significance in a liberal education coincide. The conception of significant writing that is at issue here is perhaps better illustrated first and defined afterwards. Though teachers of composition disagree hopelessly on theory and method, they tend to agree remarkably on what is first-rate prose. We agree that our students would do well to read books like Kazin's *Walker in the City*, Baldwin's *Notes of a Native Son*, Eiseley's *The Immense Journey*, Thoreau's *Walden*. We also know that ours is the only discipline in the college directly responsible for guiding the student to this sort of prose. We further readily distinguish between the expert, who may or may not communicate, and the writer who is a writer first and a specialist, if at all, second. Thus, in philosophy, William James seems more relevant to the concerns of rhetoric than John Dewey; in politics, George Orwell is more of a writer than Richard Nixon.

Among the topics that writing of general significance explores are the writer's observation of and reaction to the scene of which he finds himself a part: the natural world, the urban environment, the social context. Other such central topics derive from the manifold human relationships which, unlike our plumbing and our space capsules, cannot safely be left to the experts. The writer may explore the purposes that gives to our lives shapes or direction; he may examine the terms on which he coexists and communicates with others. He may write on these topics on the level of elementary but authentic observation; or he may treat them on a high level of abstraction and sophistication. What counts is that subjects of general human significance should matter to him, that they should absorb his attention. We are sometimes asked what is the "content" of the student's reading and writing in a rhetoric course. The answer is that the themes explored in the kind of prose most relevant to our purposes are often the same as those of imaginative literature. (This is why a course centered on rhetoric may include imaginative literature without the need for elaborate apologies and rationalizations.) The answer is further that setting up a dichotomy of content and form is no more fruitful in rhetoric than in literary criticism. A rhetoric course, in taking up descriptive writing, for instance, can no more treat matters of form and structure wthout reference to what is being described than a literature course can treat Romantic nature poetry without reference to nature.

Even the most incompletely rationalized composition course can provide the setting for the crucial contact between writer and reader. It is sometimes said that critical thinking and sensitivity to values cannot be taught, that they are "catching." This would seem to be an excellent argument for exposing the student to the work of writers who are known to be carriers of infection. The teaching of writing at its least methodical can work with what the student derives from substantial and significant reading. When the teacher takes the demand for concrete subject-matter too literally, he is often in the position of asking the students for good writing without ever having shown them any. His first task in the composition course is to convince the student that good writing exists—and that it matters.

Once the instructor has appropriate materials to work with, he can obviously try to work out some of the criteria that *make for* forceful and significant prose. A rather obvious but often slighted preliminary requirement is fluency. This does not imply a marvelous substitution of ease for the more usual toil of composition. It merely reminds us that the effective writer is typically one who has done much previous writing. We are defeated from the start unless the student ceases to regard writing as a special task, to be accomplished only with the most strenuous contortions. We should encourage anything that promotes the student's familiarity with composition: "free writing" in student journals or logs; copious note-taking in all college courses; the habit of formulating—while walking along or taking a shower—sentences and paragraphs to be put down on paper before prolonged staring at a blank sheet produces paralysis of the cerebral cortex.

Moving on from the prerequisites, we can formulate some more specific criteria. The first such criterion is that good writing carries conviction. This requirement may sound too vaguely inspirational to be relevant on the first Monday of a new semester, but it is basic to even elementary progress and can be concretely applied to every piece of prose the student produces. Even on the most elementary level, and in the most poorly prepared class, the instructor can establish the point that whatever good writing is, it is *not* the docile repetition of a few appallingly thin generalities about the American way of life. The student's writing must be something that he himself is willing to stand up for, something to which in some way or other he is personally committed. If this commitment is missing, the result is what Jacques Barzun, in *Teacher in America*, calls "hokum." In the more advanced

kind of student writing, this staple commodity in our educational en-
deavors takes the form of a judicious selection of second-hand opinions and third-hand facts, woven into a graceful pattern. Conviction
is slighted in the subject-matter course that teaches the student to
work with information whose origins and implications he must not
question. It is slighted in the issues course that teaches him to express
approved opinions in approved ways. It never has a chance in the
course that, in Leslie Fiedler's phrase, teaches a "non-functional, unreal
Academese," shaped "by antiquated rules of etiquette" and "capable of
uttering only the most correctly tepid Protestant banalities." (*CCC*,
13, [Feb. 1962] 2). The teacher in freshman English must convince
the student that writing means recording one's own observations,
pinning down one's own reactions, interpreting one's own experience,
formulating one's own judgments, questioning one's own premises, and
making one's own mistakes. In short, the writer must realize that the
mind he must put in gear is his own. All else is journalism, editorializ-
ing, and *belles-lettres*.

A second criterion of good writing is concreteness. The natural in-
stinct of the first-rate writer is to anchor what he says to concrete
reference. He thus corrects the arbitrariness of subjective impressions.
Similarly, the search of the philosophically or semantically trained for
specific reference in definition gives substance to otherwise largely
verbal controversies. The ability to translate abstract idea into vivid
image makes writing graspable, intelligible, and readable. It is this
feature of good writing that the instructor can most graphically illustrate by reference to "models," that is, simply, to first-rate prose.
It is this feature that the instructor, as editor, can most persistently
encourage in the work of the student, as writer. Rhetoric makes an
important contribution to the student's education even if it never gets
beyond a constant bombardment of the student with admonitions like
"give an example," "be specific," "illustrate," "produce evidence," "who
said?" and "say when and where."

A third crucial quality of good writing is that it has focus, or coherence. It is true that many of our students need to learn first of all
to write with some degree of spontaneity and conviction. This instructor has to be wise enough to realize, with Holden Caulfield, that
it is often the "relevant" comment that is faked or perfunctory and the
"digression" that is revealing and worth reading. But at some stage
every writer needs to be coaxed or cudgelled into following up one
point at a time. It is by encouraging sustained and focused discussion
that the instructor begins to counteract the tendency toward hasty
sampling, superficial induction, one-sided or slanted evidence, and

logical nonsequiturs. Though the student theme is necessarily too short and tentative to do justice to any topic, the student can at least begin to understand the catastrophic skimpiness of the two-sentence paragraph or of the one-sentence judgment. He can begin to see why a dazzling display of opinionated comment is more effective as ego-building than as communication. He can begin to develop the habit of making clear where he stands and backing up what he has to say.

A fourth quality of good writing that the teacher of rhetoric starts to work on at the very beginning of the course is expressiveness, that is, resourcefulness and flexibility of idiom. A writer must be able to express himself—if possible aptly and precisely and vigorously. He needs a feeling for words. He must be in control of the resources of language and take pleasure in their richness and variety. Such a love and respect for language is the result neither of following arbitrary rules nor of studying usage statistics. By alerting the student to distinctions and implications and overtones, the instructor can attempt to train the student's eye and ear. A practitioner of contemporary American prose is the poorer for not having explored the inflammatory rhetoric of Thomas Paine, the satirical marksmanship of Mark Twain, the denunciatory gusto of H. L. Mencken, the wistful ironies of James Thurber. No one can be a forceful writer unless language means something more to him than a prosaic vehicle for communication.

Finally, however gingerly we may wish to approach the subject, good writing involves responsibility. The final caricature of a subject-matter course would be the objective study of linguistic patterns and rhetorical techniques to be then used by eager learners in the selling of quack medicines and prepackaged political candidates. Teachers are understandably reluctant to leave the solid ground of a rigorously defined specialty and to venture into the area where students learn to distinguish the responsible from the irresponsible, the critical from the snide. Many of us would rather not deal with such matters as the byways of innuendo. No college department, in fact, recognizes as its specialty the responsible use of language in nontechnical communication. On the other hand, our graduates, as school board members, newspaper editors, PTA chairmen, and chamber of commerce presidents, will participate in such communication—though they may never have been led to examine its rhetorical structure for moral implications. The major difference that a college education will then have made is that they will be irresponsible not with the diffidence of the untutored but with the smugness of the half-educated.

All these various aspects of rhetoric can be studied more or less inductively in a program organized around substantial reading. Though not following a rigid pattern, a course will progress more or less naturally from the simple to the more complex, from the most concrete to the more abstract, from straight exposition through interpretation to controversy and questions of some philosophical or ethical consequence. This does not mean that the teacher may not fruitfully employ well-planned systematic instruction in rhetorical principles, making use of what he considers most important from the large body of significant material in various relevant fields. He will find it indispensable to work out a meaningful rationale of usage, reinforced by detailed study and exploration. He may want to spend considerable time in word study, ranging from etymology and the study of synonyms to the kinds of semantics clearly focused on verbal resources, on levels and kinds of meaning. He may want to teach systematically the logic of rhetoric, that is, the kind of logic that is at work in the selection, interpretation, and organization of the writer's materials. He may want to conduct an analysis of prose style, paying attention to such matters as rhythm and figurative language.

All these things can be treated in the most solid, down-to-earth fashion, satisfying the perennial demand for specific "things to teach." They can be dealt with on various levels of complexity and sophistication. Lately, it has become fashionable at professional conferences to make ironic remarks about such lowly rhetorical devices as the topic sentence. One may well grant that no one is likely to produce immortal prose by filling in paragraphs starting with a predetermined topic sentence. But in much powerful writing key phrases and key sentences paraphrase and re-echo a major theme; often a crucial sentence sums up a key point. The student who traces in a well-organized essay the network of synonyms and near-synonyms that keep pointing to the topic at hand learns something important about the difference between rambling and structured prose. The student who notices the key sentence that holds a crucial paragraph together is learning how to read. In designing the course, the instructor must choose whether to provide above all systematic coverage of such rhetorical elements and devices and categories, or whether to work into the discipline of rhetoric from the other end by first involving the students in the discussion of ideas, of themes, of issues. Whatever strategy he adopts, he will try to do justice to both content and structure, theme and form.

In thus introducing the students to a discipline of great intrinsic interest and practical importance, the instructor will not be disturbed by the possibility that their reading of the prose of John Donne will not be reflected at the end of one semester in a statistically significant change in their command of sentence structure. He will in fact be skeptical of all attempts to measure objectively what is by definition complex, intangible, and subjective. Style *is* the man when defined not in a narrowly technical sense but as the expression of the writer's commitment and experience and skill. A writing course cannot miraculously widen and enrich the student's experience, but neither can it teach skill in a vacuum. What it can at least start to do is to teach disciplined self-expression, responsible interpretation of experience, articulate participation in the public dialogue.

Good writing requires personal involvement. It is thus influenced by complex psychological variables. The teacher of composition can set these aside only at the risk of drastically narrowing and distorting the subject-matter of his course. He cannot be content with conveying factual knowledge about language; he must try to translate it into an informed awareness of language at work. He cannot be content with charting patterns of organization and logic; he must cultivate in his students habits of sensitive, responsible, informed critical thought. There is something futile in a mastery of correct English without emotional literacy. There is something depressng about a student who has a perfect command of the patterns of the English sentence but not a thought in his head. Freshman English, which at its least inspiring dwindles into a service course, can be a crucial part of the student's liberal education. The most pressing need in freshman English is not for a more rigid definition of the course but for an improvement in the teacher's self-confidence and self-respect.

Objectives and Structure
in Freshman Composition

E. JAY JERNIGAN

MANY OF THE DIALOGUES about the teaching of composition that I have listened to and participated in remind me of Alice's experience as a pawn in the surrealistic chess game of *Through the Looking Glass:*

> Alice never could quite make out, in thinking it over afterwards, how it was that they began: all she remembers is, that they were running hand in hand, and the queen went so fast that it was all she could do to keep up with her: . . . suddenly, just as Alice was getting quite exhausted, they stopped, and she found herself sitting on the ground, breathless and giddy.
>
> The Queen propped her up against the tree, and said kindly, "You may rest a little now."
>
> Alice looked round her in great surprise. "Why, I do believe we've been under this tree the whole time! Everything's just as it was!"[1]

Too often, after a spirited discussion of freshman composition, I have found myself, like Alice, "breathless and giddy" and painfully aware that my colleagues and I are still sitting under the same tree. So before I embark upon my primary topic, an apologia for structure in the teaching of composition, I should like to hesitate for a moment to ask with Alice, "Where are we going and why?" In other words, what are our objectives in freshman composition?

I

First, I believe that in teaching composition, even on the high school level, we should be concerned primarily with exposition and argument

Adapted especially for this volume from a paper delivered at the 1969 Conference on College Composition and Communication in Miami.

and should devote attention to narration and description only insofar as they are methods of development and support. Unfortunately, the term *exposition* conjures up for some of us artificially rigid rhetorical categories—analysis, classification, division, definition—while *argument* evokes the lock-step shuffle of enthymemic syllogisms or the clinical strait jacket of Baconian induction. As practiced, though, both types of writing can be expedient blends of facts, personal opinions, anecdotes, descriptions, and the like, as ordered by tools such as cause and effect, comparison and contrast, or logic, with both subject and structure contributing to the overall purpose of explaining or convincing. To sidestep any possible quibble about the terms *exposition* and *argument,* I shall use in this essay the more general and thereby more useful phrase, *discursive prose.* Thus, to restate my first assumption, in teaching freshman composition we should be concerned primarily with the techniques of discursive prose.

That may sound like the hoariest of platitudes, but, as Mrs. Anna Klein has pointed out in the *English Journal,*

> so formless is the composition program, such a stepchild, that many students even today are set to describing a sunset in glowing colors or a street scene in drab ones, balancing sentences, using sparkling adjectives and Tom Swifty adverbs, writing dialogue for punctuation practice, attempting poetry, and in general struggling to learn writing techniques that they will never again use. In other words, despite the obvious needs of the student, lack of clearly defined objectives often results in tricks of "fine" writing being taught to students who can't be counted on for coherence.[2]

Coherence, then, should be our touchstone when teaching composition. To function effectively as a writer, a student must be able to present his material clearly and with some indication of order, whether that order is organic or imposed. But some teachers disagree; they put emotional impact or provocative style before clarity and coherence. Professor Ken McCrorie, for instance, advocates the capturing of "fabulous reality" as the primary goal of his non-structured approach to teaching composition.[3] Yet the samples of student writing he cites seem mere patchworks of figures of speech in loosely chronological patterns; they may have imaginative impact, but their manner is necessarily oblique, their content circumscribed. Such descriptive narrative, however well written, is not the basic kind of writing college students are asked to produce. That is the finding of the College Entrance Examination Board's Commission on English, contained in its report, *Freedom and Discipline in English:* the expository essay, the report states, best serves the other parts of the student's education; it prepares him best for the writing he will do in college; it allows the best definition of problems and permits the most helpful exercise of informed criticism by the teacher; it provides the best classroom exercise because its discipline is the best understood; and it is, in however corrupted condition, the most common form of human discourse.[4]

Student essays must necessarily be expository and/or argumentative vehicles.

If discursive prose is our medium, then our objective must be proficiency in the handling of that medium. Last year I was a member of the Michigan College English Association's ad hoc Committee on English Proficiency. The Committee's method of determining what constitutes proficiency in English composition was to draft answers to the following question: "What minimum requirements for proficiency in English composition do we expect at the end of the sophomore year from students who are pursuing the baccalaureate degree?" In phrasing this question we wished to include all junior college students who plan to transfer to four-year institutions, yet exclude all students in various two-year terminal programs for whom different standards apply. We were not concerned with the method or amount of the student's required instruction in composition; we were concerned only with the results of this instruction. After four regional meetings and a final coordinating session, the Committee drew up a list of six minimum expectations entitled "Basic Proficiency Guidelines." I should like to submit these requirements, in slightly modified forms, as the basic objectives toward which a freshman composition program should be directed:

1. *Fluency:* An hour's writing in class (50 minutes) should result in an essay of 400 words on a given subject. The subjects assigned should be of significance and should allow for a variety of student interests.
2. *Unity:* The essay should be built around an identifiable main idea or thesis.
3. *Development:* The essay should contain an appropriate number of related paragraphs (three to five), each paragraph containing a clearly stated topic sentence or conspicuous topic idea, each developing relevant parts of the thesis in some sequential order.
4. *Diction:* The essay should clearly indicate that the writer's recognition of his audience governs his selection of appropriate language and the amount and kind of explanation he provides.

5. *Syntax:* Sentences should demonstrate the writer's awareness of the basic conventions of English syntax: subject-verb agreement; proper pronoun references and agreement; freedom from dangling modifiers, unintentional fragments, and comma splices.
6. *Mechanics:* The essay should exhibit conventional spelling and punctuation. I believe these requirements should be met by a student at the end of his mandatory composition sequence, whatever its length and however it is organized.

So, if you will grant me, for the moment at least, first, that freshman composition should be concerned with discursive prose only and, second, that this prose should meet the minimum objectives I've just outlined, then I'm ready to ask my central question, "How?" In expanded form I should like to ask: can we so structure a composition course that college freshmen can learn the techniques of discursive prose well enough to meet basic proficiency objectives? That is a large question—to which I have a brave answer: yes. But my *yes* is hesitant, much qualified, modest.

II

Deluged by the unconscionable flood of composition texts, new and revised, that pours from publishing houses each spring, I sometimes panic momentarily and long for the false security of unquestioned tradition. Then it is that I admire the accountant in Conrad's *Heart of Darkness* who managed to live in the midst of a palpable moral chaos by concentrating fervidly on keeping his accounts neat, his collar starched, his cuffs clean. His solution tempts me even now: following unexamined habits, I could order my small part of our mutual chaos and pretend that the many imponderables of freshman composition, our own heart of darkness, do not exist. But that kind of security, attained by compulsive cleanliness and lobotomized order, is intellectually and morally bankrupt—it can crumple under any energetic wave from the next flood of texts. It is not that kind of structured freshman composition program I wish to promote. On the other hand, I don't wish to pretend I have found a natural ordering principle for our chaos; even philosophic Marlow came to no definitive conclusion about Kurtz's despairing cry, "The horror! The horror!" Yet, if we are to find an honest, functional approach to the teaching of composition, we must leave the accountant behind and, like Marlow, journey up river into the darkness.

Diversity is the cardinal problem. Being a "service" course, freshman

composition includes the entire spectrum of student abilities, from the
nearly illiterate to the quite sophisticated, often within the same class.
And nearly every experienced teacher of the course has a pet approach
different enough to justify writing a new text, the patent commercialism
of publish or languish notwithstanding. Thus every year multitudes
of texts appear, appealing to a wide assortment of educational philosophies, most of them easily grouped under such simplistic categories as
"Communication Skills," "Semantics and the Media," "Writing about
Literature," "Writing about Language," "The Rhetoric of Writing," or,
by far the most popular, "Stimulation for Evocation." Too often these
types remind me of Polonius's foolish "pastoral-comical, historical-pas-
toral, tragical-historical, tragical-comical-historical-pastoral," and even he
did not "character" his own precepts. Compounding such diversity are
the varied problems of administration. The course is staffed by people
as different in ability and experience as its students, by a first-year
graduate student in one classroom, by a soon-to-retire Ph.D. in the next.
It is offered in small, homogeneous liberal arts colleges with an English
staff of ten or fewer; it is offered in wildly heterogeneous community
colleges, large and small, with multi-track, variable-credit programs; it
is offered in sprawling state universities with 200 or more sections scattered widely over the campus.

Obviously, if we are to achieve a consensus in any discussion of
freshman composition, we must specify clearly the kind of composition program under discussion, we must separate remedial tracks from
the normal academic offering, and we must acknowledge differences
in academic milieu. For example, my own limited experience with
remedial programs suggests that a semi-tutorial approach using programmed materials on an individual basis is a viable one. But that is
only an impression, because, for me at least, programmed materials are
themselves an unexplored heart of darkness. Likewise, from my observations as an outsider, it seems to me that a small residential liberal arts
college with an energetic English staff, with a flexible schedule, and
with adequate classroom and office space could successfully correlate
and utilize informal, semi-tutorial methods of teaching the course. But
that too is only an assumption; thus both of these teaching situations
must remain outside the scope of my discussion. What I have experienced and am personally concerned about is the regular college course
in freshman composition as it is widely taught at schools scheduling
numerous sections. My question is how this course should be taught;
my assertion is that it should be taught in a clearly structured fashion
toward explicit objectives. For I continually rediscover in working
with students that if they can understand the goals and can recognize

the methods of a course, then with minimum anxiety they can master the methods to attain the goals. But if they don't understand the goals or the methods, or both, then they progress haphazardly, if at all, with maximum *angst* and/or *ennui*.

We can all agree, as Professor Albert Kitzhaber has pointed out, that the fundamental dilemma of freshman composition resides in the fact that the first essay embodies all the problems of the course, yet suggests no inherent approach to these problems. Nevertheless, some method of approach, some sort of sequential order, however arbitrary, is imperative if the student is to develop his writing ability beyond that first essay. Not only has method in freshman composition courses been indefinite, but subject matter, far from inherent, has ranged from oratorical skills to transformational grammar to belles lettres, with many stops along the way. What is needed is selection and focus. Sociology and imaginative literature particularly I would like to rule out of freshman composition because of their insidious seductiveness. Both enthrall the intellectual libidoes of teaching fellows and drive them far off the course into the shallow rapids of the New Left or the perilous seas of the New Criticism. If literature is a necessary ingredient in a basic studies program (and I believe it is), then we should require a separate introduction to literature course and neither blush about it nor stoop to subterfuge when we teach it. If sociology is necessary, then we should do as Professor John Sherman suggests:

> if it is necessary to give such a course, it ought to be treated quite frankly for what it is and appear in the catalogue under its proper colors: "Sociology 1 and 2. *Stimulation of Immature Minds.* Eradication of bourgeois prejudices. Casual reading of provocative essays. Lively discussions. Three hours each semester." To call such a thing composition is a fraud. . . .[5]

Essentially, I agree with Professor Robert Gorrell in his assessment of freshman English, in the NCTE Curriculum Series Study, *The College Teaching of English:*

> The subjects to be selected as especially pertinent for a course in composition seem to me to be the ancient trivium—rhetoric, grammar, and logic. And the focus for them seems to me to be rhetoric, developed in the light of new knowledge in semantics, psychology, linguistics.[6]

Rhetoric, then, should be our focus, and, if it is, we are in good company. We are, for example, with Professor Kitzhaber, who based the composition sequence of his Oregon Curriculum Study on five rhetorical principles: purpose, audience, substance, structure, and style.[7] Whatever order we use in teaching such principles will be arbitrary, but that should not keep us from giving them sequence and coherence. Order is especially necessary in a multi-section program involving a large, heterogeneous staff situated in scattered offices, prey to difficult communications and awkwardly ineffectual staff meetings. Yet, in imposing order on any composition program, we must accommodate the experienced teacher: we must allow him sufficient room to establish his own proven brand of rapport. Certainly, no systematic approach, no orderly syllabus can substitute for the sensitivity of a truly competent instructor. But if any mutuality of goals or methods for freshman composition is to be assumed, we ought judiciously to designate certain mutual requirements; otherwise each instructor will teach a different course toward different goals, and we will be unable to assume anything about the common final product, a student's writing proficiency.

Because we need a flexible structure for the course, I should like to suggest a general one, tentative and brief, which is based upon the objectives I outlined above.

1. *Fluency:* The course should demand a sufficient number of student essays to be read closely and commented on by the instructor, then revised by the student—let's say ten discursive prose essays of about 500 words each in a one-semester course. The subjects assigned should be significant and challenging, and they should allow for a variety of students' interests. This means that the puerile personal experience (My Summer Vacation), the stultifying description (Room 235 in Horsefeather Hall), and the simplistic process (How To Sew on a Button) will be relegated to the attic of a bygone era. At least half of the essays should be written in class, but not as impromptus; each assignment should be announced in advance and some preparation allowed, for no one writes even essay examinations without a preliminary focus or an inherent vantage point. Ten essays do not guarantee fluency, of course, but that is about all instructors have time to comment on significantly and all that students have time to revise meaningfully. Ten essays treated seriously are far better than twenty unread and unrevised assignments.
2, 3, and 4. *Unity, Development, and Diction:* The order in which we take up these three units seems to me immaterial. I happen to follow the order used in the fourth edition of Perrin's *Writer's Guide,* where diction or audience is considered first. But Professor Sheridan Baker may be equally right, in his text *The Practical Stylist,* to start with thesis, then move to structure, then diction: machts nichts.

After establishing with my students the need to recognize audience, I next consider unity and development through a discussion of the modus operandi of the 500 word essay, its purpose, its structure. The best treatment of the rationale of the 500 word student essay that I have read is Duane Nichols's article "The 5 Paragraph Essay" in the *English Journal,* October, 1966. As Professor Nichols points out, the most difficult yet important element of composition to teach is the introduction, where to be successful the student must announce his purpose, his scope and limitation, his plan of procedure, and his thesis. I emphasize the features of a good introduction and then explore the various ways of developing the essay. Here I use a rhetorically arranged reader and I relate my writing assignments to the standard methods of support, such as comparison and contrast, or cause and effect, or classification and division, and to the subject matter of the readings. In preparing a class for these structured writing assignments, I try to stress the great flexibility of discursive prose and to put the methods of support in broad perspective, referring students to articles in such familiar periodicals as *Playboy* or *Harper's* (for example, Norman Mailer's report of the 1968 political conventions). Also I use the students' own essays, transferred to plastic transparencies and shown by means of an overhead projector, as a focus for teaching the relevance of unity to development and to diction. I try to use affirmative examples when working with student writing, for I have discovered that I create much better student morale by accenting the positive. This general approach to unity, development and diction, of course, is neither new nor profound, but it does follow an explicit order. However or wherever one discusses these three rhetorical elements, it seems to me imperative to demonstrate early and in an orderly fashion the intimate relationship between them.

5 and 6. *Syntax and Mechanics:* These, I believe, should be confined to an occasional classroom discussion and to individual referrals to a handbook. When the average student finds that lack of subject-verb agreement threatens the sense of his essay, he will take steps to overcome the problem, if a handbook is readily available and he is confident in its use. Indeed only when such mistakes become immediately relevant to him is he likely to try actively to understand and correct them—no amount of sterile classroom drill will do that. And, too, the percentage of our entering freshmen who have at least a passable grasp of syntax and mechanics seems to be slowly increasing; these matters should therefore be taught only to those who need such instruction and taught in the context of their own

writing. Most entering freshmen do need extensive classroom help with the rhetoric of discursive prose, though, and that's what we should concentrate on.

Such is my rationale in defense of structure in a freshman composition program. There is nothing imperative about my particular approach, but I am sure that there is an imperative for order, for structure *per se.* Unless freshmen sense the goals and the methods of their composition course, they are destined to thrash about in a heart of darkness as bewildering as Kurtz's. And we, their mentors, are destined to run hand in hand with Alice.

REFERENCES

[1] New York: New American Library, 1960, pp. 143–45.
[2] "Expository Writing for Amateurs," *English Journal* (January, 1964), 17.
[3] "To Be Read," *English Jonrnal* (May, 1968), 688.
[4] New York: College Entrance Examination Board, 1965, pp. 96–7.
[5] "How to Escape Teaching Composition," *AAUP Bulletin* (Summer, 1954), 287.
[6] New York: Appleton-Century-Crofts, 1965, p. 112.
[7] "Search for Better Ways to Teach Writing," *CTA Journal* (March, 1967), 14.

Clear Writing Is Clear Thinking

RICHARD M. BOSSONE

TEACHING composition is undoubtedly one of the English teacher's most important tasks; yet it is undoubtedly one of the tasks that he is often unprepared to do. "The blame for this state of affairs must rest squarely with the college departments of English that have given these teachers their undergraduate and graduate education," states Kitzhaber in his recent book, *Themes, Theories, and Therapy*.[1] "Preoccupied with the study of literature, English departments seldom require the future English teacher—high school or college—to take courses that would give him a genuine professional competence in teaching either language or composition."

After working with student teachers and in-service training teachers for a period of years, I am inclined to agree with Mr. Kitzhaber's statement. But what can we do about it? What suggestions can we offer to assist the befuddled teacher who suddenly realizes that the student's study of grammatical principles and his writing of compositions may have little effect on the quality of his writing?[2]

CLEAR THINKING ESSENTIAL

Common sense should tell us that a student cannot write clearly without first thinking clearly; therefore the English teacher's first ob-

[1]Albert R. Kitzhaber, *Themes, Theories, and Therapy*, (New York: McGraw-Hill, 1963), p. 15.
[2]For further information see Ruth Gates Baird, "A Survey of Errors in English Composition," *The Journal of Educational Research*, LVI (January, 1963), pp. 228–235.

jective is to teach clear thinking. However he cannot simply say to the student "I want you to think clearly." Instead, he must have a plan to assist the student in achieving this goal.

Let's face it—the average student needs definite guidance; he is usually convinced in his own mind that he knows what he wants to say and he knows that he wants to say it, but somehow he just cannot express it in writing. In short, he fails to do justice to himself because he does not know how to explain and arrange his ideas when he is confronted with expositional directives.[3]

To assist the student in achieving the goal of clear writing through clear thinking, I have set forth in my English methods class a plan that has proved to be effective. There are indeed other ways to teach good writing, but the plan outlined below is simple and has brought results.

SELECTION OF A SUBJECT

Let the student begin with a subject with which he is familiar and about which he would enjoy writing. Probably he will not know all he wishes to know about the subject; therefore, he must be encouraged to extend his knowledge by reading, by observing, by interviewing, or by doing research.

Once the student has focused on the subject and gathered material for it, he must begin to limit the subject so he can handle it adequately. For example, he cannot write about modern literature—a topic far too broad and all-inclusive to be handled in a regular assignment. Instead he must limit his subject to some aspect of modern literature.

The teacher should illustrate this by showing the student specifically how to do this. For example, the teacher might place the following illustration on the blackboard in order that the student can see how one moves toward a greater limitation of the subject: Modern Literature, The World of William Faulkner, Novels of William Faulkner, The Major Themes of William Faulkner.

FRAMING A THESIS STATEMENT

As soon as the student has an idea of what he wants to say, he must put it into a single statement—in the form of a simple or complex

[3]The emphasis has been placed on expository writing because exposition plays the predominant role in the student's reading and writing. Everyone knows from his own school experience that one is asked to explain much more often than he is asked to argue, to describe, or to narrate; further it is obvious that these forms of discourse are not exclusive of each other and that exposition is the basis of them all; therefore one can conclude it should be mastered first.

sentence but not a compound sentence. The student has one idea to explain, not two. For example, his thesis might read, "The major theme of William Faulkner's novels is the decline of the South," not, "The major theme of William Faulkner's novels is the decline of the South and southern aristocrats suffered many economic hardships during the twenties." The student must be made to realize that he must focus his writing upon the explanation of one major idea, which in turn will help to insure unity as nothing else will.

ORGANIZATION

Once the student has an idea of what he is planning to say he can begin to check the relevance of the material he has gathered in view of the thesis, and he can think about the order in which the various points should stand.

It should be noted at this point that different kinds of expository writing require different plans, but a certain general plan is common to all types, that is, expository writing must have a beginning, a middle, and end (introduction, development, and conclusion).

I. *Introduction.* A good beginning will gain the reader's attention or interest. Though the thesis will be stated in the introduction, the student must be cautioned not to plunge abruptly into the subject. Instead he must create enough interest so that the reader will want to pursue the subject.

This may be achieved by use of one or more of the following: (1) a question (to set the reader thinking in terms of the subject); (2) a dramatic statement (to capture his interest); (3) an anecdote (to arouse his interest); (4) an apt quotation (to illustrate the subject). As the reader's interest is gained, the thesis is stated and the plan of development is made clear.

II. *Development.* The thesis set forth in the introduction should be expanded in accordance with various patterns and methods of development. Using the basic patterns of paragraph development, the student's writing should reflect his thinking as he proceeds from: (1) the specific to the general (inductive pattern); (2) the specific to the general and back to the specific (inductive-deductive pattern); (3) the general to the specific (deductive pattern).

However, the student cannot develop these basic patterns logically and effectively without being specific; in other words, he must develop his thesis is accordance with various methods of paragraph development: concrete detail or illustration, definition, enumeration, cause and effect, contrast and/or comparison, and analogy.

The various patterns and methods of development might be discussed separately, but the student must be made to see that the end result of studying these various patterns and methods of development is to write paragraphs that fit well into the entire composition and that, in order to do this, experienced writers often combine these patterns and methods to achieve their aim.

Here the teacher should assist the student in analyzing how experienced writers do this and then demonstrate how he, the teacher, would do this. Experience has taught me that if the beginning student is to learn how to write clearly, he must not only analyze examples of excellent writings, he must also study examples of something being written. No one learns to cook simply by eating; one must observe and study how the cook prepares the food.

After this explanation and exercise, the student should be ready to construct a sentence outline and write the major portion of his composition for which he has already done the necessary reading or research, limiting of subject, and framing of thesis.

At this point the student should realize what hè has gained from the analysis of excellent writings; that is, he should see that development is not only a matter of understanding patterns and methods of development, recognizing divisions of thought and their relationships, but also a matter of addition and omission of certain material. As he makes a rough list of topics, groups them, chooses the main and subtopics, he will see that he must constantly add and omit material.

In short, he will come to see that development is not only a matter of order, specification, division, addition, and omission. It is also a matter of constant revision, a matter of organization which requires constant analysis, a matter of clear thinking.

III. *Conclusion.* A good composition should no more end abruptly with the last point than it should open abruptly with the first one. It should finish with some kind of conclusion that will give the reader a sense of completion and keep him from searching for another page. In a fairly long paper the conclusion should summarize the material developed, making certain the major ideas are clear in the reader's mind. In short papers, as well as long papers, the final statement should make evident that the material presented was worth discussing.

REVISION

The student can best judge whether or not he has achieved his purpose by much proofreading and self-criticism and, more specifically, by checking to see if he has kept in mind the criteria of clear writing: *unity, coherence,* and *emphasis.*

The student must check to see if the central idea or thesis statement is clearly established at the beginning and adhered to throughout his paper—*unity*. He must check to see that he has no unnecessary discussion of ideas or that he has not discussed ideas only slightly related to the thesis.

After checking to see that all the major and minor points are related to the thesis, the student must check to see that there is a natural and easy flow from one idea to another—*coherence*. The student should be reminded that coherence is achieved not only by logical arrangement of sentences but also by one of the following: repetition of key words from previous sentences; use of a pronoun or synonym referring to a word or idea in the preceding sentence; use of transitional expressions to point out thought relationships between sentences; and consistency in grammatical structure.

The student must then check to see if he has consciously arranged his material to achieve appropriate *emphasis* by proper proportion, repetition, and placement. Proportion is the allocation of the proper amount of space to major and minor ideas.

Repetition is the judicious reiteration of major points at various times in one's writing. Position is the arrangement of ideas climactically. And, of course, in revision the student must check such obvious things as grammar, punctuation, mechanics, spelling, and diction—all the details.

CONCLUSION

The above plan of providing guidance in this step-by-step procedure has proved to be effective in my English methods class and in high school English classes. A student cannot write clearly without first thinking clearly, but in order to think clearly he must be given this type of specific guidance in analyzing the writing process.

When this is done the student will realize that he can now crystallize and order his own thoughts and experiences and in so doing produce some crystallization and order in the thoughts and experiences of his readers.

Finding Your Own Voice:
Teaching Composition
in an Age of Dissent

DONALD M. MURRAY

STUDENT POWER is no longer an issue, it is a fact. The war is being won—or lost—depending on your viewpoint, and one of the major weapons in the war is rhetoric that is crude, vigorous, usually uninformed, frequently obscene, and often threatening.

Most of us wonder what this educational revolution means for the composition teacher, who has often seen himself the principal defender of good taste, an evangelist of tradition, an heroic voice speaking up for order. Is our cause lost in an Age of Mailer?

No, but the implications of the student revolt for English Departments are clear. We are freed from an obligation to teach etiquette and forced to design a curriculum which trains students to accept the responsibilities of free speech through the experience of writing—the most disciplined form of thinking—and publication—the most revealing act of the intellectual life.

I do not speak from an isolated position. I teach in conference, close to my students. I am adviser to the college newspaper, and I suppose I am one of the New Left's enemy liberals, for I've been confronted, polarized, perhaps even co-opted. I am not over thirty; I'm over forty, and I feel it. I do get discouraged, mostly because the students have had no freedom, and when they find their own voice it has not been tempered by experience.

It is ironic that a nation built by teen-age pioneers, sea captains in

From *College Composition and Communication*, May, 1969, pp. 118–123. Reprinted with the permission of the National Council of Teachers of English and Donald M. Murray.

their twenties, and statesmen in their early thirties has created a teacher-centered educational system which keeps most of its students in a state of permanent adolescence through, and sometimes beyond, the awarding of the Ph.D. Too often our students have not been allowed to speak, and when they have spoken no one has listened, and when we have listened we have not allowed the freedom of action which encourages responsibility.

Our students need to discover, before graduation, that freedom is the greatest tyrant of all. Too often the composition teacher not only denies his students freedom, he even goes further and performs the key writing tasks for his students. He gives an assignment; he lists sources; he dictates the form; and, by irresponsibly conscientious correcting, he actually revises his students' papers. Is it not surprising that the student does not learn to write when the teacher, with destructive virtue, has done most of his student's writing?

The times indeed are revolutionary, cleansingly so. And they uniquely offer the composition teacher the opportunity to play a pioneer role in constructing an educational system which removes students' responsibilities from the teacher and places them firmly on the student.

Democracy is forged out of a responsible Babel, and the mature English teacher welcomes a diversity of contradictory voices, each student speaking of his own concerns in his own way. There is no single standard, no one way to think or to write, and we must not give our students the illusion there is. We must glory in contradiction and confusion, the human cacophony. Graham Greene has asked, "Isn't disloyalty as much the writer's virtue as loyalty is the soldier's?" Each writing teacher should be a revolutionary, doubting, questioning, challenging, and, above all, encouraging his students to be individuals. He creates a constructive chaos which will allow the students to achieve effective communication.

THE FOUR RESPONSIBILITIES OF THE STUDENT

The writing course is student-centered, but this does not imply a lack of standards or a casual permissiveness. Just the opposite. It places the obligation to learn on the student. It gives him four fundamental freedoms which he will discover are also responsibilities.

THE STUDENT'S FIRST RESPONSIBILITY

The teacher should show the student how writers find their subjects. But the student must find his own subject. The teacher cannot see the student's world with the student's eyes and evaluate it with the student's mind. Every time the teacher gives an assignment he cheats the student, since each step in the writing process—form, style, tone, effectiveness—stems from what the student has to say.

The student may be shown how to perceive, but he has to do his own perceiving. The writing course is a tough course, perhaps the toughest the student will face, for he is made to look at his world and to react to it, honestly, critically, specifically, personally. If the student writer has nothing to say, he is a mute animal, uncritical, unspeaking, and he must realize it. It is the student's responsibility to find his own subject.

THE STUDENT'S SECOND RESPONSIBILITY

The student should also document his own subject so that he will build, in Lucile Vaughan Payne's words, "an informed opinion." The sturdy fact, the relevant detail, the esthetic insight, the revealing incident are the raw materials which he must collect to construct a piece of writing which supports his subject and convinces his reader.

Creativity is a tough business, and it all starts with a solid inventory of specifics. The student must either find the concrete details which he can arrange into a pattern of significance, or he can perceive a generalization and then nail it down with evidence. The poet is the most specific writer, the most accurate marksman, catching meanings on the wing. The novelist, the lawyer, the dramatist, the executive, the scientist, all depend on illuminating, revealing, relevant details as they write.

We can show our students how to search, but they must mine the nuggets of information themselves and refine the images or the facts which communicate meaning with authority, the smells and the sounds which give immediacy, the citations and statistics which persuade.

The search for information should not merely be autobiographical in a limited sense. The student does learn from the street corner, but he also learns from books. The coed who has worked as a waitress may be handed Orwell's *Down and Out in Paris and London,* or sent to an article on restaurant management. The intellectual process does not mean just reading; it certainly does not mean just feeling.

Content always comes before form, and the student should begin to discover that the vigor of writing doesn't come so much from the graceful stroke of his pen as from the incisive bite of his intellect.

THE STUDENT'S THIRD RESPONSIBILITY

The act of writing is incomplete without a reader, but it is not the teacher's job to be a receptive audience of dull writing or force others to listen when nothing is being said. It is the student's responsibility to earn an audience, winning respect for what he has on the page.

The teacher of writing will break the class up so that individual students exchange papers. He will have his class read each other's papers in small groups. He will be an audience himself in conference. He will have his students write for the class, and perhaps write outside of the class.

No group is more peer-conscious than a covey of college professors. We should expect no less of our students. We learn as our publications are evaluated by our peers, the equals we respect. Our students will teach each other and learn from the same process. Often a student will understand another student's problem and its solution better than the instructor, for the student is working on the same level. It is the student's job to try to learn and to be a constructively critical audience so his classmates will learn.

THE STUDENT'S FOURTH RESPONSIBILITY

I teach a course called Expository Writing, and students pre-register in May to exposit in October, when they may need to lyricize, report, narrate and not exposit at all. The writer cannot predict the form in which he will express himself months in advance. When he sits down knowing his subject, knowing his audience, he may write narrative, poetry, argument, critical analysis, even exposition. During any writing course the student should practice many forms, each appropriate to what he has to say.

Perhaps, at times, it is appropriate for those who are interested in a particular form to sit down together. But there is something corrupt in forcing this, for the writer first has to have something to say to an audience before he can choose his form. He cannot choose the form until he knows the audience, knows the quantity and the quality of his evidence, knows his subject. You don't buy a wedding dress and then look for a wife. And yet I, too, fall into the pattern of asking my students to write description when they have nothing to describe, editorials when they have no opinions, reportage when they have nothing to report.

I am always tempted to return to this teaching method, dictating the form and, therefore, the content, for it is neat and comforting to the teacher. I know what I am doing, and the fact that it may not be relevant seems a lesser burden than doubt. Ultimately, however, I cheat the student, and somehow I must make him see that there are many forms which he is capable of choosing. Each artistic form is inherent, arising out of the artistic situation. It is third down and four;

you are behind 17 to 14; the defensive team has over shifted to the left—the writer processes as much information as the quarterback, or more, and then chooses his form. It arises out of what he has to say and to whom he wishes to say it. And the choice of form belongs to him.

In this age of dissent the student must be given four freedoms—the freedom to find his own subject, to find his own evidence, to find his own audience, and to find his own form. These freedoms are his opportunity and his obligation.

THE FOUR RESPONSIBILITIES OF THE TEACHER

The teacher who has the courage to place the student's responsibilities on the student's shoulders finds himself in a frightening position. He can not take the aggressive role of pouring information into the students' heads; he must wait for them to write so that he can react.

Students are promoted and rewarded in our educational system for their ability to follow directions; taking orders, not taking the initiative, is the way to get into college. When the teacher forces a responsible role on his students they will at first resent and distrust the teacher— he is not doing his job—and they will be frightened—what does teacher want? But the professor should not compound the felonies of the past. If he is patient, at first a few, and then a majority, of his students will accept and even enjoy their freedom and its attendant responsibility to learn by primarily teaching themselves.

THE TEACHER'S FIRST RESPONSIBILITY

The teacher's primary responsibility is to create a psychological and physical environment in which the student can fulfill his responsibilities.

At the University of New Hampshire we have created a writing laboratory with twenty-four typewriters around the walls and a hollow square of movable tables which can be adapted to group activity. There is good lighting and good soundproofing, so that many people can work and talk and criticize simultaneously. There is a 40-foot-long wall of corkboard for articles on writing. An office opens off the laboratory where there are four file cabinets full of materials which can be given to the student during conference, a library on writing, an unabridged dictionary, and comfortable chairs where the student and the teacher can sit side by side to examine a paper. Most important, there is a dittoed sheet on the door with at least 44 fifteen-minute conference slots a week.

The psychological implications of this writing laboratory are more important than the physical setting, and they can be duplicated in the ordinary classroom. The emphasis in the writing course is on conferences which are held at the student's initiative. Teaching is done individually or around a table. The writing lab dramatizes the intellectual act of writing. Everything is designed to help the individual student find his own way to satisfy the essential discipline of the course.

THE TEACHER'S SECONDARY RESPONSIBILITY

Once the teacher has created an environment in which the student can write, then he must enforce the deadline. The student must write frequently, and probably to a minimum daily deadline, an artificial necessity. A paper a day, or five pages a week, or ten pages every two weeks. I've not had much success with a class deadline much beyond that. Formal outlines, carefully done notes, sloppy first-drafts, total revisions—all count toward the number of pages.

Once students understand the system and are convinced of the need of the deadline, they will experience the process of writing and welcome the discipline of frequent papers. They will learn to write by writing. Most students who come to me with critical writing problems have never had an intensive writing experience, while the students who enter the course writing well have passed through a course where they wrote and wrote and wrote. The teacher cannot shirk his responsibility to force the student to write. He must create artificial pressure which makes the student commit himself on paper again and again and again.

THE TEACHER'S THIRD RESPONSIBILITY

The writing teacher has to stop trying to create a world in which success for the majority day by day is the norm. He has to cultivate a climate of failure. The writer fails all the time, but he fails to succeed. He learns to shape the failure of his drafts into the successes of his final copy.

Grades, of course, are ridiculous during the writing course. They are much more than irrelevant, they do positive harm. An "A" deludes a student into thinking an early draft is final copy, while an "F" convinces another student that there is no hope. The teachers I know who have experimented with eliminating grades on individual pieces of writing never return to conventional grading. The productivity and the quality of student writing increases when grades are left off each paper. Of course, when the time comes for a final standard, it is easy enough to evaluate papers chosen by the students at the end of the course.

THE TEACHER'S FOURTH RESPONSIBILITY

The teacher is a diagnostician. Ideally, the teacher reads only those papers on which the student is having problems. He knows those papers because his students select them from their folder in conference. He does not write long, careful, but easily misinterpreted comments on papers most of the time. He listens to the student in conference, reads the papers selected by the student, listens to the student's own diagnosis of his writing problems, confirms it or proposes an alternate diagnosis, listens to the student as he proposes his own solutions, and possibly suggests alternate treatments.

The experienced composition teacher does not see all writing problems—spelling and structure, and lack of subject matter—of equal importance. He encourages the student to see that on most pieces of writing there is one fundamental problem which must be dealt with before the next problem can be spotted, and then solved. For example, an incoherent paper will be ungrammatical; once the logic of the writing is developed, grammatical problems tend to disappear.

The effective teacher rarely corrects a paper. That's too easy for him. Sometimes he will edit a paragraph or a page, particularly on a good paper, to show how it may be shaped into a still better paper, but this must be done with discretion. The teacher who corrects an entire paper is doing the student's job of editing. He is cheating the student of the opportunity to learn, for ultimately the student must be able to diagnose and treat his own problems when he has escaped the protective custody of his writing teacher.

THE RESPONSIBILITY SHARED BY TEACHER AND STUDENT

The central act of the writing course is publication. This is the crucible where the student is tested, tried and taught. And the teacher, as well as the student, must publish and share criticism from careful readers.

The teacher, by writing with his students and by failing with them, will not lose but earn their respect. He will have the enviable opportunity to share the experience of learning with his students. Together they can establish an environment of exploration and discovery.

Publication within the classroom may be performed with ditto, xerox, carbon paper, overhead projector, wall display, or merely student folders open to all members of the class. The means are not important; the ends are. The writer must face his audience. He must hear the contradictory counsel of his readers, so that he learns when to ignore his teacher and his peers, listening to himself after evaluating what has been said about his writing and considering what he can do to make it work.

Slowly, painfully, the student will discover he can achieve an audience. If he has something to say, if he says it honestly, if his opinions are informed, if he brings order to chaos, if he entertains, if he is able to give the reader information or an esthetic experience, he will be read.

The free speech movement may start with dirty words, but a cliché is a chiché, and if the audience is not shocked or frightened by short transitive verbs, then the student can go on to say what he has to say. He will reveal, as we all do, our lack of information, our naivete, our clumsiness, our dishonesties. He will experience criticism, failure, and enough success—those nice small moments of completion—to give him courage, in the right environment, to face the agonies of exposure on the printed page and to learn from it.

The teacher of composition should welcome an age of dissent. He should glory in diversity, and he should discover that by giving his students freedom they will accept responsibility. Perhaps in this age when students are using their voices to attack and transform the educational establishment, the teacher of composition may return to his important educational role when rhetoric—the art of effective and responsible argument—was the foundation of a classical education.

The Beginning Begets:
Making Composition Assignments

EDMUND J. FARRELL

WHY teachers give so little time and thought to creating composition assignments has often perplexed me. Justifiably they protest the inordinate demands made upon them in the evaluation of students' themes, the laborious hours given to the written work of the too many students in the too many classes they daily meet. Yet, rather than mitigating this load by furnishing assignments that would stimulate students to write clearly and imaginatively, they seem to compound it eagerly with slap-dash assignments composed in the spur of the half-hour before school begins or, worse, in the five minutes between classes. I have even observed a few intrepid souls risk instantaneous creation during the few precious seconds they were able to turn their backs on classes, chalk in hand, to scribble furiously before chaos triumphed.

All teachers deserve respite from the daily sound of their own voices. It is a comfort indeed to wander aisles observing students quietly writing, to surfeit on silence, and not feel the pangs of guilt that showing a movie or spinning a record provoke. One can justify his existence: rather than mulcting the citizenry of tax revenues, he is having students write, an activity endorsed by the most conservative parental group in favor of bettering the education of the nation's youth.

But after the tranquility of the day comes the gnashing of the night, when the teacher who has lugged home the illiterate and puerile products he inadvertently has encouraged, suffers to find grace and sense where none exist. Their summer vacations were vacuous, their families a bore, their hobbies morally questionable, their syntax tor-

From *English Journal*, March, 1969, pp. 428–431. Reprinted with the permission of the National Council of Teachers of English and Edmund J. Farrell.

tured, and their styles atrocious. And so, bleary-eyed to bed, red pencil blunted, morale dissipated, give-em-hell lecture contemplated, and source of problem ignored.

For some time now in the methods course I conduct on the teaching of English in secondary schools, I have had student teachers write lesson plans for a few short stories—Shirley Jackson's "The Lottery," J. D. Salinger's "The Laughing Man," and Hawthorne's "The Minister's Black Veil." Included with each plan have been two composition assignments which the student teacher believed might suitably follow the teaching of the selection. From these hypothetical assignments I have culled and ordered those which exemplify a failure on the part of student teachers to anticipate what they are asking of students, to imagine themselves adolescents trying with as little cerebral friction as possible to fulfill the demands being made upon them. Based upon the work of the student teachers, the admonitions which follow are offered humbly, for I believe that each of us can find examples of his own pedagogical aberrations in the list and can recall the profitless hours of evaluating papers which resulted therefrom:

1. *Avoid assignments that can be answered yes-no, true-false:*
   Does man's need for self-preservation ever justify sacrificing others in order that he may live?
   People are the creation of their environment.
2. *Avoid assignments that lead to short, often fragmentary, responses:*
   How did you feel when you finished "The Lottery"? Why?
3. *Avoid assignments that lead to idle speculation or that may be treated frivolously:*
   Factors which might have caused Shirley Jackson to write such a story.
   The day I (my friends, our country, etc.) threw rocks at Tessie Hutchinson.
4. *Avoid assignments which are vague or which assume knowledge students may not possess:*
   Elaborate on the symbolism in "The Lottery."
   Trace the development of imagery in "The Lottery."
   Emphasize the recurring themes.
5. *Avoid assignments which, by posing numerous questions, provoke incoherency:*
   Compare the hero image of the Laughing Man with the movie hero image of James Bond. In your discussion, you may want to consider some of the following questions: What ingredients does the Laughing Man have or not have in comparison? Would the young

boy in the story find James Bond a satisfying hero? Why or why not? Which image do you find more satisfying?

6. *Avoid assignments which a student may regard as too personal:*

Relate the feelings of guilt experienced and expressed by Mr. Hooper and the townspeople to a personal experience in which you felt the pangs of guilt (e.g., cheating on an exam, lying to teacher or parent, defaming the character of a fellow student, receiving unearned praise for work which is not your own). Be specific. Use examples from the story to make comparisons.

Relate an instance in your own experience where you have inflicted injury (not necessarily physical) on another person as a member of a group. How did you feel at the time? How did you feel afterwards when you were alone?

7. *Avoid assignments which pit a novice writer against a professional:*

Decide what is the central idea, or cluster of ideas, carried by the story and then sketch out in several paragraphs a short story form, differing from that of 'The Lottery,' which might also be appropriate to carry these ideas. You may want to consider whether the story might be developed as a mood piece, as a strongly didactic piece, as a characterization, or whatever. To get started, you might consider how the short story authors we have studied so far might have presented such an idea—Saroyan, Steele, or Poe, for instance.

Write a story of your own, patterned after "The Lottery," but with the situation, events, and people that exist today in the South.

Select one part of the story, e.g., congregating of the people to distribute the lottery papers, the selection of Tessie Hutchinson as the victim and the consequent action. Write the selection as Hitchcock might write for presentation on TV.

Common to these assignments is the absence of a stipulated audience and/or purpose which would help the student to define himself in context, which would lead him to adopt an appropriate persona or "speaking voice" in his composition. Without prior knowledge as to why and/or to whom he is writing, even the professional author would be incapable of maintaining consistent tone, tone depending upon the individual's decision about who he is, a decision which can be made only in relationship to an occasion and audience. To belabor the obvious, an adolescent's discourse or the "self" he presents, is different on a date from what it is at home, different at home from what it is in the classroom.

Speaking at the CEE luncheon at the Honolulu convention of NCTE, Professor Walker Gibson observed:

> . . . When we can recognize that choices of language are dictated not alone by subject matter, and not alone by audience, but involve as well as a self-creating act, the taking on of a role with a personality, an attitude, an identity—for some of us, at any rate, that perception offers a part way out of the woods. Thus a central activity of the composition course becomes the encouraging of students to take on various roles in their writing through exercises that may simply force upon them, however crudely, various rhetorical characters.

If Walker is correct, and I believe he is, then it behooves us to create composition assignments which stimulate students to role play, to indulge themselves in a gamut of personalities during their adolescent years. Only thus will they discover the range of rhetorical voices available to them in writing.

Let me now offer some composition assignments with built-in "selves" and indicate some of the available options as to audience and purpose. Again, the assignments were written by student teachers, some for classes they were teaching, but only after their initial efforts at composing assignments had been critically discussed in class:

1. *The "self" of an assignment may be internal to the selection, the purpose unspecified, and the audience private:*
   Assume that you are Lady Macbeth and that you keep a diary. Write the five entries which precede your suicide.

   Assume that you are the narrator in "The Laughing Man." You are in the bathtub on the evening after John Geduski has recounted the last episode of the Laughing Man story. What passes through your mind?
2. *The "self" and the audience may be internal to the selection and the purpose specified:*
   Word has reached the church fathers that Parson Hooper is dead. The Reverend Mr. Clark, who tended him at the end, was so impressed that he has petitioned the synod for permission to don a black veil and follow in Parson Hooper's footsteps. You have been asked to submit a report to a committee of church leaders stating why Mr. Clark should or should not be allowed to don a black veil.

You are Tom and have been away from home now for three months. Write to Laura trying to explain to her why you left.

3. *The "self," audience, and purpose may be external to the selection:*

A friend of yours comes to you with a copy of *Macbeth* and says, "I understand you've read this play in class. What should I look for in it so I can most fully understand it?" What advice would you offer?

You have a pen pal in a foreign country. He asks you to recommend a book which captures the spirit of this country. From your reading in English III this semester, select the novel which you believe best satisfies your friend's request. Write to him, explaining why you are recommending the novel you have chosen.

4. *The "self" may be internal to the selection and the audience and purpose external:*

You are Sanger Rainsford and have undergone the experiences narrated in "The Most Dangerous Game." A group of high-school students, interested in starting a Rifle Club, have written to you, requesting that you speak to them. You accept the invitation. What have you to say?

You are one of the inhabitants of Spoon River who have died. You have an opportunity to speak out from the grave, summarizing your life in a paragraph or two. What comments have you to make?

In short, if assignments are composed carefully so as to assist students to produce appropriate voices or "selves" in their writing, if students are not asked to do what the teacher would not want to do, if they are given a choice of assignments as well as the opportunity to create their own, then their writing should be more pleasurable to read and much easier to evaluate.

But lest the reader be left believing that he has been furnished a panacea for all students' prose, he should be reminded of the anecdote about the teacher who asked that each of her students assume he was a famous personage in history writing to a beloved one in a time of crisis. From one boy came this memorable epistle: "Dear Josephine, I just wanted to let you know things didn't go so hot at Waterloo."

Humility, saith the preacher, in all things.

A Generative Rhetoric
of the Sentence

FRANCIS CHRISTENSEN

IF THE NEW GRAMMAR is to be brought to bear on composition, it must be brought to bear on the rhetoric of the sentence. We have a workable and teachable, if not a definitive, modern grammar; but we do not have, despite several titles, a modern rhetoric.

In composition courses we do not really teach our captive charges to write better—we merely *expect* them to. And we do not teach them how to write better because we do not know how to teach them to write better. And so we merely go through the motions. Our courses with their tear-out workbooks and four-pound anthologies are elaborate evasions of the real problem. They permit us to put in our time and do almost anything else we'd rather be doing instead of buckling down to the hard work of making a difference in the student's understanding and manipulation of language.

With hundreds of handbooks and rhetorics to draw from, I have never been able to work out a program for teaching the sentence as I find it in the work of contemporary writers. The chapters on the sentence all adduce the traditional rhetorical classification of sentences as loose, balanced, and periodic. But the term *loose* seems to be taken as a pejorative (it sounds immoral); our students, no Bacons or Johnsons, have little occasion for balanced sentences; and some of our worst perversions of style come from the attempt to teach them to write periodic sentences. The traditional grammatical classification of sentences is equally barren. Its use in teaching composition rests on a semantic confusion, equating complexity of structure with complexity of thought and vice versa. But very simple thoughts may call for very complex grammatical constructions. Any moron can say "I don't know who done it." And some of us might be puzzled to work out the grammar of "All I want is all there is," although any chit can think it and say it and act on it.

The chapters on the sentence all appear to assume that we think naturally in primer sentences, progress naturally to compound sentences, and must be taught to combine the primer sentences into complex sentences—and that complex sentences are the mark of maturity. We need a rhetoric of the sentence that will do more than combine the ideas of primer sentences. We need one that will *generate* ideas.

For the foundation of such a generative or productive rhetoric I take the statement from John Erskine, the originator of the Great Books courses, himself a novelist. In an essay "The Craft of Writing" (*Twentieth Century English,* Philosophical Library, 1946) he discusses a principle of the writer's craft, which though known he says to all practitioners, he has never seen discussed in print. The principle is this: "When you write, you make a point, not by subtracting as though you sharpened a pencil, but by adding." We have all been told that the formula for good writing is the concrete noun and the active verb. Yet Erskine says, "What you say is found not in the noun but in what you add to qualify the noun . . . The noun, the verb, and the main clause serve merely as the base on which meaning will rise . . . The modifier is the essential part of any sentence." The foundation, then, for a generative or productive rhetoric of the sentence is that composition is essentially a process of *addition.*

But speech is linear, moving in time, and writing moves in linear space, which is analogous to time. When you add a modifier, whether to the noun, the verb, or the main clause, you must add it either before the head or after it. If you add it before the head, the direction of modification can be indicated by an arrow pointing forward; if you add it after, by an arrow pointing backward. Thus we have the second principle of a generative rhetoric—the principle of *direction of modification* or *direction of movement.*

Within the clause there is not much scope for operating with this principle. The positions of the various sorts of close, or restrictive, modifiers are generally fixed and the modifiers are often obligatory— "The man who came to dinner remained till midnight." Often the only choice is whether to add modifiers. What I have seen of attempts to bring structural grammar to bear on composition usually boils down to the injunction to "load the patterns." Thus "pattern practice" sets students to accreting sentences like this: "The small boy on the red bicycle who lives with his happy parents on our shady street often coasts down the steep street until he comes to the city park." This will never do. It has no rhythm and hence no life; it is tone-deaf. It is the seed that will burgeon into gobbledygook. One of the hardest things in writing is to keep the noun clusters and verb clusters short.

It is with modifiers added to the clause—that is, with sentence modifiers—that the principle comes into full play. The typical sentence of modern English, the kind we can best spend our efforts trying to teach, is what we may call the *cumulative sentence*. The main clause, which may or may not have a sentence modifier before it, advances the discussion; but the additions move backward, as in this clause, to modify the statement of the main clause or more often to explicate or exemplify it, so that the sentence has a flowing and ebbing movement, advancing to a new position and then pausing to consolidate it, leaping and lingering as the popular ballad does. The first part of the preceding compound sentence has one addition, placed within it; the second part has 4 words in the main clause and 49 in the five additions placed after it.

The cumulative sentence is the opposite of the periodic sentence. It does not represent the idea as conceived, pondered over, reshaped, packaged, and delivered cold. It is dynamic rather than static, representing the mind thinking. The main clause ("the additions move backward" above) exhausts the mere fact of the idea; logically, there is nothing more to say. The additions stay with the same idea, probing its bearings and implications, exemplifying it or seeking an analogy or metaphor for it, or reducing it to details. Thus the mere form of the sentence generates ideas. It serves the needs of both the writer and the reader, the writer by compelling him to examine his thought, the reader by letting him into the writer's thought.

Addition and direction of movement are structural principles. They involve the grammatical character of the sentence. Before going on to other principles, I must say a word about the best grammar as the foundation for rhetoric. I cannot conceive any useful transactions between teacher and students unless they have in common a language for talking about sentences. The best grammar is the grammar that best displays the layers of structure of the English sentence. The best I have found in a textbook is the combination of immediate constituent and transformation grammar in Paul Robert's *English Sentences*. Traditional grammar, whether over-simple as in the school tradition or over-complex as in the scholarly tradition, does not reveal the language as it operates; it leaves everything, to borrow a phrase from Wordsworth, "in disconnection dead and spiritless." *English Sentences* is oversimplified and it has gaps, but it displays admirably the structures that rhetoric must work with—primarily sentence modifiers, including relative and subordinate clauses, but, far more important, the array of noun, verb, and adjective clusters. It is paradoxical that Professor Roberts, who has done so much to make the teaching of composition possible, should himself be one of those who think that it cannot be taught. Unlike Ulysses, he doesn't see any work for Telemachus to work.

Layers of structure, as I have said, is a grammatical concept. To bring in the dimension of meaning, we need a third principle—that of *levels of generality* or *levels of abstraction*. The main clause is likely to be stated in general or abstract or plural terms. With the main clause stated, the forward movement of the sentence stops, the writer shifts down to a lower level of generality or abstraction or to singular terms, and goes back over the same ground at this lower level.[1] "He has just bought a new car, a 1963½ Ford, a Galaxie, a fastback hardtop with four-on-the-floor shift." There is no theoretical limit to the number of structural layers or levels, each at a lower level of generality, any or all of them compounded, that a speaker or writer may use. For a speaker, listen to Lowell Thomas; for a writer, study William Faulkner. To a single independent clause he may append a page of additions, but usually all clear, all grammatical, once we have learned how to read him. Or, if you prefer, study Hemingway, the master of the simple sentence: "George was coming down in the telemark position, kneeling, one leg forward and bent, the other trailing, his sticks hanging like some insect's thin legs, kicking up puffs of snow, and finally the whole kneeling, trailing figure coming around in a beautiful right curve, crouching, the legs shot forward and back, the body leaning out against the swing, the sticks accenting the curve like points of light, all in a wild cloud of snow."

This brings me to the fourth, and last, principle, that of texture. *Texture* provides a descriptive or evaluative term. If a writer adds to few of his nouns or verbs or main clauses and adds little, the texture may be said to be thin. The style will be plain or bare. The writing of most of our students is thin—even threadbare. But if he adds fre-

[1]Cf. Leo Rockas, "Abstract and Concrete Sentences," *CCC*, May 1963. Rockas describes sentences as abstract or concrete, the abstract implying the concrete and vice versa. Readers and writers, he says, must have the knack of apprehending the concrete in the abstract and the abstract in the concrete. This is true and valuable. I am saying that within a single sentence the writer may present more than one level of generality, translating the abstract into the more concrete in added levels.

quently or much or, both, then the texture may be said to be dense or rich. One of the marks of an effective style, especially in narrative, is variety in the texture, the texture varying with the change in pace, the variation in texture producing the change in pace. It is not true, as I have seen it asserted, that fast action calls for short sentences; the action is fast in the sentence by Hemingway above. In our classes, we have to work for greater density and variety in texture and greater concreteness and particularity in what is added.

I have been operating at a fairly high level of generality. Now I must downshift and go over the same points with examples. The most graphic way to exhibit the layers of structure is to indent the word groups of a sentence and to number the levels. Since in the narrow columns of this journal indentation is possible only with short sentences whose additions are short, I have used it with only the first three sentences; the reader is urged to copy out the others for himself. I have added symbols to mark the grammatical character of the additions: SC, subordinate clause; RC, relative clause; NC, noun cluster; VC, verb cluster; AC, adjective cluster; Abs absolute (i.e., a VC with a subject of its own); PP, prepositional phrase. With only a few exceptions (in some the punctuation may be questioned) the elements set off as on a lower level are marked by junctures or punctuation. The examples have been chosen to illustrate the range of constructions used in the lower levels; after the first few they are arranged by the number of levels. The examples could have been drawn from poetry as well as from prose. Those not attributed are by students.

1

1 He shook his hands,
    2 a quick shake, (NC)
        3 fingers down, (Abs)
            4 like a pianist. (PP)—Sinclair Lewis

2

    2 Calico-coated, (AC)
    2 small bodied, (AC)
    2 with delicate legs and pink faces (PP)
        3 in which their mismatched eyes rolled wild and subdued, (RC)
1 they huddled,
    2 gaudy motionless and alert, (AC)
    2 wild as deer, (AC)
    2 deadly as rattlesnakes, (AC)
    2 quiet as doves. (AC)—William Faulkner

3

1 The bird's eye, /, remained fixed upon him;
    2 bright and silly as a sequin (AC)

1 its little bones, /, seemed swooning in his hand.—Stella Benson
   2 wrapped . . . in a warm padding of feathers (VC)

4

1) The jockeys sat bowed and relaxed, moving a little at the waist with the movement of their horses[2-VC].—Katherine Anne Porter

5

1) The flame sidled up the match, driving a film of moisture and a thin strip of darker grey before it[2-VC].

6

1) She came among them behind the man, gaunt in the gray shapeless garment and the sunbonnet[2-AC], wearing stained canvas gymnasium shoes.[2-VC]—Faulkner

7

1) The Texan turned to the nearest gatepost and climbed to the top of it, his alternate thighs thick and bulging in the tight jeans[2-Abs], the butt of his pistol catching and losing the sun in pearly gleams[2-Abs].—Faulkner

8

1) He could sail for hours, searching the blanched grasses below him with his telescopic eyes[2-VC], gaining height against the wind[2-VC], descending in mile-long, gently declining swoops when he curved and rode back[2-VC], never beating a wing[2-VC].—Walter Van Tilburg Clark

9

1) The gay-sweatered skaters are quick-silvering around the frosty rink, the girls gliding and spinning[2-Abs], the boys swooping and darting[2-Abs], their arms flailing like wings[3-Abs].

10

1) He stood at the top of the stairs and watched me, I waiting for him to call me up[2-Abs], he hesitating to come down[2-Abs], his lips nervous with the suggestion of a smile[3-Abs], mine asking whether the smile meant come, or go away[3-Abs].

11

1) Joad's lips stretched tight over his long teeth for a moment, and (1) he licked his lips, like a dog[2-PP], two licks [3-NC], one in each direction from the middle[4-NC].—Steinbeck

12

1) We all live in two realities: one of seeming fixity[2-NC], with institutions, dogmas, rules of punctuation, and routines[3-PP], the calendared and clockwise world of all but futile round on round[4-NC]; and one of whirling and flying electrons, dreams, and possibilities[2-NC], behind the clock[3-PP].—Sidney Cox

13

1) It was as though someone, somewhere, had touched a lever and shifted gears, and (2) the hospital was set for night running, smooth and silent[2-AC], its normal clatter and hum muffled[2-Abs], the only sounds heard in the whitewalled room distant and unreal[2-Abs]: a low hum of voices from the nurse's desk[3-NC], quickly stifled[4-VC], the soft squish of rubber-soled

shoes on the tiled corridor[3-NC], starched white cloth rustling against itself[3-NC], and outside, the lonesome whine of wind in the country night[3-NC], and the Kansas dust beating against the windows[3-NC].

14

1) The beach sounds are jazzy, percussion fixing the mode[2-Abs]—the surf cracking and booming in the distance[3-Abs], a little nearer dropped bar-bells clanking[3-Abs], steel gym rings, flung together[4-VC], ringing[3-Abs], palm fronds rustling above me[3-Abs], like steel brushes washing over a snare drum[4-PP], troupes of sandals splatting and shuffling on the sandy cement[3-Abs], their beat varying[4-Abs], syncopation emerging and disappearing with changing paces[5-Abs].

15

1) A small negro girl develops from the sheet of glare-frosted walk, walking barefooted[2-VC], her bare legs striking and coiling from the hot cement[3-Abs], her feet curling in[4-Abs], only the outer edges touching[5-Abs].

16

1) The swells moved rhythmically toward us irregularly faceted[2-VC], sparkling[2-VC], growing taller and more powerful[2-VC], until the shining crest bursts[3-SC], a transparent sheet of pale green water spilling over the top[4-Abs], breaking into blue-white foam as it cascades down the front of the wave[5-VC], piling up in a frothy mound that the diminishing wave pushes up against the pilings[5-VC], with a swishmash[6-PP], the foam drifting back[5-Abs], like a lace fan opened over a shimmering water as the spent wave returns whispering to the sea[6-PP].

The best starting point for a composition unit based on these four principles is with two-level narrative sentences, first with one second-level addition (sentences 4, 5), then with two or more parallel ones (6, 7, 8). Anyone sitting in his room with his eyes closed could write the main clause of most of the examples; the discipline comes with the additions, provided they are based at first on immediate observation, requiring the student to phrase an exact observation in exact language. This can hardly fail to be exciting to a class: it is life, with the variety and complexity of life; the workbook exercise is death. The situation is ideal also for teaching diction—abstract-concrete, general-specific, literal-metaphorical, denotative-connotative. When the sentences begin to come out right, it is time to examine the additions for their grammatical character. From then on the grammar comes to the aid of the writing and the writing reinforces the grammar. One can soon go on to multi-level narrative sentences (1, 3, 9–11, 15, 16) and then to brief narratives of three to six or seven sentences on actions that can be observed over and over again—beating eggs, making a cut with a power saw, or following a record changer's cycle or a wave's flow and ebb. Bring the record changer to class. Description, by contrast, is static, picturing appearance rather than behavior. The constructions to master are the noun and adjective clusters and the absolute (13, 14). Then the descriptive noun clusters must be taught to ride piggy-back on the narrative sentence, so that description and narration are interleaved: "In the morning we went out into a new world, a glistening crystal and white world, each skeleton tree, each leafless bush, even the heavy, drooping power lines sheathed in icy crystal." The next step is to develop the sense for variety in texture and change in pace that all good narrative demands.

In the next unit, the same four principles can be applied to the expository paragraph. But this is a subject for another paper.

I want to anticipate two possible objections. One is that the sentences are long. By freshman English standards they are long, but I could have produced far longer ones from works freshmen are expected to read. Of the sentences by students, most were written as finger exercises in the first few weeks of the course. I try in narrative sentences to push to level after level, not just two or three, but four, five, or six, even more, as far as the students' powers of observation will take them. I want them to become sentence acrobats, to dazzle by their syntactic dexterity. I'd rather have to deal with hyperemia than anemia. I want to add my voice to that of James Coleman (*CCC*, December 1962) deploring our concentration on the plain style.

The other objection is that my examples are mainly descriptive and narrative—and today in freshman English we teach only exposition. I deplore this limitation as much as I deplore our limitation to the plain style. Both are a sign that we have sold our proper heritage for a pot of message. In permitting them, the English department undercuts its own discipline. Even if our goal is only utilitarian prose, we can teach diction and sentence structure far more effectively through a few controlled exercises in description and narration than we can by starting right off with exposition (Theme One, 500 words, precipitates *all* the problems of writing). The student has something to communicate— his immediate sense impressions, which can stand a bit of exercising. The material is not already verbalized—he has to match language to sense impressions. His acuteness in observation and in choice of words can be judged by fairly objective standards—is the sound of a bottle of milk being set down on a concrete step suggested better by *clink* or *clank*? In the examples, study the diction for its accuracy, rising at times to the truly imaginative. Study the use of metaphor, of comparison. This verbal virtuosity and syntactical ingenuity can be made to carry over into expository writing.

But this is still utilitarian. What I am proposing carries over of itself into the study of literature. It makes the student a better reader of literature. It helps him thread the syntactical mazes of much mature writing, and it gives him insight into that elusive thing we call style. Last year a student told of re-reading a book by her favorite author, Willa Cather, and of realizing for the first time *why* she liked reading her: she could understand and appreciate the style. For some students, moreover, such writing makes life more interesting as well as giving them a way to share their interest with others. When they learn how to put concrete details into a sentence, they begin to look at life with more alertness. If it is liberal education we are concerned with, it is just possible that these things are more important than anything we can achieve when we set our sights on the plain style in expository prose.

I want to conclude with a historical note. My thesis in this paragraph is that modern prose like modern poetry has more in common with the seventeenth than with the eighteenth century and that we fail largely because we are operating from an eighteenth century base. The shift from the complex to the cumulative sentence is more profound than it seems. It goes deep in grammar, requiring a shift from the subordinate clause (the staple of our trade) to the cluster (so little understood as to go almost unnoticed in our textbooks). And I have only lately come to see that this shift has historical implications. The cumulative sentence is the modern form of the loose sentence that characterized the anti-Ciceronian movement in the seventeenth century. This movement, according to Morris W. Croll,[2] began with Montaigne and Bacon and continued with such men as Donne, Brown, Taylor, Pascal. Croll calls their prose baroque. To Montaigne, its art was the art of being natural; to Pascal, its eloquence was the eloquence that mocks formal eloquence; to Bacon, it presented knowledge so that it could be examined, not so that it must be accepted.

But the Senecan amble was banished from England when "the direct sensuous apprehension of thought" (T. S. Eliot's words) gave way to Cartesian reason or intellect. The consequences of this shift in sensibility are well summarized by Croll:

To this mode of thought we are to trace almost all the features of modern literary education and criticism, or at least of what we should have called modern a generation ago: the study of the precise meaning of words; the

2"The Baroque Style in Prose," Studies in *English Philology: A Miscellany in Honor of Frederick Klaeber* (1929), reprinted in A. M. Witherspoon and F. J. Warnke, *Seventeenth-Century Prose and Poetry*, 2nd ed. (1963). I have used the latter, and I have borrowed from Croll in my description of the cumulative sentence.

reference to dictionaries as literary authorities; the study of the sentence as a logical unit alone; the careful circumscription of its limits and the gradual reduction of its length; . . .[3] the attempt to reduce grammar to an exact science; the idea that forms of speech are always either correct or incorrect; the complete subjection of the laws of motion and expression in style to the laws of logic and standardization—in short, the triumph, during two centuries, of grammatical over rhetorical ideas. (p. 1077)

Here is a seven-point scale any teacher of composition can use to take stock. He can find whether he is based in the eighteenth century or in the twentieth and whether he is consistent—completely either an ancient or a modern—or is just a crazy mixed-up kid.

[3]The omitted item concerns punctuation and is not relevant here. In using this scale, note the phrase "what we should have called modern a generation ago" and remember that Croll was writing in 1929.

Grading and Measuring

PAUL B. DIEDERICH

COLLEGE BOARD EXPERIENCE

THE COLLEGE ENTRANCE EXAMINATION BOARD used nothing but essay examinations from 1900 to 1926, then used a mixture of essays and objective tests, and since 1941 has used chiefly objective tests. Although the latter yielded better predictions of academic success, and although their wide sampling of content gave teachers greater freedom, there was continual pressure to return to the essay in at least one examination. Several costly experiments were conducted using essays up to two hours in length, each graded by two or more College Board readers. But these readers did not agree very closely on the merit of the papers, and the students were even more erratic. The quality of their writing varied a great deal from one occasion or topic to another. As a result, final grades on two long essays agreed only 0.45 with one another, whereas scores on two objective tests of verbal ability, taken at the time of writing the essays, agreed 0.88.

It became obvious that further progress could be made only by finding out what qualities in student writing affect readers differently, causing a difference in their grading. It seemed unlikely that capable readers would disagree so wildly unless they were looking at different things or weighting them differently.

MATERIALS FOR A STUDY OF READER REACTIONS

To study this question, the writer and two colleagues[1] in the Re-

From *Improving English Composition*, ed. Arno Jewett, 1965, pp. 81–91. Reprinted with the permission of the National Education Association.

[1]Diederich, Paul B.; French, John W.; and Carlton, Sydell T. *Factors in Judgments of Writing Ability.* Research Bulletin 61–15. Princeton, N. J.: Educational Testing Service, 1961. (Out of print.)

search Division of Educational Testing Service secured 600 papers written as homework between one class meeting and the next by freshmen at Cornell, Middlebury, and the University of Pennsylvania. There were four topics, but only two were chosen by enough students: "Who Should Go to College?" and "When Should Teenagers Be Treated as Adults?" They were told that their papers would be read by 60 distinguished readers in six different fields: college English teachers, social science teachers, natural science teachers, writers and editors, lawyers, and business executives. The students were more stimulated than frightened by such an audience because they knew that their papers would be typed and reproduced without identification and that grades would not be reported to anyone.

We reduced the 600 papers to 300 (150 on each topic) without reading them: first, by dropping papers on the two less popular topics; second, by looking at the Scholastic Aptitude Test verbal scores of the writers. Since we wanted as wide a range as possible, we kept all papers written by students with either high or low SAT verbal scores and reduced the number with middle scores in such fashion that the distribution of verbal ability on one topic was parallel to that on the other. The remaining papers on both topics represented a wider range in verbal ability than any one teacher would be likely to encounter in a selective college. It may be said at once that we found no significant difference of any kind between one topic and the other. Hence our conclusions can be generalized at least to the types of short expository papers that are commonly assigned in both high schools and colleges.

HOW THE PAPERS WERE GRADED

The readers were told to sort the papers into nine piles in order of general merit. No instructions were given as to what to look for, since we wanted to find out what the readers looked for when they were free to grade as they liked. The only rules were that all nine piles must be used, and not less than six papers on each topic must appear in the smallest piles. The readers were also asked to comment on anything they liked or disliked in as many papers as possible.

The result was nearly chaos. Of the 300 papers, 101 received all nine grades, 111 received eight, 70 received seven, and no paper received less than five. The average agreement (correlation) among all readers was 0.31; among the college English teachers, 0.41. Readers in the other five fields agreed with the English teachers slightly better than they agreed with other readers in their own field.

This procedure has been criticized on the ground that we could have secured a higher level of agreement had we defined each topic more precisely, used only English teachers as readers, and spent some time in coming to agreements upon common standards. So we could, but then we would have found only the qualities we agreed to look for— possibly with a few surprises. We wanted each reader to go his own way so that differences in grading standards would come to light. We used readers in five fields in addition to English teachers because our colleagues also have opinions on the writing ability of our students, and so do representatives of the educated public.

THE FACTOR ANALYSIS

We correlated the grades of each reader with the grades of every other reader and put this large table of agreements and disagreements through the mathematical procedure known as "factor analysis." This is too complicated to explain briefly, but the effect is as though the computer scanned all the correlations and picked out clusters of readers who agreed with one another and disagreed with other clusters to a greater degree than could come about by chance. There proved to be only five such clusters. They were clearly agreeing on something, and on something different in each cluster. What was it?

We found out by tabulating the comments of the three readers who stood highest on each factor (who came closest to the central tendency of each cluster) and only on papers graded either high (7–8–9) or low (1–2–3). We checked our conclusions by similarly tabulating the comments of the three readers who stood lowest on each factor. Comments were tabulated under 55 headings by a person who did not know the standing of any reader on any factor. In all, 11,018 comments on 3,557 papers were tabulated. They were reduced to percentages of total comments written by each reader so that readers who wrote the most comments would not unduly influence the interpretation.

It then became quite clear that the largest cluster (16 readers) was influenced primarily by the *ideas* expressed: their richness, soundness, clarity, development, and relevance. The next largest (13 readers) was most influenced by *mechanics:* the number of errors in grammar or usage, punctuation, and spelling. Seven of the ten English teachers stood high on this factor. The third (9 readers) showed the highest interest in *organization* and analysis. Four of the business executives stood high on this factor. (They were also especially sensitive to poor spelling but not to other elements of mechanics.) The fourth (9 readers) stood highest in specific comments on *wording* and phrasing: on verbal felicity or infelicity. The fifth (7 readers) emphasized style, individuality, interest, sincerity, the personal qualities of the writing,

which we decided to call *flavor*. The four readers who stood highest
on this factor were all writers or editors. They also had the lowest percentage of specific comments on mechanical errors.

Here, evidently, were some of the reasons why expert College Board
readers had so long failed to agree. Like the distinguished readers
assembled for this study, they were responding to different qualities in the papers, or they differed in the weights they attached to
these qualities. One possible conclusion might be that papers in important tests of writing ability should be rated by five different readers,
each of whom was especially sensitive to one of these factors. Since
this was hardly feasible, it was comforting to find no solid evidence
that any reader was entirely blind to any of these qualities. There
were only differences in emphasis, heightened by the absence of directives and amplified by the technique of factor analysis. If readers were
asked for a rating on each factor or on some of its principal components, it seemed likely that all but a few readers would be able
to follow these instructions.

This policy was tried out in three large high schools the following
year. The principal new finding was that, under the pressure of time
and the teaching tradition, these five factors collapsed into two: a
general merit factor and a distinct mechanics factor. The ratings that
had the highest "loadings" on the general merit factor were, however,
four of our five original factors: ideas, organization, flavor, and wording. While we might have settled for a single rating on merit and
another on mechanics, we decided to ask for a separate rating on the
four main components of each in order to make the totals more reliable.
Since we were now dealing with handwritten papers, the mechanics
factor was broadened to include a rating on handwriting and neatness
as well as on grammar and sentence structure, punctuation, and spelling.

DEFINITION OF POINTS ON THE RATING SCALE

During the past year, English departments in 17 high schools have
rated monthly test papers written in class for these eight qualities,
each on a scale of 1 (low) to 5 (high). For the benefit of students,
high, middle, and low points on each quality were defined in very
simple terms, as follows:

GENERAL MERIT

1. Ideas
   High. The student has given some thought to the topic and has
   written what he really thinks. He discusses each main point long

enough to show clearly what he means. He supports each main point with arguments, examples, or details; he gives the reader some reason for believing it. His points are clearly related to the topic and to the main idea or impression he is trying to get across. No necessary points are overlooked and there is no padding.

Middle. The paper gives the impression that the student does not really believe what he is writing or does not fully realize what it means. He tries to guess what the teacher wants and writes what he thinks will get by. He does not explain his points very clearly or make them come alive to the reader. He writes what he thinks will sound good, not what he believes or knows.

Low. It is either hard to tell what points the student is trying to make or else they are so silly that he would have realized that they made no sense if he had only stopped to think. He is only trying to get something down on paper. He does not explain his points; he only writes them and then goes on to something else, or he repeats them in slightly different words. He does not bother to check his facts, and much of what he writes is obviously untrue. No one believes this sort of writing—not even the student who wrote it.

2. Organization

High. The paper starts at a good point, moves in a straight line, gets somewhere, and stops at a good point. The paper has a plan that the reader can follow; he is never in doubt as to where he is or where he is going. Sometimes there is a little twist near the end that makes the paper come out in a way that the reader does not expect, but it seems quite logical. Main points are treated at greatest length or with greatest emphasis; others, in proportion to their importance.

Middle. The organization of this paper is standardized and conventional. There is usually a one-paragraph introduction, then three main points each treated in one paragraph, and then a conclusion, which often seems tacked on or forced. Some trivial points may be treated in greater detail than important points, and there is usually some dead wood that might better be cut out.

Low. This paper starts anywhere and never gets anywhere. The main points are not clearly separated from one another, and they come in a random order—as though the student had not given any thought to what he intended to say before he sat down to write. The paper seems to start in one direction, then another, then another, until the reader is lost.

3. Flavor

High. The writing sounds like a person, not a committee. The writer seems quite sincere and candid, and he writes about something he knows—often from personal experience. You could never mistake this writing for the writing of anyone else. Although the writer may play different roles in different papers, he does not put on airs. He is brave enough to reveal himself just as he is.

Middle. The writer usually tries to appear better or wiser than he really is. He tends to write lofty sentiments and broad generalities. He does not put in the little, homely details that show that he knows what he is talking about. His writing tries to sound impressive. Sometimes it is impersonal and correct but colorless, without personal feeling or imagination.

Low. The writer reveals himself well enough but without meaning to. His thoughts and feelings are those of an uneducated person who does not realize how bad they sound. His way of expressing himself differs from standard English, but it is not his personal style; it is the way uneducated people talk in his neighborhood.

4. Wording

High. The writer uses a sprinkling of uncommon words or of familiar words in an uncommon setting. He shows an interest in words and in putting them together in slightly unusual ways. Some of his experiments with words may not quite come off, but this is such a promising trait in a young writer that a few mistakes may be forgiven. For the most part he uses words correctly, but he also uses them with imagination.

Middle. The writer is addicted to tired old phrases and hackneyed expressions. If you left a blank in one of his sentences, almost anyone could guess what word he would use at that point. He does not stop to think how to say something; he just says it in the same way as everyone else. A writer may also get a middle rating on this quality if he overdoes his experiments with uncommon words: if he always uses a big word when a little word would serve his purpose better.

Low. The writer uses words so carelessly or inexactly that he gets far too many wrong. These are not intentional experiments with words in which failure may be forgiven; they represent groping for words and using them without regard to their fitness. A paper written entirely in a childish vocabulary may also get a low rating, even if no word is clearly wrong.

MECHANICS

5. Grammar, Sentence Structure

High. There are no vulgar or "illiterate" errors in grammar or usage by present standards of informal written English, and there are very few errors in points that have been emphasized in class. The sentence structure is usually correct, even in varied and complicated sentence patterns.

Middle. There are a few serious errors in grammar and several in points that have been emphasized in class, but not enough to obscure meaning. The sentence structure is usually correct in the more familiar sentence patterns, but there are occasional errors in more complicated patterns such as parallelism, subordination, consistency of tenses, reference of pronouns, etc.

Low. There are so many serious errors in grammar and sentence structure that the paper is hard to understand.

6. Punctuation

High. There are no serious violations of rules that have been taught —except slips of the pen. Note, however, that modern editors do not require commas after short introductory phrases, around nonrestrictive clauses, or between short coordinate clauses unless their omission leads to ambiguity or makes the sentence hard to read.

Middle. There are several violations of rules that have been taught— as many as usually occur in the average paper.

Low. Basic punctuation is omitted or haphazard, resulting in fragments, run-on sentences, etc.

7. Spelling

High. Since this rating scale is most often used for test papers written in class, when there is insufficient time to use the dictionary, spelling standards should be more lenient than for papers written at home. The high paper usually has not more than five misspellings, and these occur in words that are hard to spell. The spelling is consistent: words are not spelled correctly in one sentence and misspelled in another, unless the misspelling appears to be a slip of the pen. If a poor paper has no misspellings, it gets a 5 in spelling.

Middle. There are several spelling errors in hard words and a few violations of basic spelling rules, but no more than one finds in the average paper.

Low. There are so many spelling errors that they interfere with comprehension.

8. Handwriting Neatness

High. The handwriting is clear, attractive, and well spaced, and the rules of manuscript form have been observed.

Middle. The handwriting is average in legibility and attractiveness. There may be a few violations of rules for manuscript form if there is evidence of some care for the appearance of the page.

Low. The paper is sloppy in appearance and difficult to read.

THE MEASUREMENT OF GROWTH IN WRITING ABILITY

The only scientific way known to the writer to measure growth in writing ability by means of essays is to have all students in a span of three grades write a paper on the same topic and on the same day, at least four times a year and preferably six or eight. To keep nervous teachers from coaching students on the topic set for each date, the department may first agree on a long list of topics as suitable for short, impromptu compositions to be written in class. Then, at the beginning of each testing day, the department head may simply announce, "Today we'll use Topic 7," or "Today we'll use Topic 18." All English teachers write this topic on their blackboards, read aloud any explanatory material that accompanies it, and devote that day to the writing of test essays. Students number their own papers with any number of six digits that pops into their heads, such as 924,332 or 001,644, and they write no other identification on their papers. They copy this number on a 3 x 5 index card and add their name, grade, curriculum, other designations such as "regular" or "honors," and their teacher's name. These cards are locked up by the principal until the grading is finished.

The papers are distributed in a random fashion to all members of the department and rated on the scale previously discussed, without knowledge of the identity of the writers or their grade, curriculum, or teacher. In experimental studies, these ratings are usually recorded on separate 3 x 5 cards and no comments or corrections are written on the papers, so as not to influence the ratings of a second reader. For ordinary school use, however, each student may be asked to write a column of numbers from 1 to 8 in the upper left-hand corner of his first page. These numbers refer to the eight qualities defined in the rating scale, and the teacher who first gets the paper records his ratings on a scale of 1 (low) to 5 (high) opposite each of these eight numbers. When the paper is returned to this student's English teacher, he rates the paper again and records his ratings to the right of those already recorded by the first reader. He then adds together both sets of ratings to get a total rating for that paper, which may range from 16 (low) through 48 (average) to 80 (high). After four test papers, the cumulative total ratings may range from 64 to 320.

At the end of each period on testing days, when students hand in their papers, their teacher sorts the papers into as many piles as there are teachers and/or readers to read them. If there are eight, he sorts the papers into eight piles. At the end of the testing day, he cross-stacks these piles and takes them to the room of the department head, who has eight chairs lined up to receive them. Each teacher drops one pile of his papers on each chair until each chair holds a random eighth of the papers written in each English class that day. Each teacher or reader picks up his eighth and rates the papers at home. After a little practice, most teachers learn to rate these short test papers in about two minutes per paper if they do not write in corrections. They may, however, write a brief comment on anything they like or dislike.

Teachers often complain that they do not know how to rate a paper if they do not know whether it comes from the tenth or twelfth grade or from regular or honors classes. They hold up a paper and say that it should get a 4 in some quality if it comes from a regular class but only 2 or 3 if it comes from an honors class. There are many replies to this objection, but the most devastating is that, if they had this knowledge, the effect would be precisely the opposite. Benjamin Rosner of Brooklyn College added such bits of information to otherwise anonymous papers to see what the effect would be; what the readers did not know was that half of his information was true and half was false. Papers labeled "boy" received the same average grades as when they were labeled "girl," but papers labeled "honors" received average grades that were significantly higher than when these same papers were labeled "regular." This deception was tried out on so many teachers in different schools that there is no doubt that this tendency is general. We find what we expect to find. If we think a paper was written by an honors student, it looks better than if we think it was written by a regular student.

Anyway, all that the rating yields is a series of numbers representing total ratings on each paper. These numbers can then be adjusted for grade and curriculum before being translated into grades that will stand in the record. One simply makes a distribution of these totals for each curriculum within each grade. Then, if it has been decided that the tenth-grade regular students include (let us say) 20 students who ought to get A's, one counts 20 ratings down from the top for that group, draws a line, and calls everything above it an A. The 20 students who stand above this line may not be the same 20 who "ought" to get A's (and who *will* get A's on the other bases that were used in coming to this decision), but at least this procedure assures the desired proportions of letter grades for each group. No one gets a D simply because he is a tenth-grade vocational student who cannot yet meet the competition of higher grades and harder curriculums. If he stands high among his own group, he gets a high grade, no matter where his total rating falls in the distribution for the entire school.

This latter distribution, however, will show him where he stands in relation to the entire student body and how his standing changes from one year to the next. In grade 10, the average student stands in the lowest third of this distribution; in grade 11, in the middle third; in grade 12, in the top third; and in all grades the academic students tend to stand far above the non-academic. This is a realistic view of one's competition, and it is the only scientific way thus far developed to measure the amount of improvement in writing from one year to the next. The idea that teachers can judge the amount of growth by the old process of marking papers severely at the beginning of a year and leniently at the end is utter nonsense that ought not to deceive a child. It does, but it is a deception that should not be practiced on the young. Growth can be plotted only when each test paper is judged against a background of a representative sample of papers from the entire school, and only when the teachers do not know which papers are which. Then, if a student accumulates 128 points in his first year, 192 in his second, and 256 in his third, the rise in his standing is meaningful.

THEME GRADING

Ordinary grading of homework assignments in composition cannot make use of the rigorous departmental procedures we have recommended for test essays. On the whole, it is better not to attempt anything of the sort, since anonymity works better in testing than in instruction. One of John McNulty's sketches is charmingly entitled "A Man Like Grady, You Got To Know Him First." To help a student, you also have to know him first. It remains to be seen, however, whether it is wise or appropriate to grade these homework assignments at all, so long as the test essays are there to give the student his bearings. Many teachers prefer to give their reactions and suggestions entirely by written or spoken comments. Others like to use the rating scale, but only as an estimate of probable ratings had this been a test essay, not as marks that stand in the record. This appears to be a matter of preference. One must only remember that the homework assignments reveal problems that have no numerical solutions. It would be unfortunate if ratings on these papers were mistaken for answers and thereby headed off any real effort to find answers.

Training New Teachers of Composition in the Writing of Comments on Themes

RICHARD L. LARSON

THE TEACHER of writing customarily writes two judgments on each student theme: a grade and a written comment. In the training of a composition staff, considerable time is usually spent in trying to assure that the teachers assign equitable, consistent grades, but often much less time is devoted to seeing that they write helpful and clear comments. No one, I think, disputes the importance of trying to make the same grade represent approximately the same standard of achievement, regardless of which teacher awards it, for, whether we like it or not, decisions about scholarships, admission to graduate work, a student's draft status, and so on continue to be based heavily on his grades. And grades can be instruments of teaching; they let students know of their success in solving the various problems presented in each assignment. But it is the comment, not the grade, that helps the student to locate exactly what he did well or ill on any assignment; the comment is what leads the student most directly to inferences about what his teacher values in a paper, and about the features of his thinking or his style that he must improve in order to better his standing in the course. Yet we have all seen papers read by inexperienced teachers—sometimes even by experienced teachers—on which comments were cursory, ill-explained, impatient, perhaps condescending, and largely useless to the student. Such comments subvert the aims of any composition course. Any training

From *College Composition and Communication*, October, 1966, pp. 152–155. Reprinted with the permission of the National Council of Teachers of English and Richard L. Larson.

program for composition teachers, therefore, ought to help teachers form perceptive judgments about students' themes and present these judgments in marginal and general comments from which the students can profit.

This is one of the central purposes of the training program for new teachers of freshman composition now provided at the University of Hawaii. Among the duplicated materials distributed to new teachers during this program is the following list of "Guides to the Writing of Comments." Since writing good comments is a skill that takes time and practice to acquire, one cannot assume that perusing a few general suggestions will infallibly provide a new teacher with the wisdom he needs in order to write effective comments. But the suggestions may help new teachers to avoid the errors frequently found in the work of inexperienced comment-writers.

The University of Hawaii employs few teaching assistants in freshman composition (and all teaching assistants must participate in a seminar in teaching composition *before* they take charge of a class). Most new teachers are fulltime instructors. But many of these teachers are as inexperienced in grading compositions as any freshly-appointed teaching assistant. The guidelines, therefore, are written for people who have not previously taught composition. The guidelines assume that an effective comment on a theme can be a powerful teaching instrument —often more influential on the student's writing than many class discussions. (Conferences, to be sure, can be more helpful than a written comment, but few of us can confer with as many students as we would like on any one assignment.) The guidelines also assume that an instructor, as he annotates a theme, ought consciously to be trying to help the author write a better theme next time; he should not be content merely with giving a subjective impression of the theme, or indicating that he has at least read the paper, or explaining the grade. In the writing of comments, the guidelines argue, it is better to explain a criticism or suggestion with excessive thoroughness than to explain it so sketchily that the student cannot learn from the criticism.

GUIDES TO THE WRITING OF COMMENTS

MARGINAL COMMENTS

In making marginal comments, remember that you are neither a proofreader (responsible for normalizing spelling, punctuation, and typographical style) nor an editor (responsible for improving diction, idiom, and possibly syntax) nor a judge (responsible for rendering a verdict of "good" or "bad"), but a teacher, from whom the student hopes to get help in improving his reasoning, his organization, his style, and so on. If the student is to learn from what you write in the margins of his paper, your observations must be clear and self-explanatory.

1. Use marginal comments primarily to call the student's attention to some particular strength or weakness in his work—usually a strength or weakness of detail, or at any rate one that can be located precisely at the point where it occurs. Usually comments that refer to the reasoning or design or style in the whole theme can best be reserved for the general (final) comment.
2. Use correction symbols *only* where the error will be obvious to the student once it is pointed out. Correction symbols can point out spelling errors, run-on sentences, misuses of the semicolon, etc. But they should not as a rule be used where the reader is exercising judgment in determining that the writing or reasoning is weak. Avoid letting "Log" stand for an unexplained and unidentified error in Logic; don't just write "cl" if you think the passage is unclear or "ambig" if the passage seems ambiguous. Instead assume that the student would not have made the error in logic or permitted the lack of clarity or tolerated the ambiguity if he had known it was present. Explain, in a phrase or two, precisely where the difficulty lies and why the passage is open to criticism. Reread your comment and ask yourself: would this comment make the source of difficulty clear to me, if I had made the mistake (without realizing that it was a mistake) in the first place?
3. Try not to limit marginal comments to matters of mechanics, unless, of course, the mechanical difficulties are so striking and frequent that comment on other features of the essay is superfluous.
4. Refer the student to a helpful section of the handbook if you can, but don't let a reference to the handbook suffice where *explanation* of a difficulty (e.g., in subordination or placement of a modifier) is needed before the student will understand his error. Occasionally, if time allows, rewrite what the student has done to show how it can be improved. Also, indicate briefly why your version is better than his.
5. Avoid using "?" and terse queries like "what? or "how come?" or "so what." If you feel that the student's reasoning is unsatisfactory (e.g., because an unsound conclusion has been drawn or the significance of an idea is not made clear), explain your judgment precisely enough to let the student know where his thinking is faulty. Don't leave the student guessing that your notation simply reveals an honest difference of opinion between the two of you, or that your opinions on the

point at issue are unjustifiably rigid. Better fewer marginal comments well explained than a large number of cryptic, uninformative jottings.

6. In general, avoid arguing with the student. Focus on passages in which the student might demonstrably have improved what he has done. If the matter on which you are tempted to comment is simply a source of disagreement between you, omit the comment. Also, avoid asking a student to "explain" a point on which his reasoning is fairly obvious or self-evident. Ask for explanation only when the reasoning is genuinely hidden and needs to be disclosed. Try not to quibble over matters of diction and sentence structure that only reflect differences between your taste and that of the student. Comment on style only when you can propose a visible improvement in the student's way of expressing an idea.

7. Don't hesitate to note places where the student's thinking is especially effective, his style especially telling, his organization notably well handled, etc.

GENERAL (FINAL) COMMENTS

The purpose of the general comment is to record your overall impression of the paper and, more important, to point out goals for the writer to seek in revising that paper or in writing his next paper. The comment ought not to be merely the statement of a judgment about the paper at hand, although, of course, some comments that analyze a paper in detail can imply constructive suggestions for revision or for the elimination of recurrent weaknesses in the student's writing. The list that follows sums up the characteristics a good general comment ought to have; it is *not* a list of items to be included in every general comment you write.

1. Unless the mechanics and syntax are hopelessly inept (sometimes, to be sure, they are), make the general comment more than a list or summary of errors in mechanics and syntax.

2. Point out the strengths or good features of the theme if you can, rather than focusing exclusively on weaknesses. This suggestion does not imply, however, that you should ransack a bad paper for a trifling virtue on which to comment. If the paper marks an improvement over the student's earlier work, tell him so and tell him why you think so.

3. In part, at least, let your general comment inform the student how well he has met the substantive, structural, and stylistic problems

posed by the assignment. Deal with this point even if you plan to devote most of the comment to matters not related to the student's handling of the specific assignment.

4. Concentrate on the most important difficulties of substance, structure and style that affect the paper as a whole. If the reason for criticism of some features of the paper is not obvious, suggest why these features are indeed weaknesses and, where possible, propose changes that would have improved the paper. Be sure that the student can see *why* you think he should have done differently than he did; make clear *how* the proposed changes improve the paper. Such comments are especially important if the student will be asked to revise his paper. Specify in the comment what the student's principal aims should be in revising.

5. Try to see that the comment is constructive—that it has "transfer value." That is, try to help the student to improve his work on future papers. To achieve this purpose, search out fundamental features that weaken the student's work: lack of coherence between paragraphs, reliance on unrecognized and undefended assumptions, excessive abstractness of diction, acceptance of unsound generalizations or of conclusions based on inadequate evidence, etc. Describe and *illustrate* these features so that the student will understand them and can learn to recognize them as he corrects rough drafts of future papers. Call particular attention, if possible, to difficulties that recur in successive themes by the same student.

6. Let your general comment support, and be supported by, the marginal comments; the two sets of observations (marginal and general) should work together. Often you will be able to illustrate criticisms of the paper by referring to difficulties pointed out in detail in marginalia. But the general comment should not be merely a disjointed summary or repetition of the marginal comments. It must bring your separate responses to the paper into focus; it must give the student a coherent evaluation of the paper as a whole.

7. See that your comment is thoughtfully, precisely, and tightly written. It may act as a model of writing for the student (it is, after all, a sample of your writing); even if it isn't a model of excellence, it ought not to be an illustration of what you have been trying to make your students avoid.

8. Unless you have developed a special relationship with the student in which irony will not be misinterpreted, take care that your comments are not ironic, sarcastic, condescending, or inclined to belittle the student as a person. Irony can only anger the student, it does

not instruct him. Slangy, flippant admonitions (e.g., "Don't slit your wrists over this grade") should be avoided; supposedly a teacher can give more tasteful and beneficial advice.

9. Focus your comment on the paper, not on the personality or motivation of its author. Even making assumptions about what led the writer to adopt a particular attitude or subject is usually unwise. Of course, if parts of a paper are ambiguous or if the emphasis is fuzzy, you can and should ask the writer which of two or three possible meanings he intended to convey, or whether you are correct in believing that he meant to emphasize a particular point.

A SUGGESTED PROCEDURE FOR HANDLING

1. Read the theme quickly, making few or no marks on it.
2. Decide what features of the theme (good and bad) you wish to emphasize in your comment. Also decide how you can best present your reactions (especially the criticisms and suggested improvements)—i.e., how you can "get into" what you have to say about the paper. (If the problems in the paper are in reasoning or structure, you may need to read the paper two or three times, in order to grasp it as a whole, before deciding how you will construct your comment.)
3. Reread, writing marginal comments as needed, and focusing on those matters you have decided to emphasize.
4. Write the general comment, summing up your reactions, and citing if possible the specific parts of the paper where difficulties (or strengths) are most clearly evident.
5. Make a note to yourself (in a sort of "journal," for example) about the prominent features of the paper and about what you said, so that you can see in the revisions or the next essay whether the student has made any progress in correcting weaknesses you have identified. Then use your notes on the student's past work to guide comments on how the student is improving and how he is not.

Writing comments according to these guidelines, of course, is not an easy task for new instructors, and the Composition Committee of the University of Hawaii gives them several opportunities to practice writing comments under supervision before the year is far along. Not only do we review with new teachers a sampling of the papers they have graded (in this review we focus attention on the comments, discussing the grade on any paper only if it seems markedly unrealistic or unfair), we also reproduce selected theme assignments and student themes, invite all new teachers to annotate these themes as if they had been written by the teachers' own students, and devote staff meetings to comparing and evaluating ways of commenting on each theme. Members of our committee look over the comments that teachers have written on themes so discussed, and offer advice based on the guidelines listed here.

These procedures take a good deal of the committee members' time, but they seem worthwhile because effective written comments are such an important part of effective teaching in freshman English. Furthermore, we recognize that we are training teachers of English for positions at other schools where they may receive little or no assistance from their colleagues. We expect that our efforts may help our staff members after they leave the University of Hawaii, possibly even in their teaching of undergraduate and graduate literature courses where the writing of papers is required but the teaching of composition by itself is not a primary purpose.

Notes on Contributors

THELMA C. ALTSHULER, Associate Professor of Humanities at Miami-Dade Junior College, has been active in encouraging the wider use of films and provocative situations to stimulate student expression of ideas in speech and writing. Her recent publications include *Prose As Experience, Responses to Drama: An Introducton to Plays and Movies, Writing Step By Step,* and *Choices.*

AMELIA ASHE is presently Coordinator of the Graduate Program in Guidance and Counseling at Richmond College of The City University of New York. Formerly a New York City high school teacher for twelve years, she is now editor of the periodical *Teacher Education* and is the author of numerous articles and book reviews.

FRANCIS CHRISTENSEN, Professor of English at Northern Illinois University, is the author of *Notes Toward a New Rhetoric: Six Essays for Teachers* and *The Christensen Rhetoric Program.* An editorial consultant to *College English* and *PMLA,* he is also a past president of the California Association of Teachers of English. In 1967 he received the University of Southern California Research and Creative Scholarship Award. Dr. Christensen's studies in the rhetoric of the sentence and the paragraph have had a profound influence on the teaching of language and composition and on the revision of English curriculums throughout the country.

PAUL B. DIEDERICH, Senior Research Associate at Educational Testing Service, is best known for his nationwide experimental use of college-educated housewives as readers to assist high school English teachers in dealing with student compositions. He is co-author with Sydell T. Carlton of *Vocabulary for College,* a series of four programmed workbooks for grades 9-12.

MARGARET J. EARLY, who is Professor of Education and Associate Director of the Reading and Language Arts Center at Syracuse University, began her teaching career in the public schools of Massachusetts and Connecticut. The recipient of a Warren Research Fellowship in English at Boston University, she teaches graduate courses in methods of teaching reading and language arts at Syracuse, where she also directs the graduate program in English Education. The author of several articles and monographs, Dr. Early is coeditor of the *Journal of Reading*.

EDMUND J. FARRELL, formerly Supervisor of Secondary English at the University of California at Berkeley, recently received a three-year appointment as Field Representative for NCTE. In this capacity he will monitor the English-teaching community for the Council, will act as speaker and consultant for affiliate groups, and will represent NCTE both inside and outside English education. Author of *English, Education, and the Electronic Revolution*, he is a coeditor of literary anthologies for secondary schools.

NICK AARON FORD is Chairman of the Department of English at Morgan State College. He has taught at colleges and universities in Florida, Texas, Oklahoma, and Massachusetts and is the author or editor of seven books, including the following texts and readers for Freshman English: *Basic Skills for Better Writing, Language in Uniform,* and *Extending Horizons*.

HANS P. GUTH, Professor of English at San Jose State College, has published widely in *College English, The English Journal,* and other professional publications. He is also well known for a number of textbooks, among them *Words and Ideas, Essay, Literature,* and *English Today and Tomorrow: A Guide for Teachers of English*.

CLARENCE W. HACH, who is Supervisor of English and Chairman of Publications at Evanston Township High School, Evanston, Illinois, is a frequent member of the summer faculty at Northwestern University. The coauthor of *Modern Composition,* a six book series for grades 7-12, and of *Scholastic Journalism,* he has long been active in the National Council of Teachers of English and the Illinois Association of Teachers of English.

ROBERT F. HOGAN, Executive Secretary of the National Council of Teachers of English and Lecturer in English at the University of Illinois, is coauthor of *Obscenity, the Law, and the English Teacher* and has contributed articles on censorship to a variety of professional publications. He is also editor of *The English Language in School Programs,* a collection of readings, and he contributed a Foreword to the present collection.

E. JAY JERNIGAN is currently Director of Freshman Courses in English at Eastern Michigan University. He has taught at a high school, a junior college and at several universities and has published articles in periodicals including *Nineteenth Century Fiction, Michigan Academician*, and the *Bulletin of the New York Public Library*.

ROBERT KARLIN, who is Professor of Education and Coordinator of Graduate Reading and Language Arts Programs at Queens College of The City University of New York, is the author of *Teaching Reading in High School, Reading for Achievement*, and *Teaching Reading in High School, Selected Articles*. He is also coauthor of the *Bookmark Reading Program* and has written for the professional journals.

DOROTHY CHENOWETH KLAUSNER, a member of the staff at Chapman College, California, is involved in the administration of an experimental counseling-reading program for Chapman's probational and provisional students. Her experience in reading has included all grade levels including work with special students—retarded, disturbed, and gifted. She has served as a reading consultant and as an instructor of adult reading skills at Fullerton Junior College.

FREDERICK P. KROEGER, Associate Professor at Illinois State University, Normal, Illinois, is presently director of The Two-Year College English EPDA Fellowship Program, a program to train prospective teachers for service in inner-city junior colleges. He has served on the governing boards of NCTE and CCCC and is one of the founders of the National Junior College Conference. Dr. Kroeger has published articles in the *Junior College Journal*, the *CCC Journal, College English, Exercise Exchange*, and academic publications in Iowa and Michigan.

ROBERT J. LACAMPAGNE, now Assistant Professor of Education at City College of The City University of New York, served until recently on the staff of the National Council of Teachers of English, where he completed a national study of attitudes and approaches to writing of high school students. The editor of *High School Departments of English*, he is also coeditor of *Language Programs for the Disadvantaged*.

RICHARD L. LARSON is Professor of English and Director of Composition at the University of Hawaii. His publications include *Rhetorical Guide to the Borzoi College Reader* and several articles on rhetoric and the teaching of composition.

RAYMOND D. LIEDLICH is Instructor in English at De Anza College, Cupertino, California. He previously taught at Fullerton Junior College and California State College at Fullerton, as well as at the high school and junior high school levels. A member of the executive committees of both the Conference on College Composition and Communication and the Pacific Coast Regional Conference on English in the Two-Year College, he is coauthor of *From Thought to Theme: A Rhetoric and Reader for College English* and is currently working on a textbook for terminal English.

NANCY LIGHTHALL, a member of the English faculty at Chicago City College, is active in adult education. Presently at work on methods of teaching composition to adults with severe English deficiencies, she is the editor of *Point of View*, a fiction anthology for this population.

CONSTANCE McCULLOUGH, who is Professor of Education at San Francisco State College, received the International Reading Association's Citation for Distinguished Service in 1967 and in 1969 its Second International Citation of Merit. Her widely known publications in the field of reading include *The Improvement of Reading* (with R. Strang and A. Traxler) and *Teaching Elementary Reading* (with M. A. Tinker).

ELISABETH McPHERSON presently teaches English at Forest Park Community College in St. Louis. She has been active in NCTE and CCCC and in the formation of the National Junior College Committee, an affiliate of CCCC. She is the author, with Gregory Cowan, of two freshman composition texts, *Plain English, Please* and *Background for Writing*.

AMELIA MELNIK is an Associate Professor at the University of Arizona where, since 1960, she has worked with Ruth Strang to initiate and develop a Department of Reading. She has studied reading programs in Europe, Russia, and the United States and has held summer appointments at numerous universities. She is presently a member of the Board of Directors of the International Reading Association and Chairman of its Regional Program Committee.

THOMAS B. MERSON, currently Dean of Instruction at Bakersfield College, previously served as Director of Research of the California Junior College Association and as Assistant Director for Commissions of the American Association of Junior Colleges.

DONALD M. MURRAY is Professor of English at the University of New Hampshire and director of a composition program for the New England School Development Council. A writer as well as a teacher, Dr. Murray has published novels, short stories, and articles. Much of his work on the teaching of writing is contained in his text *A Writer*

Teaches Writing. He has received the Pulitzer Prize as an editorial writer.

SIDNEY J. RAUCH, Professor of Reading and Education at Hofstra University, is active as a lecturer and reading consultant. He has co-authored and edited a number of texts, among them *Guiding the Reading Program, Mastering Reading Skills, Study-Type of Reading Exercises, College Level, Corrective Reading in the High School Classroom,* and *Handbook for the Volunteer Tutor.* At present, his major interest is the evaluation of reading programs.

H. ALAN ROBINSON is Professor of Reading at Hofstra University, where he is active in a new doctoral program in reading. A past President of the International Reading Association, he is the author of books including *Guiding the Reading Program, Corrective Reading in the High School Classroom, Reading: 75 Years of Progress,* and *Recent Developments in Reading.*

HELEN M. ROBINSON, formerly William S. Gray Research Professor of Reading and Director of the Reading Research Center, is Professor Emeritus at the University of Chicago. She is the author of *Why Pupils Fail in Reading* and has edited numerous books and monographs in reading, the most recent being the 68th yearbook of the NSSE, *Innovation and Change in Reading Instruction.*

AUDREY J. ROTH, Assistant Professor of English at Miami-Dade Junior College, is especially interested in developing teaching materials and techniques for basic English courses and has contributed numerous books and articles on this subject. Her recent publications include *Prose As Experience, The Research Paper: Form and Content. Writing Step by Step,* and the "Search for Values" series including *Success, Alienation and Belonging,* and *Dignity.*

BONNIE RUBINSTEIN is Professor of English and Education at Merritt College in Oakland, California. Currently, she is working on an experimental program there in Experiential Arts. She has published articles in *Integrated Education* and in a humanities text *Human Value in the Atomic Age.* Most recently, she completed a collection of original children's songs for the Berkeley Unified School District.

DAVID H. RUSSELL, late Professor of Education at the University of California at Berkeley and President of the National Council of Teachers of English, published a number of articles and books in reading, among them *The Ginn Basic Readers, Children's Thinking,* and *Children Learn to Read.*

PHILLIP SHAW, Professor of English and former supervisor of the developmental reading program at Brooklyn College of The City University of New York, has been an officer of several reading associations. He has published articles and books on the development of the ability to read school assignments, the latest of which is *Effective Reading for College.*

JAMES R. SQUIRE, now Vice President and Editor-in-Chief at Ginn and Company, was a former Executive Secretary of the National Council of Teachers of English and was Professor of English at the University of Illinois from 1959 to 1967. During this period he directed the National Study of High School English Programs in the United States as well as a companion Study of English Teaching in the United Kingdom. His publications include *Teaching Language and Literature, High School English Instruction Today,* and *Teaching English in the United Kingdom.*

RUTH STRANG, Professor Emeritus of Education at Teachers College, Columbia University, is the author of numerous articles and textbooks on the teaching of reading. She has served as President of the National Association for Remedial Teaching.

SAMUEL WEINGARTEN is Professor of English and Humanities at Wright Junior College, a campus of the Chicago City College. He has been a member of the College Section Executive Committee of the National Council of Teachers of English and is presently a member of the Executive Committee of the Conference on College Composition and Communication Courses, and the National Committee on Junior College English. Dr. Weingarten's publications in the field of reading include *English in the Two-Year College, Response in Reading,* and many articles in professional journals.

CHARLES WEINGARTNER is Associate Professor of Education at Queens College of The City University of New York. The author of numerous articles, he is also coauthor with Neil Postman of *Linguistics: A Revolution in Teaching, Teaching As a Subversive Activity,* and *Language in America.*

RICHARD M. BOSSONE, editor of this volume, is Professor of English at Baruch College of The City University of New York. He has taught Methods of Teaching English and reading courses at the University of California and has published national research studies dealing with the training of English teachers and with the reading and writing problems of community college students. The author of numerous articles on the teaching of English and reading, Dr. Bossone is senior author of *Basic English*, a program of computer-assisted instruction in remedial English grammar for high school and college students, published recently, and coauthor of *The Handbook of Basic English Skills*, in press.